Chivalry, Kingship and Crusade

WARFARE IN HISTORY

ISSN 1358–779X

Series editors
Matthew Bennett, Royal Military Academy, Sandhurst, UK
Anne Curry, University of Southampton, UK
Stephen Morillo, Wabash College, Crawfordsville, USA

This series aims to provide a wide-ranging and scholarly approach to military history, offering both individual studies of topics or wars, and volumes giving a selection of contemporary and later accounts of particular battles; its scope ranges from the early medieval to the early modern period.

New proposals for the series are welcomed; they should be sent to the publisher at the address below.

Boydell and Brewer Limited, PO Box 9, Woodbridge, Suffolk, IP12 3DF

Previously published titles in this series are listed at the back of this volume

Chivalry, Kingship and Crusade

The English Experience in the Fourteenth Century

Timothy Guard

THE BOYDELL PRESS

First published 2013
The Boydell Press, Woodbridge
Paperback edition 2016

ISBN 978 1 84383 824 1 hardback
ISBN 978 1 78327 091 0 paperback

The Boydell Press is an imprint of Boydell & Brewer Ltd
PO Box 9, Woodbridge, Suffolk IP12 3DF, UK
and of Boydell & Brewer Inc.
668 Mt Hope Avenue, Rochester, NY 14620–2731, USA
website: www.boydellandbrewer.com

A CIP catalogue record for this book is available
from the British Library

The publisher has no responsibility for the continued existence or accuracy of
URLs for external or third-party internet websites referred to in this book,
and does not guarantee that any content on such websites is,
or will remain, accurate or appropriate

Typeset by Frances Hackeson Freelance Publishing Services, Brinscall, Lancs

This publication is printed on acid-free paper

Contents

List of Maps

Acknowledgements

The AHRC provided financial support for much of the research upon which this book is based. My examiners, Malcolm Vale and Chris Given-Wilson, saved me from a host of very embarrassing errors and offered encouragement. Chris Given-Wilson and the Medieval History Department at the University of St Andrews first inspired my interest in the world of fourteenth-century England. The late Maurice Keen listened, with a great deal of kindness, to some of my initial ideas forming. My principal academic debt is owed to Christopher Tyerman, who first suggested the late-medieval crusade as an area of research. A model supervisor, his unshakeable faith in the project, and in my ability to bring it to fruition, stiffened my resolve during some dark days. If the book has any merit, it is due to his generous help. Robert Brandon and my colleagues in the history department at Wolverhampton Grammar School provided encouragement as the thesis was being turned into a book. Myriam Bell designed the maps. Christopher Tyerman and Robert Brandon heroically tramped through various drafts. That there is a book at all is down to the patience and understanding of Julie, Emily, Alice and the rest of my family.

List of Abbreviations

Full details of books listed are given in the bibliography.

ASV	Archivio Segreto Vaticano
Barberi	A. Barberi, *Illustrazioni della spedizione in oriente di Amedeo VI* ed. F. E. Bollati di Saint-Pierre
BIHR	*Bulletin of the Institute of Historical Research*
BL	British Library
CA	College of Arms
CChW	*Calendar of Chancery Warrants*
CCR	*Calendar of Entries on the Close Rolls*
CIPM	*Calendar of Inquisitions Post Mortem*
Clément VI: Lettres rapportant à la France	*Lettres closes, patentes et curiales du pape Clément VI se rapportant à la France* eds E. Déprez et al.
CPL	*Calendar of Papal Letters*
CPP	*Calendar of Papal Petitions*
CPR	*Calendar of Entries on the Patent Rolls*
CUL	Cambridge University Library
Diplomatic Correspondence	*Diplomatic Correspondence of Richard II* ed. E. Perroy
DNB	*Oxford Dictionary of National Biography*
Documents nouveaux	*Documents nouveaux servant de Preuves à l'Histoire de l'Ile de Chypre sous le Reigne de la Maison de Lusignan* ed. M. L. de Mas Latrie
EETS	Early English Text Society
EHR	*English Historical Review*
Eulogium	*Eulogium Historiarum* ... ed. F. S. Haydon
Expeditions	*Expeditions to Prussia and the Holy Land made by Henry, Earl of Derby* ed. L. Toulmin-Smith
Foedera	*Foedera, conventiones, literae etc.* ed. T. Rymer
Froissart	Jean Froissart, *Oeuvres*, ed. K. Lettenhove
Gough	S. Gough, *Sepulchral Monuments in Great Britain*
Henry of Hervod	'Chronicon Henrici de Hervodia' *Sciptores Rerum Prussicarum* eds T. Hirsch et al. vol. III
HMC	Historical Manuscripts Commission
Indentures	*Private Indentures for Life Service in Peace and War, 1278–1476* eds M. Jones and S. Walker
Knighton	*Knighton's Chronicle, 1337–1396* ed. G. H. Martin

Londoniensis	'Annales Londonienses' *Chronicles of the Reigns of Edward I and Edward II* ed. W. Stubbs
MGH	*Monumenta Germaniae Historica: Scriptores* eds G. Pertz et al.
Middle English Romances	*Six Middle English Romances* ed. M. Mills
NA	The National Archives
Cabaret d'Orville	Cabaret d'Orville, *La Chronique du Bon Duc Loys de Bourbon* ed. A.-M. Chazaud
Oxford Bod.	Bodleian Library, Oxford
Paulini	'Annales Paulini' *Chronicles of the Reigns of Edward I and Edward II* ed. W. Stubbs
Peerage	*Complete Peerage* ed. G. E. Cokayne
John of Reading	*Chronica Johannis de Reading et Anonymi Cantuarensis 1346–1367* ed. J. Tait
reg. avin.	*Registra Avinionensia*
Reg. Baldock	*Registrum Radulphi Baldock, Gilberti Segrave, Ricardi Newport et Stephani Gravesend* ed. R. C. Fowler
Reg. Bransford	*Register of Wolstan de Bransford, Bishop of Worcester, 1339–1349* ed. R. M. Haines
Reg. Clem.	*Regestum Clementis Papae V* ed. Ordinis St Benedicti
Reg. Droxford	*Register of John de Droxford, Bishop of Bath and Wells, 1309–1329* ed. B. Hobhouse
Reg. Dunelmense	*Registrum Palatinum Dunelmense* ed. T. D. Hardy
Reg. Edington	*Register of William Edington, Bishop of Winchester, 1346–1366* ed. S. F. Hockey
Reg. Gilbert	*Registrum Johannis Gilbert, Episcopi Herefordensis, 1375–1389* ed. J. H. Parry
Reg. Halton	*Register of John de Halton, Bishop of Carlisle, 1292–1324* eds W. N. Thompson and T. F. Tout
Reg. Hethe	*Registrum Hamonis Hethe, Diocesis Roffensis, 1319–1352* ed. C. Johnson
Reg. Kirkby	*Register of John Kirkby, Bishop of Carlisle, 1332–1352 and the Register of John Ross, Bishop of Carlisle, 1325–1332* ed. R. L. Storey
Reg. Langley	*Register of Thomas Langley, Bishop of Durham, 1406–1437* ed. R. L. Storey
reg. lat.	*Registra Lateran*
Reg. Melton	*Register of William Melton, Archbishop of York, 1317–1340* eds R. M. T. Hill et al.
Reg. Montacute	*Register of Simon de Montacute, Bishop of Worcester, 1334–1337* ed. R. M. Haines
r.s.	*Rerum Britannicarum medii aevi scriptores*

Reg. Shrewsbury	*Register of Ralph of Shrewsbury, Bishop of Bath and Wells, 1329–1363* ed. T. S. Holmes
reg. supp.	*Registra Supplicationem*
Reg. Trefnant	*Register of John Trefnant, Bishop of Hereford, 1389–1404* ed. W. W. Capes
reg. vat.	*Registra Vaticana*
Reg. Wakefield	*Register of Henry Wakefield, Bishop of Worcester, 1375–1395* ed. W. P. Marett
Rot. Parl.	*Rotuli Parliamentum* eds J. Strachey et al.
Scrope and Grosvenor	*Controversy Between Sir Richard Scrope and Sir Robert Grosvenor in the Court of Chivalry* ed. N. H. Nicolas
Servion	Jean Servion, 'Chroniques de Savoy' *Monumenta Historiae Patriae* eds C. Albert et al.
SRO	Staffordshire Record Office
SRP	*Sciptores Rerum Prussicarum* eds T. Hirsch et al.
TRHS	*Transactions of the Royal Historical Society*
Urbain V: Lettres closes	*Lettres closes, secrètes et curiales du pape Urbain V* eds P. Lecacheux and G. Mollat
Urbain V: Lettres communes	*Urbain V: Lettres communes* eds M.-H. Laurent et al.
Vitae paparum	*Vitae paparum Avenionensium* ed. G. Mollat
West. Chron.	*The Westminster Chronicle, 1381–1394* eds L. Hector and B. F Harvey
Wigands von Marburg	'Chronik Wigands von Marburg' *Sciptores Rerum Prussicarum* eds T. Hirsch et al. vol. II

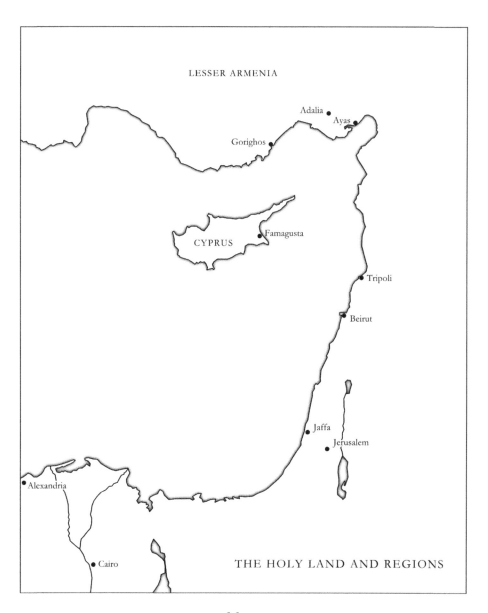

THE HOLY LAND AND REGIONS

Map 1

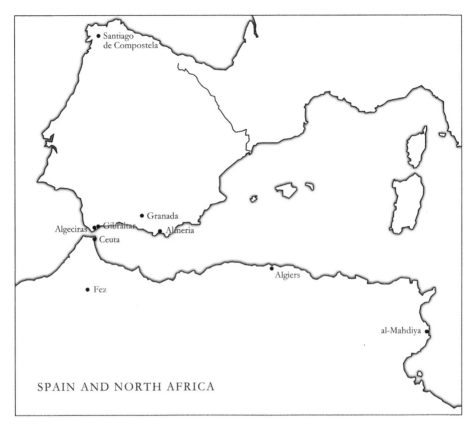

Santiago
de Compostela

Granada

Algeciras • Gibraltar
Ceuta • Almeria

Fez

Algiers

al-Mahdiya

SPAIN AND NORTH AFRICA

Map 2

Map 3

Nicopolis •

Varna •

Sozopolis •

THRACE   Constantinople

Thessalonica •   Gallipoli   SEA OF
                                                        MARMARA
THESSALY   • Lampsacus

                                        Lesbos

                        • Negroponte   • Smyrna

                                        Chios
                        • Athens

MOREA   Bodrum

Modon •   Rhodes
    • Coron

CONSTANTINOPLE   Crete
AND THE AEGEAN

Map 4

Introduction

This book is a study of the outlook and development of late-medieval English chivalric society, and its appetite for warring against the 'enemies of Christ'. It is an account of English military involvement in the later crusades and an attempt to show how crusading remained a defining function of chivalric society, particularly during the fourteenth century, the so-called 'golden age' of English chivalry. It contributes to the growing corpus of literature on the late-medieval crusade movement, supplying a case study from a local and regional perspective, centred largely on the experiences of crusading's most active constituents, the military elite, and it looks mainly from that perspective at English contributions to the crusade campaigns themselves. It presents a mixed picture of continuity and change. Failure to launch a grand Jerusalem crusade after the fall of Acre and the destruction of Christendom's hold on the Holy Land (1291), or later to field a meaningful force against the Turks, contrasts sharply with crusading's tenacious appeal across courtly and magnate circles. Here it continued to colour attitudes towards chivalry, personal honour and religion, despite such disruptive factors as the Anglo-French war, plague, church schism and political revolt. As a normative value of military society, the vogue for far-flung crusading (or at least the idea of far-flung crusading) was the route to paradise, worldly fame and the prettiest girls – if contemporary poets and churchmen were to be believed. The popularity of the theme provided knights with a deep well of enthusiasm and moral support. In general terms, the book argues, as an interpretation of the fourteenth century, England's withdrawal from the crusade has been largely exaggerated.

The primary aim is to assess the crusade's contemporary impact as a military and cultural enterprise. Denied the traditional Holy Land campaign, the impulse to cross swords with the infidel was expressed in numerous expeditions fought along other frontiers of Christendom, in the evocative landscape of romance and pilgrimage, the so-called *hethenesse* (i.e. non-Christian regions of the Mediterranean, Balkans, Iberian peninsula, Baltic). Investment in such wars – both materially and psychologically – served various secular and religious purposes and effects, creating significant demands. Its imprint can be seen in government and church bureaucracies, private

finances, legal measures and a wide range of personal gambles and sacrifices. The
impact left upon men's domestic and private lives suggests a historical reality quite at
odds with the well-known caricatures of chivalric literature – the love-struck bachelor,
the mercenary warrior or the wandering hermit knight. The book's secondary focus
recognises the tight grip that the crusade idea possessed at the height of political society, as an animating force of English kingship. It disputes the common assumption
that by the age of the Hundred Years War loyalty to crusading was mainly a decorative
ideal, ill-treated by English monarchs, and adopted as a double-speak of diplomacy or
as a means of raiding church coffers. Instead, it will be argued, throughout the period
there was directed at the court and the figure of the English king a fairly consistent
mixture of expectation, speculation and pressure centred on the crusade goal. Insofar
as the preoccupations of the military and political community helped stamp character upon English kingship (rather than vice-versa), the crusade remained central to
the self-image and assigned function of king and court.

Made up of two sections, *Chivalry, Kingship and Crusade* builds a composite picture. The first part makes a detailed, front-by-front study of *hethenesse* campaigning
in the fourteenth century. The extent and variety of individual experience – much of
it uncovered for the first time – is striking. At the very height of society, for example,
of the fifty-two men elevated to the rank of earl between 1337 and 1399, twenty-one
(40.4%) undertook campaigns in the *hethenesse*, some several times. Applying this
yardstick to 1215–1300, a period far better known for English crusading, the rate of
comital participation stands at 22.4% (11 of 49).[1] English knights and esquires did
not move in a backwater of idealism or play the junior partner to continental nobility,
as traditionally depicted in textbook histories of the later crusades. In the fourteenth
century English warriors held positions of high command in crusade flotillas in the
Mediterranean and Black Sea; spied for the pope behind enemy lines in Egypt and
Syria; fought on north African beaches, in Iberian river valleys and mountainous
plains; made embassies to the distant far east; and became expert in the society and

---

[1]   E.g. John Beaufort (Somerset) fought at al-Mahdiya (Tunis) (1390), in Prussia (1391–1392, 1394) and
perhaps at Nicopolis (1396). The others are Thomas Beauchamp II (Warwick), Humphrey Bohun V
(Hereford/Essex/Northampton), Henry Bolingbroke (Derby/Hereford/Lancaster/Leicester/Lincoln),
Enguerrand Coucy (Bedford), Edward Courtenay (Devon), Thomas Despenser (Gloucester), Henry
Grosmont (Derby/Lancaster/Leicester/Lincoln), John Holand (Huntingdon), Thomas Holand I
(Kent), William of Jülich (Cambridge), John Montagu (Salisbury), William Montagu I (Salisbury),
William Montagu II (Salisbury), Thomas Percy (Worcester), Michael de la Pole (Suffolk), William
Scrope (Wiltshire), Thomas Stafford (Stafford), Robert Ufford (Suffolk), William Ufford (Suffolk),
Thomas Woodstock (Buckingham/Essex). To illustrate this point I have chosen not to include John of
Gaunt's Castile crusade (1386). No earls accompanied Bishop Despenser's crusade to Flanders in 1383.
See also the appendix. Cf. S. D. Lloyd, *English Society and the Crusade 1216–1307* (Oxford, 1988) pp.
82–4, 113–53. Some adjustment must be made (overall the number of earls increased by about 30% up to
1399 – as opposed to the increase in comital titles, cumulatively nearly 55%), but the rough sums show
enough. *Handbook of British Chronology* eds F. M. Powicke and E. B. Fryde (2nd edn, London, 1961) pp.
414–546 conveniently tabulates the genealogical data.

politics of the Mamluk state. In Lithuania, they helped build forts and navigate freez-ing waterways. To some extent, this diversity of experience was replicated in patterns of recruitment. As well as the famous names of English chivalry, crusading had a robust following among lesser figures of gentry society and those families keen to establish knightly credentials for the first time. It also attracted careerist clerks – men normally to be found in the chancery court – and that new breed of jobbing soldier, the much-maligned *routier*. The fighting varied significantly in scale, peaking during periods of peace and truce in the Anglo-French war. High-profile campaigns, such as the sack of Alexandria (1365), or Alfonso XI's onslaught against Granada (1342–1344), attracted the grandest names, and the wide acclaim of poets and chroniclers. Traffic in the direction of Prussia was at times so thick that, after France and Scotland, it is reason-able to talk of the Baltic crusade as being the third frontier of English chivalry in the fourteenth century. At the other end of the spectrum are the isolated experiences of men like Sir William de la Pole of Castle Ashby, who (for pay) held church outposts near Athens against Turks, Greeks and Catalan settlers, and planned to lead a com-pany to Egypt, or Hugh, Lord FitzHugh, the gentleman arms-dealer who helped to supply the Knights Hospitaller at Rhodes in 1409. These remain shadowy at best, and perhaps hard to distinguish from older patterns of military privateering or Christian aggression.[2] Amongst other things, what becomes apparent is that the start of the Hundred Years War was not the breakwater to crusading commonly thought. On the contrary, judging by the numbers of English recruits and their cosmopolitan outlook, the confidence gained through campaigning in the French war and the social contact obtained through associated truces, alliances, embassies, tournaments and battlefield exchanges actually helped spur a new period of activism. It thrust English knights squarely into the orbit of continental chivalry, and wider currents of idealism and crusade enthusiasm. Crusading engaged the knightly order far more in activity and self-image than is often understood.

The second part sets out the local political and organisational context of individ-ual decisions to embark, analysing church policy, crusading's social spread and the challenges confronting would-be crusader knights in fourteenth-century England. Evidence of organisation and of controls and restraints reveals a texture of response and impact far richer than the simple assessment of numerical commitment or mili-tary success and failure. Crusading's diffuse cultural impact is also considered. Besides the material culture of knightly campaigning, with its stress upon display, conspicu-ous consumption and entertainment, the crusade 'ethos' rested on a raft of supporting influences and common values embedded as part of the environment at home. Court pageantry and ceremony, imaginative literature, myth, military competition, the expectations of lineage, the decorative arts and patterns of social advancement all spoke to crusading's higher calling, instilling in knights an ethos of admiration and

---

[2]   For Pole see *Correspondance de Pierre Ameilh, archevêque de Naples puis d'Embrun 1363–1369* ed. H. Bresc (Paris, 1972) pp. 366–9. For Fitzhugh see *CCR 1409–1413* pp. 2–3.

material response. Of course, what provided a large measure of cohesion among participants were the various codes of behaviour and expectation held up for emulation in the tenets of chivalry, and the pressures of prestige and competition between men. It is hard to exaggerate the extent to which the crusade remained rooted in contemporary chivalric culture. Here, crusading was not an 'optional extra' to Christian knighthood, but intrinsic to its very warp and essence. Few in military society can have escaped its impact entirely. This book sets out some of the main avenues by which idealism travelled. One aspect of this consumption was burgeoning interest in ancestral crusading and the famous events of Richard I's crusade, as attested in the production of romance literature, depictions of the Lionheart in tapestries and manuscripts, and in the reports of family genealogies.

This impulse to memorialise spoke forcefully to the currency afforded to *hethenesse* crusading in contemporary public life, and the emulatory pressures of local and national chivalry. The final chapter analyses its function in royal circles, charting what was a quite insistent argument about crusade and political power, subject to various influences from within and around the court. Here kingship is seen as an institution inseparable from the fight for the faith – a cause that was hard to divorce from intervening, fluid political priorities or competing expressions of royal authority, despite burgeoning pressures of national war or deteriorating relations with the papacy. Cutting across a lively historiographical debate over the shifting nature and substance of fourteenth-century kingship and English royal power, conclusions presented in Chapter 9 open perspectives on such related issues as the crown's chivalric identity and sacral function. This range of engagement with the crusade idea has generally been overlooked, not least because the traditional chronicle sources are quiet on the subject and the evidence of romance and imaginative literature is tricky to interpret. (Continental sources are generally more informative.) Loyal service in the crown's wars, the strengthening bonds of patriotism, growing legal constraints, changing religious tastes and troubled Anglo-papal relations would seem to militate decisively against large-scale participation in wars *contra paganos*. Yet, as will become clear, with the exception of Richard I's Palestine expedition, English knights enjoyed probably their greatest degree of crusade involvement from 1307 to 1399, the variety of war-frontiers and briefer terms of service encouraging a pattern of traffic which rivalled the late twelfth and early thirteenth centuries, the 'heyday' of crusading, for its wide distribution of campaign experience among knightly families. Prussia and the coastal marches of the eastern Mediterranean replaced Syria and Palestine as principal destinations, but it is fair to think of the fourteenth century as a golden period of English crusading, integral to the apparent 'full-flowering' of English chivalry.[3] As such, insofar as it touched on England's standing as a leading western power, the crown was protective of its historic and diplomatic links with Christian powers in

---

[3]   For English chivalry's florescence in the fourteenth century see N. Saul, *For Honour and Fame: Chivalry in England 1066–1500* (London, 2011).

the east, and with other nations along the borders of Christendom. Partly about the projection of honourable knighthood and kingship, lip-service to the crusade spoke directly to the tastes and ambitions of leading nobles, courtiers and visitor knights.

The wider implications for a study of this kind include such diverse subjects as medieval travel, popular literary tastes, public and private religion, church exceptionalism, Baltic trade, sermon propaganda, private finance, papal and secular bureaucracy, the moral 'decline' of chivalry, royal diplomacy and the testimony of tombstone brasses. Although it is often hard to gauge, the cost borne by families and local communities through prolonged or permanent absence, or the subsidy of crusading's enormous expense, is another underlying consideration. Inevitably, limitations of space mean there are several gaps. Little is said about crusade taxation and related mechanisms of vow redemptions and indulgence sales, aspects of church finance exhaustively studied by the American historian William Lunt over fifty years ago. Similarly, there is no room for an institutional history of the Knights Hospitaller, or other military orders, in fourteenth-century England, except insofar as they provided potential channels for crusade activism. Increasingly, as Simon Philips has shown, the English Hospitallers' roles as landlords, royal administrators and religious brethren left larger imprints on English society than their manifestation of the crusade ideal. Likewise, I touch on the so-called 'national crusades' to Flanders (1383) and Castile (1386) only in passing, mainly to highlight points of contrast. Both campaigns have received generous attention elsewhere, usually in relation to the history of the Anglo-French war. Finally, there is little said about English participation in the crusades against papal enemies in Italy, a front attractive to the mercenary companies, but never acquiring the chivalric aura of part of the *hethenesse*.[4]

---

[4]   W. E. Lunt, *Financial Relations of the Papacy with England* (Cambridge, Mass., 1939–1962); id. *Papal Revenues in the Middle Ages* (New York, 1965); S. Philips, *The Prior of the Knights Hospitaller in Late Medieval England* (Woodbridge, 2009); M. Aston, 'The Impeachment of Bishop Despenser' *BIHR* 38 (1965) pp. 127–48; K. DeVries, 'The Reasons for the Bishop of Norwich's attack on Flanders in 1383' *Fourteenth Century England III* ed. W. M. Ormrod (Woodbridge, 2004) pp. 155–65; A. Goodman, *John of Gaunt: The Exercise of Princely Power in Fourteenth-Century England* (Harlow, 1992) chap. 8; P. E. Russell, *English Intervention in Spain during the Reigns of Edward III and Richard II* (Oxford, 1955).

PART I

1

Questions and Perspectives

In 1349 the Ely chronicler recorded a new miracle. His account is worth quoting in full:

> In the 23rd year of King Edward III's reign ... Sir William Hinton was fighting against the enemies of the cross in Spain when he summoned his brother Hugh, a highly spirited esquire (*armiger*). The young man rushed to Spain and joined the Christian army, soon acquitting himself courageously against the Saracens. One day, however, battle was particularly hard fought and, as happens in war, the sword swung calamitously, felling many on both sides. Among those killed was the valiant knight William Hinton. His brother Hugh was horribly wounded by a lance driven hard into the groin (*osse lumborum*). Stuck deep in his flesh the weapon was impossible to tear out without inflicting terrible pain. In despair, Hugh appealed for divine aid, and prayed fervently to the blessed St Æthelreda and God for comfort ... Having made his prayer, he put a hand to the offending lance and it came away with ease. Nevertheless, the injury was grave, and, exhausted by battle, Hugh retired to bed, close to death. Doctors and surgeons (*medicos et chirurigicos*) failed to heal his wound, but Hugh kept up prayer to St Æthelreda, so that God might show mercy and lessen his pain. One night four nuns appeared at Hugh's bedside. One of them, saint-like in virtue, spoke kindly to the young man, saying, 'Have faith, soon you will be well.' With some silken cloth she dressed his wound, her touch giving such miraculous comfort that the hurt was immediately dulled. Making ready to leave, the blessed lady whispered to Hugh, 'Find the weapon that inflicted this wound and bring it to me at Ely.' Bandaged and anointed, Hugh's injury soon healed. After a three-day search Hugh found the lance in the keeping of a companion. Breaking off the tip he returned with it home to England. Visiting the Isle of Ely, Hugh came to the cathedral with Ralph, another brother. With great devotion they offered the iron lance-head (*paxillum ferreum*) at St Æthelreda's shrine, fastening it overhead as a pious memorial of this miracle.[1]

Battlefield relics are commonly the stuff of saints' legends. The annals of military saints were packed with examples of such saintly interventions. Yet this notice of St Æthelreda's latest miracle smacked more of an eye-watering reality. Numerous English knights participated in the fitful fourteenth-century war against Spanish Islam and

---

[1] 'Continuatio Historiae Eliensis' *Anglia Sacra, sive Collectio Historiarum* ed. H. Wharton (London, 1691) p. 653. Translated by the author.

experienced its attendant dangers. Writing about the siege of Muslim-held Algeciras in 1342 to 1344, for instance, the Florentine chronicler Giovanni Villani described the arrival of a stream of English soldiers at Alfonso XI of Castile's crusade camp. Most stayed between four and six months, and won Castilian praise after fighting a Moorish fleet anchored off the Moroccan coast at Ceuta. The conflict attracted glamorous figures of English chivalry such as the earls of Derby and Salisbury, as well as the retinues of the less well known.[2] Sir William Hinton probably lost his life during the Castilian attack upon Gibraltar (1349–1350). Other documented careers include John Hampton of Mortimer, who was badly disfigured at the battle of Vega (1319) and then imprisoned for several years in a Granadan cell. Such risks were part of the danger many other English knights and esquires expected to face. As part of this tradition, so long as foreign knights were drawn to the southern frontier, Anglo-Saxon saints were kept busy on Iberian battlefields.[3]

Not much else of Hugh Hinton is known, but the chronicle story shows some familiar soldierly impulses.[4] Martial ambition, Christian fortitude and familial duty each feature prominently, as well as exemplary devotion to Ely's foundress. As such, little separated fighting 'enemies of the cross' from other forms of organised violence, including the crown's wars in Scotland and France. Yet, as implied by the story of Hinton's miraculous vision and healing, holy war on the rim of Christendom – and especially in the east – possessed singular psychological significance. In this respect the middle of the fourteenth century was no different from earlier periods. In February 1343, for example, Sir John Fauconberg, former sheriff of Yorkshire, got leave to travel *ad terram sanctam*, vowing 'not to bear arms again' until he had fought 'the enemies of God'. Shortly afterwards Sir Thomas Wale neglected to do homage for his Northamptonshire estate because he was 'busy' warring with '*enemis de dieu et de la crestienetes*' in Spain; and in June 1346 the Gloucestershire knight John de la Ryvere embarked against the Turks in *Romania* (Western Anatolia), hoping to 'save his soul'. This is formal chancery-talk, not carbonated *élan*. What motivated Wale and Fauconberg is uncertain, but Ryvere wanted to expiate crimes committed during his former soldiering career.[5]

[2]   Giovanni Villani, *Cronica* ed. F. Gheradi Dragomanni (Milan, 1848) vol. IV pp. 57–8; *Cronica del Roy Don Alfonso el Onceno. Cronicas de los Reyes de Castilla* ed. C. Rosell (Madrid, 1875, 1877) vol. I pp. 360–70.

[3]   J. N. Hillgarth, *The Spanish Kingdoms 1250–1516* (London, 1971) vol. I p. 344; D. Romano, 'Un Inglés en la Guerra contro el Moro: 1324' *Al-Qantara* 2 (1981) pp. 457–9.

[4]   It is probable that Hugh was a son of the gentry family of Hinton Manor a few miles south of Ely. See *The Victoria History of the County of Cambridge and the Isle of Ely* vol. X eds A. F. Wareham, A. P. M. Wright et al. (London, 2002) pp. 106–9.

[5]   Licence to travel to the Holy Land (Fauconberg) 3 February 1343, NA, C66/209 m. 40; chancery warrant (Wale) 24 August 1343, NA, C81/291/15587; licence to travel overseas 'propter votum ob salutem anime sue' (Ryvere) 20 June 1346, NA, C66/217 m. 27; safe conduct for journeying 'in subsidium fidelium Romanie contra Turchos' (Ryvere) 16 August 1346, ASV, reg. vat. 140 fol. 311ᵛ. For John

Of course literary representations raise more questions and issues than answers about the nature of holy war, the crusades and the societies in which they were promoted. Interested in St Æthelreda's holy powers, the Ely chronicler conveys little recognition of the fourteenth-century Iberian *reconquista* as a crusade war; he does not mention his protagonist making a vow, taking the cross or receiving indulgences.[6] The Moors are styled *inimicos Crucis*, pitched against an *exercitus christiani* – perhaps a recognisable 'crusade' periphrasis – but age, temperament and landscape establish character and atmosphere, not Hinton's position in canon law. Wider traditions of English campaigning in Moorish Spain are simply assumed. Other questions follow. How does the story relate to the mainstream context of later medieval society, to popular religion and wider cultural values? How did politics, the church, law, commerce and the economy, for instance, affect attitudes towards and involvement in what Edward III described as 'the Lord's wars'?[7] Was involvement confined to particular families, certain localities and/or other social groupings? To what extent was there tension between knightly independence and military service to the crown? How far was there a decline in enthusiasm for crusading? How was the crusade retinue organised, supplied and transported? How were the chivalric code and the crusade related? And if, as F. M. Powicke memorably put it, the crusade ideal 'pervaded' thirteenth-century minds, 'being inseparable from the air that was breathed', what was the outlook of succeeding generations?[8]

Chivalry and the late-medieval crusade

Thanks to its near-ubiquity in chivalric and romance literature, the stereotype of the crusading knight-errant is perhaps as familiar to modern historians as it was to fourteenth-century audiences. Probably more than at any other time, knights and esquires, such as the Hinton brothers, were exposed to messages of what constituted ideal martial behaviour, and, along with lessons in knightly stamina and Christian piety, the theme summed up the outlook of an age when the cult of arms achieved perhaps its richest expression – as witnessed in the flourishing of secular orders of chivalry, the market in knightly treatises, the codification of rules of war and increasingly formalised tournament play.[9] It is, though, necessary to peel away the literary and ceremonial in order to examine the wider historical context of such knightly

de la Ryvere see *DNB* 'John de la Ryvere' http://www.oxforddnb.com/view/article/92453, accessed 20 Dec. 2011.

[6]   Castilian sources are more certain, e.g. it was thought Derby and Salisbury were at Algeciras in 1343 'por salvacion de sus almas', as well as to meet Alfonso XI ('conoscer al Rey'). *Cronica Alfonso* p. 360.

[7]   Letter to Alfonso XI, 12 June 1341, *Foedera* vol. II pt. 4 pp. 102–3.

[8]   F. M. Powicke, *The Thirteenth Century, 1216–1307* (2nd edn, Oxford, 1962) p. 80.

[9]   E.g. the oft-quoted 'crusade' topos in Chaucer's Knight's Prologue. J. H. Pratt, *Chaucer and War* (Lanham, 2000) pp. 97–133.

idealism. Several broad historiographical themes help form part of the general background. First, a recent burgeoning of interest in the history of the later crusades has made large parts of a previously neglected subject much more familiar, charting key political and strategic developments, and raising an assortment of questions. Important in this respect is the exploratory work of Kenneth Setton and Norman Housley, whose minute analysis of papal policy and bureaucracy in the fourteenth century chronicles a complex crusade movement with shifting strategic priorities and fronts, and ongoing appeal among western princes and knights. A great deal is now known of the efforts made by popes to shape events, particularly in Italy and the eastern Mediterranean.[10] The Baltic crusades are now also much better documented, thanks to the research of a number of German historians, most notably Werner Paravicini.[11] In practice, the challenges in this period were daunting. Recovery of the Christian east remained the ultimate dream, notwithstanding the period of crisis and abortive planning following the fall of Acre in 1291, but whether western bureaucracies could absorb the necessary fiscal and political costs of mounting a general crusade remained doubtful. Long periods of internal conflict and decline in papal influence undermined efforts to organise unified action. Exceptions were most regularly made for those crusade expeditions directed against political enemies of the pope, in Italy and elsewhere, where local interests were at stake and obvious gains could be made. Nevertheless, despite the problems besetting Holy Land crusading, growing numbers of western noblemen and knights were drawn to the diverse crusade wars fought *contra paganos* on Christendom's borders in the years 1300–1400.

Secondly, insofar as these wars intruded upon the course of English politics, historians of English aristocracy have taken a closer interest, such as with the career of Henry Bolingbroke, the future Henry IV, whose reputation for chivalry was cultivated largely around his fights against pagans in Lithuania in 1391. Most important in this respect is the work of Maurice Keen, J. J. N. Palmer, and Christopher Tyerman.[12]

---

[10] K. M. Setton, *The Papacy and the Levant 1204–1571* (Philadelphia, 1976–1984); *History of the Crusades* ed. K. M. Setton (Madison, Wis., 1969–1989); N. Housley, *The Italian Crusades: The Papal-Angevin Alliance and the Crusades against Christian Lay Powers, 1254–1343* (Oxford, 1982); id. *The Avignon Papacy and the Crusades, 1305–1378* (Oxford, 1986); id. *The Later Crusades, 1274–1580: From Lyons to Alcazar* (Oxford, 1992). For an assessment see G. Constable, 'The Historiography of the Crusades' *The Crusades from the Perspective of Byzantium and the Muslim World* eds A. E. Laiou and R. P. Mottahedeh (Washington D. C., 2001) pp. 1–22. The field continues to expand: more recent works in English include N. Housley, *Religious Warfare in Europe 1400–1536* (Oxford, 2002); *Crusading in the Fifteenth Century: Message and Impact* ed. N. Housley (Basingstoke and New York, 2004). For a broader chronological perspective cf. J. France, *The Crusades and the Expansion of Catholic Christendom, 1000–1714* (London, 2005); C. J. Tyerman, *God's War: A New History of the Crusades* (London, 2006).

[11] W. Paravicini, *Die Pruessenreisen des Europäischen Adels* (Sigmaringen, 1989–). For full references see Chapter 4 below.

[12] M. H. Keen, 'Chaucer's Knight, the English Aristocracy and the Crusade' *English Court Culture in the Later Middle Ages* eds V. J. Scattergood and J. W. Sherborne (London, 1983) pp. 45–63; C. J. Tyerman, *England and the Crusades, 1095–1588* (Chicago, 1988), chap. 10; J. J. N. Palmer, *England, France and*

Keen's seminal work on late-medieval chivalry first uncovered evidence for wider English and French participation, questioning the stereotype of the opportunist or light-hearted crusader knight, and suggesting various avenues for research. Tyerman gives the best introduction to the topic so far, displacing the cynicism usually ascribed to late-medieval crusading with explanations of nostalgia, competition and political necessity. Yet, compared to the late twelfth and thirteenth centuries, the pattern of knightly involvement and its wider cultural imprint in the 1300s remains a relatively neglected area. Instead, concepts of decline and disillusion have continued to colour modern interpretations – the failure to launch an effective crusade to Syria and later against the Ottoman Turks being generally accepted as evidence of the institution's eroded significance.

There is a wider interpretative difficulty with this analysis. Distrust of the stereotype of the questing knight-errant received its most strident statement at the hands of the Dutch historian Johan Huizinga, who characterised late-medieval crusading as a largely empty function of social class and display, confined to lobbyists and chivalry's more delusional elements, remote from what he called the 'harsh realities' of the period, and like other cultural forms in the later middle ages, a pale impression of former achievements and feats. Abandonment of the Jerusalem crusade was a symptom of his famous 'waning of the middle ages'.[13] The emphasis of a contrasting historiographical tradition – that identifying the fourteenth century as a period of positive political and cultural development, not decline – allows equally little room for such ambition: enthusiasm for the international crusade appearing somewhat out of touch with evidence of emergent patriotism, changing religious tastes, and the proliferation of national wars. Until relatively recently, the best that could be said was that the later crusades and their participants were 'a kind of cultural convention' quite 'out of tune' with developments in European life.[14] Alongside this, the construct of chivalry itself is an awkwardly slippery one. Taken variously to mean rehearsal for battle, a rationalisation of knightly violence, a code of manners or *courtoisie*, a vehicle of literary fancy, a category of landed society and a doctrine of Christian behaviour, it is most often written about in isolation from other social, military and political currents of the day, caught awkwardly in a haze between perceived ideals and realities. It is the material functionings of chivalrous, or arms-bearing, society and its wide social contract with crusading, rather than the literary or theoretical abstractions of

---

Christendom 1377–1399 (London, 1972); F. R. H. Du Boulay, 'Henry of Derby's Expeditions to Prussia, 1390–1391 and 1392' *The Reign of Richard II* eds F. R. H. Du Boulay and C. M. Barron (London, 1971) pp. 153–72. See also the articles of A. Luttrell, 'English Levantine Crusaders, 1363-1367' *Renaissance Studies* 2 (1988) pp. 143–53; 'Chaucer's Knight and the Mediterranean' *Library of Mediterranean History* 1 (1994) pp. 127–60. For the interest and participation of French and Burgundian chivalry see J. Paviot, *Les Ducs de Bourgogne, la Croisade el l'Orient* (Paris, 2003).

[13]   J. H. Huizinga, *The Waning of the Middle Ages* tr. F. J. Hopman (London, 1938) p. 87.

[14]   J. Prawer, *World of the Crusaders* (London, 1972) p. 150. This view was echoed more recently by A. Jotischky, *Crusading and the Crusader States* (Harlow, 2004) p. 259.

chivalry, that will be the main emphasis below. Nonetheless, that the wars of the cross intersected with the Christian roots of idealised martial behaviour is clear enough, and crusading's relationship with other chivalric forms also throws light on a composite set of values that are notoriously difficult to define, despite their prevailing influence over medieval society.[15]

One of the central claims of this book is continuity. Expectations that a royal Holy Land *passagium* would sail survived Edward II, the outbreak of the Anglo-French war, plague and the dotage of Edward III, despite increasingly unpromising conditions. Even after the full escalation of the Anglo-French war, a compound of strategic, economic and political factors kept the ideal current at court, an instrument of statecraft as much as a focus of aristocratic ambition. So long as crusade militancy was bound up with social and political aspiration, it is suggested, it makes little sense to treat the subject as an 'ideal in decay'. Court rhetoric, and the views articulated from beyond, acknowledged the pre-eminence of the crusade cause among princely and knightly obligations, showing an appetite for themes of national salvation, royal heroism and ascendancy over Christendom. This did not necessarily make for easy kingship.

Other issues and questions remain open to investigation. For the participants and campaigns themselves, historians are still reliant on general and largely untested characterisations. In the absence of central retinue rolls or *vadia guerre* accounts, little is understood about the functioning of fourteenth-century crusade expeditions in the field, for example. Scant detail survives of combatants, itineraries or conditions of service. It is hard to get beyond the impressionistic description of chroniclers and their suspiciously rounded numbers, or the pronouncements of the papacy and other apologists.[16] Nor is much known about the functioning of traditional crusade institutions. There is no systematic study of the promotion and preaching of fourteenth-century expeditions. Dozens of preaching campaigns were launched, leaving traces upon diocesan registers and other ecclesiastical sources across the western church, including in England; yet, with the exception of the more sensational crusades against schismat-

---

[15] The central text remains M. H. Keen, *Chivalry* (New Haven, 1984). See too M. G. A. Vale, *War and Chivalry: Warfare and Aristocratic Culture in England, France, and Burgundy at the End of the Middle Ages* (London, 1981); P. R. Coss, *The Knight in Medieval England, 1000–1400* (Stroud, 1993); Saul, *For Honour and Fame* pp. 1–20 and passim. Cf. F. Cardini, 'The Warrior and the Knight' *The Medieval World* ed. J. le Goff, tr. L. G. Cochrane (2nd edn, London, 1997) pp. 75–112, for a chapter-length introduction to the competing guises of chivalry.

[16] The best documented of the eastern crusades is Amadeo of Savoy's 1366 expedition. See A. Barberi, *Illustrazioni della spedizione in oriente di Amedeo VI* ed. F. E. Bollati di Saint-Pierre (Turin, 1900). Papal registers are occasionally forthcoming about magnate retinues, e.g. ASV, reg. supp. 42 fols 145ʳ–179ʳ 'rotulus comitis Warrewici' (May 1364). Amongst the English sources, household accounts preserve many details of Derby's campaign in Lithuania (1390–1391). *Expeditions to Prussia and the Holy Land made by Henry, Earl of Derby* ed. L. Toulmin-Smith, Camden Society 52 (London, new series 1894). Less well known is the account relating to the earl of Stafford's abortive 1391 'viagio versus Prucem', SRO, D641/1/2/4.

ics, not much is known about the reception and application of crusade indulgences on the ground, or the content and form of preaching messages and sermons.[17] The transition from large-scale centrally recruited crusades to the mainly independent aristocratic expeditions of the fourteenth century raises questions over the degree of church and secular control, as well as levels of knightly enthusiasm or participation. More broadly, modern historians of crusading talk generally of an enduring 'crusading ethos', and describe it in action, but only modest attempts have been made to study its cultural mainsprings, or position it within the framework of late-medieval secular and devotional aspirations and needs.

Crusading fragmented: Expansion and retraction

Fourteenth-century crusading is hard to interpret. It has been characterised as a 'golden age of crusading'; 'an epoch of crises and confusions'; an 'incoherent and diffuse' period; but also one of 'remarkable panache'.[18] To those wishing to impose neat categories over crusade and religious warfare, the reality of late-medieval campaigning resists easy typology. Historians adhering to a strict canonical definition, where papal leadership, the crusade vow and attendant spiritual and secular privileges (particularly the plenary indulgence) form the *sine qua non* of crusading, might find the meaning stretched when faced with spontaneous, unauthorised expressions of popular enthusiasm to recover the Holy Land, such as the People's crusades of 1309 and 1320, for instance. As with earlier periods, not all crusading uniformly involved traditional mechanisms of church funding and control. Two foci of English military activity, the campaigns against Moorish Granada in Spain and the seasonal incursions into pagan Lithuania, were never formally preached in England and were run by local expansionist powers, albeit under licence from the papacy. Similarly, crusade recruitment in the 1390s ran through the wider channels of diplomacy and contact between courtiers and nobles of England and France, not the ecclesiastical authorities – a necessary measure given that a state of church schism had unhelpfully supplied two rival popes. By contrast, those favouring a view of crusading as, in origin and essence, holy wars concerned with the Holy Land, lacking full credibility after the fall of the Latin East, struggle to accommodate the contemporary religiosity of wars on other frontiers, and the ready appropriation there of crusade symbolism, language and canon law. Other historians stress the political importance of the traditional

---

[17] The classic studies end c.1300. See P. J. Cole, *The Preaching of the Crusades* (Cambridge, Mass., 1991); C. T. Maier, *Preaching the Crusades* (Cambridge, 1994); J. A. Brundage, *Medieval Canon Law and the Crusader* (Madison, 1969); E. Bridrey, *La Condition juridique des croisés et le privilège de croix* (Paris, 1900); M. Purcell, *Papal Crusading Policy: The Chief Instruments of Papal Crusading Policy, 1244–1291* (Leiden, 1975).

[18] Housley, *Later Crusades* pp. 402, 420; id., 'The Crusading Movement, 1274–1700' *Oxford Illustrated History of the Crusades* ed. J. S. C. Riley-Smith (Oxford, 1995) pp. 267 (quoting A. Luttrell), 277.

image of Christendom under siege, perhaps deflecting from the emotional intensity that the Holy Land retained in popular piety. Much ink has been spilt on the issue, not all of it edifying.[19] Partly a function of different research tastes, it is also a problem of filtering sources and synthesising local and regional responses.

One example from the English evidence helps bear this out. Of those that can be shown to have joined crusade expeditions in the later middle ages, or intended to do so, many are known only or chiefly through references in the crown's records of the chancery and exchequer. Here, problematically, the term *crucesignatus* (i.e. marked with the cross, or avowed crusader), which achieved fairly extensive use in the thirteenth century, drops out of currency, disappearing from governmental rolls altogether after 1307. In the absence of either a general expedition to the east, or a royal crusade, the reasons for this are not hard to find, royal clerks and legal experts apparently keeping to a narrow view of when the financial and legal immunities of a *crucesignatus* might be applied. The presumption in 'Bracton', the 'Fleta' and later legal treatises – e.g. 'Modus Tenendi Curias' (c.1310) and 'Mirror of Justices' (c.1321), for instance – is that the crusader's privileges applied only to campaigns to the Holy Land. More specifically, the 'Fleta' (c.1290) advises independent campaigners to sue out for royal licences and juridical protections because, in their case, the traditional immunities awarded for a royal crusade did not apply.[20] This circumscribed application of crusading's legal apparatus may not have met with approval from papal lawyers (or some modern analysts), but it reflects practice as it developed in England, and there is usually little in the record to distinguish those in royal service, or those conducting some other business overseas, from men embarking under licence to fight in defence of the faith. The bureaucratic change attracts little comment, largely because taking the cross, becoming a *crucesignatus*, retained a cultural ubiquity outside the juridical realm, but it makes the task of positive identification rather more difficult.[21]

[19]   Constable, 'The Historiography of the Crusades'; N. Housley, *Contesting the Crusades* (Oxford, 2006); C. J. Tyerman, *The Invention of the Crusades* (Basingstoke, 1998); id. *The Debate on the Crusades* (Manchester, 2011) pp. 218–28.

[20]   Henry de Bracton, *De legibus et consuetudinibus Angliae* ed. T. Twiss, r.s. 70 (London, 1878–1883) vol. V pp. 159–65; Andrew Horn, *The Mirror of Justices* ed. W. J. Whittaker, Seldon Society 7 (London, 1895) pp. 82–4; *The Court Baron: Being precedents for use in seignorial and other local courts, together with select pleas from the Bishop of Ely's Court of Littleport* eds F. W. Maitland and W. P. Baildon, Seldon Society 4 (London, 1891) pp. 81–2; *Fleta* eds H. G. Richardson and G. O. Sayles, Seldon Society 72, 89, 99 (London, 1955–1983) vol. VI pp. 122–4, esp. p. 122.

[21]   E.g. the brass cross riveted onto the duke of Gloucester's armour (1391), or, for contrast, the flesh-cross cut into the shoulder of the fictional Sir Isumbras, preparatory to his heroic ordeals in the east. See *Testamenta Vetusta* ed. N. H. Nicolas (London, 1826) vol. I pp. 146ff; 'Sir Isumbras' *Six Middle English Romances* ed. M. Mills (London, 1992) pp. 125–47. The sources are full of references to the cru-sader's cross, both as the object of devotion and as a banner of holy war. See the inclusion of the rite for cross-taking in various contemporary cathedral and chapter house missals. J. A. Brundage, 'Cruce Signari: The Rite for Taking the Cross in England' *Traditio* 26 (1966) pp. 289–310. The following four-teenth-century examples may be added to Brundage's inventory: *Missale ad usum Percelebris Ecclesiae*

Of course, medieval or modern, theory alone did little to animate the experiences of active participants. Crusading's impact on the culture of aristocratic society involves categories of behaviour and thought outside the confines of narrow technical interpretations. Faced with a diversity of campaign frontiers and a host of logistical and material preparations, what was important was the settling of affairs at home, purchase of safe conducts, adequate transportation, equipping of a fighting retinue and a general confidence that the warfare embarked on was spiritually and socially meritorious, as backed by papal pronouncements, analogies to the Holy Land crusade, or other various continuities of crusade and holy war. These are the active links that surface repeatedly in the pages below. There is no reason to stray far from this understanding of wars in the *hethenesse*. It seems sane here to allow the evidence and preoccupations of knightly combatants to be our principal guide. What was inescapable was the scale of the challenge surrounding Christendom in the fourteenth century. The topography of late-medieval crusading can be dizzying. Campaigning spanned several geographical regions, and can be divided into three periods of heightened activity broadly synonymous with the ebb and flow of the Anglo-French conflict: 1307–1346, 1360–1375 and 1389–1403. As a venue of English chivalry each frontier is examined in much greater detail below, but it is useful here to provide a preliminary overview.[22]

Failure to organise a mass eastern crusade, following the loss of Acre in 1291, characterised the first period (1307–1346). Franco-papal plans for general crusades to embark in 1319 and 1336 received extensive diplomacy and church support but disintegrated on grounds of poor finance, domestic unrest and conflict between neighbouring powers. A ceremonial highlight came in 1313 when Edward II took the cross with his father-in-law, Philip IV, and an assembly of French nobles in Paris, but this was to prove an empty display of zeal. Otherwise, the English court adopted a more cautious approach. Edward III's rejection of traditional politics with France, his refusal to accept a junior role and his subsequent audacious claim to the French crown represented the sternest test of Franco-papal crusade plans. Paranoid about being branded an obstacle to the crusade, Edward's government commissioned a dossier of legal defences to contest their good intentions, but ultimately co-operation proved impossible.[23] Accusations of bad faith in the 'business of the cross' featured largely in the propaganda of both sides in the build-up to open war. Nevertheless, traditional concentration on the objective of Jerusalem did not blinker strategists

---

Herfordensis ed. W. G. Henderson (Leeds, 1874) pp. 443–5; *The Sarum Missal* ed. J. W. Legg (Oxford, 1916) pp. 451–3; *Manuale et Processionale ad usum insignis Ecclesiae Eboracensis* ed. W. G. Henderson, Surtees Society (Durham, 1875) pp. 103–6; HMC, *Fifth Report* (London, 1887) p. 505; *The Register of Thomas Langley, Bishop of Durham, 1406–1437* ed. R. L. Storey, Surtees Society (Durham, 1949–1962) vol. III pp. 12–147.

[22] Secondary literature for the following paragraphs is found in the notes of Chapters 2–5.

[23] See below p. 188.

to wider threats in the eastern Mediterranean. The plight of Christian Armenia and the activity of Turkish shipping in the coastal waters of the Aegean caused particular alarm, and brighter points of this first phase included the successful launch of a Hospitaller-led expedition to Rhodes in 1309 and the co-operation of local maritime powers in crusade leagues of the 1330s and 1340s. These relatively small-scale operations had far larger western roots than is usually thought. Fundraising in aid of the Hospitaller crusade caused a significant stir in the English dioceses between 1309 and 1313, for instance, calling to mind the periodic appeals of earlier decades, and a number of Edward II's knights volunteered for action. Some years later, campaigning between 1343 and 1346 witnessed a combined army of Italian, English and French knights establishing a bridgehead at Muslim-held Smyrna, probably the most prized position along the coastline of Turkish Anatolia. This was highly promising, but escalation of the French war following the battle of Crécy (1346) and the onset of the Black Death at the end of the decade, extinguished the possibility of turning it into a genuine challenge for regional control.

The pause in the Anglo-French war in the 1360s opened the second period of raised expectations and activity. Alongside optimistic proposals for a new Holy Land expedition there surfaced more modest plans based on tested methods of amphibious assault and western recruitment. The most famous of these was the expedition to Alexandria led by King Peter of Cyprus in 1365. Plans for English participation were far-reaching, with a major component of the Cypriot crusade to be formed of an Anglo-Gascon army led by Thomas Beauchamp, the earl of Warwick. Other campaigns included a flotilla sent in aid of Constantinople (1366) and Cypriot raids along the Syrian coast (1367), targeting places such as Jaffa and Tripoli, old names in crusading history. The years 1363–1368 were a high point in English involvement, with scores of nobles and knights embarking from Venice and other Italian ports, and many combining experience of the Mediterranean with time spent fighting on the Baltic frontier. Crusading received a charismatic figurehead in the form of Peter of Cyprus. Twice he visited Edward III's court to drum up support.

An Anglo-French truce was once more the context of activism during the 1390s, the third period of heightened activity. With the onset of peace, the governments of England and France took steps to protect their interests in what promised to be an impressive revival of eastern crusading, despatching spies and agents to the Balkans and other parts, and publicly entertaining talk of a joint expedition. The powerful John of Gaunt became implicated in Burgundian plans for a campaign for the relief of Hungary and the city of Constantinople. Halted at Nicopolis in 1396, the crusade failed to live up to hopes, but it formed part of the vogue arising for pilgrimage and crusading in other theatres among the knights and nobles of Richard II's court. A hothouse atmosphere of competition, honour and display helped instil commitment, the *hethenesse* crusade providing an attractive alternative to recent disappointments in the Hundred Years War. Confidence was boosted with participation in a Genoese-led attack upon the north African port of al-Mahdiya (Tunis) in 1390. While of residual importance in the fight against Islam, it allowed for close contact between English knights and illustrious figures of continental chivalry.[24]

By contrast with the eastern frontier, the crusades in the Baltic and Spain depended less upon the stop-start pattern of the Hundred Years War. The Teutonic Knights, the military order domiciled in Prussia and Livonia, faced significant military challenges in the 1330s and 1360s, after a long period of territorial expansion. Despite the Order's formidable financial and military resources, and its ability to control the main routes into pagan territory, Lithuanian war-bands were capable of disrupting Christian colonisation and even raiding the interior of Prussia itself. In reality a condition of military stalemate persisted and the fighting continued apace after 1386, when the unification of Lithuania with Christian Poland technically removed the religious argument. The wars against Muslim Granada did not acquire the pattern of regular semi-seasonal campaigning seen in the Baltic. Early engagements included James II of Aragon's attack upon Granada in 1309, and the disastrous Castilian assault at Vega in 1319. The arrival of a large invading Moorish army in the southern foothills of Castile in 1340 opened a period of more sustained war, and the subsequent struggle to gain control of the straits of Gibraltar attracted significant western involvement. As already seen, English nobles and knights were among those welcomed by the crusade *lumière* Alfonso XI. This could not last, however, and only a decade later, political divisions between the peninsular kingdoms and the growing distraction of fighting in northern Europe meant that the Moors of Granada and Morocco had little to fear. Only in the fifteenth century did the tempo of Christian attack increase. Other fronts included the war in Italy, where the majority of papally preached crusades in this period were directed, and new 'interior' crusades against the *routiers*, mercenary companies active in France and other regions during the 1360s and 1390s.[25]

Lest the diversity of crusade fronts and activity in the fourteenth century lapse into incoherence, crusade theorists turned to the concept of the *passagium particulare*: a limited specific campaign with experienced fighters that would clear the way for a general crusade or a *passagium generale*. This was not accepted everywhere; for instance, the author of the chivalric treatise *Tree of Battles* (c.1389) deemed it too dangerous on the grounds that local Christians would suffer reprisals before any major western relief could arrive.[26] And to some extent this was theory making a virtue out of necessity, the difficulties in producing a massed crusade encouraging apologists to adopt more compact expeditions as the most practical option. Arguably, within the context of English crusading, the *passagium particulare* had been standard practice since the early thirteenth century, when baronial campaigns such as those led by the earl of Chester and William Longsword attached themselves to the Fifth Crusade

---

[24]   Cf. Luttrell, 'Chaucer's Knight'.

[25]   For an introduction see N. Housley, 'Mercenary Companies, the Papacy and the Crusades, 1356–1378' *Traditio* 38 (1982) pp. 253–80.

[26]   Honoré Bonet, *The Tree of Battles* ed. G. W. Coopland (Liverpool, 1949) pp. 126–7.

(1217–1221) and Louis IX's expedition to Egypt (1249–1250). The Lord Edward's crusade of 1270 also belonged to this category, although it possessed the advantages of national lay and ecclesiastical taxation. Dominated by the associates of leading members of the royal family, Edward's small army was primarily constructed around household contingents and his band of personal followers.[27] The proliferation of English crusading in the fourteenth century departed little from this model, recruitment running though tested channels of clientage, friendship and kinship. None had the resources of a taxation state at their disposal, but in other respects military continuities went hand in hand with political and religious ones.

Less easy to reconstruct is the crusade's impact on domestic settings and the normal running of men's affairs, the sources barely hinting at the predicament facing families, relatives, friends and neighbours when plans failed, mishaps struck or the dangers of the *hethenesse* became fatal. It is only possible to guess at the level of disruption caused to the family of Sir Francis Villiers (d. c.1327), for instance, when his ambitions to fight in the Mediterranean inadvertently rendered his wife and children nearly penniless. Their plight eventually came to the attention of parliament.[28] Perhaps still less approachable is the fate of Elizabeth, the wife of Alexander Mowbray, a young knight killed while fighting outside Constantinople. A desperate whirlwind of events, including an incident of rape and abduction, overtook her in the months following her husband's departure for the east. It is hard to see this happening had he stayed closer to home.[29] Indeed, while the emphasis below is on military objectives and purposes, it is worth keeping in mind the gaps opened in local communities and the disruption caused to private and public relationships. One of the distinctive features of the crusade – unlike most other forms of contemporary European war – was its limited impact on the course of long-standing struggles for regional or political control. Far greater was its effect on the domestic lives of its participants and their private interests at home.

[27] Lloyd, *English Society and the Crusade* chap. 4 offers the best account of the organisation of the expedition.
[28] See below p. 28 n. 25.
[29] For Alexander Mowbray see below p. 101.

2

Eastern Mediterranean and the Holy Land

In 1319 the noted crusade enthusiast and former companion of Edward I, Sir Otto Grandson, finally retired from political life, making the gloomy prediction that the general *passagium* to the Holy Land appeared unlikely to embark in the near future. Close to the royal courts of England and France, he was well placed to judge, and installing a large part of his seignorial treasure at the papal camera, over 20,000 gold florins, Grandson redeemed his crusade vow.[1] Wider expectations were more robust. Throughout the fourteenth century the allure of the *partes de terra sancta*, an area roughly corresponding with the coastal strip of northern Syria and Palestine but also bridging the region of the Nile delta, continued to inspire military dreaming of the most ardent sort. It spawned very muddled but potent notions of politics and events. Against periodic rumours of mammoth Christian success and sudden Muslim collapse, Latin rule conducted a piecemeal retreat, becoming eventually reduced to a clutch of island dependencies in the Aegean and the kingdom of Cyprus. By the 1370s war-torn Constantinople and Armenia were the political remnants of eastern Christendom. Prophecy, Jerusalem-centric piety and honoured military tradition gave the greatly diversified frontier a straightforward significance, however. In 1364, according to the Evesham chronicler, all the rulers of the infidel world (the sultan of Egypt; the 'kings' of Turkey, Morocco, Tunisia and Lithuania; the Tartars; and the king of north Africa and Spain) converged on the border of Armenia to fight a Christian host led partly by the Knights Hospitaller and a small band of western knights and 'pilgrims'. The source of the story is not clear, and the stunning defeat of forty thousand pagans was wishful thinking, but it suited the writer's purpose to place Christendom's global struggle on the outskirts of the *terra sancta*. This was where the ultimate question of salvation would be decided. Little of the structural tensions in

---

[1] *Jean XXII, 1316–1334: Lettres Communes*, ed. G. Mollat (Paris, 1904–1947) no. 9566. For Grandson's career see E. Clifford, *A Knight of Great Renown* (Chicago, 1961).

Anatolian and Mamluk politics or the divided loyalties of local Christian powers is acknowledged in western sources.[2]

Eastern crusading remained firmly in vogue throughout the fourteenth century, drawing a ready supply of English recruits to its fragmentary borders, even as the grander Jerusalem schemes continued to run into the sand.[3] The absence of concerted action from western governments meant that active crusading was confined to the maritime powers of Venice, Genoa and Cyprus, joined by the Hospitallers at Rhodes after 1310. The conquest of Rhodes (1308–1313) set the pattern for future enterprises, attracting a mixed range of recruits but favouring those knights with reliable access to court and the various channels of power. Emphasis lay upon highly mobile ship-borne expeditionary forces, and impressive numbers were sometimes achieved, with several hundred vessels and around eight thousand fighters contributing to Peter of Cyprus's crusade in 1365, for example. However, of the scattered direct attacks on enemy shores, Smyrna (1344), Lampsacus (1359), Adalia (1361), Alexandria (1365), Ayas (1361, 1367), Jaffa (1367), Tripoli (1367, 1403), Beirut (1403) and Bodrum (1407), only the capture of Smyrna resulted in the occupation of a significant strategic site (1344–1402). Dependence on the Italian maritime states, the expense of sea-travel and limits of seasonal sailings inevitably narrowed the scope for participation, particularly from north of the Alps, and English knights depended upon unmolested passage through Piedmont and Lombardy to the embarkation ports of Genoa and Venice, or less commonly to the French seaports of Marseilles and Aigues Mortes. The traditional dream of reinvading the Holy Land remained relevant, but for most of the period the Christian powers could only react defensively against the menace of Turkish piracy, and occasionally bring relief to the beleaguered Greeks. A papally preached Jerusalem crusade was resurrected for a final time in 1363, when John II of France and Peter of Cyprus took the cross, together with large numbers of continental and English knights. As ever, conditions in the west had a determinate effect. Edward III, always primed for war, needed little encouragement to see French crusade alliances with the Genoese and Visconti in the 1340s and 1360s as a veiled threat to his regional influence in Gascony, and later in the Iberian peninsula. These suspicions were not much lightened in times of peace. On the other hand, where they were able, English crusaders continued to feature centrally in multi-national expeditions, alongside French, Italian, Greek, Cypriot, German and Scottish forces. The

[2]   *Eulogium Historiarum* ... ed. F. S. Haydon, r.s. 9 (London, 1858–1863) vol. III pp. 237–8.

[3]   For the background to this, good starting points include M. Balard, *Les latins en Orient XIe–XVe siècle* (Paris, 2006); *Ibn Khaldun: The Mediterranean in the 14th Century: Rise and Fall of Empires* eds M. Viguera et al. (Seville, 2006); J. H. Pryor, *Geography, Technology and War: Studies in the Maritime History of the Mediterranean 649–1571* (Cambridge, 1988); P. Lock, *The Franks in the Aegean, 1204–1500* (London, 1995); Setton, *Papacy and the Levant*; Housley, *Avignon Papacy*; Tyerman, *God's War*; Luttrell, 'English Levantine Crusaders' pp. 143–53; id. 'Chaucer's Knight' pp. 127–60.

antagonism that sometimes surfaced between rival nations on the northern crusade is largely unrecorded in the east.[4]

Innovation and tradition

The first expedition to depart for the east in the fourteenth century, a Hospitaller-commanded force of several thousand fighters, has gone almost entirely unnoticed in the history of English crusading. It possessed many features of traditional campaigning, including widespread crusade preaching, indulgence sales, vow redemptions, dubious Italian mercantile interests, a pope desperate to achieve something for the Christians of the east, and a self-serving political leadership. Scheduled to sail on 24 June 1309, the official objective was the relief of Christian Armenia and the establishment of an entry-point to northern Syria, though the Hospitallers regarded completion of their conquest of Rhodes to be of greater importance. Money was to be found from several sources: the papal exchequer, the French king, Philip IV, and funds raised through the universal sale of indulgences. An unusually liberal scheme of indulgences formed the heart of the initiative and was aimed at extracting as large a profit as possible from non-embarking penitents through vow-redemption and alms-giving. General participation of the faithful was discouraged. That privilege was reserved for western knights and noblemen acceptable to the Order. Instead, the chaotic 'Crusade of the Poor' would become a focus for responses lower down the social scale (see below pp. 137–9).[5]

In contrast to France and Spain, where it faced resistance from the royal authorities, the Hospitaller expedition received extensive promotion in the English dioceses.[6] The crusade bulls probably arrived in England with the bishop of Nazareth, whose presence in London during January 1309 triggered the start of fundraising across the dioceses. Church collecting boxes were installed, a dedicated liturgy imposed and local ecclesiastics instructed to preach in support of the *passagium*.[7] It was the first

---

[4]   See below pp. 90–1.

[5]   Housley, *Avignon Papacy* pp. 15–16; *Regestum Clementis Papae V* ed. Ordinis St Benedicti (Rome, 1885–1892) nos 2987–92, 2996–7; *Papsttum und Untergang des Templeordens* ed. H. Finke (Münster, 1907) vol. II pp. 157–8.

[6]   For an overview of the European context see N. Housley, 'Pope Clement and the Crusades of 1309–1310' *Journal of Medieval History* 8 (1982) pp. 29–43.

[7]   'Annales Paulini' and 'Annales Londonienses' in *Chronicles of the Reigns of Edward I and Edward II* ed. W. Stubbs, r.s. 76 (London, 1882–1883) pp. 156, 266; *The Chronicle of St. Mary's Abbey, York* eds H. H. E. Craster and M. E. Thornton, Surtees Society (Durham, 1934) pp. 46–7; *Reg. Clem.* nos 4769, 4772–3; *Register of John de Halton, Bishop of Carlisle 1292–1324* eds W. N. Thompson and T. F. Tout, Canterbury and York Society (London, 1913) vol. I p. 317, vol. II p. 41; *Registrum Radulphi Baldock, Gilberti Segrave, Ricardi Newport et Stephani Gravesend* ed. R. C. Fowler, Canterbury and York Society (London, 1911) pp. 109–10; *Registrum Simonis Gandavo, Diocesis Saresbiriensis, 1297–1315* eds C. T. Flower and M. C. B. Dawes, Canterbury and York Society (Oxford and London 1914–1934) vol. II pp.

time crusade indulgences had been widely promoted since 1291, and a fast trade seems to have quickly developed. In London it was profitable enough to attract a criminal element, with sham preachers seen haunting taverns, hostels and other disreputable places in a bid to separate cash from the faithful. Elsewhere the authorities collected healthy sums, particularly during the first two years, though the recorded amounts vary widely.[8] For men of independent standing, it was an opportunity to fulfil old vows and engage in warfare more satisfying than Edward II's early dismal outings against the Scots. Service in the Hospitallers' relief raids and strategic island conquests had, by contrast, all the appearance and appeals of a private military enterprise. As a specific, specialised campaign with discrete objectives manned by professional soldiers, it was recognition of the innovations demanded by crusade planners. Limited in scale and difficult to trace in the sources, it nonetheless would set the mould of English crusading for much of the period.

A series of open-ended truces with Robert the Bruce (October 1308–January 1310) provided scope for participation of twelve months or more, if not the expedition's intended extent of five years.[9] A wartime ban on the export of bullion, horses and war equipment was lifted in favour of the expedition, and several knights with connections to Edward II's household received warrants to depart for the east. The official letters do not mention their status as crusaders, referring to their objective merely as the Holy Land – which emotionally, if not militarily, it was – but their intentions are clear. Sir John Elsfield was specially commended to the pope because he was going 'against the enemies of Christ', and, together with an unnamed companion, William Chesney, 'the king's cousin and yeoman', carried letters of introduction to the master of the Hospitallers.[10] Another knight of the household, Francis Villiers, was issued with a safe conduct valid for five years in respect of his journey to the east 'in the service of the Almighty', his intention apparently to serve the duration of the crusade.

303–12; *Registrum Henrici Woodlock, Diocesis Wintoniensis, 1305–1316* ed. A. W. Goodman, Canterbury and York Society (Oxford, 1940–1941) vol. II pp. 348, 539–41; *Register of John de Droxford, Bishop of Bath and Wells, 1309–1329* ed. B. Hobhouse, Somerset Record Society (London, 1887) vol. I p. 67; *The Register of William Greenfield, Lord Archbishop of York, 1306–1315* eds W. Brown and A. H. Thompson, Surtees Society (Durham, 1931–1940) vol. IV pp. 284–5, 363, vol. V pp. 134–5.

[8]   According to the 'Paulini' p. 266, the indulgences were of the sort 'a saeculo non erant auditae'; *Reg. Gandavo* vol. II pp. 312–13; *Reg. Baldock* p. 134. The bishop of Salisbury was disappointed to find only 25 marks in the parish chests of Berkshire archdeaconry in June 1309. This was put down to the shortness of time, the collecting chests having been installed in his churches for only a matter of weeks. In the diocese of York, on the other hand, nearly £500 was accounted for between 1309 and 1311, an impressive tally considering that the region was suffering the twin ravages of famine and the Scots war. In 1318 the new valuation of the clerical tenth in the four northern dioceses was barely £2,400. See Lunt, *Financial Relations* vol. I p. 405; *Reg. Greenfield* vol. IV p. 363. After 1313 Edward II could not raise taxes in the north of England because of wide impoverishment.

[9]   C. McNamee, *The Wars of the Bruces: Scotland, England and Ireland, 1306–1328* (East Linton, 1997) pp. 43–8.

[10]   NA, C70/2 m.4; *Foedera* vol. I pt. 4 pp. 141–3; *CChW 1244–1326* p. 292.

The knights John Roches, Giles Trumpeton and Payn Turberville possessed similar grants, though their licences term them as pilgrims, which, mindful of their status in canon law, technically they were.[11]

The activities of Elsfield and Chesney in Avignon (Chesney also fielded letters of introduction to the curia) towards the end of the summer of 1309 provide strong evidence that the court took close interest. Already in June 1308 one of Edward II's household sergeants was bound for the region of Cyprus, purportedly to 'service a vow' in the Holy Land, but also perhaps to gather first-hand knowledge of the crisis in the east. Information of delay to the *passagium* because of a lack of ships passed freely between the papal authorities and English officials, so that recruitment could proceed after the original embarkation date, and men taking out royal licences early could postpone their departure, though a number may have followed the lead of an impatient Sir Francis Villiers and set out anyway.[12] In fact, a plan for a sizeable English army was in the air as early as August 1308. It originated in royal circles under the auspices of Robert, Lord Fitzpayn, steward of the household, but it also gathered the support of the French king, Philip IV, the evidence first emerging from papal correspondence with the French court. What transpired was an early example of high-level crusade enthusiasm largely hidden from view in the official sources. Fitzpayn, 'burning with fervour for the faith', approached Philip IV with the plan while travelling en route to the curia at the beginning of September 1308.[13] Armed with letters of recommendation from the French king, Fitzpayn travelled to Avignon and received an audience with the pope sometime before 30 September 1308, where, on his own behalf, and on behalf of 'many other English magnates', he submitted that for one year starting 24 June 1309 a party of up to five hundred noblemen would embark with the Hospitallers in aid of the Holy Land. Impressed with the nobleman's credentials but noting that he had no firm evidence of wider support, Clement V bestowed crusade indulgences upon him and his collaborators to take immediate effect on their departure for the east. The suggestion – apparently forwarded by Philip IV – that Fitzpayn might be given leadership of the Hospitaller expedition was rejected.[14]

If the French held out hope of Fitzpayn wresting control of the Hospitaller *passagium* from the curia, Clement V dismissed it out of hand. Edward II's part in the initiative is perhaps less easy to gauge. Fitzpayn's activity at the curia had official status, his party of five carried letters of protection for travelling 'on the king's service', and it is conceivable that the steward's mission was to apprise Philip IV and Clement V of Edward's reaction to the recent exile of royal favourite, the hated Piers Gaveston.[15]

[11]   *CPR 1307–1313* pp. 102 (Turberville), 107 (Villiers), 115 (Roches) 121–2 (Trumpeton).
[12]   The unnamed yeoman also carried letters of introduction to the Hospitallers: *CChW 1244–1326* p. 273.
[13]   *Vitae paparum Avenionesium* ed. G. Mollat (Paris, 1914–1927) vol. III pp. 87–90.
[14]   Ibid. p. 90; *Reg. Clem.* no. 3054.
[15]   *CPR 1307–1313* p. 93.

The English embassy may have been sent to argue that Gaveston should be exonerated from blame. The four months stipulated by royal licence provided enough time for the journey to Paris and Avignon for this purpose. Fitzpayn was, though, an unusual choice for such a mission, his coolness towards Gaveston later leading him to align with Edward II's critics in 1310.[16] Fitzpayn's activity at the curia in fact fits much more closely with the court's ongoing pattern of contact with the crusade, i.e. through personal and semi-official channels. Whether or not it originated with Edward II or his advisors, the plan was reminiscent of his father's policy in the 1290s of enlisting courtiers to participate in the king's name and was consistent with the activity of royal servants in the Mediterranean. The ambition seems to have been to forge closer links to Philip IV and impose a joint leadership over the *negotium terrae sanctae*. As the official in charge of the corps of household knights, Fitzpayn was an obvious representative of royal intentions. It is difficult to be more conclusive: Robert carried Edward II's letters of introduction to Clement V but record of their content is lost.[17]

Fitzpayn's leadership is nonetheless instructive. A baron with extensive parliamentary experience and a career in arms stretching back to the 1270s, he rose to prominence in the final decade of Edward I's reign as custodian of several royal castles and envoy to France. Too young to have accompanied the Lord Edward on crusade, and a seasoned campaigner by the time of the fall of Acre, Fitzpayn belonged to a generation of men who identified themselves with the martial spirit of Edward I and his avowed devotion to the Holy Land.[18] For knights of his age it was becoming obvious that opportunity to perform active service on crusade was beginning to run out. He began passing the names of men requiring licences to travel to the east to the king at the end of February 1309.[19] The record sources are scanty, and the steward's name is absent from some of the warrants, but the shape of a fairly coherent grouping emerges, including some of the prominent figures already named. The influential marcher-lord Payn Turberville and John Elsfield, for instance, both came to royal service from the earl of Gloucester's retinue, and were probably known to Fitzpayn at court. William Gritton (licence to travel to the east, 23 June) was a retainer of Sir Giles Trumpeton, a veteran of the Scottish war and an experienced royal envoy; another recruit, Sir Simon Montagu, held land in Fitzpayn's native Somerset and, like the steward, was a former keeper of Corfe Castle.[20] The west country connection was enlarged with Sir John Beauchamp of Hatch, a prominent figure of Edward I's Scottish campaigns

[16] 'Londonienses' pp. 170–1; J. R. Maddicott, *Thomas of Lancaster, 1307–1322: A Study in the Reign of Edward II* (Oxford, 1970) pp. 106–20.

[17] For Edward I see Tyerman, *England and the Crusades* pp. 230–40; *Vitae paparum* vol. III p. 90.

[18] C. Moor, *Knights of Edward I*, Harleian Society (London, 1929–1932) vol. II pp. 50–1.

[19] E.g. the enrolled protections for Payn Turberville and Sir John Beauchamp of Hatch. See *CPR 1307–1313* p. 102.

[20] *Glamorgan County History* ed. T. B. Pugh (Cardiff, 1971) vol. III p. 690 (Turberville); Moor, *Knights of Edward I* vol. I p. 303 (Elsfield); ibid. vol. V pp. 50–1 (Trumpeton); *CPR 1307–1313* p. 122 (Gritton); *Complete Peerage* ed. G. E. Cokayne (London, 1910–1957) vol. IX pp. 78–9 (Montague).

who held his baronial lands in Somerset and Devon. Robert, Lord Fitzwalter, also prepared to embark, appointing attorneys to manage his affairs during his absence in the east for four years starting 24 June 1309. Other *peregre* with licences to travel *ad terram Jerosolomitanam* include the figures of John Dyve and Nicholas Alneto (alias Dauney), royal servants of standing at county level.[21] William Paris of Castle Homby (Lancs.) and John Roches represented the wealthier sort of gentleman, able to commit private resources to the *passagium*.[22]

Although writs of protection are an unreliable guide to the numbers involved and the relationships between would-be participants, a picture is formed of a loose confederation of crusade militants probably known to Fitzpayn either through common military service in Scotland, Wales and Gascony, or through the circles of royal government and bureaucracy at court. Another marcher-lord, Fulk Fitzwarin, apparently had an active role. His experience of fighting 'Saracens' was reportedly of practical use twenty years later when advising Edward III's commanders on battle tactics against the Scots. The leadership of at least five barons with extensive military experience (Fitzpayn, Turberville, Montagu, Fitzwalter, Beauchamp) provided the grouping with a natural core. It was probably expected that paid retainers, tenurial dependants and family relations would make up the bulk of manpower. Surviving household indentures show that service on crusade could be obligatory for some of Fitzpayn's contemporaries, and even with the limited resources of a private enterprise, Edward II's noblemen could probably expect to field a fighting force of several hundred men. This is less than the total promised to Clement V, but nevertheless in keeping with the scale of the Hospitaller *passagium*.[23]

In the event, the proportions of this early scheme are more significant as a marker of courtly and military aspirations than of actual contributions at the front. Fitzpayn's grouping may have been buoyed by displays of popular crusade enthusiasm in London and other urban centres (see below pp. 137–9), and they possibly helped to stoke it,

---

[21] *CPR 1307–1313* pp. 102, 111; *Peerage* vol. II pp. 48–9 (Beauchamp). Fitzwalter had yet to depart in April 1310: *CPR 1307–1313* p. 224. Appointed commissioner of peace for Oxford (March 1308), Dyve held two knights' fees in that county: *CIPM* vol. V p. 144 no. 268; *CPR 1307–1313* p. 54. Alneto was a commissioner of array in co. Devon (March 1316): *CPR 1313–1317* p. 461.

[22] *CPR 1307–1313* pp. 114 (Paris), 115 (Roches). Roches held most of his lands in Hampshire: *CIPM* vol. V no. 298.

[23] For Fitzwarin, 'a baron renowned in arms', see *Brut* ed. F. W. D. Brie EETS o.s. 131, 136 (London, 1906–1908) vol. I pp. 277–8. He commanded Edward II's army at Boroughbridge (1318) and fought at Dupplin Moor (1332). Examples of indentures are printed in *Private Indentures for Life Service in Peace and War, 1278–1476* eds M. Jones and S. Walker, Camden Miscellany 32 (London, fifth series 1994) pp. 48–52 nos 14, 17, 18: Sir Bartholomew de Enfield with Humphrey Bohun, earl of Hereford (February 1307); John Darcy with Aymer Valence, earl of Pembroke (November 1309); and, for contrast, showing care to explicitly exclude war in the Holy Land, Sir John Bracebridge with Robert, Lord Mohaut, for service 'en toutes terres et en touz regions hors pris la Terre Seynte' (August 1310). Bracebridge had perhaps indented to crusade with another noble household, or alternatively, he wanted indemnity against otherwise expected demands of knightly service.

but circumstances worked against the baronial army. The steward's appointment as Edward II's envoy to Avignon in March 1309 allowed for the further developing of his plan at the curia, but prolonged absence from England over the spring months threatened arrangements at home, and the household direction of the initiative appears to have broken down.[24] Despite this setback and an apparent loss of focus, by mid-summer 1309 more than a dozen English knights and their followers were in possession of warrants to embark for the east, and some of them set out. Francis Villiers reached enemy lines as early as May 1309, whereupon he lost his baggage in a skirmish with Turkish pirates. After limping back to Avignon he was forced on the charity of the cardinals.[25] Sir John Roches embarked for the east sometime after 17 June. One year later he was thought dead, and proceedings were started to place his Hampshire estate into the king's hands. When news eventually filtered through that John was alive and well, still *in partibus transmarinas*, perhaps with the Hospitallers, the royal escheator was ordered to stop 'meddling' with the Roches lands – proof that chancery protections worked, but also a reminder of the risks of lengthy absence in the east.[26] The withdrawal of Payn Turberville from public life also points towards lengthy absence abroad. His amassing of 300 marks for his pilgrimage to the 'regions of Jerusalem' is in keeping with the sort of retinue and equipage appropriate for military action.[27]

Whether part of a baronial grouping or not, other English knights continued to be attracted by the conquest of Rhodes and Hospitaller attacks upon the adjacent Turkish emirate of Menteshe over the five years of Clement V's crusade indulgences (1308–1313) and beyond. Edward II's circle remained a main hub of activity. In February 1311, for instance, a close friend of Piers Gaveston, the famous Giles d'Argentein – 'the third best knight in Christendom' – withdrew from Edward's army at Berwick to travel *ad terram sanctam*. D'Argentein's objective was service with the Hospitallers, and it was when travelling on a galley near Rhodes that he was captured and imprisoned at Thessalonica by Greek forces, enemies of the Order's expansion across the Rhodian archipelago (1313). D'Argentein was returned to the king's side the following summer – in time to lead a suicidal charge at Bannockburn and earn a permanent place in the annals of chivalry.[28] Few had the profile of d'Argentein or

[24] *Foedera* vol. I pt. 4 pp. 136–7; Maddicott, *Thomas of Lancaster* pp. 90–106.

[25] *Reg. Clem.* no. 4118. The mishap ruined his family: Francis's widow, Agnes, appealed to Edward III for help in escaping poverty, making a plea on the basis of Francis's loyal service to the court in the Holy Land, Gascony, Wales, Scotland, Flanders and England (n.d. but sometime after 1327): *Rot. Parl.*vol. II p. 381.

[26] *CPR 1307–1313* p. 379; NA, C54/129 m. 31; *CCR 1308–1313* p. 366 (20 August 1311); *CIPM* vol. V no. 298.

[27] *CCR 1308–1313* p. 122 (12 August 1308); following the terminology on roll NA, C54/126 m. 22ᵈ.

[28] *CPR 1307–1313* p. 324; *Foedera* vol. II pt. 1 p. 50; A. Luttrell, 'Hospitallers in Rhodes, 1306–1421' *History of the Crusades* ed. Setton vol. III pp. 278–313. D'Argentein's career is summarised in J. R. V. Barker, *The Tournament in England 1100–1400* (Woodbridge, 1986) pp. 127–8. See also J. S. Hamilton,

Fitzpayn, but others passed from England to fulfil crusade vows. Besides the east, the war against Muslim Granada apparently attracted considerable interest. According to Aragonese sources at the curia, many English *cavallers* were eager to take advantage of papal indulgences announced for a new offensive against the Moors in the spring of 1309. The court was represented with the expedition of Sir Robert Tony, another of Edward II's close associates. Royal letters opened the way to an audience with Ferdinand IV, a cousin of Edward II, as part of an effort to breathe fresh life into the historic alliance with Castile and to gain English entry to the holy war.[29] Tony and his companion, Sir Walter Kingsmeade, were reported dead by the beginning of December 1309, possibly casualties of a disastrous Christian attack on Almería. A third member of Tony's mission, Sir Walter Haket, survived, though his influence at court was soon eclipsed, and in 1318 he sided against Edward II with the rebellious earl of Lancaster.[30]

Knightly fervour – knightly torpor?

Insofar as it signalled commitment to traditional chivalry, the dubious reputation of military culture at Edward II's court should perhaps be modified to take into account the crusade. Men such as d'Argentein, Elsfield, Fitzwarin and Beauchamp were regulars on the tournament circuit (word of Fitzpayn's project may have spread at the large meetings at Dunstable and Stepney, spring 1309), and they probably saw the Hospitaller *passagium* as an opportunity to enhance their standing at home. Elsfield's willingness to interrupt a promising career in royal service for the sake of the Holy Land points to this frame of mind.[31] There was the usual mixed-bag of motivations. At least one of Fitzpayn's associates solemnised his commitment with a religious vow. Two years and one week after he failed to embark, Sir Simon Montagu sought absolution for breaking his vow to start for the Holy Land on the feast of St John the Baptist

---

Piers Gaveston: Earl of Cornwall, 1307–1312 (Detroit, 1988) p. 142; *The Bruce of John Barbour*, ed. W. W. Skeat, EETS e.s. 11, 21, 29, 55 (London, 1870–1889) vol. I pp. 264, 317. The crusader John Elsfield was also killed at Bannockburn: 'Londoniensis' p. 231.

[29]   *Acta Aragonensia* ed. H. Finke (Berlin-Leipzig, 1908–1922) vol. I pp. 263–4; *CChW 1244–1326* p. 287; *CPR 1307–1313* p. 117; *Reg. Clem.* nos 3819, 3988-91. In 1311 Ferdinand IV sought to deepen Anglo-Castilian co-operation, making his shared lineage with Edward II and 'la guerre des sarazins' the basis of an appeal for a substantial loan: NA, C47/27/8/13. Edward declined, citing the expenses of war in Scotland (9 October 1311): *Foedera* vol. I pt. 4 p. 195.

[30]   *CPR 1307–1313* pp. 190, 197, 239. Haket and Tony witnessed numerous royal charters in the first year of Edward's reign. See J. S. Hamilton 'Charter Witness Lists for the Reign of Edward II' *Fourteenth Century England* vol. I ed. N. Saul (Woodbridge, 2000) pp. 1–20; Moor, *Knights of Edward I* vol. II p. 172.

[31]   For the politics surrounding the Dunstable and Stepney tournaments see Maddicott, *Thomas of Lancaster* pp. 90–106 and references there; *Foedera* vol. I pt. 4 p. 143.

1309.[32] A packed career in royal service, including captaincy of the English fleet and custody of Beaumaris Castle in Anglesey, had apparently intruded.[33] Hereditary tradition was perhaps another important motivating factor: Giles Trumpeton, Fulk Fitzwarin and Payn Turberville were elder sons of participants on the Lord Edward's crusade of 1271–1274. John Roches could count Peter des Roches, the crusading bishop of Winchester (d. 1238), among his distant kin. Robert Fitzwalter's ancestor and namesake was a participant of the Fifth Crusade (1217–1221).[34]

Some of this was carried over later in Edward II's reign. In 1317 Sir Edmund Kendale, a king's bachelor, in order to fulfil a crusade vow made 'when he was in peril in Scotland', was released from six years' rent on a royal manor in Rutland, which he was allowed to lease out for the same period.[35] Others at Edward II's court became knowledgeable about eastern affairs. One servant of the king, the sea-captain William Badin, was able to peddle his expertise to the count of Clermont, grandson of Louis IX, in the early 1330s, consulting on the *holy viage* and undertaking a fact-finding mission of the entire Mediterranean region and Persia, ranging between Constantinople, Trebiz, Baghdad and Egypt.[36] Living reminders of Latin Palestine and English crusading, Otto Grandson and Antony Bek, the bishop of Carlisle, stalked the diplomatic arena, employed as mouthpieces of Edward II's regime. As Patriarch of Jerusalem and twice *crucesignatus*, Bek captained efforts to broker the king's French marriage (1306–1308). Grandson was held in particularly high esteem, still commanding great admiration in courtly circles, judging by Edward II's letters. He met the king at least twice after Edward II's coronation, at Edward's cross-taking in 1313 and during a trip to England on papal business in 1317. He was well regarded by prominent Levantine Christians as well as other western rulers.[37]

In this respect, Edward II's involvement and the involvement of his circle followed directly on from the policies of Edward I. Participation in schemes for a grand eastern crusade was inescapable if the English court was to continue claiming church tenths and papal support. Confirmation of this position, Edward II's cross-taking in Paris

[32]   *Reg. Droxford* vol. I p. 65.
[33]   Montagu was obviously something of a loose cannon: he was subsequently arrested for 'diverse felonies and trespasses against the king', including an attempted invasion of the Isle of Man. Montagu still occupied a cell in Windsor castle when a papal penitentiary entrusted him to the bishop of Bath and Wells for penance, with the stipulation that he must be ready to join the next *passagium generale* (31 June 1311): *Reg. Droxford* p. 65. He was released in December 1311 and formally pardoned in April 1313: *CCR 1308–1313* p. 389; *CPR 1307–1313* p. 505.
[34]   Peter des Roches led an English contingent as part of Frederick II's Holy Land crusade (1227–1229). See Lloyd, *English Society and the Crusade* pp. 75, 83 (Roches), 99 (Trumpeton), 122 (Turberville); Tyerman, *England and the Crusades* pp. 99-101.
[35]   *CPR 1313–1317* p. 628; *CChW 1244–1326* p. 462.
[36]   As noted in Paviot, *Ducs de Bourgogne* p. 64; cf. *CPR 1327–1330* p. 9.
[37]   For Bek's life see C. M. Fraser, *A History of Antony Bek, Bishop of Durham, 1283–1311* (Oxford, 1957); T. Stapleton, 'A Brief Summary of the Wardrobe Accounts of the Tenth, Eleventh and Fourteenth Years of King Edward the Second' *Archaeologia* 26 (1836) pp. 318–44; *Foedera* vol. II pt. 1 pp. 104–5.

1313, was an obvious signal of continuity, as well as an acknowledgement of his host Philip IV's political pre-eminence. Afterwards the king's relationship with the French general *passagium* suffered the same sort of evasion and dilatoriness as other matters of government. But even sceptical observers, like Pope John XXII, believed in crusading's capacity to transform political reputations, as well as to produce results for the church. No-one expressed surprise at the king's crusade vow, despite the unfavourable beginnings of his reign. Nor was Edward immune to the competitive psychology that saw each of the main European monarchies take up the crusade cause at various points in the fourteenth century. His envoys at the curia had sweeping powers to treat on the Holy Land as a matter of royal and, by implication, national honour. In private, Edward spoke of the proposed *voiage a la terre seint* with a matter of factness that veers away from the sort of mendacity usually suspected of paper crusader kings.[38]

This is not to say that Edward had any serious ambition of going on crusade or came close to the level of practical action. In aligning himself with the crusade Edward II was capable, perhaps more than most, of possessing contradictory impulses and motivations. Within various settings, optimism that the liberation of the Holy Places was imminent served as a focus of ceremonial and religious display, and Edward, like other kings of England after him, did not belittle crusading's devotional aspects (see below pp. 186, 190–2). When Edward took the cross in 1313, among his entourage of advisors, for instance, were individuals like the Carmelite John Boukhil, who was preparing for a pilgrimage to the Holy Land 'for the salvation of the king and his subjects', and William Villeneuve, bishop *in partibus persarum*, whom the pope was sending to convert the Tartars. Villeneuve look leave from Edward armed with a handsome gift of money and letters of introduction as *zelator servidus Sanctae Fidei*.[39] The presence of such figures at court helped fix the mood. A few days after receiving the cross, Edward made a payment of 10 marks to Boukhil for his journey to the east. He travelled in the 'service of Christ', but it was also for Edward's peace of mind, probably in partial fulfilment of his vow. At other times, particularly periods of crisis, royal servants were despatched as pilgrims to the east.[40]

This was the partly the context for English participation in the Hospitaller expedition, the royal chamber providing a natural place for consolidating such sentiment.

---

[38] NA, SC1/45/192 (December 1316).

[39] *CPR 1307–1313* p. 566; NA, E101/375/8 fol. 30ʳ; *Foedera* vol. II pt. 1 p. 40; cf. J. Paviot, 'England and the Mongols (1260–1330)' *Journal of the Royal Asiatic Society* 3rd series 10 (2000) pp. 305–18. For Villeneuve see J. Richard, *La Papauté et les Missions D'Orient au Moyen Âge* (2nd edn, Rome, 1998) p. 148.

[40] NA, E101/375/8 fol. 32ʳ. The Carmelite also appears in the records variously as 'Bonkhil' and 'Dunkhull'. Nearness to the anniversary of Gaveston's death (19 June) may also have been a factor. Cf. Boukhil's first royal commission to travel 'ad terram sanctam' (23 July 1312): *CCR 1307–1313* p. 542; *CPR 1307–1313* p. 481. Other eastern pilgrimages on behalf of the king include that of John Boseham, yeoman of the chamber (n.d. but before 1314), and that of Adam of Cokerham, Hospitaller 'for the health of the soul of the late king' (May 1331): *CCR 1313–1317* p. 277; *CPR 1330–1333* p. 315.

A final example, the case of former Mamluk captive and Hospitaller knight, Roger Stanegrave, helps illustrate the point. Testifying before Edward II at York in 1318, Stanegrave was able to cut a sensational figure. Recounting the story of his capture by the Mamluks in the 1280s, his imprisonment over the course of three decades, and the crippling ransom of 10,000 gold florins set for his release, remarkably, Stanegrave could claim to have been in attendance on Edward II's father at Acre in the autumn of 1271 as part of a bodyguard that brought Persian ambassadors through Christian defences.[41] After nearly four decades in captivity, he was able to report on conditions behind the enemy lines, the strength of Muslim armies and the prospects of an attack upon Egypt. He also described the squalor of Mamluk jails, forced apostasy and the fate of other Hospitaller knights. The king was suitably impressed to write of his case in letters to the curia and the master of Hospitallers (first in 1318 and then again in 1320),[42] the emotive aspects of the eastern crusade rousing in Edward II a rare display of energy. Helped by the court, Stanegrave seems to have paid off his ransom and then retired from public life, probably in the custody of the Order; he and 'Isaac', the Jewish broker of his release, both disappear from the official record. All that is known of his last years is his writing of the remarkable crusade treatise *Li Charboclois d'armes du conquest precious de la terre sainte de promisson* (n.d. but c.1327/1333), a text which deserves a place alongside better-known crusade proposals like Pierre Dubois's *De recuperatione terre sancte* (1306) and Marino Sanudo Torsello's *Liber secretorum fidelium crucis* (1321).[43]

Contained in Stanegrave's text was an urgent and systematic appeal to English chivalry and to Edward's son (styled 'Edward of Wyndsore'), to whom the manuscript was dedicated. Devotion to the Holy Land would be the path towards Christian and knightly recovery, Stanegrave argued. Next to themes of renewal and ethical reform, there was comment on the topography, climate and social structure of the Cairo sultanate, including the strength of Mamluk armies, the hubris of the sultan, the places where water was plentiful, and other details apparently gatherable from a

---

[41] 'Roger of Stanegrave' *DNB* http://www.oxforddnb.com/view/article/92443, accessed 10 Dec. 2011; NA, C66/150 m. 8; *CPR 1317–1321* p. 254. The interview at Acre is recalled in Stanegrave's crusade treatise *Li Charboclois d'armes du conquest precious de la terre sainte de promisson*, BL, MS Cotton Otho D V fol. 1ʳ; now published in *Projets de Croisade (v.1200–v. 1330)* ed. J. Paviot (Paris, 2008) pp. 293–387. A contingent of English Hospitallers sailed with Edward I in 1270; the sources do not show if Stanegrave was amongst them. See *CPR 1268–1272* p. 438.

[42] In *Li Charboclois* Stanegrave describes his passage to Cyprus from Alexandria after being ransomed: BL, MS Cotton Otho D V fol. 2ᵛ. On prisoner exchange see L. Fernandes, 'On Conducting the Affairs of the State: A Guideline of the Fourteenth Century' *Annales Islamologiques* 24 (1988) pp. 81–91; Ibn Taymiyya, *Lettre à un roi croisé* (al-Risâlat al-Qubrusiyya) ed. J. Michot, (Louvain-la-Neuve and Lyon, 1995); G. Cipollone, *La liberazione dei 'captivi' tra Cristianità e Islam: Oltre la crociata e il Ǧihād: Toleranza e servizio umanitario* (Rome, 2000). Edward II's letters are found in the Roman Rolls, NA, C70/4 m. 10.

[43] See n. 41 above and in general cf. A. Leopold, *How to Recover the Holy Land: The Crusade Proposals of the Late Thirteenth and Early Fourteenth Centuries* (Aldershot, 2000).

cell window.[44] An attack against the cities of the Nile delta, the port of Alexandria, Cairo and Damietta was recommended, thus unlocking Syria in a single expedition. There was advice on how to achieve tactical surprise, the type of shipping required, the workings of the Egyptian fiscal state (the 'tresure de Mahimet') and its ripeness for plunder. Above all, however, the text was a manifesto for Christian knighthood. Subtitling his text *Oevres des le armes a guerroier les sarrazines*, there was enough to satisfy most practitioners of chivalry. The paragons of crusade history, medieval and epic romance – Tristam, Lancelot, Roland, Charlemagne, Godfrey de Bouillon, Arthur and Alexander – are held up for emulation. Fighting in the east was the best way to demonstrate 'corage', 'noble lignage' and gain 'le haute renown'. By the same token, slackness in the cause was the same as cowardice. Blended with Stanegrave's practical advice, this was not a fuddled view. It answered mounting political uncertainties with its clarity and comprehensiveness of vision. Knightly heroism, courtly leadership and the call of 'noble lignage' lay central to perceptions of crusading for the rest of the period. The expectation was that it would garner sympathy and action where politics had failed.[45]

Athletae Dei: Chivalry awakened?

Li Charboclois anticipated a major step change in English military culture, including the crusade. After the domestic turbulence and humiliations of Edward II's rule, the first years of Edward III's reign did indeed promise to open a new chapter in Mediterranean crusading, stoked in part by the young king's reputation for high chivalry. Plans for a joint Anglo-French *passagium* to the Holy Land received serious consideration at the courts of England and France during the 1330s. As Tyerman has shown, expectations were at first permitted to run high.[46] However it was not until the 1340s that much of military significance was achieved for the east. With plans for the recovery crusade shelved because of the outbreak of the Hundred Years War, the focus was allowed to return once more to meeting the maritime threat of the Turkish emirates, and defending key Christian sea-lanes. Jointly financed by Venice, Cyprus, the Hospitallers and Clement VI, a naval league was formally incepted in the summer of 1343 under the leadership of Henry of Asti, the Latin Patriarch of Constantinople. Among western recruits to the league, English links were strong, tallying with a wider stirring of crusade adventurism in Spain and the Baltic, and the burgeoning martial spirit of Edward III's court. The flotilla performed well in its

[44] BL, MS Cotton Otho D V fols. 1ʳ, 11ᵛ–12ʳ.
[45] Ibid. fols 2ʳ, 6ᵛ, 12ᵛ, 13ʳ.
[46] C. J. Tyerman, 'Philip VI and the Recovery of the Holy Land' *EHR* 100 (1985) pp. 25–52; id. 'The French and the Crusade 1313–1336' DPhil. thesis (Oxford, 1981). Edward III's most recent biographer is, quite rightly, sympathetic to Edward III's crusade claims: W. M. Ormrod, *Edward III* (New Haven, 2011) pp. 181–2.

first engagements, scattering a Turkish fleet off the Aegean islet of Kassandra in May 1344, but the biggest success arrived in November 1344 when the Christians block-aded and captured the port of Smyrna on the Turkish mainland. Although crusade indulgences were not preached in England or France, a pause in the Anglo-French war following the treaty of Malestroit (January 1343) cleared the way for significant knightly involvement. English diplomacy stimulated additional interest: gathered for peace talks at Avignon during the spring and autumn of 1344, Henry Grosmont and other royal diplomats went so far as to suggest a joint Anglo-papal expedition under the leadership of Clement VI himself.[47]

One of the first to sail was the king's private secretary and friend, William Kilsby, one-time candidate for the archdiocese of York. Kilsby took letters of accreditation to the leading Christian powers of the east, evidently combining diplomacy with the crusade. A sceptical Edward III may have wanted information on the true inten-tions of the Holy League, or used Kilsby in an attempt to counter any propaganda advantage gained by the French because of their support for the enterprise. Kilsby also banked on doing some fighting. Royal letters stated that after seeing the Holy Sites, the Englishman wanted to remain in the region to perform certain 'other pious labours', perhaps finding a berth with the Holy League or in one of the Hospitallers' patrols in the Aegean.[48] Others followed Kilsby's lead. By the spring of 1344 a sub-stantial grouping of English knights had passed en route to the east, probably aiming for the Holy League's main base at Negroponte (Euboea), the Venetian trading sta-tion on the Thessalian coast. For the better-connected, Avignon was the first calling point, Clement VI's active role in establishing the flotilla making the papal court a good source of information about transportation and military objectives. It was also the site of a thriving weapons market. Most participants left little trace in the surviv-ing English records, but their impact was clearly felt at the papal chancery, where the business of purchasing safe conducts and individual grants of indulgence was a major preoccupation. The volume of English petitions was so great that a *pro forma* sched-ule of crusade indulgences was drafted specifically to meet the demand of English and

[47]   Setton, *Papacy and the Levant* vol. I pp. 177–94. The main text for Derby's crusade negotiations is *Lettres closes, patentes et curiales du pape Clément VI se rapportant à la France* eds E. Déprez et al. (Paris, 1901–1961) no. 1844 but also cf. nos 1155, 1158, 1462, 1590; *CPL* vol. III pp. 15, 16; ASV, reg. vat. 138, fol.152ʳ–152ᵛ; Adam Murimuth, *Continuatio Chronicarum* ed. E. M. Thompson, r.s. 93 (London, 1889) pp. 177–88; *CPL* vol. III p. 2; NA, SC7/11/5 (misdated to 1305 in *Foedera*); NA, SC7/13/8 (misdated to 1306 in *Foedera*); vol. II pt. 4 pp. 141, 148, 152; John of Thoresby's journal (November 1344) printed in Jean Froissart, *Oeuvres* ed. K. Lettenhove (Brussels, 1866–1867) vol. XVIII pp. 235–56, esp. p. 255; R. M. Haines, *Archbishop Stratford: Political Revolutionary* (Toronto, 1986) pp. 343–5. Because of wide dis-crepancies in the papal calendars produced by the English and French schools, the crusade negotiations have generally escaped attention. See J. R. L. Highfield's notice in *EHR* 77 (1962) pp. 140–1.
[48]   *CCR 1343–1346* pp. 106–7, 361; *Foedera* vol. II pt. 4 pp. 141–2. Kilsby was also keeper of the privy seal (1338–1342). See T. F. Tout, *Chapters in Medieval Administrative History* (Manchester, 1920–1933) vol. III p. 163.

French knights. For brevity, chancery clerks shortened their register enrolments of indulgences and other privileges, making reference only to a standard crusader grant which was 'given to those of England and France', attesting to their dominant presence among western knights.[49] Most of the names that come to light had significant court or aristocratic connections; these were men familiar with the juridical mechanisms of government and church bureaucracy.

Prominent among them was Sir John Fauconberg, a royal chamber knight, who took leave to go against the 'enemies of God' almost immediately after the signing of the Anglo-French truce at the beginning of 1343. A veteran of fighting in Scotland and Flanders, his early departure may have been prompted by premature news that plans for a crusade fleet were already close to fruition. His preparations for embarkation included a £100 loan secured on Fauconberg lands in Yorkshire.[50] It is likely that he travelled with fellow Yorkshireman and royal servant Sir Robert Littlebirs, who petitioned for a crusade indulgence at the curia towards the end of February. Others with close links to the court (this time via the Black Prince's household) included Sir Ralph Cromwell and Sir John Bond of Norwich.[51] As a detachment from court, it had much the appearance of Fitzpayn's proposed 1309 expedition, though at Smyrna the dimensions of English involvement were significantly larger. Court stalwarts such as Bartholomew Burghersh and William Clinton, the earl of Huntingdon, made ready to embark, for example, suing out papal licences and indulgences. Burghersh wanted to discharge an old crusade vow, and Clinton successfully lobbied for papal letters so that he could embark on the *saint voyage* in the protection of the church. Together with the men going in his company, Clinton was awarded the full crusade indulgence, though there is no positive evidence he actually sailed.[52] Less prominent men also made the crossing, apparently independently. Sir John Garin, of the Welsh marches, reached Avignon at the end of the summer 1344, reportedly 'burning with zealous devotion for the faith'. He had testified his wish to embark against the 'blasphemers of Christ's name' in the apostolic chambers, perhaps in a formal ceremony that took place before papal letters could be issued. Whether he received the cross is unclear, but under safe conduct, Garin's person and possessions were to be preserved from secular attack or infringement, and he was entrusted to the care of prelates and other churchmen en route to the east.[53]

As a larger grouping, the English evidently made their presence felt. One admiring account of the fighting at Smyrna gives the impression that the decisive assault

---

[49]   E.g. *CPP* vol. I p. 52; ASV, reg. supp. 6 fol. 341ʳ 'in forma concessa aliis qui de Regnis Anglie et Francie' (May 1344).

[50]   *CPR 1343–1345* p. 6; *CCR 1343–1346* p. 82.

[51]   *CPP* vol. I p. 14, vol. II p. 574. Littlebirs took part in a royal embassy to the pope in 1339. For Cromwell and Bond see below nn. 55–6.

[52]   *CPL* vol. III p. 115; *CPP* vol. I p. 45; ASV, reg. supp. 6 fol. 319ᵛ.

[53]   ASV, reg. vat. 138 fol. 272ʳ.

was fought by the Hospitallers and *anglici* alone, without the aid of other nations. Combined, their prowess forced the Turks and other pagan fighters from their hidey-holes as if they were no more than 'yelping dogs'. Besides the Hospitallers, Martin Zaccaria, a fighter famed in the west and captain of the papal galleys, was another magnet for English crusaders.[54] The wealthy Ralph Cromwell attached his retinue of seven English knights, and an unspecified number of archers and other fighting men, to Zaccaria's command, evidently giving cause to impress. It was a reflection of his high standing that Cromwell was put in charge of rebuilding Smyrna's defences after the Christian army had successfully stormed the port and lower town.[55] Other Englishmen enhanced their chivalric reputations. Great praise was heaped upon Sir John Bond when he returned to Avignon in January 1345. Singled out for his heroic bravery against the Turks, Clement VI despatched Bond as a messenger to Edward III, hoping that a first-hand report, together with Bond's household connections, might turn royal attention towards the new beachhead in the east and away from conflict with France.[56] If the capture of Smyrna afforded traditional opportunities to cross swords with the infidel and gain knightly fame, it also possessed the old dangers. In January 1345 an enemy raid trapped many crusaders between the harbour walls and a column of Turkish cavalry. Most of the Holy League's leadership and numerous other ranks were killed. Among the English casualties was the humble chaplain, William Toli of Dunmow (Essex), who was left badly wounded across his body. Probably in Smyrna as part of a knightly retinue, on getting home he received a benefice in the bishopric of London out of consideration for his grave disfigurement.[57]

The postlude to Smyrna, a relief crusade under the powerful Prince Humbert I of Vienne between 1345 and 1347, faced greater diplomatic challenges, partly because of Edward III's decision to reopen the offensive in northern France and Gascony in 1345. It was a sign of optimism, however, that the diminutive English crusading Order of St Thomas (militarised by Peter des Roches in the 1220s, but now stationed on Cyprus) planned some sort of armed contribution, judging from letters to collectors in England. Fundraisers were supposed to cast about for pledges of money, gold, silver and weaponry, of which the Order was especially starved (August 1344).[58] The arrival

---

[54]   *Biblioteca bio-bibliografica della Terra Sancta e dell' Oriente francescano* ed. G. Golubovich (Quaracchi, 1906–1954) p. 445; *Foedera* vol. II pt. 4 p. 141; Housley, *Avignon Papacy* p. 119 and references there.

[55]   *CPP* vol. I p. 213.

[56]   *Clément VI: Lettres rapportant à la France* no. 1462; *CPL* vol. III pp. 15, 160.

[57]   For a Latin account of the St Antony's day massacre see *Biblioteca bio-bibliografica della Terra Sancta* p. 445; *CPL* vol. III p. 186.

[58]   *Documents nouveaux servant de Preuves à l'Histoire de l'Ile de Chypre sous le Reigne de la Maison de Lusignan*, ed. M. L. de Mas Latrie *Mèlanges Historiques* (Paris, 1882) vol. IV pp. 360–1. The fraternity kept up a regular search for alms for 'their wars against Saracens'. E.g. in 1320 agents of St Thomas embarked on a ten-year preaching tour, visiting the dioceses of York (1320–1321), Coventry and Lichfield (1322–1323), Bath and Wells (1323 and 1326), and Carlisle (1331): *The Register of William Melton, Archbishop of*

of Edward III's armies in Bordeaux (August 1345) did not persuade Clement VI to suspend crusade recruitment, and, despite the obstacles, the English contribution to the Holy League of 1345–1347 was not negligible. Indeed, in contrast to Philip VI, who insisted that Humbert's expedition should not be promoted in France, Edward III's government imposed no restriction on crusade preaching when it was initiated in the English dioceses during the winter of 1345–1346. Nor was there any indication of royal interference in the collection of donations and alms *contra Turchos*. In January 1346, as part of a wider recruitment drive, the prior provincial of the English Carmelites appointed brethren to preach the cross in London and Colchester and across the southern dioceses of Canterbury, Winchester and Rochester.[59]

Among the English recruits the expeditions of two Gloucestershire knights, Sir John de la Ryvere and Robert Bradestone, offer a good illustration of crusading's contrasting fortunes. Accompanied by a small retinue, Ryvere took the familiar course to the Mediterranean ports, reaching Avignon in August 1346 and taking out a safe conduct to go against the Turks at Smyrna (*Romanie*). Two of his party, John Wayfor, an esquire from one of Ryvere's scattered Dorset estates, and his chaplain John Noble, received similar licences. Ryvere reached the east in time to establish a dazzling international reputation for his prowess against the infidel. This indomitable 'athleta Dei' fought zealously for the faith, not only in Turkish lands but also as a spy behind enemy lines in Mamluk Syria and Egypt, where he travelled as a pilgrim.[60] Moving in elite channels, the Englishman became a patron of the increasingly popular, but thinly documented, international knightly fraternity, the Order of the Holy Sepulchre, and took part in the dubbing of several noble pilgrims in Jerusalem. Here his path crossed with the high-born Étienne de Lucing, Humbert of Vienne's chamberlain, Robert, count of Namur, and a young Philippe de Mézières, future crusade propagandist and advisor to the Lusignan and Valois courts. He may even have

York, 1317–1340 ed. R. M. T. Hill et al. Canterbury and York Society (Woodbridge, 1977–) vol. III p. 23; E. Hobhouse 'The Register of Roger de Norbury' *Collections for a History of Staffordshire* William Salt Society (Birmingham, 1880) p. 270; *Reg. Droxford* vol. I p. 220; *The Register of John Kirkby, Bishop of Carlisle 1332–1352 and the Register of John Ross, Bishop of Carlisle, 1325–1332* ed. R. L. Storey, Canterbury and York Society (Woodbridge, 1993–1995) vol. I p. 9. Forey perhaps understates the Order's military character in the fourteenth century: A. Forey, 'The Military Order of St. Thomas of Acre' *EHR* 92 (1977) pp. 481–503.

[59] *Clément VI: Lettres rapportant à la France* nos 1462, 1704; *Registrum Hamonis Hethe, Diocesis Roffensis, 1319–1352* ed. C. Johnson, Canterbury and York Society (Oxford, 1948) vol. II pp. 770–5.

[60] 'John de la Ryvere' *DNB* http://www.oxforddnb.com/view/article/92453, accessed 20 Dec. 2011; *Lettres closes, patentes et curiales du pape Clément VI intéressant les pays autres que la France* ed. E. Déprez et al. (Paris, 1960–1961) nos 1155, 1156, 1605, 1608; with supplementary detail, ASV, reg. vat. 141 fols 222ʳ–223ᵛ, esp. 223ᵛ; O. Raynaldi, *Annales Ecclesiastici* (Lucca, 1750) vol. VI anno 1348 § xxix; *CPL* vol. III p. 36. Ryvere's clerical companion can probably be identified as the John Noble appointed Master of the collegiate church of St Mark's, Billeswick (Gloucs.) in 1339. See *The Register of Wolstan de Bransford, Bishop of Worcester 1339–1349* ed. R. M. Haines, Worcestershire Historical Society (London, 1966) p. 186.

rubbed shoulders with the feted *auteur* of chivalry, Geoffrey de Charny, another of Vienne's crusade recruits.[61]

By contrast, Robert Bradestone's crossing was beset with difficulties. The most serious occurred when his party were arrested by Pisan officials as they made their way through Tuscany, travelling towards Venice. The episode apparently had roots in a dispute over a Pisan vessel impounded in English waters (Bradestone's strong connections to Bristol, an outpost of Italian commerce, were perhaps incriminating), but it was a chastening reminder of crusading's attendant risks. Clement VI argued vigorously for their release on the grounds that they were bound for the east, whence they had embarked 'for wreaking vengeance upon the Turks' (April, 1345), but the appeal fell on deaf ears. The incident took on significance because Robert's father, Lord Bradestone, was one of Edward III's *familiares*. There is no way of telling how many other English crusaders became stranded in the 1340s, or at other times, unable to attract the attention of the authorities. Bradestone's group were not released until the end of 1347, long after the follow-up crusade had broken up and Humbert of Vienne had returned home.[62]

The Gloucestershire example opens another perspective. The fact that Ryvere and Bradestone possessed adjacent lands, shared the same social milieu and were both prominent figures in county society perhaps points to a regional response. Conclusions are obviously difficult from such a narrow sample, but a sharp congruence of kinship and locality amongst crusade recruits can be clearly observed in other decades of the fourteenth century. Alternatively, it speaks to the knights' vertical connections with aristocratic patrons (both had dealings with the powerful Berkeley family), and particularly at court. While Ryvere apparently had Edward III's ear, Bradestone's *iter* won the blessing of the young Prince Edward.[63]

Optimism and responses: The Alexandria crusade

A great expansion in eastern crusading seemed possible in the 1360s. A lengthy pause in the Anglo-French conflict after the Rheims campaign (1359) encouraged the French

---

[61]   *Lettres ... du Clément VI intéressant les pays autres que la France* no. 1605. Ryvere's name may be added to Gennes's list of fourteenth-century pilgrim-knights. J.-P. de Gennes, *Les Chevaliers du Saint-Sépulcre de Jérusalem* (Herault, 1995) vol. I pp. 272–5; N. Iorga, *Philippe de Mézières et la croisade au XIVe siècle* (Paris, 1896), p. 73; *The Book of Chivalry of Geoffroi de Charny* eds R. W. Kaeuper and E. Kennedy (Philadelphia, 1996) pp. 7–8.

[62]   *Clément VI: Lettres rapportant à la France* no. 1617; *CPL* vol. III p. 160; *CPR 1345–1348* pp. 21, 330; Thomas, Lord Bradestone, was one of Edward III's councillors and friends (the king had been known to wear Bradestone's arms while tourneying). See J. Vale, *Edward III and Chivalry: Chivalric Society and its Context 1270–1350* (Woodbridge, 1982) p. 61.

[63]   For the knights' place in county society see N. Saul, *Knights and Esquires: The Gloucestershire Gentry in the Fourteenth Century* (Oxford, 1981) pp. 76–7, 228–9; R. W. Barber, *Edward Prince of Wales and Aquitaine* (Woodbridge, 1996) p. 40; BL, MS Harley 4304 fols 16ᵛ–20 (sixteenth-century copy of Prince Edward's household account, 1344–1345).

court to start talking of a Holy Land *passagium* once more, though much more as a symbol of political and moral regeneration than as a practical goal. Racked by the mercenary *routiers* (or the 'Free' companies) and suffering political disarray, the dire internal condition of France made it hard to look upon John II's taking of the cross in March 1363 with much hope.[64] Rather more promising as far as practitioners of chivalry were concerned were the subsidiary crusade plans of Peter I of Cyprus. The Cypriot king's desire to recruit a western army won papal backing in 1363, first as a preliminary *passagium* to John II's expedition, but then as the main focus of crusade activity following King John's death in April 1364. Two tours of the west, including visits to Edward III's court in 1363 and 1367, gave Peter a platform for propaganda and recruitment. Ostensibly, conditions in England were ripe. Riding high from their famous victories against the Scots and French, Edward III's nobles had built an unrivalled reputation for valour and battlefield success. Rising enthusiasm for crusading elsewhere was evident in the 1360s, especially in the Baltic, and King Peter was able to capitalise upon a strong culture of competition and support, particularly among the Black Prince's circle at Bordeaux. As a frontier of chivalry, the eastern crusade offered the traditional fruits of high renown, fraternisation with foreign knights, access to papal indulgences and contact with the Italian trading powers. Expectations of social advancement and opportunities for pilgrimage widened the appeal. Less conspicuous were other rewards of high chivalry – ransoms, plunder, pensions and the carving out of new lands – but while many of the French nobility were kept busy with Charles V's difficult accession, English crusaders embarked for the Mediterranean in the greatest numbers since Richard I's crusade of the 1190s.[65]

In 1359, English knights were already playing a role in the Holy League resurrected by Innocent VI and the Hospitallers under the direction of the celebrated papal legate and crusade enthusiast Pierre Thomas. A large English contingent took part in the attack upon the Turkish stronghold at Lampsacus on the Asiatic side of the Dardenelles, opposite Gallipoli. According to eyewitnesses, their presence was the main contribution of the northern nations, although among the 'English' there may have been Gascon or German participants. Compared to the Italian mariners, who fled at the first sign of Turkish resistance, the westerners showed proper mettle as soldiers, repulsing the garrison troops of Lampsacus and killing over three hundred

[64]   One of the reasons given by John II for his voluntary return to captivity in England in January 1364 was discussion of the crusade. See *Les Grandes Chroniques de France* ed. R. Delachenal (Paris, 1910–1920) vol. I pp. 339–41. The Westminster chronicler suggests that greed, not a love for God, was John II's true motive: John of Reading, *Chronica Johannis de Reading et Anonymi Cantuarensis 1346–1367* ed. J. Tait (Manchester, 1914) p. 156.

[65]   For the diplomatic background see Tyerman, *God's War* pp. 831–4; P. W. Edbury, *The Kingdom of Cyprus and the Crusades 1191–1374* (Cambridge, 1991) pp. 147–79; Setton, *Papacy and the Levant* vol. I pp. 224–84.

of the enemy.[66] Some took longer term service in the league when it moved to join Cypriot attacks on the southern coast of Anatolia, where Peter occupied the town of Gorighos in 1360 and captured Adalia in 1361. An 'English' or Gascon knight, Robert de Louza (alias Toulouse or 'le Ros'), was sent with two galleys and four companies of archers to take command of Gorighos in 1361.[67] Paid out of Venetian, papal or Cypriot coffers, the foreign recruits were eligible for crusade indulgences and other privileges by virtue of Pierre Thomas's powers as papal legate, and the penetration of northern knights into the by now regular cycle of sea-borne attack and raid was recognisable from the naval flotillas of the 1340s.[68] It persuaded the Cypriot court that there was sufficient interest north of the Alps for opening a much wider eastern campaign. In 1362 Cypriot and Armenian knights converged upon a royal tournament outside London, seeking aid against the pagan enemies of their homelands.[69]

This was the backdrop for the delegation of Peter of Cyprus in England in November 1363. Part of his agenda was to act as broker between the pope, John II and Edward III, but the main objective lay in recruiting for a Cypriot-controlled expedition that was to precede a larger western *passagium*. It was laid down that he could recruit no more than 200 nobles, 2,000 horse and 6,000 foot in the west (despite what the chronicler Froissart says, King Peter did not expect to enlist Edward III), and his host was suitably lavish.[70] A tournament marked the embassy's arrival. Edward indulged Peter's taste for the hunt, feasted him and loaded him down with presents and fine words. Possibly the absence of Edward III's eldest sons robbed the audience of some momentum, but Peter kept close company with royal advisors and knights.[71] He made use of familiar arguments: as titular king of Jerusalem and Cyprus, his rightful inheritance and kingdom had been stolen. On moral, legal and historic grounds, the fight against the 'unbelievers' was both necessary and just, and the Holy Land remained the ultimate objective. An appeal to the kings' shared lineage (via the house of Anjou) provided an additional spur. Despite his instinctive caution, Edward was prepared to provide Peter with what he wanted. Assurances were passed around that when the crusade sailed it would be accompanied by as many English knights as

---

[66]   Mézières reports the contributing nations as Venice, Genoa, England, Greece and various other Christian groupings: *Life of St. Peter Thomas by Philippe de Mézières* ed. J. Smet (Rome, 1954) p. 85.

[67]   *Recital concerning the Sweet Land of Cyprus entitled 'Chronicle'* ed. R. M. Dawkins (Oxford, 1932) vol. I p. 100, vol. II pp. 98–9; G. F. Hill, *A History of Cyprus* (Cambridge, 1940–1952) vol. II p. 320.

[68]   Housley, *Avignon Papacy* p. 139.

[69]   John of Reading, pp. 152–3.

[70]   *Lettres closes, secrètes et curiales du pape Urbain V* eds P. Lecacheux and G. Mollat (Paris, 1954–1955) nos 476, 477; Froissart, vol. VI pp. 380–1; Tyerman, *England and the Crusades* pp. 290–3.

[71]   Henry Knighton, *Knighton's Chronicle, 1337–1396* ed. G. H. Martin (Oxford, 1995) p. 187. The tournament was held at Smithfield on the feast of St Martin (11 November): NA, E36/4 9d (wardrobe account). Peter presented King Edward with a live leopard, a play upon the Plantagenet badge: NA, E403/417 m. 13. Peter's brother, Philip of Ibelin, received three ceremonial cups of silver and gold worth £29 1s 6d and a courser with bridle and saddle worth £17 7s 3d: NA, E403/417 m. 19.

wished to embark.[72] A number of ceremonial ties were established, underlining the brief prominence of the Cypriot crusade in diplomatic channels. Several of Edward III's esquires were retained by King Peter. At least one of them, William Welles, travelled with Peter to Paris, where he took service with a third king, the newly installed Charles V, the triangular association between the English, Cypriot and French courts providing a potential platform for contact with Charles's young regime.[73] Another household esquire, Thomas Alberton, received papal indulgences to accompany the king *in terre sancte subsidium*, and a third was knighted by Peter immediately after the crusade fleet landed on the beaches outside Alexandria. Such links papered over the question of more substantial royal aid.[74]

There was close contact with other courtiers, including the young crusade enthusiast Humphrey Bohun, earl of Hereford, who greeted Peter at Dover and escorted him to London. Concrete evidence of vows is elusive, but many of Edward III's men made preparations to go to the east. In January 1364 Sir Miles Stapleton took out a licence to be abroad for three years, a term traditional for Levantine expeditions. He embarked with his cousin and namesake Miles Stapleton of Haddlesey, sometimes identified as *le seigneur*. It was the latter who fought in the train of Pierre Thomas at Alexandria.[75] Another royal servant, Sir William Trussel, set his sights on going to the east and was apparently joined by his son-in-law, Fulk Pembridge, and a contingent from the Welsh borders. The group splintered during their journey towards the Mediterranean, but Pembridge reached Avignon in May 1364, where he petitioned Urban V for a grant of crusade indulgences.[76] The earl of Hereford was Peter's most eminent recruit. In the view of the crusade leadership, Bohun's kinship to the king and close friendship with Edward's elder sons probably compensated for his youth and relative inexperience. A passage in the *Anonimalle Chronicle* places him at Alexandria with Miles Stapleton and Sir John Argent, a Bohun man. The earl's withdrawal from public life between January 1365 and the first months of 1366 almost certainly relates

---

[72]   Froissart, vol. VI pp. 380–1; *Chronique des quatre premiers Valois* ed. S. Luce (Paris, 1862) p. 128.

[73]   *CPP* vol. I p. 416. *Mandements et actes divers de Charles V (1364–1380)* ed. L. Delisle (Paris, 1874) no. 121 (Welles).

[74]   *CPP* vol. I p. 490; ASV, reg. supp. 42 fol. 113; ASV, reg. vat. 251 fol. 258 (Alberton); *Controversy Between Sir Richard Scrope and Sir Robert Grosvenor in the Court of Chivalry* ed. N. H. Nicolas (London, 1832) vol. I pp. 124–5, vol. II pp. 323–5 (Stephen Scrope). Froissart's claim that Edward gave King Peter a war galley worth 12,000 florins (the 'Catherine') is far-fetched. At any rate, Froissart says that the vessel remained rotting at its moorings at Sandwich after Peter's departure: Froissart, vol. VI p. 381.

[75]   Stapleton of Bedale died 'in parts overseas' at the end of October 1364; his heir, Miles, was nine: *CIPM* vol. XII no. 45. The Anonimalle writer, understandably, confuses Stapleton of Bedale with his cousin of Haddlesey: *The Anonimalle Chronicle 1333 to 1381* ed. V. H. Galbraith (Manchester, 1970) p. 51.

[76]   NA, C61/76 mm. 3 (Trussel). Trussel was a knight of the chamber and a life retainer of the Black Prince: *CPR 1364–1367* pp. 331, 472; *Register of Edward the Black Prince, 1346–1365* ed. M. C. B. Dawes et al., HMSO (London, 1930–1933) vol. IV pp. 178, 261; ASV, reg. supp. 42 fol. 109[v] (Pembridge).

to the Cypriot crusade. A clerical writer with Bohun links described the departure of numerous English knights 'contra inimicos Christi', and gloomily prophesied the death of their 'Dux'.[77]

Much more was expected of the Black Prince's court. The king's eldest son had exchanged courtesies with three of Peter's nuncios in 1362, presenting them with honorific belts during the tournament festivities at Smithfield, and he was probably at the private crusade conference held afterwards with Edward III.[78] The Cypriot embassy reached Aquitaine in the early months of 1364, finding the prince in an ebullient mood as he progressed through the ducal lands, taking homage from the Gascon nobility. King Peter would later journey to Flanders, Brabant, Germany, Prague, Cracow and Vienna, but the Black Prince's court, newly established at Bordeaux, held the most attraction for aspiring knights and esquires. A tournament was again the focus of crusade recruitment, fitting with the pageantry that the prince used to establish himself in the duchy. According to one account, the Cypriots received a sensational response. The Gascon lords, led by Louis Harcourt, Guichard d'Angle, Guillaume of Parthenay and Florimond de Lesparre, lined up to take the cross, their ardour inspired by the eloquence and prowess of King Peter. Similarly, English luminaries such as Sir Thomas Felton, Sir Nigel Loring, Sir Simon Burley, Sir Baldwin Freville and Richard Punchardoun, heroes of Crécy and Poitiers, announced their desire to fight in the Holy Land, the Black Prince's inner circle vying with visiting knights to show the greater zeal.

The religious fervour may have gained something in the telling (the main source is Froissart), but the crusade possessed special attraction in the contested politics of Gascony, where the swapping of loyalties from Paris to Bordeaux was still very much a delicate affair. The *negotium crucis* was a satisfactory way for former supporters of the Valois to show common purpose with their English counterparts and fix additional links with their new duke. Louis Harcourt and Guichard d'Angle, for instance, were both wanting to distance themselves from their former liege-lord, John II.[79] Tournaments and chivalric festivals provided one way of doing this, crusade recruitment traditionally going hand in hand with jousting's military training and competition. There was face-saving here too, with some taking the cross or seeking far-flung frontiers as an honourable excuse for absence from the Black Prince's incoming regime. Representatives of several notable Gascon families featured in Peter's Alexandrian fleet, others travelled to the Baltic, and a substantial Anglo-

---

[77] *Anonimalle* p. 51; Luttrell, 'English Levantine Crusaders' pp. 150–2; John Erghome's commentary on St John of Bridlington, *Political Poems and Songs Relating to English History* ed. T. Wright, r.s. 14 (London, 1859–1861) vol. I pp. 182–4.

[78] John of Reading, pp. 152–3. For part of their stay the Cypriot knights were accommodated at the prince's lavish residence at Kennington: *Register of the Black Prince* vol. IV p. 428.

[79] Froissart, vol. III pp. 393–6; Iorga, *Philippe de Mézières* p. 184. Guichard d'Angle served as the Black Prince's lieutenant in Saintonge (1364), and Harcourt eventually became Marshal of Aquitane. See J. Sumption, *The Hundred Years War* (London, 1990–2009) vol. II p. 474.

Gascon contingent sailed with Amadeo of Savoy's expedition to Constantinople in 1366 (see below pp. 102–7).[80]

If responses were partly coloured by the purposes of fraternal display, an imposing figurehead for western recruitment was nonetheless found in Thomas Beauchamp, earl of Warwick, the most senior – and perhaps the most feared – of all Edward III's noblemen (the French dubbed him 'the devil').[81] Stationed in Gascony since June 1363, Beauchamp had earlier shown interest in the pope's war against the Visconti in Italy, offering to take a force against Milan in the autumn of 1363. The Cypriot crusade now provided a more attractive target.[82] Thomas's younger brother and companion in arms, John Beauchamp, probably carried news of the London audiences when he arrived in Gascony at the end of 1363.[83] It was easy enough for the earl of Warwick to turn his sights to the east, and at the end of a contracted twelve months in royal service there was no reason for the court to withhold support. Like his father, the Black Prince had given his word that men would be free to join the crusade. Shortly after King Peter's departure from Aquitaine, Warwick travelled to Avignon to receive Urban V's blessing for an army to be drawn mainly from the English retinues in Gascony. Talks at the curia culminated in a cross-taking ceremony in May 1364 and a grant of plenary indulgence *in articulo mortis* (at the hour of death) for all those going in the earl's company, as well as the award of various other privileges.[84]

The outlines of an impressive expeditionary army can be reconstructed from papal sources, constituting the largest English military undertaking in the Mediterranean in over a century. Grouped around the earl of Warwick's large household were a number of the Black Prince's companion knights, including Nigel Loring, his chamberlain; Ralph Basset, lord of Sapcote, one of the heroes of Crécy; and Edward Courtenay, son of the earl of Devon. Sir Baldwin Freville and the fiery Gascon Florimond de Lesparre were other notable associates. This represented the military core. A far larger and more heterogeneous grouping of English knights congregated at Avignon during April and May.[85] Amongst those suing out for crusade indulgences 'in the customary form' were high-ranking soldiers such as Thomas Ufford, son of the earl of Suffolk, the entrepreneurial William de la Pole and Sir Thomas Alberton. A grouping of one hundred men, planning to journey to the Holy Sepulchre under the leadership of Sir Baldwin Burford and Sir William Flambard can also be connected to the Cypriot

---

[80] Besides Florimond de Lesparre, A. S. Atiya lists Guillaume Roger, viscount of Turenne; Bertrand de Grailly, son of the viscount of Benauges; and several cadets of the Montegiscard family: Atiya, *The Crusade in the Later Middle Ages* (London, 1938), pp. 517–19.

[81] *Anonimalle* p. 61.

[82] *CPL* vol. IV p. 5.

[83] NA, C61/76 mm. 2, 3.

[84] Froissart, vol. III pp. 393–6; *CPL* vol. IV pp. 9–10; ASV, reg. vat. 246 fols 179ᵛ, 208ᵛ; *CPP* vol. I pp. 494–500; ASV, reg. supp. 40 fols. 145ʳ–179ʳ 'Rotulus Comitis Warrewici'.

[85] ASV, reg. supp. 40 fols. 147ʳ–147ᵛ, 176ʳ. For Freville see A. Gundy, 'The Rule of Thomas Beauchamp 1369–1398' Phd thesis (Cambridge, 2000) pp. 46, 65.

expedition (March 1364).[86] It is almost certain Beauchamp was their figurehead. Ranks of infantry also joined the march. When issuing safe conducts for the earl and his knights, the governor of the Dauphiné gave passage to the earl's company of three hundred 'lances' – a lance referring to the military unit of three mounted soldiers (the man-at-arms, his squire and page). In total Beauchamp may have boasted a camp-following of around one thousand crusaders, a highly impressive number in an age when few English field armies counted more than six to seven thousand men. Papal letters were needed to smooth the way for the host to travel to Venice, where King Peter was due to arrive in August. Requests for safe conduct through the provinces of the Dauphiné, Savoy and Lombardy chart Warwick's progress across the alpine passes towards the republic. The earl's messengers arrived in Venice by the middle of July, where the senate answered his request for the equipping of war galleys for the eastern *passagium*. Some of his wealthier associates probably contracted separately. One of them, Florimond de Lesparre, chartered a galley for his contingent of thirty knights and other ranks some time later.[87]

Watching events in Venice, the great Italian poet Francesco Petrarch gave a vivid record of the Englishmen gathered during the first two weeks of August in expectation of the crusade's departure. Among the crowds he spied a number of high-ranking English noblemen, including an earl and a cousin of the king. The identity of the earl is clear enough; the 'cousin' is probably Edward Courtenay, the earl of Devon's son, related to Edward III by virtue of his father's marriage.[88] Warwick's arrival was marked by jousts and other festivities in Venice, including trials of horsemanship (*labori equoreo*), a significant recognition of his seniority and wide renown. Beauchamp's importance to the crusade was confirmed when he was recognised by the pope along-side Amadeo of Savoy and King Peter as the leading nobleman with command in the crusade. To this end, Urban V wrote to Beauchamp commending Pierre Thomas, titular Patriarch of Constantinople, as his new appointment as papal legate, and for-malising the terms of Thomas's jurisdiction within the army (30 June 1364). The earl's enterprise lacked only a large-scale grant of church funds, though Petrarch writes that the earl had 'contraxerat' for the crusade expedition, perhaps indicating a private financial arrangement with the pope or King Peter.[89]

Beauchamp's expedition received the most attention in diplomatic circles, but it was not the only element with English leadership. According to Philippe de Mézières, now Peter of Cyprus's chancellor, by December 1363 Venice was brimful

---

[86]   *CPP* vol. I pp. 483, 489 (Burford and Flambard), 490 (Alberton and Ufford); *Urbain V: Lettres communes* ed. M.-H. Laurent et al. (Paris, 1954–1985) nos 11463–4; *CPL* vol. IV pp. 8–9 (Pole).

[87]   John of Reading, p. 339; Iorga, *Philippe de Mézières* p. 206 n. 8. For Florimond de Lesparre see Atiya, *Crusade in the Later Middle Ages* p. 370.

[88]   Francesco Petrarca, *Prose* ed. G. Martellotti et al. (Milan, 1955) p. 1086; Iorga, *Philippe de Mézières* p. 254.

[89]   Petrarca, *Prose* p. 1086; ASV, reg. vat. 246 fol. 242.

with English and Germans waiting for the crusade leaders to embark for the east.[90] Delays, secrecy over the crusade's objective and the division of leadership between King Peter, Amadeo of Savoy and Thomas Beauchamp made for a confused scene. Urban V further complicated matters by issuing indulgences for an attack upon the Turkish emirate of Aydin even as men gathered to join the Cypriot crusade – part of a rushed plan to divert the *routier* bands in aid of Constantinople (September 1364).[91] Attracted by reports of church subsidies and the chance of gainful employment, a steady stream of unemployed soldiers swelled the numbers waiting at Venice, most seeking passage with King Peter. Details survive where individuals came into contact with the authorities. The presence of the Pembrokeshire crusader Sir Henry Sturmy (alias Stromin), for instance, is known because one of his man-servants was killed in a knife-fight outside the English hostel ('the Dragon') where he was staying. Some of those waiting to embark for the east found employment when the Venetians raised an army to put down a revolt on Crete in early 1364. One English military contractor named only as 'Lord Thomas' agreed to furnish 110 men-at-arms, an indication of the reserves of foreign soldiery camping at Venice. Profit was the first motive, but it was not the only one. The Doge promised free shipping to 'Lord Thomas' and his English company to join the crusade fleet either at Cyprus or Rhodes at the end of their six-month contract, 'so that they may have more cause for coming, and for seeking our honour'.[92] It is not clear how the various English groups responded to the approach of the earl of Warwick, but the crusade leadership clearly thought Beauchamp capable of imposing control over a significant part of the army, replacing Amadeo of Savoy, who had temporarily withdrawn from campaigning, as a focus for western knighthood. None of the French or German crusader knights could match his reputation or high-birth. First steps towards imposing discipline and increasing group cohesion were probably marked by the pageantry on Warwick's arrival.

In the event, however, Warwick was unable to delay in Italy beyond the summer months of 1364. The cost of a prolonged wait for Peter I (who had unexpectedly extended his travels), and the need to uphold English interests in a precarious civil war in Brittany forced him to withdraw, probably with a large part of his military household. His absence substantially increased the burden of responsibility upon the Cypriot command, and attracted the wrath of King Peter's chancellor, Mézières, but Urban V acknowledged the Englishman's devotion to the cross and the great sums Warwick had already committed to the cause. The earl was given licence to fulfil his crusade vow in Prussia instead.[93] Even without Beauchamp, however, the English crusaders remained a formidable grouping. According to one chronicler, Peter's brother,

[90]   Mézières, *Life of St. Peter Thomas* (§50).
[91]   *Urban V: Lettres closes* no. 1265.
[92]   *Calendar of State Papers and Manuscripts relating to English Affairs: Venice* ed. R. Brown, HMSO (London, 1864–1947) vol. VI pt. 3 pp. 1578–80.
[93]   ASV, reg. vat. 248 fol. 9ʳ-9ᵛ.

John of Antioch, had gathered nearly two hundred additional English volunteers in the east as part of a mixed force of Greeks, Cypriots and Hospitallers. These may have included men who had fought at Lampsacus in 1359, at Gorghios and Adalia in 1360 and 1361, or on Crete in 1364. The pilgrim traffic between Cyprus and other Mediterranean outposts was another likely source. In Italy, Peter retained a large company of English mercenaries for a year.[94] The names of a number of other English recruits have survived: Stephen Scrope of Masham, probably attached to King Peter's suite; Nicholas Sabraham, who was never a knight but had an extensive military career at Crécy and elsewhere in the west, in Prussia, Hungary and Constantinople; John, Lord Grey of Codnor; Sir Alexander Goldingham; Sir William Scrope, Stephen's uncle; and English Hospitallers, including the Prior of England, Robert Hales, whose reputation was made by the expedition, and William Middleton, Turcoplier of Rhodes. Between the Scrope family, Nicholas Sabraham and Miles Stapleton *le seigneur* there ran a common thread of service in the Bohun retinues of the 1340s and 1350s, and it is reasonable to assume some sort of affiliation with the young earl remained. When the fleet set sail in June 1365, Mézières reported a somewhat exaggerated total of ten thousand men, including 'English, Cypriots, French and Germans', in that order.[95]

This impression was probably sharpened in the aftermath of the attack upon Alexandria, the *anglici* playing a conspicuous part in the sacking of the city, and in the hotly contested decision to withdraw after a few days. Following the strategy advocated by Stanegrave thirty years earlier, Peter I mustered his fleet at Rhodes for supply and launched a beach assault using specially adapted craft with ramps (*husseria*) to allow mounted knights to disembark fully armed. Despite meeting little Mamluk resistance, the English refused to spend a single night in the town, instead keeping close to the protection of the fleet in the harbour. According to Mézières, English knights also sabotaged Peter's council of war at the critical point, swaying the Hospitallers, most of the French and even the king's brothers into abandoning the city after holding it for little more than a week. In fact, Guillaume Roger, viscount of Turenne, one of the Gascon contingent, probably echoed the majority view when he pointed out the crusaders' exposed position after the destruction of the city's two land gates. Indefensible from approaches to the south and the east, the continued occupation of Alexandria was futile. The seasonal flooding of the Nile delta ruled out significant progress into the interior, and with the mutiny of the Anglo-Gascon retinues and pillage of the city's great riches, the crusaders' solidarity quickly disintegrated, and the army returned to their boats loaded down with plunder. This did little to commend Edward III's knights to European commentators (reports reached

[94]   *Chronique Valois* pp. 164–5; Luttrell, 'English Levantine Crusaders' p. 144.
[95]   'Nicholas Sabraham' *DNB* http://www.oxforddnb.com/view/article/92452, accessed 11 Dec. 2011; *Scrope and Grosvenor* vol. I pp. 70, 124–5, 181–2, vol. II pp. 227, 323–5, 425–7; Mézières, *Life of St. Peter Thomas* (§§89, 91).

Germany, for instance, that the city had been lost because the English took their booty and fled), but public opinion in England was generally sympathetic, where the involvement of *multi strenui milites et armigeri de Anglia* was proudly pointed out.[96] It was the severest blow that the Mamluks ever received at the hands of a Christian army.

King Peter cut a forlorn figure at Alexandria, isolated by English plotting and assiduous looting. Yet, despite the recriminations, it did not weaken Peter's faith in western aid, nor did it sour his relations with the English retinues. Not all returned expeditiously to the west, weighed down by Egyptian cloths, exotic silks and precious stones. Some men stood out for their idealism. John, Lord Grey of Codnor, a baron with a rich crusade pedigree, enjoyed an exalted reputation for piety, as well as for his record in arms in Scotland and France, for example. A close relationship to the English Carmelites recommended him to the crusade legate and Carmelite preacher Pierre Thomas. Grey went on to win great praise for his valour at Alexandria, being entrusted with the office of carrying the *vexillum ecclesiae* into battle. He returned to England with high battle honours and a treasured copy of Pierre Thomas's *vita*, a freshly composed blend of hagiography, homily and crusade propaganda.[97] In the meantime, a half-hearted effort at diplomacy with Cairo allowed Peter time to regroup. Crusade bulls highlighting the urgent dangers of Mamluk reprisals were issued in the west, including England and Gascony.[98] The enclaves of Rhodes and Cyprus were most at risk. In 1367 Peter launched fresh attacks upon the Anatolian and Syrian coasts, sailing from Famagusta and Rhodes. A force of four hundred English, Germans and others under a captain named Philpot burned Jaffa, and Humphrey Bohun, again in the east, played a conspicuous part in the sack of Tripoli in September. With the earl of Hereford were Sir Richard Waldegrave, Alexander Goldingham, lord of Chigwell (Essex), Sir William Lucy of Dorset, Sir John Goddard, Nicholas Sabraham, at least one of the Scropes and possibly Sir John Burley. Others, like Sir Walter Malbis, who alienated his Yorkshire estate to pay for his crusade, and the Garter knight John, Lord Grey of Rotherfield (a cousin of Lord Grey of Codnor), apparently planned to get involved. Englishmen achieved some prominence in Cypriot diplomacy: Hereford's entourage was present when King Peter signed a truce with the emir of Tekke in

---

[96] Ibid. (§§103, 104); *Chronicon Moguntinum* ed. C. Hegel (Hanover, 1885), p. 14; Ranulf Higden, *Polychronicon,* ed. J. R. Lumby, r.s. 41 (London, 1865–1886) vol. VIII p. 365.

[97] Richard, Lord Grey, John's great-grandfather, founded the first Carmelite house in England after returning from the east with disciples of the order in 1242. He had campaigned in Syria with Richard of Cornwall in the 1240s. John's maternal grandfather was Robert Fitzpayn, the crusade enthusiast of Edward II's household. See Iorga, *Philippe de Mézières* p. 279; F. J. Boehlke, *Pierre de Thomas, Scholar, Diplomat and Crusader* (Philadelphia, 1966) pp. 267–8; *CPR 1364–1367* p. 127; *De Visione Sancti Simonis Stock* ed. B. M. Xiberta (Rome, 1950) pp. 245–5, 306.

[98] *CPL* vol. IV pp. 25–6; *Urbain V: Lettres closes,* nos 2416, 2418; NA, SC7/34/7.

August 1367, and Robert le Ros went as the Christian envoy to Cairo after renewed fighting at Gorghios.[99]

Despite being the toast of such poets as Petrarch, Geoffrey Chaucer and Guillaume Machaut, the conditions of King Peter's second trip to the west were less favourable than those of 1363–1364. The kings of England and France were occupied with the prospect of fresh military confrontation, which in the winter months of 1367–1368 looked increasingly likely, and the confidence of Edward III's court following the treaty of Brétigny was starting to fade. Attempts by Edward III to secure a marriage alliance with Flanders had resulted in a bitter struggle with Urban V and increasing diplomatic isolation for the English king. Arriving in England sometime before January 1368, the presence of Peter's troupe of officials and knights is attested in a single exchequer account. Royal brothers, Princes John of Antioch and Philip of Ibelin, Peter's chamberlain Brémond de la Voulte, noblemen James 'le Petit', Pierre de Sur, and master Guy de Bagnulo of Reggio numbered among the party, making a suitably glittered group. Guy de Bagnulo had replaced the charismatic Mézières as Peter's chancellor.[100] The Cypriot nursing of crusade ambitions now included the occupation of Cilician Armenia, a target that had never fully captured the imagination of the west, and Peter struggled to hold the attention of Edward III and the royal household. There was no evidence of papal backing or a maritime alliance (though Venice apparently sold Peter weapons), and a newly concocted claim to Armenia's crown fell on unsympathetic ears. English ambivalence is perhaps reflected in Edward III's expedient plundering of Westminster Abbey for silverware to present to the Cypriot entourage.[101] The atmosphere in Bordeaux was hardly more promising. The Black Prince's recent triumphs in Spain could not disguise the parlous state of the principality's finances, and after the conciliation of the first years, his rule had settled down into a trying pattern of quarrel and confrontation with the lords of Albret and Armagnac. It is not known whether Peter visited there. Peter's deteriorating relations with his own nobility cast further gloom.[102]

The end of the eastern crusade?

Even so, after the dramatic inflammation of chivalric crusading in the 1360s, such a dispiriting response was hardly inevitable. The successful signing of a peace treaty

[99]   *Chronique Valois* pp. 188–91; Guillaume Machaut, *The Capture of Alexandria* tr. J. Shirley (Aldershot, 2001) pp. 138, 178, 193, 204 (le Ros); *Scrope and Grosvenor* vol. I pp. 70, 77, 124–5, 165–6, 171–2 (Henry Scrope), vol. II pp. 171–2, 272, 261, 323–5, 377; S. Gough, *Sepulchral Monuments in Great Britain* (London, 1796) vol. I pt. 2 p. 122 (Malbis). Grey received papal indulgences to go against the infidels (August 1366): *CPP* vol. I p. 531.

[100] NA, E403/417 m. 19; NA, E403/433 m. 18, which provides a new terminus ante quem for Mézières's service.

[101] Sir Robert Knolles also parted with a number of his decorative goblets of gold and silver. The total cost of Edward's presentational gifts was valued at over £200: NA, E403/433 m. 18.

[102] R. W. Barber, *Edward Prince of Wales* pp. 207–20; Sumption *Hundred Years War* vol. II pp. 540–85; Hill, *History of Cyprus*, vol. III pp. 362–9; Edbury, *Cyprus and the Crusades* pp. 168–72.

between Cyprus and the Mamluk sultanate in 1370 would ultimately prove fatal to the 'recovery' crusade in its eastern context, uncoupling traditional military, economic and political objectives, but there was no sense of a pivotal moment in crusade history passing. The logic of Urban V's bull of 1366 – that Latin Cyprus and Rhodes could be stepping stones to Jerusalem – sustained expectations for many decades. What closed off eastern crusading to European chivalry were the problems of control evident in the aftermath of the attack upon Alexandria – not so much in the behaviour of crusade retinues, as in the politics of the Italian maritime powers, who clamoured to appease the Mamluk authorities and restore trade. At the same time, the battle had moved elsewhere, to the defence of Constantinople and eastern Europe against the Ottomans.

Denied much larger investment, the escalation of anti-Turkish operations on Hospitaller Rhodes in the 1370s and 1390s provided the best avenue for continued English participation. Regular embarkation of soldiers under the auspices of the English Hospitallers provided a focus for recruitment, strengthening the already well-established relations between English knights and the Order. In 1397, for example, Prior Walter Grendon took a retinue of fifty knights to Rhodes to serve for three years. Another party left in 1401, laden with jewels, gold, silver and other equipment necessary for their journey 'contra inimicos Christi Saracenorum et Turcorum.' Grendon remained in the east for another eleven years, and, according to royal letters, was involved in the Order's efforts to expand into Despotate of the Morea (south-eastern Pelopennese); in 1417 his successor embarked with a further group of thirty knightly followers. The numbers appear small, but a distinction can be made between those serving for a fixed term, Hospitallers and lay, and the fairly regular traffic of men looking to combine pilgrimage with a worthy fight. The courtly poet John Gower thought that campaigning at Rhodes was as glamorous as the war in Prussia and *Tartarie*.[103] The English priors may have hoped to expand enlistment significantly, making use of their excellent links to court, but such schemes seem to have sat uncomfortably with a conservative leadership at Rhodes. Some English knights may have taken part in the French nobleman Marshal Boucicaut's circulatory raids upon Greece, the Cyclades, Cyprus and Syria in 1403; soon after this date an (unnamed) English dignitary at Florence claimed that he was going to redeem 'certain noblemen' of his country from Turkish imprisonment. The single example of Sir Walter Fitzwalter, captured by the 'Saracens' while still in Italian waters and

---

[103]   *Foedera* vol. III pt. 4 p. 141, vol. IV pt. 1 p. 19, vol. IV pt. 2 p. 201. In 1395 Prior John Raddington was given leave to go to Rhodes with as many fighting men as was fitting for his rank and dignity: ibid. vol. III pt. 4 p. 109. The earl of Gloucester included terms of military service in 'Sprws, Rodes ou vers aucuns autres parties quelconques hors du roiaume Dengleterre' in his life indentures (1399): *Indentures* pp. 123–4; *The English Works of John Gower* ed. G. C. Macaulay, EETS e.s. 81, 82 (London, 1900–1901) vol. I pp. 345–7. For the fifteenth century see A. Luttrell, 'English Contributions to the Hospitaller Castle at Bodrum in Turkey: 1407–1437' *Military Orders: II* ed. H. Nicholson (Aldershot, 1998) pp. 163–72.

released on bond in 1402, perhaps stands for numerous others. He died a few years
later in Venice, apparently still trying to raise capital for his ransom.[104] Such dangers
did not necessarily put men off, but the combination of political factors weighing
against larger western involvement was decisive: the annexation of Cyprus by Genoa
in 1374; the outbreak of war between Venice and Genoa (1374–1381); the resumption
of the Anglo-French conflict; the collapse of lesser Armenia in 1375; and the opening
of the Great Schism in 1378. After a period of nearly three centuries and strong surges
of activism in the fourteenth century, without concerted papal leadership or the support of the Mediterranean maritime powers, a drying up of western crusader traffic
was difficult to stem.

An exception might still be found in the service of the crown, where the passage
to the east retained a moral and practical value for the purposes of diplomacy and
propaganda. In the course of 1391, for example, chamber knight Sir Henry Percy
('Hotspur') travelled between northern Syria (h'antioc) and the coast of western
Maghrib. He was accompanied for the second part of his journey by Sir John Paveley,
a veteran of campaigning in Prussia and Tunis, north Africa. Similarly, royal servants
John Clanvow and William Neville toured the Levant (including Rhodes) before
mysteriously meeting their ends near Constantinople, perhaps victim to the plague.
Ambassadors rather than crusaders, they were nonetheless the crown's best means
of discovering the military strength of the Mamluk state and the necessary conditions for a recovery crusade. Links were retained with Cyprus when Henry Percy
travelled there on behalf of Richard II (1393). Such travels strike a direct parallel
with the intelligence gathering recommended by Mézières in his lengthy moral allegory on Christian kingship, political renewal and the eastern crusade (*Songe du vieil
Pèlerin*).[105] Repeated failure to transform these exploratory, diplomatic impulses into
decisive action would remain the dominant problem of eastern crusading.

---

[104]   In 1435 Sir John Falstof claimed to have served in the east at a young age, possibly with Boucicaut:
English Suits before the Paris Parlement, 1420–1436 eds C. T. Allmand and C. A. J. Armstrong, Camden
Society 26 (London, fourth series 1982) p. 263; *Epistolario di Coluccio Salutati* ed. F. Novati (Rome,
1891–1911) vol. III p. 672; Adam Usk, *The Chronicle of Adam Usk* ed. C. Given-Wilson (Oxford, 1997)
p. 163 (FitzWalter).

[105]   NA, E404/14/96; NA, E403/533 m. 13 (Percy, Paveley). The connection between pilgrimage and
diplomacy strongly suspected by Palmer, Tyerman and Luttrell can be traced in the relevant chancery
protections and exchequer writs: e.g. Clanvow and Neville received a royal licence to go to Rhodes, 5
May 1390: NA, C81/514 no. 6150. Their status as servants of the crown was verified the following year (10
May 1391) when their licences of royal protection were renewed for another year because of continued
absence 'in partibus ultramarinas, in obsequis regis': NA, C81/1057/29; C76/75 mm. 2, 3. The pair died
in October 1391: *Westminster Chronicle, 1381–1394* eds L. C. Hector and B. F. Harvey (Oxford, 1982) p.
481. For Percy in Cyprus see E. F. Jacob, *The Fifteenth Century, 1399–1485* (Oxford, 1961) p. 10. Other
important crusade informants were also drawn from Richard's household knights. See below pp. 110–11,
169–71; Palmer, *England, France and Christendom*, p. 198; Tyerman, *England and the Crusades* p. 296;
Luttrell, 'Chaucer's Knight' p. 145; Philippe de Mézières, *Le songe du vieil pèlerin* ed. G. W. Coopland
(Cambridge, 1969) vol. II pp. 422–9.

3

Spain and North Africa

Compared to the entrepreneurial, polyglot character of the crusade in the eastern Mediterranean, crusades against the Moors of Spain and north Africa remained largely the monopoly of Spanish kings. Dynasticism and political unrest dictated the pace of fourteenth-century campaigning, which was fitful, but the strategic objective of seizing the Straits of Gibraltar and severing Muslim Granada's life-line to north Africa provided grounds for co-operation. Only later, when the conflict promised to move along the shores of Berber Morocco and Tunisia, could other powers, most notably the Genoese, intervene.[1] Historic contacts of diplomacy and trade paved the way for English involvement in this period. Formally, expectations of involvement were high. Edward II and Edward III were both sensitive to the prestige of the Iberian *reconquista*, viewing it, theoretically, as a suitable field of honour for a royal crusade, not least because of their strong dynastic links to Castile. The traditional popularity of the Spanish frontier among French and Gascon nobles could be a source of extra pressure. This was amply illustrated in 1330–1331, when Philip Valois recruited a number of Edward III's Gascon vassals for a proposed expedition to Granada. The thorny issue of Edward's homage, together with French designs upon Gascony, meant that much more was at stake than chivalric war, and the English king stood to lose influence over important regional clients, like the hitherto pro-English count of Hainault and the influential lords of Craon, Albret, Isle Jourdain and Armagnac. Edward III

---

[1]   The *reconquista* has attracted a wealth of modern research: in general see T. F. Ruiz, *Spain's Centuries of Crisis, 1300–1474* (Oxford, 2007); *Ibn Jaldún: el Mediterráneo en el siglo XIV: La Peninsula Ibérica El entorno mediterráneo* eds M. Viguera et al. (Seville, 2006); R. S. i-Lluch, 'Caballeros Cristianos en el Occidente europeo e islámico' *'Das kommt mir Spanisch vor': Eigenes und Fremdes in den deutsch-spanischen Beziehungen des späten mittelalters* eds N. Jaspert and K. Herbers (Münster, 2004) pp. 217–90; J. F. O'Callaghan, *Reconquest and Crusade in Medieval Spain* (Philadelphia, 2003); P. Linehan, *History and the Historians of Medieval Spain* (Oxford, 1993); M. Manzano *La intervención de los benimerines an la peninsula ibérica* (Madrid, 1992); L. P. Harvey, *Islamic Spain, 1250-1500* (Chicago, 1990); D. W. Lomax, *The Reconquest of Spain* (London, 1978); M. Riquer, *Caballeros andantes españoles* (Madrid, 1967); Tyerman, *England and the Crusades* pp. 276–81.

put on a face-saving show of crusade enthusiasm.[2] With the outbreak of the Hundred
Years War, Anglo-Iberian relations entered a new phase. The need to command the
sea-lanes along the French coast attracted the competing courts of England and
France to the powerful Castilian navy. Alongside the regular diplomatic avenues of
marriage and military alliance, collaboration in the crusade promised to strengthen
relations. Anglo-French rivalry lay behind other acts of intervention in this period,
including the Black Prince's invasion of Castile in 1367, Sir Thomas Trivet's expedition to Navarre in 1378–1379, the earl of Cambridge's arrival in Lisbon in 1381, and
John of Gaunt's Urbanist crusade in 1386. An attempt to clothe the Black Prince's
Nájera campaign (1367) with a crusading mantle reflected the efforts of French propagandists, who accused Pedro I and his English allies of being puppets of Granada
and north Africa. Both sides drew ideological capital from the intrusion of English
chivalry into a traditional theatre of French crusading.[3]

Despite its relative proximity, the geography of the Granada frontier was less
accessible to English knights than the Baltic, or even the eastern Mediterranean. The
shipping ports of the Basque region and Galicia steered commercial and pilgrim traffic along the narrow northern corridors, towards Burgos and Santiago de Compostela,
and away from the southern plains and the contested fringes of Granada. There was
not the free, if hazardous, movement associated with travel across Italy for passage
to the east, the mountainous regions of Navarre and Aragon providing formidable
geographical and cultural barriers to voyages over land. The sense of remoteness may
have been heightened by the strong local flavour of campaigning on the frontier,
which was a vehicle first for Iberian nationalism and then for cross-border commercial and territorial control.[4] The large English incursions of the 1360s and 1380s did
little to transform this. Nonetheless, foreign knights continued to fulfil their crusade vows against the Moors. An underlying tradition of chivalry is reflected in the
careers of Englishmen fighting on the outskirts of Granada, such as John Hampton
of Mortimer, wounded and captured at the battle of Vega (1319); the knights fighting
at Teba, where the Scots earl James Douglas and his kinsmen were killed (1330); and
the Cambridgeshire crusaders at Gibraltar (1349), who travelled with Hugh Hinton
and his brother, Sir William. There may have been an English element at the battle of
Salado (1340).[5] Some, like Sir Robert Tony, kept a family tradition alive. Descended

[2]   *CCR 1330–1333* p. 137; Tyerman, *England and the Crusades* pp. 246–7.

[3]   J. B. Valdeón, *Pedro I, el Cruel, y Enrique de Trastámara: la primera guerra civil española?* (Madrid,
2002). See Russell, *English Intervention in Spain* for a still excellent overview.

[4]   A. Mackay, 'Religion, Culture and Ideology on the Late Medieval Castilian-Granadan Frontier'
Medieval Frontier Societies eds R. Bartlett and A. Mackay (Oxford, 1989) pp. 228–43; J. Molina, 'The
Frontier of Granada' *Ibn Khaldun: The Mediterranean in the 14th Century* pp. 154–63; Ruiz, *Spain's
Centuries of Crisis* pp. 28–50, 139–63.

[5]   'Continuatio Historiae Eliensis' p. 653; Romano, 'Un Inglés en la Guerra contro el Moro' pp. 457–9;
J. E. López de Coca and B. Krauel, 'Cruzados escoceses en la frontera de Granada (1330)' *Anuario de
Estudios Medievales* 18 (1988) pp. 245–61; Geoffrey le Baker, *Chronicon Galfridi le Baker de Swynebroke*

from the renowned Norman knight Roger de Tosney (nicknamed 'the Spaniard' for his terrorising of Iberian Muslims in the 1030s), Tony took Edward II's leave in June 1309 'to serve God against the Saracens in Spain'. The pattern was generally of much more limited fighting than that of the early thirteenth century, the heyday of Iberian re-conquest, but chivalric participation still had significant scope. The Spanish authorities lobbied hard to attract international support, particularly in the period before 1350. Coincidentally or not, there was sufficient contact in this period to permit the transmission of Andalusian folklore and custom into areas north of the Pyrenees. One of crusading's less likely legacies was the appearance in central England, by the end of the fourteenth century, of fragmented forms of Moorish drama and dance.[6]

Granada: Civil war, holy war

Sheltered by ongoing war in northern Europe and periodic conflict within the peninsular kingdoms, the Granadan Moors in their fortress kingdom could enjoy a considerable degree of security. The pattern of English participation in the crusade was confined mainly to the episodic and subsidiary. The one significant campaign of the 1340s is instructive. Following a period of political resurgence in the mid 1330s, Alfonso XI of Castile (r. 1312–1350) galvanised a Christian attack against Muslim-held territory close to the Straits of Gibraltar. An alliance of combined land and naval forces from Castile, Aragon and Portugal attempted to dislodge the Moors from ports and river-valleys that served as points of control and entryways for expeditionary forces from Morocco. Utilising the tested tactics of a massed frontal charge, in October 1340 the Christian army scored an impressive victory over an invading Berber force along the Salado river, the weight of horse and armour shattering the Muslim centre. Next to fall was the port of Algeciras in 1344, following a siege of two years. Papal indulgences and Alfonso XI's growing reputation for chivalry helped draw knights from wider parts, including, in May 1343, a grouping headed by Henry Grosmont, earl of Derby, and William Montagu, earl of Salisbury, 'men of great standing in the kingdom of England', as Alfonso's biographer put it.[7] The appearance of English knights at the siege was partly explained by the onset of an Anglo-French

ed. E. M. Thompson (Oxford, 1889) p. 41. See Murimuth, *Continuatio* pp. 263–9 for an English newsletter to Edward III purportedly sent from Christian lines in the aftermath of Salado.

[6] *CChW 1244–1326* p. 287; *CPR 1307–1313* p. 117; Orderic Vitalis, *Historia Ecclesiastica* ed. M. Chibnall (Oxford, 1969–80) vol. I pp. 24, 34. Another Roger Tosney sailed with Richard I to Acre in 1191: 'Itinerarium Peregrinorum' *Chronicles and Memorials of the Reign of Richard I* ed. W. Stubbs, r.s. 38 (London, 1864–1865) vol. I pp. 217–18. Cf. the processional drama/dance 'moros y Cristianos' first performed in Lérida in 1149, emphasising the martial and exotic. For its currency in England during the fifteenth century and scholarly discussion of origins see J. Forrest, *A History of Morris Dancing, 1458–1750* (Cambridge, 1999) pp. 99–101.

[7] Villani, *Cronica* vol. IV pp. 57–8; *Cronica Alfonso* vol. I pp. 360–70; Russell, *English Intervention in Spain* pp. 1–11; K. A. Fowler, *The King's Lieutenant: Henry of Grosmont, First Duke of Lancaster*

truce. They were joined by prominent knights from Germany and France, including the count of Foix and Philip of Navarre, a cousin of Philip VI. Outwardly, relations remained cordial, but distrust split the crusade camp, the French allying under the count of Foix, and a German contingent keeping close to the English. The reason for coolness was not hard to find. Edward III's noblemen were following orders to lobby the Castilian court, competing with Foix to win Alfonso's affection and access to the Castilian navy. They were equipped with the offer of one of Edward III's daughters for marriage to Alfonso's eldest son. Business of lesser importance – the settling of outstanding maritime disputes and 'other necessities and charges' – was to help ease the way.[8]

Compared to Foix and Philip of Navarre, the English made a strong impression. Wanting to make the siege of Algeciras and his court a magnet for European chivalry, Alfonso was delighted at their arrival. The Castilian chroniclers too were attracted by the earls' reputation and displays of gallantry. Much was made of Alfonso's decision to conduct some Moorish emissaries through the English camp, presumably because of its richness and impressive scale. The elaborate military regalia erected outside the visitors' tents reportedly had the desired demoralising effect. Not content to merely spectate, the earls played a highly praised part in attacks upon the Muslim fortifications and took the opportunity to see for themselves the quality of Castilian naval power when joining in a galley raid upon a Berber fleet anchored at Ceuta on the Moroccan coast.[9] Such actions generated goodwill, and the diplomatic mission was a success: Alfonso agreed to treat on a marriage alliance despite Franco-papal protests, and his Genoese admiral, Egidio Boccanegra, promised his ships and crews for service against Philip VI. Edward III's daughter Joan was eventually affianced to Don Pedro in 1346, and departed to marry the Castilian heir in 1348 (only to fall victim to the plague en route to Spain).[10]

The political context deserves emphasis, but the scale of English involvement at Algeciras went far beyond that of a simple embassy. Grosmont and Salisbury spent at least six months at the crusade camp, and sought numerous opportunities to fight. According to one well-informed chronicler, the earls had come 'por salvacion de sus almas, et otrosi por ver et conoscer al Rey' ('for salvation of their souls, besides to meet and befriend the king'). Their retinues were inflated by a stream of other English knights reportedly attracted by the publishing of papal indulgences, perhaps journeying down from Compostela. According to Castilian sources, most performed tours of service of either four or six months, typical terms for campaigning during the

(London, 1969) pp. 45–7. Alfonso sported the moniker 'He of Salado River' after his famous victory of 1340. See *Foedera* vol. II pt. 2 pp. 102–3 for English reactions to the news of Salado.

[8]   Tyerman, *England and the Crusades* pp. 276–81; *CCR 1343–1346* p. 226; *CPR 1343–1345* p. 449.

[9]   *Cronica Alfonso* vol. I pp. 360–70.

[10]   *CCR 1343–1346* p. 456; Russell, *English Intervention in Spain* pp. 1–11.

Hundred Years War.[11] Those closest to the earls included Sir Thomas Holand (future earl of Kent), Sir Matthew Gourney, Sir William Cusance, Sir Thomas Colvill and Sir Thomas Cok, known to Froissart as *un bon chevalier engles*.[12] Despite the courtliness, the dangers were real enough. Two of Grosmont's household were killed. The earl himself was wounded in the face, and disease raged through the crusader camp, afflicting a number of English knights, including the earl of Salisbury. He died the following year, perhaps still suffering the effects.[13] Every effort was made to cross swords with the Moors: one report had the English earls leading a daring charge to rescue some of Alfonso's siege-engineers trapped in a surprise Muslim attack; another told of the English themselves needing to be plucked from death, the weight of enemy numbers threatening to overwhelm Grosmont's men, despite their steady discipline.[14] Advancing against Moorish positions in formation and often on foot, Edward III's knights showcased the battle tactics newly honed in the Scottish and French wars.

As such, the niceties of diplomacy were not always at the front of their minds. Grosmont valued the chivalric and spiritual prize of crusading, and, steeped in the mythology of Charlemagne and Roland, the war against the Moors exerted a strong psychological pull. Every knight knew from the poet the ominous atmospheres of the Pyrenees, Oliver's bravery and Roland's heroic, temple-bursting blast on his horn.[15] The story, in its various forms and derivations, remained the archetype for the fourteenth-century warrior-code. Thus it was (in the eyes of chronicler Geoffrey le Baker) that the death of Scottish nobleman James Douglas from five wounds at the battle of Teba (1330) called to mind the martyrdom of Roland as well as Christ's suffering on the cross. A more urbane treatment – that of Chaucer's Knight – set the war in Granada and *Bel marye* (i.e. Marinid Morocco) as a compass-point of true chivalry, alongside the fighting in Prussia, Turkey and the Levant. This imaginative, historic dimension added appreciably to its mystique. And the double vision was shared in other circles. Edward III permitted Sir Thomas Wale to postpone the homage ceremony for his Northamptonshire lands because of his absence in Spain (August 1343). Officially, Wale was taking part in the 'guerre contre les enemis de dieu et de la crestienetes', not royal diplomacy, the chancery choosing to ignore the siege of Algeciras's political dimension in favour of brighter religious gloss.[16]

After the conclusion of the siege of Algeciras in 1344, this identity with the vocabulary and sentiment of the *reconquista* found its richest expression in the 1360s,

---

[11] Tyerman, *England and the Crusades* p. 278; *Cronica Alfonso* vol. I pp. 360–1; Villani, *Cronica* vol. IV pp. 57–8.

[12] *CPR 1343–1345* pp. 16, 18; Gough, vol. II p. 20 (Gourney); Froissart, vol. IV p. 303.

[13] *Cronica Alfonso* vol. I pp. 362–3. Montagu's rapid decline and death (30 January 1344) was not the result of wounds received at a royal tournament at Windsor as is usually claimed. See Ormrod, *Edward III* p. 301.

[14] *Cronica Alfonso* vol. I pp. 362–4.

[15] See in general W. R. J. Barron, *English Medieval Romance* (London, 1987) pp. 89–108, 114–19 and references there.

[16] *CCR 1343–1346* p. 159; NA, C81/291/15587. Wale was a retainer of Salisbury: NA, C81/1738/29.

during the civil war between Henry Trastamara and Pedro I of Castile. Propagandists on both sides went to significant lengths to present their cause as a war partly aimed at Granada, capitalising on the sentiment stirred by other crusade appeals, notably the Cypriot expedition of 1365 and the *passagium* to Constantinople simultaneously being promoted in Gascony. The treaty which brought the Black Prince into the war on the side of Pedro I affirmed the vision in operation, stipulating the prince's right to lead the Christian army against the Moors of *Granata* when the moment was ripe. The expense of maintaining war equipment for this purpose was allotted to Pedro I and his successors (September 1366).[17] Such gestures helped harness the idealism and energy unbottled when Peter of Cyprus visited the English court at Bordeaux, turning it to national and dynastic ends. Rumours added to the belief that intervention in Spain might involve fully fledged war against Islam, and English commanders were among those apparently willing to trust the double-speak. The Black Prince's brother, John of Gaunt, sealed indentures with retainers stipulating terms in case they should take the 'chemyn sur les enemys Dieux' (May 1366), for example.[18] On the opposing side, the famous Bertrand Du Guesclin, captain of Henry Trastamara's army, was publicly crowned 'king of Granada' as part of Trastamara's military and political coup, the ceremony clearly designed to confer additional legitimacy on the Pretender's bid for power. Twenty years later the memory of the Black Prince's biographer also ordered events in this way. Trastamara's invasion was a 'holy expedition' fought 'to open the passes and defiles of Granada' as well as to avenge the tyranny of Pedro I. Of course, none of this made a military conquest of Granada any more plausible. Foreign intervention merely exacerbated Christian disunity in the Peninsula. Instead, glutted with the ransoms won at the battle of Nájera, English veterans carried their enthusiasm over to the Baltic crusade, embarking to fight there in unprecedented numbers (see below pp. 76–80). In France, however, the fiction apparently stuck. In 1371 Charles V paid Du Guesclin 30,000 gold francs towards his outstanding costs. In practice it was to help the nobleman with repayment of his £20,000 ransom, owed to the Black Prince. But officially royal funds were released in honour of Du Guesclin's loyal service in leading the Christians 'against Granada'.[19]

With the escalation of civil war in Castile and ongoing hostility between the Peninsular kingdoms, the fourteenth-century war against Spanish Islam slipped into abeyance, devolving into a series of minor skirmishes (*razzia*) and confrontations. English involvement conformed to this pattern – intermittent and of strictly local consequence. With the rest of Europe, English enthusiasts had to await the revival of Spanish crusading in the late fifteenth century for the conclusion of the

---

[17] For Pedro I's alliance with Muhammed V of Granada see Russell, *English Intervention in Spain* pp. 138, 147, 153; *Foedera* vol. III pt. 2 pp. 122–3.

[18] S. Walker, *The Lancastrian Affinity, 1361–1399* (Oxford, 1990) appendix 3 pp. 294–5.

[19] Chandos Herald, *Life of the Black Prince* eds M. K. Pope and E. C. Lodge (Oxford, 1910) lines 45, 1641, 2030, 2049–103, 2783; Froissart, vol. VII p. 145; *Mandements et actes* p. 437.

reconquista and the destruction of Granada. In the meantime dynastic links were the main avenue for continuing associations, and these ran largely through the house of Lancaster, perhaps fittingly, given the early campaign honours of Henry Grosmont, the first duke. John of Gaunt's marriage to Pedro I's daughter Constance and subsequent claim to the throne of Castile made a requirement of showing formal interest in the *reconquista* as part of Gaunt's projected Spanish kingship. In the 1370s he was patronising the Castilian crusading orders, bestowing gifts, holding audiences and seeking to cultivate goodwill. The Spanish émigrés that joined his household in the 1370s and 1380s imported a knightly ethos that included traditions of fighting the Moors, though little prospect of active campaigning against Granada existed until the 1390s, when a new spate of cross-border war suddenly flared. Here, again, contact was largely anecdotal. Perhaps representative was the case of Diego Fernández, a son of one of Gaunt's bachelors, Sir Juan Fernández of Portugal. He was among the survivors of a massacre inflicted in 1394, when members of the military order of Alcantara marched, with suicidal intent, up to the gates of the Muslim capital and were cut to pieces by the Moors. Kept bound in chains and tortured, Fernández spent years in prison awaiting payment of a ransom. A spotlight was thrown on his fate because of his family's prestigious connections. At the end of 1397 the bishop of Winchester, who had an ear for knightly daring-do and news at court, published an appeal in aid of the foreign hostage. Diocesan indulgences were issued to church-goers who gave alms to assist Fernández's release. Fundraising may have been started in other dioceses where John of Gaunt had strong influence. Any money gathered was funnelled to Sir Juan Fernández, now entering his third decade in Gaunt's service. In such ways the struggle for Christian Spain remained in the public domain.[20] Ongoing loyalties would surface again in the late fifteenth century, when the names of numerous English knights, along with those of other nations, appeared in the Aragonese records as volunteers fighting against the Moors. Several won battle honours from Ferdinand II during Granada's final stand of 1485–1492.[21]

'Bone compaignie et bone chere': Louis of Bourbon's crusade

While the Spanish *reconquista* entered a period of relative quiet, the promotion of a Genoese-sponsored attack on Tunis (al-Mahdiya) on the coastline of north Africa in 1390 showed the alternative possibilities open to crusade planners in the final decades

---

[20]   For Fernández see *John of Gaunt's Register, 1379–1383*, eds E. C. Lodge and R. Somerville, Camden Society 56, 57 (London, 1911) vol. I p. 8; Walker, *Lancastrian Affinity* p. 269; Russell, *English Intervention in Spain* p. 297; Goodman, *John of Gaunt* p. 135 and references there; *Wykeham's Register* ed. T. F. Kirby, Hampshire Record Society (London, 1896–1899) vol. II pp. 476. Wykeham also published prayers in aid of Thomas Woodstock's *passagium* to Prussia and for captives of the French war (vol. II p. 430).

[21]   A. Gutiérrez de Velasco, 'Los ingleses en España' *Estudios de Edad Media de la Corona de Aragon* vol. IV (Saragossa, 1951) pp. 309–10.

of the fourteenth century. It preceded the more sustained Portuguese and Castilian efforts to conquer the coast of Morocco and Tunisia in the early fifteenth century. Even more than the iconic Nicopolis expedition of 1396, the campaign embodied the resurgence of knightly enthusiasm for crusading following the tentative Anglo-French truce of 1389. Traditional crusade indulgences and the invoking of the crusader king *non pareil*, St Louis, could not disguise the expedition's limited aims – the destruction of one of Genoa's commercial rivals and its resident nest of Berber pirates – yet, arriving at a tipping point in Anglo-French relations, the expedition possessed strong attractions. Besides the traditional vision of old enemies unified under the banner of the cross, co-operation in the *hethenesse* was held up as an essential step towards church unity and the healing of the papal schism, now entering its second decade. The defence of Christendom would help cement peace between England and France while at the same time providing employment for western soldiery, thus reconciling the more militant of the king's subjects to an unaccustomed peace, so crusade propagandists claimed.[22]

As such, as an exercise of chivalry the Tunis expedition fitted into a wider debate about military culture going on in some quarters. Against the growing disenchantment with the French war, and the perceived gap between high chivalry and the murderousness of fourteenth-century warfare, an international crusade offered its participants special glamour and martial prestige.[23] Perhaps more than any other fourteenth-century crusade, politics and a heated atmosphere at court shaped responses. Richard II was well disposed to it, using English participation in the Tunis crusade and on other far-flung frontiers to help establish his credentials as a patron of righteous causes, and demonstrate the military character of his court (see below pp. 67–8, 169–72). Similar matters of prestige encouraged the powerful John of Gaunt to take close interest. His promotion to the duchy of Gascony in 1390 and courtly contact with the uncles of Charles VI placed him increasingly in the circles of the Valois princes, close to crusade enthusiasm at the French court. Gaunt would act as a figurehead for English involvement in 1390, liaising with Louis II, duke of Bourbon, the chosen candidate to command the Genoese-backed crusade. Neglecting to take personal command (Froissart made the excuse he was too old), he planned for his sons, Henry Bolingbroke and John Beaufort, to take part. For the English nobility more generally, the Tunis expedition chimed with a mood of renewal and reconciliation after the collapse of the ruling Appellant regime and Richard II's resumption of personal authority in 1389. For the king's closer associates, it was a chance to rub out the political humiliations of 1386–1389 and repair knightly reputations; for others, it was an expression of enthusiasm for settlement with France and growing exasperation at the schism.

---

[22]   Atiya, *Crusade in the Later Middle Ages* pp. 398–434; M. L. Mirot, *Le Siège de Mahdia: une expédition Française en Tunisie au XIVᵉ siècle* (Paris, 1932). The English sources remain largely unexplored.

[23]   For the crisis of high chivalry (and its literary expression) see Saul, *For Honour and Fame* pp. 128–34, 193–6.

Recruitment centred upon courtier and elite circles. There was no preaching or widespread publication of indulgences. It is probable that Gaunt brought back news of the Tunis expedition when he returned from Aquitaine at the end of 1389. His departure from France coincided with Genoa's search for western military aid, and Gaunt kept in close contact with the crusade leadership once Bourbon had been nominated as expedition leader. One of Louis II's messengers left England at the beginning of March in the company of Gaunt's heralds, 'Lancastre' and 'Leycestre', probably carrying assurances of English support and a plan for Lancastrian participation.[24] Richard II's informers in Paris supplied the English nobility with further details. Besides the usual variety of transport and merchant vessels, Genoa was to contribute forty war galleys from its own fleet and ten galleys pooled from 'other parts'. Charles VI's restrictions upon French recruitment meant that the French contingent would number no more than one thousand knights and esquires (in contrast to the chronicle reports of fifteen thousand), but an impressive roll of French noblemen, including the counts of Eu and Harcourt, Marshal Boucicaut, Charles III of Navarre, and the lord of Trémouille, had already displayed their interest. The Italians undertook to pay for shipping and other expenses (excepting wages) for four months only, putting the campaign on a relatively short-term footing, particularly if African conquests proved unprofitable or difficult to effect. The date for sailing was set for 15 May 1390. English newsletters hinted at a possible connection between Bourbon's crusade and the ambition of the duke of Anjou in the kingdom of Naples, but this was an overly subtle reading of events.[25]

News of the expedition reached a wider chivalric audience through a series of tournaments held to celebrate the sealing of the Anglo-French truce in the spring months of 1390. Marshal Boucicaut hosted a grand meeting at St Inglevert near Calais towards the end of March. Invitations went out in November 1389, and a brief visit to London enabled Boucicaut to attract many of the younger figures of Richard II's court. Henry Bolingbroke, the earls of Nottingham and Huntingdon, and Henry Percy 'Hotspur' travelled to St Inglevert with impressive retinues. Huntingdon, the king's half-brother, apparently took sixty knights. Another large grouping of one hundred knights and esquires accompanied the prominent courtiers Sir John Beaumont; Sir Lewis Clifford; and Sir Peter Courtenay.[26] The premium placed upon military spectacle and Anglo-French fraternity concealed the level of care to forward the business of the crusade: Gaunt sent letters of introduction with his sons, arranging for a conference between Boucicaut and Bolingbroke. The presence of Sir Peter Courtenay, chief chamberlain of the royal household, signified Richard II's interest, providing a figurehead for other chamber knights and nobles as well. The strong correlation between

[24] Gaunt was in England by 19 November 1389. Goodman, *John of Gaunt* p. 144; NA, C81/514/6167 (safe conducts).

[25] NA, SC1/51/37 (chancery memo); *West. Chron.* p. 433.

[26] *Foedera* vol. III pt. 4 pp. 55–6. Froissart gives the fullest account: vol. XIV pp. 151–9, 211–53.

those taking out licences to participate at St Inglevert and English recruits to the Tunis crusade points to the precedence of the project in diplomatic and social channels. As such, it is significant that Froissart later sought information on the fighting at Tunis in the marcher lands of English Calais, not in the Low Countries or in the French capital; it was here that memories of the campaign were evidently freshest.[27]

Preparations for a sizeable English force to embark were finalised in the weeks immediately after St Inglevert. A second tournament, this time held in London at Smithfield, enabled Richard II to preside, the presence of a number of foreign knights further charging the atmosphere. Men linked to the crusade, such as Sir Peter Courtenay and John, Lord Welles, were prominent combatants.[28] An outline of the response is gleaned from chancery writs issued under the privy seal. The records are incomplete but amongst those taking out licences to go *vers les parties des Barbarie* were the royal esquires Thomas Trewin and Henry Scrope, and the prominent soldiers Sir John Russell, Sir John Heveningham, Thomas, Lord Camoys, and John, Lord Bourchier. Richard II's courtiers John Clanvow and William Neville also received commissions to go east.[29] Evidence of a larger grouping, including Camoys and Bourchier, is found in the treaty rolls, where a flurry of legal activity relates to the crusade's imminent sailing. Men with strong Lancastrian credentials, such as Sir Richard Abberbury, William, Lord Willoughby, and John Norbury, appointed attorneys to attend to their affairs during their absence *transmarinas*. The well-connected esquire Richard Fotheringhay, Sir William Elmham and Sir Baldwin Seint George made similar arrangements.[30] Although leadership of the enterprise was largely centred upon Bolingbroke, the involvement of figures close to other Appellant lords, Thomas Mowbray and Thomas Woodstock, duke of Gloucester, points to a wider base of interest. Would-be participants moving in Gloucester's circle were Sir John Heveningham, the young Henry Scrope and his Essex neighbour, Lord Bourchier.[31] The overall response mirrored the new cohesion imposed upon politics in the early 1390s after the rupture of the Merciless Parliament, particularly between Richard II and the younger Appellants. Three of the knights forcibly removed from Richard's household in 1388 appointed attorneys for their absence on crusade (Camoys,

[27]   Beaumont, Courtenay and Clifford petitioned for a royal safe conduct to the Calais march on behalf of Boucicaut, Jean de Sempy and Regnault de Roye, the organisers of St Inglevert: NA, C76/74 m.8; Goodman, *John of Gaunt* p. 170. n. 8; Froissart, vol. XIV p. 217.

[28]   *West. Chron.* pp. 432–7. Welles was probably not alone in taking out private letters of indulgence for the crusaders' irruption into north Africa, the land of 'Prester John': BL, MS Royal 20 D IX fol. 190ᵛ.

[29]   NA, C81/515/6266–9; C81/515/6289; C81/515/6291; C81/515/6150. Clanvow and Neville are placed at al-Mahdiya by the monk of Westminster: *West. Chron.* p. 433; corroborated by Cabaret d'Orville, *La Chronique du Bon Duc Loys de Bourbon* ed. A.-M. Chazaud (Paris, 1876) p. 222.

[30]   NA, C76/74 mm. 12, 7, 4. Fotheringhay was made a life retainer by Richard II in 1389. He was also an annuitant of the duke of Brittany: *CPR 1388–1392* p. 106.

[31]   For political connections see A. Goodman, *The Loyal Conspiracy: The Lords Appellant under Richard II* (London, 1971) pp. 97 (Heveningham), 81 (Scrope), 57 and 124 (Bourchier).

Elmham and Abberbury), and another intimate of the king, Sir William Bagot, sent ten esquires as a contribution to Bolingbroke's retinue, his open-handedness apparently chiming with the co-operative spirit.[32]

Officially, the crown placed the enterprise under its control, the chancery deeming those embarking with Louis II as going to foreign parts 'in the service of the king', a formula which adequately preserved royal dignity as well as reflecting Richard II's personal interest. Sympathetic towards the crusade (and perhaps alert to the attractions of Lancastrian pay), Richard II helped offset the campaign expenses of some in his inner circle, despite the tight constraints imposed on royal spending. Terms of service do not survive, but on their return from the east, Sir John Paveley and Henry Scrope received sizeable gratuities to relieve their costs in 'coming out of Barbary', paid from the exchequer rather than the privy purse, probably in light of official commissions. The prominence of the senior chamber knight Lewis Clifford, amongst the crusaders at al-Mahdiya (another victim of the 1388 purge) and Sir Bernard Brocas, chamberlain to Queen Anne, also attests to the household's strong influence.[33] More distant from the political centre and keen to enhance his knightly reputation, Edward Courtenay, earl of Devon, was another to set his sights on the Tunis expedition, appointing his powerful uncles, William Courtenay, archbishop of Canterbury, and the chamber knights Peter and Philip Courtenay as his attorneys. If he did indeed embark, it was the earl's final military enterprise before slipping into political retirement, increasingly confined by the onset of blindness.[34]

In the absence of church funds or lay subsidies, the English participants resorted to various expediencies to raise money. None could rival the scale of funding available to John of Gaunt's sons, whose war-chest was siphoned from Gaunt's ducal treasury and probably exceeded £5,000, enough to finance a small army for several months (though even this required very careful husbandry).[35] The crusade terms found in some English life-indentures, putting the burden of extra costs, such as transportation and ancillary wages, on to retainers, reflected the situation of some Lancastrian knights who were expected to add their own retinues at their own expense.[36] Genoa's stipulation that recruits had to be knights, squires or others qualified by gentle birth who

---

[32] NA, C76/74 m. 4; *Expeditions* pp. xxxvii–xliii, 118–27.

[33] NA, C76/74 m. 4 (John Norbury); NA, E404/14/96 (Paveley); E403/533 mm. 13, (Paveley) 14 (Scrope). Before committing to the eastern *passagium*, Paveley and chamber knights William Neville and John Clanvow considered campaigning in Prussia. Neville and Clanvow received gifts of £71 13s 4d towards their costs in going to *Pruys*, and Paveley received £20 (April 1390): NA, E403/531 m.7; NA, C81/514/6150. The Bourbon chronicler describes Clifford as the 'chief de Anglois': Cabaret d'Orville, p. 249. The part of Brocas (d. 1395) in the crusade was recorded on the memorial brass at his tomb in Westminster Abbey. He was said to have beaten the 'king of Morocco' in a personal combat: Gough, vol. I pt. 1 p. 160.

[34] NA, C76/74 m. 14; NA, C66/329 mm. 5, 7; *West. Chron.* pp. 432–3.

[35] *Expeditions* pp. lxxxvi–lxxxvii; Du Boulay, 'Henry of Derby's Expeditions to Prussia' pp. 168–70.

[36] E.g. *Indentures* nos 40, 85, 87, 93; Walker, *Lancastrian Affinity* appendix 3 no. 1 pp. 294–5.

could afford to pay for themselves, and thus provide 'good company and good cheer', was largely decorative. Few outside these groupings could hope to absorb the necessary expenditure. Thomas, Lord Camoys, pursued the problem with energy, placing his southern manors in trust with a wealthy group of lawyers and clerks, including the bishop of London, probably as surety for a loan. He made a personal visit to the chancery to certify the transfer of all his moveable possessions to two of his associates, either as part of a monetary transaction or to preserve their safe-keeping during his absence. On the same day Camoys sued out for a licence to cross *vers les parties de Barbarie* with £400 in gold or coin, his asset-stripping evidently producing a sizeable sum for his crusade retinue.[37] The evidence of more marginal cases such as the esquire Thomas Trewin, who embarked carrying only 30 marks 'of English or French money', probably disguises a dependency upon a wealthier retinue leader or an alternative financial device, such as a letter of exchange. It is likely that Trewin could command a significantly larger fortune. He was sufficiently eminent to attract a royal annuity and livery of retainer in 1393.[38]

Taken at face value, the scale of English involvement was going to be impressive. The evidence of Bolingbroke's accounts show that his agents, William Willoughby and Thomas Swinford, disbursed wages for about 120 men – knights, squires and at least forty-one archers.[39] Bolingbroke's half-brother, John Beaufort, travelled with a large knightly following, and a conglomerate of courtiers, including Lewis Clifford, John, Lord Clinton, and Sir John Cornwall, offered Bourbon a retinue of twenty-five knights and one hundred archers. Another English knight, Baldwin Seint George, undertook to join Bourbon with twenty-five knights and esquires.[40] The earl of Devon travelled with a smaller grouping, perhaps intending to attract further recruits in Calais, a clearing house of English soldiery, and Lord Bourchier headed a party of thirty, made up of six esquires, fifteen valets and eight man-servants. For this he allocated £300. The retinues of Sir John Harpendon, seneschal of Aquitaine, Sir Thomas Botiller, lord of Sudeley (Gloucs.), John, Lord Welles, Sir John Paveley, the royal ward Nicholas Lovein and possibly a contingent of English Hospitallers further fleshed out the numbers.[41] Together with their archers, it is conceivable that the English retinue leaders fielded a force of at least six hundred to seven hundred men.

Recruitment ran through established social and political channels. A detailed contract between Sir Alexander Stewart of Swaffham (Norf.) and the Scottish lord George Douglas outlined the terms for their participation. Stewart agreed to serve

---

[37]   NA, C54/231 m. 12ᵈ; NA, C81/515/6291; NA, C76/74 m. 4.
[38]   NA, C81/515/6266; *CPR 1391–1396* pp. 193, 225, 328.
[39]   *Expeditions* pp. xxxvii–xliii, 118–27.
[40]   Froissart, vol. XIV pp. 156–7; Cabaret d'Orville, p. 222.
[41]   *CPR 1388–1392* p. 199; Mirot, *Siège de Mahdia* p. 16; NA, C76/74 m. 4; Froissart, vol. XIV p. 225; BL, MS Royal 20 D IX fol. 190ᵛ. *West. Chron.* p. 433 connects the English prior of the Hospitallers, John Raddington, to the Tunis expedition, but this is perhaps confused. Raddington embarked for Rhodes before the end of March 1390: *CPR 1388–1392* p. 205; *CCR 1389–1392* p. 126.

with Douglas in Bourbon's expedition *contra Saracenos*, and if necessary to remain in north Africa for up to one year. In the event of illness or some other incapacity, however, Stewart was to forfeit a bond of 1,000 marks, or furnish Douglas with two knights of good repute in his place, the terms suggesting that the agreement was of a reciprocal nature, possibly made as a pact between the knights as brothers-in-arms. The crusade pledge was almost certainly agreed at the March tournament at Smithfield, where Scottish, French and English knights mingled freely.[42] Particular religious currents may have drawn some of the crusaders into an equally intimate association. Men such as Clanvow, Neville, Clifford and Scrope were known sympathisers of John Wyclif's heterodox teachings, for example, and the vogue amongst some of Richard II's knights for puritanical religion may have set down larger roots in the crusade. One of Sir John Paveley's attorneys was Sir Richard Stury, royal councillor and reputed 'Lollard' knight; Sir John Golafre, a noted ascetic, acted in the same capacity for Sir John Russell. A taste for war in the *hethenesse* as a purifying ideal is evident in the careers of other knights known for heterodox belief (e.g. John Montagu and William Beauchamp), despite the pacifism of some Wyclifite preachers and the abhorrence for warfare assumed in certain radical circles, such as the audience of Langland's *Piers Plowman*.[43]

Homogeneity marked other elements of the enterprise – not just at court but also at the regional and local levels. Interaction as neighbouring property-holders and their varying associations with the magnate affinity of Thomas II, earl of Warwick (d.1401), kept the midland knights Thomas Botiller, John, Lord Clinton, and John Russell locked in a close social circle, for example. The trio were each patrons of the town guild of the Holy Trinity at Coventry, a civic body founded by the Beauchamps, where ideals of public honour and military character, including the crusade, were incubated. A number of other noble-born crusaders, including the elderly Henry Ferrers, Lord Groby, and Thomas, earl of Stafford, featured among the guild's regional membership.[44] An element of central organisation is evident in the decision of some crusade recruits to take out letters of exchange with the London branch of the same Lombard bankers, the Christofori – the company's extensive links with Bourbon's Genoese contractors perhaps giving them something of a monopoly over financial arrangements. Cashed in the ports of Calais, Marseilles or Genoa, the letters obviated the various practical and legal obstacles to exporting sums in bulk and were in

---

[42]   BL, MS Add. 15644 fol. 3ᵛ (sixteenth-century copy).

[43]   NA, C76/74 mm. 8 (Paveley), 7 (Russell). Paveley's father, John senior, possessed somewhat stronger links to the 'Lollard' knights Lewis Clifford, Richard Stury and Thomas Latimer, enfeoffing the trio with his Northamptonshire lands sometime before 1395: *CIPM* vol. XX p. 41 no. 127. See below pp. 80–5, 92–3, 76–7, 125, 132, 180 (Montagu and Beauchamp).

[44]   *The Register of the Trinity Guild, Coventry* ed. M. Dormer-Harris, (London, 1935–1944) vol. I pp. 11, 27, 76–7; Gundy, 'Rule of Thomas Beauchamp' p. 280. Besides the Coventry guild, Thomas Botiller possessed other links to the earl of Stafford, appointing Stafford's steward, John Knyghtly, as his attorney for the term of his absence on crusade in April 1390: NA, C76/74 m. 4.

common use by men embarking on all manner of other business, including the crusade, throughout the period.[45] In a different example, the fact that the earl of Devon was married to a daughter of Thomas, Lord Camoys, almost certainly encouraged both men to embark, kinship links helping to frame individual responses.

Gathered at Calais in the middle of May, the size of the English army elicited a nervous response from Charles VI of France. The presence of John of Gaunt accompanying Henry Bolingbroke and John Beaufort, together with a substantial expeditionary force, was particularly unwelcome, in spite of recent Anglo-French cordiality.[46] The speed at which Richard II's nobles mustered for the eastern expedition perhaps took Paris by surprise. For Charles VI's alarmist councillors, an English force massing on the northern march automatically attracted suspicion, Gaunt's arrival at the head of an English crusade perhaps stirring memories of Bishop Despenser's expedition to Flanders in 1383. Gaunt's only interest was to supervise the embarkation of his sons, but while the English knights waited for their safe conducts to journey to the Mediterranean, Charles VI chanced a diplomatic snub and refused passage to Henry Bolingbroke, the expedition's figurehead. The reasons are nowhere explicit, but the *Westminster Chronicle* states that disagreement arose over the terms of the earl's safe conduct, the scale of his military retinue probably being the sticking point. There may have been a plan for Bolingbroke to levy troops from Gascony, thus capitalising upon his father's recent promotion as duke there, a course of action calling to mind crusade recruitment in the 1360s and also bound to elicit a cagey response from the French.[47] Henry's brother, the less-distinguished John Beaufort, was allowed to proceed with a large cohort of knights, and a significant number of other Englishmen received safe conducts, though care was taken to marshal them across the kingdom quickly. Philippe Pelourde, one of Charles VI's courtiers, personally supervised Beaufort's journey to Genoa.[48] The effect was not so much to fragment the army as to diminish its profile as a vehicle for Lancastrian power. Bolingbroke took the disappointment with good grace, knowing the delicate state of affairs between governments, and in June he disbanded his retinue at Calais, returning to England to prepare for his alternative scheme of campaigning in Prussia. He was in esteemed company. Also barred from sailing, Marshal Boucicaut and Sir Jean Sempy, the authors of St Inglevert, turned to the northern crusade a few months later.[49]

Although weakened, the English force at al-Mahdiya was not negligible, and, grouped around John Beaufort, the captains and their retinues played a praiseworthy

---

[45]   E.g. the earl of Devon and Lord Bourchier: *CPR 1388–1392* pp. 195, 199; NA, C81/515/6289. The Christofori were a presence in England from the 1260s. See R. J. Whitwell, 'Italian Bankers and the English Crown' *TRHS* 17 (1903) p. 41.

[46]   See Gaunt's letters patent dated Calais, 18 May 1390: BL, Add. Ch. 7487.

[47]   *West. Chron.* pp. 432–5. French anxiety was heightened by the terms of Gaunt's elevation to the duchy of Aquitaine (March 1390), granted by Richard as king of France, not of England.

[48]   Mirot, *Siège de Mahdia* p. 16 (quoting Bibl. Nat. MS fr. 205090 no. 10).

[49]   Paravicini, *Die Preussenreisen* vol. II p. 216.

part. The fighting was brisk but inconclusive, the Christians fencing themselves in between the enemy port and the Hafsid armies sent to repel the invaders.[50] Italian engineers and sailors took charge of the assault upon the harbour and citadel, leaving the French and other contingents to fend off forces arriving from the interior. The confrontation soon reached a deadlock, however, with both sides content to observe their own blockade. Many of the horses boarded with the English and French knights were lost to the heat, hampering the crusaders' manoeuvrability and making it hard to tempt the Berber generals into open battle. For over three months, from July through September, the crusaders fought skirmishes around the perimeter of their camp, and accounts of the siege mention the important English military contribution. In Bourbon's ordinances for battle, John Beaufort held command of the Christian flank as banneret, with the experienced Gloucestershire soldier Sir Thomas Botiller taking charge of the English pennon. From his exposed position, Beaufort probably saw testing action. The English archers reportedly did well, fending off the enemy cavalry and proving their worth as a potent battlefield weapon.[51] There was also room for individual heroism. 'Jehannicot' Courtenay (one of the earl of Devon's men), Sir John Cornwall (a future Garter knight) and Lord Clifford stood out for their great deeds of chivalry, according to the Bourbon chronicler. The irrepressible Sir John Russell also showed spirit, answering a challenge for a hand-to-hand combat between Christian and Muslim champions, though the contest was prohibited by Louis II before the two sides could meet. Veteran campaigner Richard Fotheringhay was slaughtered in a bloody encounter that followed soon afterwards, along with various other unnamed Englishmen.[52] Casualties were relatively light, despite the incessant harrying, but the western knights showed their thirst for warfare. In the end, fetid conditions at camp proved the biggest enemy, disease and heat taking a greater toll than the Muslim assaults. Illness continued to deplete the ranks, even after the army reached Italian waters – a large part of Sir Baldwin Seint George's military retinue died at Genoa, unable to recover their health after exiting the desert.[53]

Failure to nullify al-Mahdiya's defences and a growing shortage of food compelled the Genoese to open negotiations with the ruler of Tunis. At Louis II's council of war, the English contingents put their weight behind a proposed treaty which placed the city under tribute to the Italians for fifteen years, extracted a large war indemnity and imposed a temporary regional truce. The French were equally enthusiastic. Bourbon

[50] Atiya, *Crusade in the Later Middle Ages* pp. 398–434; Tyerman, *England and the Crusades* pp. 279–80.
[51] Froissart vol. XIV p. 225; Juvenal des Ursins, *Histoire de Charles VI, roy de France* eds J. Michaud et al. (Paris, 1836) vol. II p. 384; *Chronique du Religieux de Saint-Denys* ed. L. F. Bellaguet (Paris, 1839–1852) vol. I pp. 656–9.
[52] Cabaret d'Orville, pp. 229–30; Froissart, vol. XIV p. 254. Russell's skill as a jouster won him the prestigious office of Master of the King's Horse. See Tout, *Chapters* vol. IV p. 38; *Chronique du Religieux de Saint-Denys* vol. I pp. 668–9; *CPR 1388–1392* p. 368.
[53] Cabaret d'Orville, p. 257.

put up an objection, citing the pious purposes of the campaign, but expectations were generally less expansive than that, the original four-month contracts and the negotiated settlement fitting closely with the pattern of war practised by English and French armies of the 1370s and 1380s.[54] Bourbon's protests that the crusaders did not come 'pour faire paatris [i.e. *patiz,* or protection money], mais pour... conquester' sounded out of touch when the dominant experience of seasoned knights since the reopening of the Hundred Years War in 1369 was economic and military blockade, not regional conquest and occupation. This was confirmed in the sentiment of the veteran nobleman and Garter knight Soudic de la Touc, who considered the terms extracted from the ruler of Tunis to be as honourable to the crusaders as the capture of the town itself. Reduced to tribute and servitude, al-Mahdiya joined the numerous strongholds and towns on the Mediterranean littoral owing tribute to a foreign mercantile power. In Touc's opinion, the honour of attacking the infidel was the equivalent of fighting in three great battles, affirmation of the *hethenesse's* superior appeal in the order of knightly merit. Contemporary commentators did not diverge far from this point of view.[55]

If there was little concept of the larger war against Islam, particularly the threat of the Ottoman Turks, the Genoese did not refrain from casting themselves as the champions of Levantine Christianity. In their judgement, the extension of a *pax Januensi* over the entire Mediterranean basin could be the precursor to the long-anticipated recovery *passagium.*[56] Some took a different view, unready to return to the west without achieving more against Islam, or at least visiting the holy sites in Syria. Elements of the crusade chartered Genoese vessels to Rhodes, Cyprus and other parts of the Latin Aegean. The Gloucestershire knight Thomas, Lord Botiller, was amongst them, wending his way to Syria and the holy places with several of his household, and probably with other English visitors such as Sir John Clanvow, Sir William Neville and Lewis Clifford. Botiller's mindset was now openly pacific. Indeed, he and his companions indulged in traditional tourist curiosity, breaking the canonical prohibition on fraternisation with the infidel – talking, drinking and even eating with the 'perfidious Saracens'. Their crime was flagrant enough to attract the wrath of local church officials in Jerusalem and the unusually harsh penalty of excommunication. Local anxiety about Muslim sensitivities perhaps accounted for the heavy-handed response. Tensions between the resident Christian community and the Mamluk authorities would boil over a few months later when four Franciscan preachers were killed on Temple Mount after proselytising to Muslim crowds (November 1391). Behind Botiller's inquisitiveness may have been a similarly risky agenda. Showing exactitude

---

54   Ibid. pp. 248–9.
55   Ibid. pp. 247–8; *West. Chron.* pp. 433, 449–51.
56   In 1392 Doge Adorno canvassed the western courts for support of a Genoese fleet to Constantinople: *Diplomatic Correspondence of Richard II* ed. E. Perroy, Camden Society 48 (London, third series 1933) no. 148.

in following the canons, Botiller returned to England with letters from the cardinal-priest of St Susanna, the papal penitentiary, placing the matter of his penance in the care of his local diocesan, the bishop of Worcester.[57]

Capitalising on the crusade

The Tunis crusade had minimal importance in the fight against Islam, yet the campaign caught the imagination of English sources close to the court. Froissart claimed that processions and prayers for the crusaders' victory were conducted in England.[58] Some of the Tunis crusaders melted back into their positions of local government and magistry, but others were propelled to greater prominence, helping to set the military and political tone at court and signalling a significant revival in aristocratic crusading. It established the career of Henry Scrope of Masham, for example, who received the honour of being dubbed a knight while fighting on infidel soil, probably in the ceremony conducted by Louis II on the beaches outside al-Mahdiya. His new status was rewarded on return to England when Richard II retained him as a king's knight. It was an apt beginning for a man whose family boasted a long crusading tradition.[59] Similarly, the heroism of Sir John Paveley and Richard Fotheringhay slipped into common currency, attracting comment in different official settings at court, both men known because of their close links to the royal household.[60] The nobleman who stood to gain most was John Beaufort. Journeys to Prussia in 1391 and 1394, when he undertook two campaigns, confirmed Beaufort's enthusiasm for the *hethenesse*. He may have fought against the Turks at Nicopolis in 1396. An annuity as king's knight in June 1392 marked his growing proximity to Richard II, and a rapid promotion into the ranks of the peerage followed his legitimisation in 1397.[61] Less eminent members of the Tunis expedition were also brought more firmly within the sphere of the court. Of the thirty-six knights retained between 1389 and 1393, for example, a cohort of ten, possibly eleven, were veterans of al-Mahdiya. Several others

---

[57]   Botiller was in Jerusalem with John Warner and John Wymondesley of his household: *Register of Henry Wakefield, Bishop of Worcester 1375–1395* ed. W. P. Marett, Worcestershire Historical Society (Worcester, 1972) p. 107; NA, C81/514/6150; *West. Chron.* p. 481. News of the atrocity reached the west in 1392 with Gerard Calvet, OM Guardian of the Holy Sepulchre: *Biblioteca bio-bibliografica della Terra Sancta* vol. IV p. 38.

[58]   Froissart, vol. XIV p. 252; Tyerman, *England and the Crusades* p. 280.

[59]   Froissart, vol. XIV p. 222; NA, E403/532 m. 3 (September 1390). On the Scropes see Keen, 'Chaucer's Knight' pp. 45–63.

[60]   *CPR 1388–1392* p. 363 (Fotheringhay); *West. Chron.* p. 511 (Paveley).

[61]   See below pp. 80, 85, 88, 112–13. Palmer, *England, France and Christendom* p. 200 puts the case for Beaufort at Nicopolis.

were veterans of Prussia.[62] Alongside gentle birth and high local standing, experience
of holy war added a conspicuous chivalric gloss.

Underpinning such responses was Richard II's strong personal empathy for the
crusade cause and a close enmeshing of royal ceremonial, politics and chivalric ambition. Officially, Richard observed the same formal commitment to the *negotium crucis*
as other crowned rulers of Europe, but the crusade ideal in his hands also offered a
means of rebuilding influence and prestige after the political setbacks of the 1380s.
Indeed, while refraining from ritual displays of crusade zeal of the sort orchestrated
by Charles VI, the king nevertheless allowed himself to be moved by the condition
of the church and the heroism of crusader knights, and was content for others to
identify him as a potential liberator of Jerusalem (see below pp. 169–73, 199–206).
Evidence of royal sympathies is scattered across the sources, contradicting modern,
largely negative, views of Richard's chivalric outlook. Crusading's various appeals
were fostered across the royal household, and will be considered in more detail below,
but some measure of the social esteem available is evident in the king's deliberate
honouring of English valour performed in the *hethenesse*. Alive to the propagandist
advantages, Richard II used the death of courtly protégé Sir John Paveley as an opportunity for royal aggrandisement, for example, arranging for the return of his bones
from Prussia to England in 1393, and their interment in a London church. A glowing
epitaph in the *Westminster Chronicle* is a reflection of the stir caused in courtly circles.
Paveley's bravery at al-Mahdiya ('the lands of Barbary') stuck at the front of men's
minds, partly because it was brought to public attention by interested parties at court.
Fitting with Richard II's unusual habit of intervening in the funerary arrangements
of royal servants and high-ranking associates, it struck a parallel with the repatriation
of another set of crusader remains, the bones of John, Lord Mowbray (d. 1368), from
Constantinople.[63] Displayed at the Carmelite church in London during the autumn
of 1397, just after the creation of his son Thomas Mowbray as duke of Nottingham, the
Mowbray ossuary was expected to attract 'very many prominent men, nobles, kinsmen
and others' for the blandishing of alms and prayers. It accorded with Nottingham's quest
for greater political stature to have the court congregate in honour of his father's crusade
chivalry. Among the well-wishers were Richard II and his queen, indicating a spectacular
reception for the shrine. A ceremonial banquet hosted by Henry Bolingbroke in the refec-
tory at Whitefriars attests to the presence of the royal couple. Held on 1 October 1397,
the event was suitably prominent to find a place in a London chronicle.[64]

[62]   The list includes Richard Fotheringhay, John Russell, Thomas Botiller, Thomas Trewin, John Beaufort,
Bernard Brocas, John Paveley, John Holand, John St John and William Elmham. See appendix for full details.
[63]   John, Lord Beaumont, received £10 16s 8d for bringing Paveley's bones back to England on his
return from Prussia (January 1393): *Issues of the Exchequer* ed. F. Devon (London, 1837) p. 250; *West.
Chron.* p. 511. Another veteran of al-Mahdiya, the chamber knight Sir Bernard Brocas, was buried in
Westminster Abbey near the royal tombs: see n. 3 above; N. Saul, *Richard II* (New Haven, 1997) pp.
461–3. For Mowbray see below pp. 100–2.
[64]   NA, E326/9376; NA, DL28/1/6 fols 8–9; BL, MS Harley 3775 fol. 87ʳ; see below pp. 201–2.

More pertinent to the Tunis crusade is the perspective opened up with the lavish tournament staged at Smithfield during October 1390, in the aftermath of the expedition. Held at the suggestion of the duke of Guelders (who was absent), the event vied with the St Inglevert tournament for international prestige, and gave a cover for Richard's burgeoning diplomacy with the Low Countries. Traditionally associated with the king's first use of his famous White Hart livery, it also substituted as a formal reception for returning Tunis crusaders. Prominent amongst these was the foreign prince William VI, count of Ostrevant, who arrived at the beginning of the month with a troupe of Hainault and Flemish knights, coming directly out of Mediterranean waters.[65] The tournament and visit tallied with the crown's attempt to build a coalition against Burgundy (1388–1392), but William's presence also reflected the close ties fostered between English knights and the Netherlander contingent at the siege of al-Mahdiya. The two groups kept close company from the outset, eschewing embarkation with Bourbon at Marseilles and travelling in tandem to Genoa. During the fighting, Flemish and other northern retinues gravitated towards John Beaufort's command, co-operation between English captains and prominent Hainaulters such as Henry d'Antoing and Francois de Aubréticourt (a relation of the Lancastrian knight John Dabridgecourt) helping to lay down the early roots of Count William's speculative alliance.[66] The lavish ceremonial at Smithfield culminated in William's appointment as a Garter knight and his oath of allegiance to Richard II, his standing as a crusader prince casting a genuine martial gleam over proceedings. With Richard II warming to his role as a patron of chivalry and holy war after a period of grave political difficulty, it provided a fitting context for his sole public appearance armed for the joust. To some degree it anticipated the enthusiastic reception of the duke of Bourbon at Charles VI's court in Paris, when the French king reportedly took the cross.[67]

Widening social and diplomatic links with the courts of Flanders, Ghent and Guelders had another implication for the crusade, helping to raise the profile of the Baltic frontier as an outlet for English arms after a generation of inactivity. The

[65] *West. Chron.* p. 451; *Historia Vitae et Regni Ricardi Secundi* ed. G. B. Stow (Philadelphia, 1977) p. 132. For Ostrevant at al-Mahdiya see Mirot, *Siège de Mahdia* p. 16; Atiya, *Crusade in the Later Middle Ages* p. 521. Froissart thought the Smithfield tournament owed its inspiration to Queen Isabella's ceremonial entry into Paris, an event loaded with crusade symbolism, including a theatrical joust between Saladin and Richard I, and perhaps orchestrated by Philippe de Mézières: Froissart, vol. XIV p. 270. For Mézières and civic pageantry see D. A. Bullough, 'Games People Played: Drama and Ritual as Propaganda in Medieval Europe' *TRHS* 24 (1974) pp. 97–119.

[66] Uberti Foglietta, *Historia Genuensium libri XII* (Genoa, 1585) pp. 348ff; *Chronique du Religieux de Saint-Denys* vol. I pp. 652–3; Cabaret d'Orville, pp. 229–30.

[67] *Historia Vitae Ricardi Secundi* p. 132; Froissart, vol. XIV pp. 279–80. The decision to hold a major procession through London before the tournament was probably an attempt to emulate the civic ceremonial of the Low Countries: S. Lindenbaum. 'The Smithfield Tournament of 1390' *Journal of Medieval and Renaissance Studies* 20 (1990) pp. 1–20.

bellicose figure of the duke of Guelders, a *persona grata* at Richard II's court, enjoyed
a military reputation built largely on the back of the northern crusade. Between 1383
and 1400, he undertook campaigns in Prussia no fewer than seven times. William
VI of Ostrevant was also a devotee of the *reyse*.[68] That both Guelders and Ostrevant
were invested as Garter knights in 1390 (they were Richard II's most distinguished
Garter creations) gave the northern crusade a commanding platform in English chivalry. Guelders's visit to London shortly before Bourbon's crusade in April 1390 was
the signal for English military traffic to Prussia to widen dramatically after a period of
decline.[69] It should be clear that none of this accords with the image of a moribund
military culture conjured by chroniclers hostile to Richard II's court and still commonly accepted by modern critics.[70]

The diplomatic possibilities opened up in the Tunis campaign and the impressive
degree of co-operation between the English and French courts were the main legacies
of crusading in the summer of 1390. Many of the characteristics of the more famous
Nicopolis crusade of 1396 were already present in Bourbon's expedition. It played
upon the same social and diplomatic channels, where an interest in the crusade combined with a growing desire to find lasting settlement in France and an end to church
schism, the latter a particular concern of French courtiers and churchmen. Froissart
found it hard to separate the two concerns in his account of European diplomacy
between 1390 and 1396.[71] The scene played out at the expedition's embarkation, where
a bishop from either side of the religious divide delivered a blessing over the mixed
army of Urbanists and Clementists, reflected the mood of collaboration. Agreement
among the Tunis crusaders to observe a tacit silence on the subject of the schism
showed a general willingness to ignore awkward realities, including the problem
of legitimate authority and separate sets of indulgences. It exposed the ideological
reach of papal schism as somewhat artificial.[72] The influence of crusade propagandist
Philippe de Mézières, now a councillor to Charles VI, is not explicit, but the inten-
sive contact established at the crusader tournaments in 1390, and in Gaunt's private

---

[68]   Paravicini, *Die Pruessenreisen* vol. I pp. 56, 60.

[69]   Guelders was at pains to promote his image as a crusader knight, not least because a huge ransom
incurred while he was in Lithuania left him searching for financial aid: see the newsletter addendum in
the *West. Chron.* pp. 371–3. Froissart, vol. XIII pp. 290–1 shields the duke from accusations that he went
to Prussia in 1389 to escape an invading French army. See also NA, C81/515/6212 (licences to royal 'familiares' Sir Walter Bitterly and Sir John Standish to cross to Prussia, 19 March 1390); and Chapter 4 below.

[70]   Thomas Walsingham, *The* Chronica Maiora *of Thomas Walsingham, 1376–1422* tr. D. Preest with
J. G. Clark (Woodbridge, 2005) p. 375. For diagnosis of Richard II's 'unmilitary' character see Saul,
Richard II pp. 330–3, 452–3; but compare C. D. Fletcher, *Richard II: Manhood, Youth and Politics, 1377–
1399* (Oxford, 2008) pp. 1–44 and below pp. 169–73.

[71]   Palmer, *England, France and Christendom* pp. 180–210 and the references collected there.

[72]   As Tyerman (*God's War* p. 853) points out, evidence for cross-taking among Bourbon's followers is
scant, but the Latin redaction of the chronicle of St Denys describes the soldiers as wearing the 'signum
crucis': *Chronique du Religieux de Saint-Denys* vol. I pp. 654–5. For blessings at embarkation see Ursins,
Histoire de Charles VI, pp. 383–4.

embassies to the duke of Bourbon, clearly anticipated the prominence enjoyed by Mézières's associates in the years before Nicopolis. Aside from revitalising the vogue of the *hethenesse*, the crusade's most tangible effect was the hardening of rhetoric for a lasting peace. Efforts at both courts would now go towards translating this mood into a decisive alliance against the Ottomans and realising the dream of recovering the Holy Land.

4

The Baltic

The crusade to Lithuania was established in the chivalric calendar throughout the Catholic world by 1350. First founded as an offshoot of campaigning during the Second Crusade, from 1147 the conquest and Christian colonisation of territory in the Baltic regions of Prussia, Lithuania, Estonia, Finland, Latvia and Russia won approval and canonical recognition from the Latin church. Sandwiched between the *Ordensstaat* of the Teutonic Knights in Prussia and Livonia, the heathen regions of Lithuania and (further east) western Rus' came under increasing pressure at the end of the thirteenth century, absorbing significant Catholic colonisation and a heavy pounding from the Order's commanderies of Königsberg in the south-east and Riga in the north. On the other side of the frontier, expansion to the west provided the Lithuanian monarchy with a degree of insulation, allowing the ruling Jagiellonian clan to consolidate power in Lithuania, and eventually steer a course towards political union with Poland in 1386. The baptism of Jogaila I in 1386 (as Wladyslaw II) accelerated the slow process of Christianisation, but this did not precipitate an immediate halt to the fighting. The war was defined by a frontier-wilderness of wasted land and forest, criss-crossed by narrow passes and river tributaries, and studded with forts and marginal settlements. For civilian contact there was an established trade network in furs, timber, amber and slaves. Ransom of wealthy captives happened at the end of campaign season. The inner reaches of Lithuania were more easily broached by missionaries, particularly the Franciscans, than by soldiers, but until the 1380s the Christian religion was tolerated there mainly as diplomatic cover, for use in courting the pope and neighbouring powers rather than as an alternative to indigenous animist beliefs. On either side of the *wildnesse*, those settled within striking distance of the enemy lived precariously, vulnerable to surprise attack, capture or forced marches.[1]

[1]   The specialist German literature is vast. Excellent starting points include the series edited by Z. H. Nowark, *Ordines Militares: Colloquia Torunensia Historica* (Torún, 1981–) and *Quellen und studien zur Geschichtes des Deutschen ordens* eds U. Arnold et al. (Bonn, 1966–). In general see S. C. Rowell, *Lithuania Ascending: A Pagan Empire within East-Central Europe, 1295–1345* (Cambridge, 1994); E.

More than any other frontier, the Baltic crusade appealed to chivalric senses. Papal appeals to punish the Baltic pagans, combined with the Teutonic Order's power to issue indulgences, drew a steady stream of western combatants, and by the 1300s the Teutonic Knights had perfected a 'knightly package tour', with visiting noblemen expected to take part in a regimen of banqueting, hunting, long-distance raids and hearing mass. Prizes were given to reward noble deeds and help buff reputations.[2] Traditionally, the majority of 'pilgrims' and 'guests' came from the empire, largely from the areas of Germany and the Netherlands which were home to the Order's convents and bailiwicks. Rhineland princes were closely involved in the wars of Edward III and the Valois, and through this network the vogue spread quickly, establishing a large following within English chivalry. Traditions of military service in the Baltic passed through English noble families and their dependencies, surfacing at court, and from time to time eclipsing in popularity all other theatres of war, though compared to France and Scotland the evidence is distributed much less evenly across the sources. Its prominence was marked by the introduction in the vernacular of the German term for the Order's seasonal campaigns, the *reyse*. Just as the Knight of Chaucer's *Canterbury Tales* had *reysed* in 'Lettow' and in 'Ruce', winning acclaim for his prowess, so moralising voices reached for a similar contemporary sound, criticising the bloody wars between Christians elsewhere as 'batels *reysed* welny3 in every lond'.[3] The *reysen* were carefully organised. They took place when the climate made the terrain passable, and coincided with the major Marian feasts, the Virgin Mary being specially honoured by the Teutonic Knights as patroness and deliverer of all conquests. Campaigns were led in the winter when the waterways froze, especially around the feast of the Purification (2 February), and in summer when the marshes were dry and the Lithuanian population was preoccupied with the harvest. Assumptiontide (15 August) and Our Lady's Birthday (8 September) marked the period of the *reyse d'esté*. Summer campaigns tended to be larger, more protracted affairs.[4]

Christiansen, *The Northern Crusades* (2nd edn, London, 1997); W. L. Urban, *The Baltic Crusade* (2nd edn, Chicago, 1994); id. *The Prussian Crusade* (Lanham, 1980); id. *The Livonian Crusade* (2nd edn, Chicago, 2004); id. *The Samogitian Crusade* (Chicago, 1989); *Crusade and Conversion on the Baltic Frontier 1150–1500* ed. A. V. Murray (Aldershot, 2001); I. Fonnesburg-Schmidt, *The Popes and the Baltic Crusades, 1147–1254* (Leiden, 2007); Paravicini, *Die Preussenreisen*; id. 'Die Preussenreisen des Europäischen Adels' *Historische Zeitschrift* 23 (1981) pp. 25–38; id. 'La Prusse et l'Europe occidentale: La participation de la noblesse d'Europe occidentale aux croisades de l'Order des Chevaliers Teutoniques contre la Lituanie' *Cahiers de Recherches Mèdievales (XIIIe-Xves.)* 1 (1996) pp. 177–91; Tyerman, *England and the Crusades* pp. 266–76. What follows draws largely on previously neglected published and unpublished documentary sources.

[2] Tyerman, *England and the Crusades* p. 267.

[3] Geoffrey Chaucer, *The Riverside Chaucer* ed. L. Benson (3rd edn, Boston, 1987) lines 43–78; *Middle English Sermons* ed. W. O. Ross, EETS o.s. 209 (London, 1940) no. 40 (anonymous sermon, c.1380); cf. 'Simonie' (c.1327) *Political Songs of England* ed. T. Wright, Camden Society 6 (London, first series 1839) p. 334.

[4] Christiansen, *Northern Crusades* p. 221.

Campaigns and recruitment (i) 1330–1370

English knights are first found in the Baltic in large numbers from the 1330s. A period of peace with Scotland and France released some knights to take part in the campaign led by John of Luxembourg in the winter of 1328–1329 (perhaps exiles of Isabella and Mortimer's regime), and two years later the adventurous Thomas Ufford, brother of Robert Ufford (earl of Suffolk from 1337 to 1369), helped terrorise the Lithuanian population along the river Nieman, with many other English 'pilgrims'. The lightning raids (conducted 'without leaving the saddle') had a passing resemblance to warfare along the Scottish border.[5] The presence of French and Burgundian knights in the following years attested to the *reyse*'s rapidly growing popularity, but the duke of Holland's campaigns in 1333, 1336, 1343 and 1345 attracted the greatest number of well-placed *anglici*, including some of Edward III's close friends and courtiers. The royal councillors Sir Reginald Cobham, William, Lord Fitzwarin (the son of crusade enthusiast Fulk Fitzwarin, d. c.1343) and Sir John Beaumont joined companies of Hainaulter and Rhenish knights mustering at Marienburg, probably as part of Edward III's diplomacy within the Low Countries (1343/1345). Free-booting types, such as Sir Thomas Holand and William, Lord Hastings, travelled more independently, drawn by the Baltic's emerging reputation as a field of valour. To pay for his journey to 'Frontier and Spruz', Hastings put his Berkshire estates out to farm for a period of forty weeks (c.1349).[6] For some, the expedition to Prussia became a habit. The younger Thomas Ufford, son of the earl of Suffolk, fought with the Teutonic Knights in 1348, 1362, 1365 and possibly in 1352. The escalation of the Anglo-French war failed to reverse the trend. English knights fought in defence of the Order's eastern lands between 1346 and 1348, despite a prohibition issued by Edward III at the siege of Calais (October 1347), and English noblemen were to be found on the winter or summer *reysen* at regular intervals for the next half-century.[7]

If English knights were generally subsumed into princely retinues from Germany and the Low Countries during the 1330s and 1340s, later participants enjoyed a greater degree of independence. The duke of Lancaster's expedition of 1352 set the benchmark, although achieving little of military worth. Accompanied by the earls of Suffolk and Salisbury, and a large portion of his northern affinity, Henry Grosmont's crusade

---

[5]   Paravicini has produced the most comprehensive study of English participation to date, conveniently tabulating nearly two hundred names, mainly of retinue leaders. No list can claim to be definitive; at least twenty-seven further names can be added to Paravicini's table. In total, several thousand English knights and esquires probably passed to the Baltic between 1330 and 1400. See Paravicini, *Die Preussenreisen* vol. I pp. 123–7; Wigands von Marburg, 'Chronik Wigands von Marburg' *Scriptores Rerum Prussicarum* ed. T. Hirsch et al. (Leipzig, 1861–) vol. II pp. 479, 483.

[6]   Wigands von Marburg, p. 490; Paravicini, *Die Preussenreisen* vol. I p. 123; Cobham and Fitzwarin formed part of Edward III's large mission to the Netherlands in the 1340s. See Tout, *Chapters* vol. III pp. 89–90; *CIPM* vol. VI p. 229.

[7]   *CCR 1346–1349* p. 403; Tyerman, *England and the Crusades* p. 268.

stood comparison with the largest German expeditions, as no doubt it was supposed to. His personal bodyguard of horse and foot numbered at least two hundred, and the retinues of the other English earls and captains may have swelled the expedition to well over three times that number.[8] Licensed by Edward III, publicised with special prayers across the northern dioceses and furnished with papal indulgences, the expedition *contra inimicos fidei* was a fitting way to mark Grosmont's recent elevation to the ducal rank, attracting positive comment from English and continental chroniclers.[9] There was also a diplomatic agenda to observe, the duke's march north through Flanders, Brabant and the imperial lands coinciding with Edward III's attempt to claw back influence lost there to the French court during the late 1340s. The pro-English counts of Jülich and Marck and a number of German knights promptly congregated under the duke's crusade banner.[10]

Unfortunately for Lancaster, the party reached the Prussian borders just as the Order suspended their summer offensive. Various chronicle reports have him redeeming his vow in Poland, allying with the Christians in Livonia, or not fighting at all. According to a French chronicle, he even reached Estonia, where local Catholic rulers made him their captain. In this account, the duke did have battle with the pagans and with the Russian kings said to have been allied with them. In one confrontation there was 'great chivalry', whereby 'the good duke' rescued the Christian standard which had fallen underfoot in the melee.[11] Whatever the case, Lancaster's expedition sealed the military and social links between English chivalry and the northern frontier, opening knightly traffic in a way which his heroics on the Spanish crusade did not quite manage to achieve. It was in this context that Edward III widened his court's influence, awarding an annuity to Henry II of Rendsburg, count of Holstein, a veteran of the Lithuanian *reyse* and a leading agitant against the Rus' – such was the pressure on Edward III to show interest in his aristocracy's foreign endeavours. He also reinstated Edward I's yearly

---

[8]   For the duke's papal indulgences and details of his armed following see ASV, reg. vat. 211 fol. 190; ASV, reg. supp. 23 fol. 47ʳ pt. II. Notable soldiers accompanying Grosmont included William, Lord Ros; William Cross; William, Lord Latimer of Corby; William, Lord Greystoke; William Bernak; Sir Nigel Loring; Sir Ralph Hemendale; Sir Walter Paveley of Hilperton; Sir Miles Stapleton; Henry, Lord Percy; John, Lord Neville; Sir Thomas Courtenay; Roger, Lord de Warre; Thomas Ufford; and Sir William Gantelion: *Foedera* vol. III pt. 1 p. 80; *CPR 1350–1354* pp. 182, 185, 187. According to Henry Knighton, Lancaster travelled with 'many of the greatest men of the realm': Knighton, p. 111. A German chronicler counted four hundred: Henry of Hervod, 'Chronicon Henrici de Hervodia' *SRP* vol. III pp. 741–2.

[9]   *CPR 1350–1354* p. 191; *Royal and Historical Letters of Henry IV* eds F. C. Hingeston et al., r.s. 18 (London, 1860–1965) vol. I pp. 402–3; *CPL* vol. III p. 459; Knighton, p. 111; Baker, *Chronicon* p. 119; Henry of Hervod, pp. 741–4.

[10]   *Chronique Valois* pp. 13–14; Fowler, *King's Lieutenant* pp. 106–10.

[11]   *Chronique Valois* pp. 13–14. A document issued by Grosmont at Stettin (Poland) on 15 January 1352 is printed in *SRP* vol. II p. 516.

donations to the Teutonic Knights at Coblenz, which had been allowed to lapse (c.1350).[12]

The numbers of Englishmen undertaking the *reyse* increased significantly in the decade after the peace of Brétigny in 1360. Royal records show demand for licences to travel to Prussia growing yearly until 1368–1369, with the winter campaign season (December–March) being markedly more popular. The largest expeditions were led by earls, each drawing deeply on personal affinities and attracting very substantial military followings. The young earl of Hereford split his time venturing between Thorn in the south of Prussia and the Order's siege-works in Samogitia in the north-east between 1362 and 1363.[13] Thomas Beauchamp, earl of Warwick, served in Prussia for over a year in 1365–1366, converting his crusade vow from the Cypriot crusade (see above pp. 43–5). A festival held at Königsberg welcomed his army and 'many other English nobles'. The earl of Suffolk probably crossed paths with Warwick in February 1366.[14] Evidence for wider involvement is impressive, suggesting that besides the Black Prince's court in Gascony, from which many knightly 'pilgrims' embarked, and the more prestigious peacetime commands, Lithuania was the main destination of aspiring knights in the 1360s. The upper ranks of military society showed remarkable enthusiasm. During the first wave of popularity (c.1348–1368), nineteen current or future members of the Order of the Garter campaigned in Prussia, including many of Edward III's most experienced war captains. Veterans of Crécy and Poitiers, such as Nigel Loring, Miles Stapleton of Bedale, Walter Paveley, William, Lord Latimer, John, Lord Neville, and Richard Pembridge, raised their banners in the *hethenesse*, reluctant to retire from military service or, like Loring on his second *reyse*, unable to gain passage with an expedition against the Mamluks; younger men, such as William Beauchamp, Peter Courtenay and William Scrope of Bolton, laid the foundations for their future careers as courtier-soldiers.[15]

Crusading in the Baltic, as elsewhere, ran in families. Maurice Keen and Christopher Tyerman have shown the lively and persistent interest in crusading of a number of noble families, including the Beauchamps, Uffords, Bohuns, Percies, Despensers, Fitzwalters, Beaumonts, Scropes, Courtenays, Hastings and Montagues, each with active representatives in the 1360s. Extended family ties were evident, and probably influenced recruitment; in the second half of the fourteenth century the

---

[12]   Christiansen, *Northern Crusades* p. 192; *CPR 1399–1401* p. 14.

[13]   NA, DL25/1989; NA, DL25/1638–9; Wigands von Marburg, p. 531; see below pp. 89–90.

[14]   Wigands von Marburg, p. 549; John of Reading, p. 172; Paravicini, *Die Preussenreisen* vol. I. p. 124.

[15]   The full list of Garter knights reaching Prussia is: Nigel Loring; William Montagu II, earl of Salisbury; Walter Paveley; Miles Stapleton; John, Lord Neville; William Latimer; John Burley; Thomas Ufford; Thomas Beauchamp, earl of Warwick; Henry Grosmont, duke of Lancaster; Robert Ufford, earl of Suffolk; Thomas Beauchamp II, earl of Warwick; William Scrope of Bolton; Peter Courtenay; Richard Pembridge; Humphrey Bohun, earl of Hereford; William Beauchamp; Henry, Lord Percy; William Ufford. The founder-knights Reginald Cobham and William Fitzwarin campaigned there in 1341, some years before Edward III established the order (1348). See the appendix.

Beauchamps, Uffords, Cliffords and Ferrers of Groby – all closely linked by marriage – all produced Baltic crusaders.[16] This emphasis was one of the Baltic's attractions, a factor shared with the publicly financed armies of the Hundred Years War. Heirs and younger sons campaigned with their fathers, cousins and uncles, partly as a means of mobilising greater numbers and partly to pool limited resources. Thomas Beauchamp's three elder sons crusaded together in the winter *reyse* of 1367–1368. They were joined by Edward Courtenay, heir of the earl of Devon (d. 1378), along with two of his brothers and a number of other family associates. Even the very young could be safely accommodated in this sort of campaign, kept back in the security of one of the Order's castles or shepherded by a heavily armed retinue. In 1368 Peter Courtenay was thirteen. His Beauchamp companion, William, was fourteen and already a veteran of the *reyse* (aged eleven in 1365) and the battle of Nájera the year before.[17] In a military culture where high-born knights looked unfavourably on garrison duty or the banditry of the mercenary companies in France, fighting in the northern crusade, one of the 'great expeditions of war', as one observer termed it, was a hallmark of genuine prestige.[18] For such reasons, a distinctive attraction was that the *reyse* offered reliable seasonal military training and experience. In 1362 Edward III appointed the veteran knights Walter, Lord Deveraux, Sir Miles Stapleton and Sir Richard Waldegrave as chaperones to accompany the young and ambitious earl of Hereford on his *reyse*, along with the earl's contemporaries John Burley and William Lucy.[19] The intention was to provide the earl with experienced counsel as he served out his military apprenticeship.

This was not the whole picture. Men of humbler means also campaigned in the *hethenesse*, the Order's English 'guests' including foot-soldiers, mounted archers, sappers and miners, as well as professional men-at-arms, like John Goddard and William Dalleson. Pay was a condition for most, usually in the service of a retinue leader or a tenurial lord, though the possibility of drawing wages in the Order's service may also have been an appealing prospect.[20] With the English ranks less 'top-heavy' than the sources sometimes suggest, there was opportunity for the middling sort to participate on more independent terms. Men with long soldiering careers, such as Thomas Boynton and Maurice le Bruyn, undertook *reysen* during periods of peace, acting largely upon private initiative. Although thinly documented, their experiences were probably replicated across wider gentry society. At the court hearing where le Bruyn

[16] Tyerman, *England and the Crusades* pp. 266–76; Keen, 'Chaucer's Knight' esp. pp. 51–6.

[17] *CPR 1367–1370* pp. 24, 56, 128, 132; Paravicini, *Die Preussenreisen* vol. I. pp. 124–5.

[18] *Scrope and Grosvenor* vol. I p. 82; cf. M. H. Keen, *Origins of the English Gentleman: Heraldry, Chivalry and Gentility in Medieval England c.1300–1500* (Stroud, 2002) pp. 50–1.

[19] R. C. Fowler, 'Seals in the Public Record Office' *Archaeologia* 74 (1923–1924) p. 115; *Scrope and Grosvenor* vol. I pp. 77–8, 165–6, vol. II pp. 171–2, 261; NA, DL25/1989; NA, DL25/1638–9; NA, DL34/1/27.

[20] Paravicini, *Die Preussenreisen* vol. I. p. 123; *Scrope and Grosvenor* vol. I pp. 125, 171–2, vol. II pp. 323, 377; *CPR 1367–1370* p. 57; *Indentures* no. 40; Christiansen, *Northern Crusades* pp. 159, 175.

gave evidence of his career-in-arms, at least a dozen other deponents could claim experience of fighting in the *hethenesse*.[21] Far-flung campaigning was esteemed among the 'professional' classes of soldier no less than in aristocratic and gentle circles. As well as fighting in Prussia, Scotland, France and Constantinople, for example, the adventurous Nicholas Sabraham saw action with the Cypriot crusade to Alexandria in 1365, and in the Black Sea against Turks and schismatics with the count of Savoy in 1366. Le Bruyn boasted an equally diverse career, serving in most known theatres of war, including Prussia, 'beyond the Great Sea' and in the Dardenelles, spending part of the time as commander in a garrison at Gallipoli. He was knighted by 1369, after a career spanning nearly thirty years.[22]

Characteristics of Baltic crusading in this period included an absence from home of five or six months, and a departure date of late autumn or early winter. Only the wealthiest knights could afford lengthier terms of service. Expense also dictated the route taken towards Prussia. A short crossing to Calais or Flanders, followed by an overland journey towards Hamburg, across Pomerania and into western Prussia was the most common approach. From here a few Englishmen made the longer, more arduous journey into the northern province of Livonia. It usually took six weeks to reach the Order's Prussian lands, although Froissart (implausibly) thought it was possible in thirteen days. Thomas, Lord Percy, reputedly achieved such a feat in 1383, but he had to discard most of his military wardrobe along the way. Alternatively, a leg of the journey could be taken at sea, from Calais to the mouth of the Elbe, or from the northern port of Lübeck along the Baltic shoreline towards Danzig or Königsberg. When English merchants began to carry regular trade to the Baltic ports in the 1370s, the direct passage was more common, usually from eastern ports of Lincolnshire, the Humber and East Anglia. Against the hazards of sea transport the overland route probably retained some attraction, at least allowing for relatively reliable travel in the winter months, but by the 1390s English recruitment for the winter *reyse* largely tailed off. The Order's longer summer campaigns became the main focus.[23]

Groups of crusaders did not necessarily form or coalesce into one retinue, but a strong local dimension was often evident. At the beginning of 1368, for example, at a peak of the northern frontier's popularity, a sizeable military contingent from Norfolk and the Lincolnshire coast embarked with the Lords Walter Fitzwalter, Henry Beaumont and William Ufford. From northern Norfolk travelled prominent knights close to Ufford, such as Sir John Sekford, Roger, Lord Scales, Sir Roger

[21]   Keen, 'Chaucer's Knight' pp. 45–63; *Scrope and Grosvenor* vol. I pp. 117, 125, 161, 171–2, vol. II pp. 310, 323, 367, 377; *CPR 1367–1370* pp. 30, 65.
[22]   *Scrope and Grosvenor* vol. I p. 125, vol. II p. 323; Barberi, p. 60; *CPR 1367–1370* p. 210.
[23]   Froissart, vol. X p. 243. Henry Bolingbroke embarked from Boston in 1390; two years later he sailed for the Baltic from the small port of Heacham, south of Hunstanton: *Expeditions* pp. xxxvi, 263. The duke of Gloucester embarked from Orwell in Suffolk in 1391: *Foedera* vol. III pt. 4 p. 71; SRO, D641/1/2/4 m. 4. Sir Richard Abberbury's esquire, Thomas Astel, was licensed to leave either from Kingston upon Hull or St Botolph (16 May 1391): NA, C81/ 525/7233.

Boys, Sir Thomas Goys and Sir Roger Felbrigg, and from Lincolnshire the wealthy Anthony Lucy, Sir John Tautheby, John Aysterby, Sir Ralph Sutton and John Multon. The most prominent among them – Felbrigg, Scales, Sekford and Lucy – held manors within a few miles of each other and were accustomed to acting together in a variety of roles: as charter witnesses, as sureties, in the formation of marriage ties, and on various county commissions.[24] These local spheres of influence helped to seed enthusiasm as much as hierarchical loyalties or dependencies on aristocratic leadership. Sir Roger Felbrigg, for instance, already had indirect knowledge of the *reyse*, after acting as an attorney for his friend Robert Howard, a recruit to Prussia from 1362 to 1364. Military recruitment followed predictable patterns. The influential Anthony Lucy of Holbeach, a kinsman of Lord Fitzwalter, was a linchpin of recruitment on the Norfolk/Lincolnshire border, associating with John Multon of Frampton and Richard Welby of Kirton – neighbours, tenants and soldiering companions. Collaboration between the trio is evident in their shared nomination of Roger Toup and Thomas Claymound as attorneys, and the co-ordinated decision to place their estates in trust. John Multon named Richard Welby amongst his feofees. The group's extensive legal provisions were well advised, considering that Lucy and Multon both left infant daughters as heirs.[25] Finally, the men took advantage of strong links at court to raise additional capital, securing loans on their Lincolnshire rents. Royal favourite and reputed embezzler Alice Perrers loaned Multon £20, while the much better off Anthony Lucy borrowed the tall sum of £600, representing almost three times his annual income. It was generous enough to equip him with a knightly retinue of fifteen men-at-arms and possibly to subsidise others.[26]

This was recruitment at a distinctly local level. Multon, Welby and Lucy lived within eight miles of each other. Friendship, clientage and overlapping patterns of tenure predisposed the group to concerted action, as it would groups embarking for other frontiers.[27] Lucy's relationship with the high-born Fitzwalter was an important component, allowing his neighbours access to the upper surfaces of county society, but insular interests and a shared local ethos typified recruitment as well, implicating men of relatively low standing. Richard Welby was in this bracket, holding title

---

[24] *CPR 1367–1370* pp. 10 (Ufford), 18 (Felbrigg), 21 (Boys), 25 (Sekford), 27 (Scales), 34 (Lucy, Multon), 41 (Tautheby), 42 (Aysterby), 43 (Goys), 54 (Ufford, Sekford), 57 (Sutton, Lucy), 58 (Multon), 72 (Goys), 129 (Fitzwalter), 132 (Beaumont). Not all of the enrolled licences for travel name Prussia as the destination, yet the case for shared purpose is compelling. Roger Boys, Lord Scales and John Sekford rarely strayed from Ufford's inner circle; similarly Felbrigg, Sutton and Lucy were important clients of Fitzwalter and Henry Beaumont; see notes to this paragraph and below.

[25] *CPR 1361–1364* p. 251; *CPR 1367–1370* pp. 34, 57–8; *CIPM* vol. XII p. 207; ibid. vol. XIII pp. 90–1. Sir John Sekford and Sir Roger Felbrigg also shared attorneys for the *reyse*, appointing Roger's brother, George Felbrigg, an influential figure at Edward III's court: *CPR 1367–1370* pp. 18, 25.

[26] *CIPM* vol. XII pp. 207, 273; ibid. vol. XIII pp. 90–1; *CCR 1364–1368* p. 396; *CPR 1367–1370* p. 57.

[27] E.g. the Lucy family held a moiety in Richard Welby's manor at Kirton, and John Multon was a tenant at Frampton, held in jointure by Lucy and Fitzwalter: *CIPM* vol. XII pp. 17, 273.

to a single manor in his own right (Kirton).[28] The extended networks of Fitzwalter's collaborators and peers – Lords Despenser, Beaumont and Ufford – operated in the same way, and the pattern can be extrapolated across gentry society in other parts of Lincolnshire, and other parts of England. In Yorkshire the aspiring gentlemen crusaders Thomas Boynton, Richard Mauleverer and Thomas Southeworth galvanised a similar cohort of knights and esquires to embark to Prussia in 1367–1368, probably with the expedition formed by the sons of the earls of Devon and Warwick.[29] Group cohesion and consistency of military experience were strong features of these expeditions. It was perhaps some testament to this that, soon after penetrating Lithuanian territory in 1368, Anthony Lucy, Sir Roger Felbrigg and John Multon were killed while fighting alongside one another in defence of a stockade on the river Nieman. Their fate mirrored that of Sir Geoffrey Scrope five years earlier, slain a few miles downstream at the Order's siege of Pillen.[30]

Campaigns and recruitment (ii) 1390–1399

Although the standing of the northern frontier as a theatre of honour grew as the period progressed, opportunities to participate were narrowing somewhat by the 1390s. Increased expense was the main factor, the passage to the Baltic by sea and the rising costs of equipping a military retinue obstructing all but the wealthiest participants. Increasingly, crusaders abandoned their independence in favour of association with, and the direct protection provided by, a great nobleman. Inflated budgets reflected the trend. Henry Bolingbroke lavished almost £4,500 on his retinue in 1390–1391, while the duke of Gloucester's winter expedition of 1391–1392 was set to cost significantly more. Less extravagant spenders, like Sir Stephen Scrope, also felt the pinch; stranded at the end of the winter *reyse* in 1394, Scrope was forced to borrow £110 just to settle his accounts in Danzig and get home.[31] Nonetheless, such constraints failed to diminish Prussia's popularity among the wealthy and ambitious, particularly at court. The future earls of Somerset (John Beaufort), Salisbury (John

[28]   Anthony Lucy was second cousin to Fitzwalter: ibid. p. 273. Welby expected to embark with at least £40, however, possibly a loan or profits of service in royal armies.
[29]   *CPR 1367–1370* pp. 30, 64–5; *Scrope and Grosvenor* vol. I. p. 117, vol. II p. 310. The northern contingent included, from Yorkshire: John Dautre, John Goddard, Thomas Fitzhenry, William Dalleson; from Lancashire: Robert Urswyck, Sir William Scrope of Bolton; from Staffordshire/Yorkshire: Sir William Furnival. See *CPR 1367–1370* pp. 30, 57, 71–2, 127; *Scrope and Grosvenor* vol. I pp. 123, 171–2, vol. II pp. 323–5, 377, 389–90.
[30]   Paravicini, *Die Preussenreisen* vol. II p. 117. The memorial brass of Roger Felbrigg in the church of St Margaret, Felbrigg (Norf.) reads that Roger 'died in Prussia and is buried there' ('qi mourut en prus e la est son corps enterre'): printed in Housley, 'The Crusading Movement, 1274–1700' p. 274 (misdated to 1380). See also *Scrope and Grosvenor* vol. I pp. 117, 188, vol. II pp. 310, 443.
[31]   *Expeditions* p. lxxxvii; T. Hirsch, *Danzigs Handels – und Gewerbs-geschichte* (Liepzig, 1858) pp. 234–5.

Montagu) and Worcester (Thomas Percy), all of whose titles were new foundations of the 1390s, performed service in the Baltic in this period, as did an impressive roll of chamber knights and household officials, including Sir Stephen Scrope, John, Lord Beaumont, Sir Walter Bitterly, John Beaufo, Sir Thomas Peytevyn, Sir Henry Percy *le filz* and Thomas, Lord Clifford. In 1390 Lord Neville and John Clanvow laid plans to fight in Prussia before turning their attention to the Tunis crusade.[32]

The best-known campaign of this period was Henry Bolingbroke's *passagium* of 1390. Not as substantial as chronicle estimates of three hundred, the earl's retinue nonetheless featured the bulk of the Lancastrian war-band originally recruited for Bourbon's Tunis crusade. The names of seventy-one knights, *armigers*, other infantry and serving staff, including musicians, appear in Bolingbroke's household accounts, retained for service on *reyse*. Added to this were the retinues (esquires and mounted archers) of the earl's knights, almost certainly drawing wages on a separate basis. One eyewitness estimated Bolingbroke's bodyguard at fifty men-at-arms and sixty bowmen. A further separate financial arrangement may have been in place for the local fighters who joined the party on the Order's lands.[33] That the earl's expedition enjoyed the support of other noblemen at Richard II's court was reflected in the participation of crusaders drawn from various aristocratic households. His uncle, the duke of Gloucester, sent one of his heralds (Croyslett) as well as his retainer Sir John Clifton; the earl of Devon released the ambitious esquire Robert Chalons, and valets of Lord Bourchier's household featured among the earl's men-at-arms. The expectation that military honours would be reflected upon noble patrons probably encouraged this practice, again attesting to a culture of mobility between military households.[34] Arriving in Danzig in August 1390 and immediately striking deep into Lithuania, Bolingbroke played a credible part in the Order's offensive against Skirgiello, the regent of Lithuania, fighting his way across a strategic river crossing and joining the eleven-week siege of the city of Vilna. The earl's bowmen proved their worth, earning the Marshal's 'copious' praise, and a flattering account credited Bolingbroke with capturing part of the enemy city, taking several high-born prisoners. On his return to England, Henry was feted with high honours, his victories bringing joy to Christians everywhere, according to one enthusiastic observer.[35] Privately, there may have been

---

[32] Wigands von Marburg, pp. 645–6; *Expeditions* pp. 36, 100 (Percy); NA, C81/515/6212 (Bitterly); NA, E403/536 m. 11 (Beaufo); Paravicini, *Die Preussenreisen* vol. I p. 125 (Peytevyn); NA, E403/531 m.7 (Neville, Clanvow); Tyerman, *England and the Crusades* p. 270. See below for details of the other knights.

[33] *Expeditions* pp. xliv, 9, 30–1, 53, 88, 105–6, 111, 142–3, 303–4; Tyerman, *England and the Crusades* pp. 270–1; Du Boulay, 'Henry of Derby's Expeditions to Prussia' pp. 168–70.

[34] *Expeditions* pp. xliv, 9, 30–1, 53, 88, 105–6, 111, 142–3, 303–4. For Robert Chalons see M. Cherry, 'The Courtenay Earls of Devon: The Formation and Disintegration of a Late Medieval Affinity' *Southern History* 1 (1979) p. 93.

[35] *West. Chron.* pp. 444–9; cf. Walsingham, *Chronica Maiora* pp. 278–9; id. *Historia Anglicana* ed. H. T. Riley, r.s. 28 (London, 1863–1864) vol. II pp. 197–8; Knighton, p. 537.

frustration. After withdrawing from Vilna, the English had endured several idle months cooped up within Prussia's boundaries before sailing home in April 1391. The late onset of winter meant that the anticipated February/March *reyse* was abandoned, despite Derby's boisterous efforts to 'sally out with the flag of St George' (as the Thorn chronicler put it). It occasionally suited the Order to put on special raids to satisfy the 'big names', but the new Grand Master, Conrad von Wallenrod, showed no interest in indulging Richard II's cousin.[36]

Potentially far more significant, though less well known, was the expedition embarked on by the duke of Gloucester from Orwell (Suffolk) in October 1391, his first foreign command in six years. Spurred by his nephew's example, Thomas Woodstock set about his plans in single-minded fashion, lobbying Richard II and other members of the royal council for support and recruiting heavily amongst his adherents and retainers in East Anglia and Essex.[37] The timing was advantageous. Putting aside his personal distrust of Woodstock, it suited Richard II to treat the project both as a token of friendship towards his uncles and as a marker of royal prestige. John of Gaunt was probably relieved at the removal of a potentially disruptive influence as peace negotiations with France passed through a delicate stage. The recent marriage of Gloucester's daughter Anne to Thomas Stafford, the new earl of Stafford, was another factor in Woodstock's ambition, causing the duke's stock to rise at court and equipping him with influence beyond his traditional political base in the south-east. Stafford was automatically part of the crusade plans. Richard showered his uncle with a slew of favours to facilitate the expedition, pardoning debts owed to the crown, relieving feudal dues related to Stafford's inheritance, and ordering the arrest of ships and sailors to assemble on the Suffolk coast for the impending voyage. There was also a moderate subsidy from the exchequer, supplemented by a payment of £500 on the duke's return. On his part, Gaunt lent a 'great sum' which, by May 1392, Woodstock was paying off five hundred marks at a time.[38] The crusade attracted a host of prominent supporters including Michael de la Pole, heir to the earldom of Suffolk, John, Lord Montagu, heir to the earldom of Salisbury, and Thomas, Lord Morley, Lieutenant of Ireland. Other recruits included the experienced retinue leaders Sir Robert Turk, Richard, Lord Caus, Sir Thomas Mauvesin, Sir Richard Hogge, Thomas Ypre, and the notorious soldiers Sir Reginald Pympe and Sampson

[36] 'Franciscani Thorunensis Annales Prussica' *SRP* vol. III pp. 164, 168; Christiansen, *Northern Crusades* p. 157.

[37] *West. Chron.* p. 479; *Foedera* vol. III pt. 4 p. 71; NA, C76/74 m. 18; NA, C76/76 mm. 12, 13, 15; NA, C81/1058/39; NA, C81/1059/4; NA, C81/1059/7; NA, C81/1059/9; NA, C81/1059/13–15; NA, C81/1059/41; NA, C81/1059/50.

[38] NA, E403/536 m. 22; *CCR 1389–1392* p. 494; BL, Add. MS 40859 pt. A m. 4; *West. Chron.* p. 481; NA, C76/76 m.12; *CPR 1388–1392*, pp. 477, 482 (10 Dec. 1391). Stafford had been retained to stay with the king for life in 1389: *CPR 1388–1392* pp. 160, 316; SRO, D641/1/2/4 m. 4.

Greenwich of Kent.[39] Festooned with Woodstock's military livery, the embarking crusade army conjured a satisfying image of ducal power. The bishop of Winchester, a member of Richard II's council, published diocesan prayers commending the nobleman's great devotion and sacrifice in going on pilgrimage against the 'enemies of the cross of Christ'. Indulgences were granted for parishioners who observed vigils for the duke's safe return.[40]

It is significant that the duke's Essex neighbours and former campaign companions Walter, Lord Fitzwalter (the younger), and John, Lord Bourchier, had already embarked for Prussia.[41] Together with Morley, Montagu, Pole and the earl of Stafford, they formed the main core of Gloucester's political support at home, men either sympathetic to the duke's personal ambition, or sharing his instinctive distaste for Richard II's government. Lords Morley, Bourchier and Fitzwalter had served together under Woodstock in the 1380s, the duke personally knighting Morley and Fitzwalter during his major Breton command of 1380. They remained firm partisans of the duke.[42] The high-born John Montagu was a member of Woodstock's council, and Michael de la Pole had given his support during the Appellant attack upon the court of 1386–1387. He was also married to the earl of Stafford's sister. Apart from John of Gaunt, or the king himself, no other English magnate could boast such an extensive or coherent bloc of support, let alone put it into the field.[43] Others awaiting the duke's arrival in Königsberg included William, Lord Botreaux, and Richard II's courtiers John, Lord Beaumont, Thomas, Lord Despenser, and Thomas, Lord Clifford. They probably travelled in tandem with Sir Simon Felbrigg, Sir John Harleston and Paul Salisbury, son of the disgraced chamber knight John Salisbury. Sir Richard Abberbury junior and Sir Henry Percy 'Hotspur', newly returned from a Mediterranean embassy, rounded out the numbers.[44] The commitment in military resources far exceeded that

---

[39] *Foedera* vol. III pt. 4 p. 71 (Pole, Morley); NA, C76/76 m. 12; NA, C81/528/7578 (Montagu); NA, C76/74 m.18 (Turk); SRO, D641/1/2/4 m. 4 (Caus, Mauvesin); NA, C81/1059/41 (Hogge); NA, C81/1059/14 (Ypre); NA, C76/76 m. 13 (Pympe, Greenwich). Mauvesin was treasurer of Stafford's household and sheriff of Stafford 1385–1386 and 1395–1396 (SRO, D641/1/2/40 A m.1); Turk was sheriff of Essex and Hertford in 1396. See *List of Sheriffs for England and Wales,* NA Lists and Indexes (London, 1898) vol. IX pp. 44, 127. For Sampson Greenwich's riotous career in Kent see *CPR 1381–1385* pp. 494–5.

[40] SRO, D641/1/4 m. 4; *Wykeham's Register* vol. II p. 430.

[41] Bourchier had originally intended to embark on the Tunis crusade: see above pp. 60, 62. In October 1390 he took out a licence for a pilgrimage to Rome and Jerusalem: NA, C81/519/6621; *West. Chron.* p. 475; NA, C76/75 m. 4.

[42] M. K. Jones, 'The Fortunes of War: The Military Career of John, second Lord of Bourchier' *Transactions of the Essex Society for Archaeology and History* 26 (1995) pp. 145–61; Goodman, *Loyal Conspiracy* pp. 12, 25, 75.

[43] 'John Montagu, third Earl of Salisbury' *DNB* http://www.oxforddnb.com/view/article/18995, accessed 11 Dec. 2011; Goodman, *Loyal Conspiracy* p. 25.

[44] Botreaux received a licence for a pilgrimage to Rome and Jerusalem in November 1390 (NA, C81/520/6733) which he perhaps completed before arriving in Prussia during the autumn of 1391:

of Henry Bolingbroke's expedition. Even within the limits of private funding, it is reasonable to hypothesise a fighting force well in excess of one thousand men. With the exception of Richard II's Irish campaigns, it was the highest-profile English expeditionary army assembled in the 1390s.[45]

It was appropriate that younger figures featured prominently. Woodstock saw the Prussian expedition as a chance to reassert himself at court. In his own mind, and in the view of some others, he was the natural spokesman for the generation of knights coming of age in the 1390s, and success in the crusade would have underlined his position as the *primum mobile* of English chivalry. At thirty-six Woodstock was one of the older knights in the party. Fitzwalter and Stafford were both aged twenty-three, Pole was twenty-four, while the highly decorated Percy was twenty-seven. Leading a sizeable retinue of fifty horse, Thomas, Lord Despenser, had yet to reach his eighteenth birthday. With the exception of Stafford, who died the following year, they all had successful futures in royal service.[46] Other factors helped shape responses. Lords Despenser, Fitzwalter, Beaumont and Sir Simon Felbrigg no doubt recognised the symmetry between their involvement and the expeditions of 1367–1368, when their fathers embarked on a *reyse* together. Robert Morley also boasted a strong pedigree in the Baltic crusade. One of his ancestors was an early pioneer of the *reyse* in the 1280s. Among the Suffolk gentry it was common knowledge that this first Morley had died in Prussia, and that his embalmed heart had been returned to England for burial. An effigy of the knight was known to stand in the family church at Reydon, close to a stained-glass memorial.[47]

In the event, Gloucester was undone by the decision to risk a winter crossing. Putting to sea in the last week of October, the duke endured a harrowing six weeks aboard his flagship, the *St Christopher*. Heavy seas and fog scattered most of the English fleet, eventually pushing the crusaders past Denmark and Norway and into the 'wilds of Scotland' (Orkney islands?). Many ships were lost, together with their

Calendar of Select Pleas and Memoranda of the City of London 1381–1412 ed. A. H. Thomas (Cambridge, 1926–1961) vol. III pp. 182–92. Clifford and Beaumont received licences for an embassy to the pope in February 1391, but they probably reached the Baltic by Christmas 1391: NA, C76/75 mm. 5–6; NA, C81/1057/6; NA, C81/1057/15; *West. Chron.* pp. 455, 475, 478; *CPR 1388–1392* p. 413 (Despenser); NA, E30/1515 (Felbrigg); NA, C76/75 m. 4 (Salisbury), *CPR 1391–1396* p. 323. Abberbury's esquire, Thomas Astel, received a licence to export 100 marks 'in gold or silver' for his lord's use in Prussia. See NA, C81/525/7233 (16 May, 1391); *West. Chron.* p. 455; *CPR 1388–1392* pp. 367–8; NA, C76/75 m. 12; NA, E403/536 m. 22 (Percy) and above p. 50.

[45]   In the event of his death abroad, Woodstock's executors were permitted to retain rents and farms on his estates for two years to satisfy outstanding debts – a measure of the anticipated strain on the ducal finances: *CPR 1388–1392* p. 482.

[46]   *CPR 1388–1392* p. 413. In addition to their offices in the royal household, Beaumont, Felbrigg and Montagu were invested as knights of the Garter in the mid 1390s: H. E. L. Collins, *The Order of the Garter, 1348–1461* (Oxford, 2000) pp. 291–2. Montagu inherited his father's title and estates as earl of Salisbury in 1397.

[47]   NA, C46/6/1 mm. 26, 36; Keen, 'Chaucer's Knight' esp. p. 50; id. *Origins* pp. 51–2.

cargoes of soldiers, horses, jewels and other rich possessions. Gloucester washed up near Bamburgh around Christmas time, chastened by the experience but thankful for his 'miraculous escape'.[48] Some elements of Gloucester's party did manage to complete the journey, navigating the Skagerrak and reaching the Baltic ports unscathed. Among them was John, Lord Montagu, who spent the first half of 1392 in Prussia taking part in Grand Master von Wallenrod's first *reyse*. He left at the beginning of June, when his money ran out. Another, Richard II's chamber knight John Harleston, suffered capture behind enemy lines; he was released by February 1393.[49]

Gloucester's costly failure did not dampen wider enthusiasm. One of the crusade proposals aired between John of Gaunt and Philip of Burgundy in the early 1390s was to undertake a joint campaign with the Teutonic Knights as a precursor to a general *passagium* against the Turks. John Beaufort and Sir Stephen Scrope visited Grand Master Jungingen in 1394 as part of these negotiations, their embassy coinciding with a Burgundian delegation.[50] Discussions centred upon a new overland crusade linking the powers of Prussia, Bohemia and Hungary, aimed ultimately at halting the Ottoman advance in the Balkans, but first nullifying Lithuanian paganism and vanquishing the schismatic Rus'. Jungingen's reply – that the nature of the terrain and climate made it impossible to guarantee the Order's co-operation – was true enough; it was also typically obstructive, the Teutonic Knights remaining allergic to foreign political interference. Even so, John Beaufort was equipped to fight, and with a company of English and German knights he waged a vindictive campaign for a few weeks, maiming and killing 'without mercy', and herding hundreds of captive peasant families back to Prussia.[51] The *reyse* remained *de rigeur* for knights in need of private adventure. In the later 1390s it was anticipated that Bolingbroke would join the winter campaign after being exiled from Richard II's court in 1398. His rival and fellow exile Thomas Mowbray embarked with royal introductions to the courts of Bohemia and Germany, probably also in expectation of fighting on the northern frontier. Similarly, in the opening weeks of Henry IV's reign, Thomas, Lord Despenser, no longer the youth of 1391, considered a second voyage to Prussia or a military expedition to Rhodes. At the same time he was also plotting against the new regime. As it happened it would have been better for him if he had gone abroad.[52]

---

[48]   BL, Add. MS 40859 pt. A m. 4 (£30 to the Master and Constable of the St Christopher of Levington, in part payment for shipping the duke's valets and mariners 'versus partes Prucie'); *West. Chron.* pp. 483–5; Walsingham, *Chronica Maiora* p. 282.

[49]   NA, E30/1515; *West. Chron.* p. 515.

[50]   Palmer, *England, France and Christendom* pp. 200, 240–2; Hirsch, *Danzigs Handels* pp. 234–5; Wigands von Marburg, p. 653.

[51]   *Codex diplomaticus Prussicus* ed. J. Voigt (Königsberg, 1836–1861) vol. V no. 57. Beaufort's party included Sir Henry Hoghton, Richard Eton and John Aclum, members of Gaunt's affinity. See Hirsch, *Danzigs Handels* pp. 234–5; Wigands von Marburg, p. 653.

[52]   Froissart, vol. XVI p. 107; *Foedera* vol. IV pt. 4 p. 148; *Indentures* no. 93 pp. 123–5, and cf. no. 87 pp. 119–20. Despenser was executed for his part in a failed uprising against Henry IV in 1400.

For various reasons the pattern could not be sustained. Disenchantment surfaced in some circles from an early date. After leading two abortive campaigns with the Teutonic Knights, the German Emperor Charles IV decreed the *reysen* to be a waste of time and money (1345). His theme was taken up by other hostile voices.[53] English recruitment to the *reyse* slowed markedly in the early 1400s, and after the Order's defeat against a joint Polish and Lithuanian army at Tannenberg (1410) it ceased completely. The pagan frontier may have held fast in men's minds, but Wladyslaw II's protestations of Christianity (he was baptised a Catholic in 1386) gradually eroded knightly support for the *Ordensstaat*. Unsettled domestic politics and deteriorating Anglo-French relations further dampened enthusiasm. News of English achievements in the Baltic received wide currency in the early 1390s, reflecting satisfaction at chivalry's exploits in the *reyse*, but over time attitudes began to swing against the Teutonic Order. When the Council of Constance (1414–1418) refused the Knights' request for a retaliatory Polish crusade, it seemed to cast an indictment over the whole enterprise.[54] Even so, for some the appeal remained strong. The celebrated soldier-adventurer Henry, Lord Fitzhugh, apparently performed on the summer *reyse* of 1408. One year later Richard Beauchamp, earl of Warwick, toured 'Russe, lettowe, Poleyn, Spruse, Westvale' and such 'coostes as his auncestry hadde labored in', following in the footsteps of his father and illustrious grandfather. He was probably one of the last Englishmen to arrive with a military following, fighting along Prussia's southern border on the eve of Tannenberg, and winning 'great worship' in many 'faites of were'.[55] Military emergencies at Henry IV's court and a less leisured chivalric culture inclined against wider participation. Although Henry IV made fond references to his 'gaddling days' in Prussia and pledged payment of the customary royal pension to the Teutonic Knights, he did nothing to encourage English involvement in the Order's wars.[56] Disaffection may have passed through the ranks. One year after returning from the Baltic, Lord Fitzhugh decided that his money was better spent shipping weapons and equipment to the Hospitallers at Rhodes, rather than on a second expedition with the Teutonic Order. Having experienced the winter *reyse* in 1391, Lord Fitzwalter also turned his arms towards the Mediterranean, undertaking an expedition there sometime before 1402. The waning of interest occurred across

[53]   S. C. Rowell, 'Baltic Europe' *The New Cambridge Medieval History, 1300–1415* vol. VI ed. M. Jones (Cambridge, 2000) pp. 729–30; id. 'Unexpected Contacts: Lithuanians at Western Courts c.1310–c.1400' *EHR* 111 (1996) p. 559; Christiansen, *Northern Crusades* pp. 159–60.

[54]   Paravicini, *Die Preussenreisen* vol. I pp. 123–7; *West. Chron.* pp. 445–9; Walsingham, *Chronica Maiora* pp. 278–9; Tyerman, *England and the Crusades* p. 271; Christiansen, *Northern Crusades* pp. 231–41.

[55]   Paravicini, *Die Preussenreisen* vol. I p. 127; Fitzhugh was elevated to the Order of the Garter on his return from Prussia. He became Henry V's chief chamberlain. See *Pageants of Richard Beauchamp, Earl of Warwick* ed. W. P. Carysfoot, Roxburghe Club (Oxford, 1908) plate XXII.

[56]   Housley, *Later Crusades* p. 355; Christiansen, *Northern Crusades* p. 229; J. H. Wylie, *The History of England under Henry the Fourth* (London, 1884–1898) vol. IV pp. 13–15.

other realms. A party of Burgundians were the last non-German 'guests' to undertake a campaign in 1413. The reopening of the Anglo-French war finally extinguished the tradition, and the territories of the *Ordensstaat* became partially absorbed into the kingdom of Poland-Lithuania with minimal foreign intervention.[57]

Chivalry, profit and religion

Conditions on the northern frontier veered from the convivial and glamorous to the appalling. The well prepared, like the earl of Stafford, travelled with numerous furs, blankets, tenting and a flagon of *aquavit* to defend against the winter cold. His household purchased military equipment from well-known London suppliers, including new plate gauntlets and a basinet for the lord's use, but the acquisition of good quality logging axes showed foreknowledge of one of the severest tests ahead – the densely afforested tracks and bogs that grooved and pocked the wilderness.[58] The pattern of warfare in the winter months was a rapid foray of some two hundred to two thousand men punching across river crossings or lightly defended routes – the object being to devastate and depopulate a given area as quickly as possible, gather intelligence and soften up the locality for a forthcoming assault. The violence of these raids, like those perpetrated by English crusaders in 1364 and 1394, could be extreme, with the Christians quite prepared to use massacre as a tool of local control.[59] In the summer months warfare was conducted on a larger scale, the masters of Prussia and Livonia mobilising all their resources for a full-scale offensive. It was usually intended to secure new ground by destroying an enemy fort or by building a new one in heathen territory. Most of the fighting took place in the lands adjacent to the rivers Dvina and Nieman, within reach of river-craft, castles and fortified crossings, though sometimes the central commercial sites such as Grodno, Novgorodok, Kaunas and Vilna were also targeted. At all times the difficulty of the terrain limited the crusaders' movement. Sleds were necessary to traverse the ice and snow over the winter months, and a range of one hundred miles was usually all that was possible without risk of breaking communications or being caught in foul weather. In 1365 the earl of Warwick's men were forced to carry one month's supplies flattened under their saddles because of the barrenness of the land, a feature of Baltic campaigning notorious enough to win the attention of contemporary English travelogues. Similarly, in the summer of 1390 Henry Bolingbroke could not be certain of finding fodder for his horses. It did not

---

[57]   *CCR 1409–1413* pp. 2–3; *Foedera* vol. IV pt. 1 p. 161; Usk, *Chronicle* p. 163; Christiansen, *Northern Crusades* pp. 229–30, 241–8.

[58]   SRO, D644/1/2/4 mm. 3, 4. Stafford stocked his weapons from Stephen Ffletcher and Thomas Coton 'Bowyer' the same arms-manufacturers used by Thomas of Woodstock and other noble-born military contractors. See BL, Add. MS 40859 pt. A m. 1.

[59]   Wigands von Marburg, pp. 544–5, 653.

help that baggage carts purchased for navigating *le Wyldrenesse* broke apart at the earl's first encounters with rough going.[60]

The military impact of the English contingents is hard to tell. Their work-a-day violence is sometimes reflected in the Prussian accounts, and the mounted archers always seemed to do well, though it was difficult to employ the English longbow as a decisive weapon on the *reyse*. One figure achieving notoriety was Sir Thomas Ufford, son of the earl of Suffolk, descended of the same branch as the Thomas Ufford who *reysed* in the 1330s. Participating on three, perhaps four *reysen* (1348–1365), Ufford was the most frequently recorded Englishman in the Baltic, his commitment to the northern crusade far outweighing any personal achievements of the French Wars. His campaign experience and high birth recommended him to John of Gaunt, the earl of Warwick and Urban VI. He received the garter in 1360, despite doing conspicuously little in Edward III's wars.[61] English crusaders sometimes played a notable part in the Order's sieges. A party of Yorkshire knights, including Henry, Lord Ferrers of Groby, John Ryther and Geoffrey Scrope were at Marshal Shindekopf's attack upon Pillen in 1363 (where the Christians used siege-engines and incendiary weapons), and Henry Bolingbroke's men showed great skill in laying siege to the defences at Vilna. English reports had the earl breaking into Vilna itself, which was wrong, but he successfully stormed one of the outlying forts.[62] Points of tension arose when visiting knights demanded a say in how the fighting was to be conducted. The hot-blooded Henry Percy tried to force a joint march in 1392 with the Order's tricky Lithuanian ally, the renegade Prince Witold, and there was always pressure on the leadership to mount exploratory raids, even if conditions of the frontier left no room for hasty or impromptu attacks. English knights occasionally recovered some of their campaign expenses by accumulating spoil, though this cannot have been worth a tremendous amount. Livestock and peasant captives, like those amassed by John Beaufort and Stephen Scrope in 1394, or Thomas Ufford senior in 1331, could be sold on, but the larger prizes, such as ransomable prisoners or merchant caravans, were usually reserved for the Order. The English chronicler Thomas Walsingham thought the *reyse* a provider of 'substantial booty', but this was a dubious moralist argument. In his view the Order's avarice was the main contributing factor in their defeat at Tannenberg.[63]

[60]   Christiansen, *Northern Crusades* p. 172; *West. Chron.* p. 477; *The Travels of Sir John Mandeville* ed. A. W. Pollard (London, 1915) pp. 87–8; *Expeditions* p. 50.

[61]   The composite horn crossbow remained the preferred long-range weapon of the Teutonic Knights: S. Ekdahl, 'Horses and Crossbows: Two Important Warfare Advantages of the Teutonic Order in Prussia' *Military Orders:II* pp. 119–50; Wigands von Marburg, pp. 514, 549; Paravicini, *Die Preussenreisen* vol. I p. 170. Collins' verdict that Ufford 'totally lacked military experience' is wrong: *Order of the Garter* p. 74.

[62]   Wigands von Marburg, pp. 539–60, 642–3; *Scrope and Grosvenor* vol. I. pp. 117, 123, 125, 144–5 171, 188, vol. II. pp. 310, 352–3, 443; *West. Chron.* pp. 445–9.

[63]   Wigands von Marburg, pp. 479, 646–8, 653; Christiansen, *Northern Crusades* p. 175; Walsingham, *Chronica Maiora* p. 380.

Away from the stockades and remote spaces of the *hethenesse*, the Teutonic Knights developed a rich reputation for honouring foreign visitors with feasts, jousts and other chivalric distractions, bringing the material culture of knightly campaigning into sharp focus. There was the *Ehrentisch*, the table of honour at which those who had arrived to fight the Lithuanians were banqueted and awarded prizes. A good place at the Grand Master's table became an object of pride and competition, the assembled host electing their champions before the onset of campaigning.[64] Further distractions could easily be found, making the time spent in Prussia before and after the fighting scarcely less appealing than the *reyse* itself. In the Order's official annals more attention was paid to the pageantry that welcomed Thomas Beauchamp to Königsberg than to Grand Master Kniprode's much-anticipated summer offensive (1365). In 1390 the pomp that accompanied Henry Bolingbroke included the parade of a live ostrich and leopard, animals associated with the heraldry of the Black Prince and the Plantagenets. Mobility within the *Ordensstaat* was easy enough, and the bustle of larger urban centres like Marienburg, Thorn, Elbing and Danzig gave relief from the tedium of long-distance travel or the physical strains of campaigning, as well as opportunity to lavish money and re-supply. In 1362 the earl of Hereford passed Christmas in Thorn, before moving north to Königsberg to muster for the outgoing campaign.[65] Henry Bolingbroke spent liberally during his eight months in Prussia. Local craftsmen provided silverware for his table, war horses were purchased from the Order's stud, and the earl indulged in many of the luxuries expected of a European prince, including fresh chicken for his falcons.[66] Tours of the churches and various Christian shrines that dotted Prussia cultivated an atmosphere of religiosity, allowing foreign knights to gain local indulgences and distribute alms. Guests were encouraged to participate in the Order's special worship of the Virgin Mary, with a redoubling of observances in the Virgin's honour before every campaign.[67] An important focus was the cathedral church of St Mary in Königsberg, where foreign visitors were permitted to display ceremonial shields on the interior walls or in decorative glass. Memorials to nobles killed on the *reyse* naturally drew strong interest, the cathedral doubling as a mausoleum and monument to the hazards of crusading. The bodies of Sir John Loudham (1390) and Geoffrey Scrope (1363) were brought back for burial there, and by the 1380s numerous armorial blazons testified to the tradition of English participation, kindling pride and national interest. Feasting, hunting and dancing occupied the rest of the time. Thomas Stafford travelled with a crossbow,

---

[64] See Peter von Suchenvirt, 'Duke Albert's Crusade' *SRP* vol. II pp. 163–4 lines 106–17, 123–9, 148–54.

[65] NA, DL25/1638–9; NA, DL34/1/27; Paravicini, *Die Preussenreisen* vol. II pp. 214–15; see below p. 90.

[66] *Expeditions* pp. lvii, 68, 86, 114–18.

[67] Ibid. pp. 194, 229; Wigands von Marburg, p. 549; Christiansen, *Northern Crusades* p. 221.

bolts and a new hunting horn; he also packed a harp (complete with travel case and spare strings). Gambling was another common addiction.[68]

There was a serious facet to this expenditure. Ritualised feasting and gift-giving between leading nobles had importance where differences of nationality or political allegiance threatened an army's cohesion. Attention was always paid to the splendour of the lord's table as a way of impressing rival nobles. In 1367 Walter Fitzwalter embarked with enough silverware for his twelve knightly companions (twelve silver dishes, bowls and spoons, six drinking cups – it being customary to share – and two serving vessels), and with sufficient grandeur to host other crusader lords. *In extremis* the silver could also be used in place of cash. A dignitary of Henry Bolingbroke's stature expected to be hosting all the major figures assembled in Königsberg, including the hierarchy of the Teutonic Knights. Smaller gestures would sometimes suffice. In February 1363 Hereford's minstrels played for John of Blois, the Brabantine nobleman, and to reciprocate, some days later Blois presented gifts to the earl's heralds.[69] Such niceties served to alleviate the animosity which might be imported from the Anglo-French war or from a myriad other quarrels. The good humour could be quickly worn down, however. An altercation between Scottish knights and Lords Bourchier and Clifford in one of the Order's churches in 1391 resulted in the maiming of an English esquire and the death of three Scotsmen, one of whom was the nobleman Sir William Douglas. Similarly, arguments over the right to bear the emblem of St George, a design favoured by English, German and Italian knights as well as the Teutonic Knights, regularly threatened to boil over into violence. In a culture where issues of rank and military bearing were inseparable from personal honour, conflict readily bubbled up.[70] In 1363 a petty dispute poisoned the early conviviality between John of Blois and the earl of Hereford, becoming so serious as to threaten the unity of the entire army. The details are difficult to recover, but knights from France, Bavaria and the Netherlands were drawn into the violent *controversiam* against the English, with tensions reaching a critical point after Hereford's men tore down an escutcheon of Blois's arms from the walls of St Mary's cathedral. The Teutonic Knights had to quickly separate the warring parties and orchestrate a peace treaty with terms set to endure until the end of the impending winter campaign. An icy cordiality held

[68] *CIPM* vol. XVI p. 411; Wigands von Marburg, p. 643 (Loudham); *Scrope and Grosvenor* vol. I pp. 117, 188, vol. II pp. 310, 443, (Scrope); cf. Grey vs. Hastings, CA, MS Processus in Curia Marescalli vol. I no. 441; Keen, *Origins* pp. 43–58, esp. 51–2; id. 'Chaucer's Knight' esp. p. 50. Stafford lost a mere 12d at gaming while waiting to embark at Orwell; he was either a dab hand or unusually timid: SRO, D644/1/2/4 m. 4. Bolingbroke spent nearly £70 at the table in Prussia: Du Boulay, 'Henry of Derby's Expeditions to Prussia' pp. 168–70.

[69] *CPR 1367–1369* pp. 131–2; Paravicini, *Die Preussenreisen* vol. I pp. 313–15.

[70] *West. Chron.* pp. 474–7; Wigands von Marburg, pp. 544, 644–6; Tyerman, *England and the Crusades* pp. 271–2.

fast, though unlike other foreign nobles, the earl of Hereford remained unwelcome at Blois's feasting table.[71]

English influence was felt in Prussia in other ways besides the fractious or spend-thrift nobleman. Commercial ties between England and the Baltic were established many years before the popular traffic of crusaders to the north. By 1300 Hanseatic merchants were settled in London, Hull and Boston, importing timber products, furs, potash and occasionally grain from the Baltic ports. At the same time the market in English exports increased substantially from the 1350s, diverted north by the Anglo-French war, and abetted by the emergence of the Baltic region as a volume consumer of cloth. Unsurprisingly, the challenge of English merchants to the monopoly of the Hanse and Teutonic Order was not met with great ease, and commercial relations became strained. The question of trading rights turned into a diplomatic issue in the 1370s, and relations hit rock bottom in 1385 when an English merchant fleet attacked Hanseatic shipping in the Zwin.[72] It was more than a matter of tallages and weights. By the 1390s English merchant colonies in the ports of Prussia and Livonia were large enough to support a network of Anglophone clergy, artisan guilds and manufactur-ing societies (including weapons makers). Exasperation on the part of the Prussian authorities led to restrictions on English rights of residence in 1396, possibly helping to cool knightly enthusiasm for the Order's seasonal wars. The sale of war goods to Scotland and France through Prussian and Lübeck merchants added an extra element of friction. Compensation for damages to Prussian shipping was twice agreed, in 1388 and 1409, though the underlying issue of liberalised trade was left unresolved.[73]

It is difficult to identify explicit links between chivalric crusading and the fight for market share. On the whole, English relations with the Teutonic Knights remained good, uninjured by the strains of commerce. The Order sought to separate diplomatic matters from its operation of the *reyse*, though visiting nobles sometimes got entan-gled in local disputes. Bolingbroke was made a target for representations by some angry English fishmongers, for example.[74] Occasionally, diplomacy broke the surface. In 1391 members of the royal council were keen to use the duke of Gloucester's voyage as an opportunity to petition the Teutonic Knights on trading rights. A few days after receiving his royal safe conduct he was empowered to treat with the Order on behalf of Richard II. The business at hand was probably the failure of the 1388 settle-ment. Gloucester was close to mercantile opinion in London and he could always be

---

[71] NA, DL34/1/27, written by a scribe in the service of Marshal Schindekopf ('Schreiber des Marschalls von Preußen') and sealed with the seal of the convent of Königsberg; Paravicini, *Die Preussenreisen* vol. I pp. 313–14.

[72] T. H. Lloyd, *England and the German Hanse, 1157–1611* (Cambridge, 1991) pp. 75–8, 96–100; Tyerman, *England and the Crusades* pp. 272–4; W. M. Ormrod, 'Finance and Trade under Richard II' *Richard II: The Art of Kingship* eds A. Goodman and J. L. Gillespie (Oxford, 1999) pp. 155–86.

[73] *CPL* vol. V p. 57; T. H. Lloyd, *England and the Hanse* pp. 96–100; Jacob, *Fifteenth Century* p. 70; *Diplomatic Correspondence* pp. 66–8; Wylie, *Henry the Fourth* vol. IV pp. 1–15, esp. p. 14.

[74] *Expeditions* p. xxxiv; Tyerman, *England and the Crusades* p. 273.

trusted to defend national interests, but the chairing of a trade summit hardly tallied with expectations of the *reyse*. Success rested on the calculation that there was always close synthesis between the economic interests of the Order and other members of the Hanse, which there was not. Expectations cannot have been very high; in contrast to the diplomatic team sent to Prussia in 1388, Gloucester's party lacked a recognised legal expert in commercial matters and maritime trade.[75]

Nonetheless, a productive relationship between Baltic commerce and knightly crusade clearly existed. For one thing, the well-developed financial institutions of the Hanseatic and Prussian merchants provided significant flexibility, giving crusaders access to the capital necessary to finance their expeditions. Numerous English knights availed themselves of the credit on hand in Thorn, Danzig and Elbing. Some of the larger borrowers, like William, Lord Kerdeston (extracting £600 in 1351), dealt in sums that dwarfed their regular incomes, probably gambling upon future fees and wages. Typically, expeditions to Prussia, as elsewhere, rested upon multiple levels of credit. Borrowing £800 from Henry Stonehals of Thorn, for example, the earl of Hereford mortgaged a significant portion of the rents and income which he had yet to obtain because of his minority (1363). Undertaking to repay his loan in Flanders, the earl had to raise fresh capital from the merchants of Bruges, again trading on the worth of his anticipated inheritance. Members of his retinue acted as sureties on the loan, spreading the burden of risk.[76] To counter their escalating expenses, some crusaders turned to commerce. In the 1360s the earl of Warwick's servants shipped consignments of cloth from London for his use in Prussia, Thomas Beauchamp apparently intending to offset some of his campaign expenses by cornering the new market for English cloth. As a mark of special favour Edward III remitted the usual export tariffs.[77]

For nobles and royal officials used to farming the profits of royal customs, or proficient with the mechanisms of trade, the expedient was obvious. In 1391 the duke of Gloucester and the earl of Stafford stowed quantities of fine cloth, and the cheaper worsteds, kersays and straits, in their vessels, along with war horses and military armaments, possibly for retail at Danzig.[78] On rare occasions crusaders attracted business investment as part of a mixed consortium of merchants and knights. In May 1392, for instance, John Montagu borrowed £57 from Peter Bixton, a merchant of Danzig. Sir Simon Felbrigg and John Skorel, a Norwich merchant, stood as Montagu's sureties,

---

[75] *Foedera* vol. III pt. 4 p. 71. On the Teutonic Knights and the Hanse see M. M. Postan, *Medieval Trade and Finance* (Cambridge, 1973) pp. 238–42.

[76] Paravicini, *Die Preussenreisen* vol. I p. 123, vol. II, p. 214 (Kerdeston); NA, DL25/1989; NA, DL25/1638–9; Fowler, 'Seals' p. 115 (Bohun); cf. C. Higounet, 'De la Rochelle à Torun: Aventure de barons en Prusse et relations économiques' *Le Moyen Age* 69 (1963) pp. 529–40.

[77] *CCR 1364–1368* p. 143.

[78] *West. Chron.* pp. 482–5; SRO, D644/1/2/4 m. 4. Alternatively, the harder-wearing worsteds may have been intended for use as outdoor pennons and war-standards. Cloth emblazons stayed mainly indoors. See Vale, *Edward III and Chivalry* p. 79.

Skorel exposing some of his commercial fortune to risk.[79] A second loan for £340 contracted with German merchant Wynard Ostinchosen implicated a larger circle of Montagu's associates as sureties, including John, Lord Beaumont, Lord Botreaux and three English merchants domiciled in Prussia. Peter Bixton, the source of the original loan, also acted as one of Montagu's guarantors, his first grant apparently serving as collateral against the larger sum. Raising two rounds of capital, and possibly a third, Montagu was therefore the principal debtor in a larger commercial transaction, almost certainly involving the export of Baltic commodities or raw materials. The multiple layers of liability, and graduated rates of investment, were standard methods for protecting merchandise against loss or damage while securing a proportional rate of return for private investors. Two months after raising funds in Danzig, Lord Montagu's agents presented payment of £340 to one of Ostinchosen's representatives in the presence of the Warden and Aldermen of the Hanse in London – the partnership with the Hanse underlining the nobleman's evidently well-respected business credentials.[80]

But knights were not merchants, and if a balance sheet of profit and loss for the crusade could be drawn up it would make sober reading. In turning to merchant groups to top up their campaign purses, nobles were merely acting along traditional lines, according to the model set out by the crown in its wars. Few Baltic crusaders can have emerged from the struggle for credit showing profit. Only the Teutonic Knights consistently gained. Bolingbroke's expenditure in the *Ordensstaat* of approximately £4,500 brings out the enormous financial saving made by the Order with their volunteer armies. For the military entrepreneur there were far greater rewards available fighting in the *routier* companies on the continent, or competing for royal offices at home.[81] One likely legacy of commercial links with the Baltic, on the other hand, was the strong distribution of combatants drawn from the eastern regions of England, particularly those areas serving the North Sea ports, where contact with Prussia had been unbroken since the early thirteenth century. Over a quarter (sixty-two) of the 223 knights and esquires identified as embarking for the *reyse* between 1330 and 1410 had tenurial or dynastic links to East Anglia or the Lincolnshire and Yorkshire coasts. If, as Michael Evans has suggested, Lincolnshire and East Anglia provided a large proportion of the English crusaders to the east during the twelfth and thirteenth centuries, then the ethic of crusading remained almost as strong in regional military society in the later period, albeit diverted towards Prussia.[82]

---

[79]   NA, E30/1515 (financial instrument: exchequer copy). Skorel nominated his wares 'bona mobilia et immobilia in mari vel circa marem' as collateral.

[80]   *Calendar of Select Pleas*, vol. III pp. 182–92.

[81]   Du Boulay, 'Henry of Derby's Expeditions to Prussia' pp. 168–70.

[82]   M. Evans, 'Crusades and Society in the English Midlands c.1150–1307' Phd thesis (Nottingham, 1997) pp. 235, 331–2.

Other imperatives propelled men to devote their physical and mental energies. Attractive for its vaunted place in chivalry, the military dangers were real enough. Besides the deaths of young knights like Anthony Lucy, John Multon and Roger Felbrigg at Neu-Kauven in 1368, the *reyse* claimed the lives of the celebrated soldiers William, Lord Ros (1351), Sir Geoffrey Scrope (1363), Sir John Loudham (1391), Thomas, Lord Clifford (1391) and Sir John Paveley (1392), as well as scores of less prominent men.[83] Captivity was a frequent hazard. In 1391 Sir John Clifton, Sir Thomas Rempston (Bolingbroke's standard-bearer) and a number of other *anglici* got cornered while sheltering at a holy site on the Lithuanian-Prussian border. The English accused Wladyslaw II of 'wolfish' entrapment, which was a bit rich, but after twelve months of imprisonment Clifton was safely returned to London, perhaps freed under one of the Order's prisoner exchanges.[84]

Part of Lithuania's appeal lay in the competitiveness of war for its own sake. The closeness of continental chivalry, particularly the military culture of the Low Countries, was important in this respect, breeding interest in fashionable courtly circles. As already seen, glamorous figures such as the duke of Guelders and Marshal Boucicaut in the 1390s, or William IV, count of Jülich, and the young John of Blois in the 1360s, were enthusiastic adherents of the *reyse*. Ironically it was perhaps through Blois that the earl of Hereford first formulated his crusade plans, adding an additional twist to their violent falling out in 1363. Both men spent time in the custody of Edward III's household in 1360–1361, Bohun as a ward of court, Blois as a prisoner of war. In Prussia, Hereford also crossed paths with the extraordinary Sir Rutger Raitz, one of Blois's associates and a fanatic of the northern frontier. Raitz boasted an exceptional record on the Baltic crusade, campaigning no fewer than thirty-two times in Lithuania and three times in Livonia by the time his career was ended in 1369.[85]

Going on a *reyse* enhanced reputations in a tangible way, even for giants of English chivalry. A wave of excitement greeted Thomas Beauchamp at the Westminster parliament of 1366, inspiring copycat vows of devotion, according to one well-placed observer. Nobles cultivated enthusiasm in domestic and local settings with specially commissioned prayers and masses, harnessing the pulpit to enhance their standing and prestige, especially amongst their regional followings (see below pp. 153–7).[86]

---

[83]   Knighton, p. 111; *CIPM* vol. X p. 32 (Ros); *West. Chron.* p. 511; NA, E404/14/96 (Paveley); *Peerage* vol. III p. 292 (Clifford).

[84]   *Diplomatic Correspondence* p. 218. Clifton made ready to join Gloucester's abortive expedition to Ireland, May 1392: NA, E101/74/1/43.

[85]   Raitz was one of those clashing with Bohun's men: NA, DL34/1/27; Paravicini, *Die Preussenreisen* vol. I p. 174 (Raitz); cf. the poetic tribute to Raitz composed by his contemporary, Claes Haenen, herald Gelre, quoted in M. H. Keen, *Nobles, Knights and Men-at-arms* (London, 1996) pp. 75–6.

[86]   John of Reading, p. 172. Henry Grosmont's clerical officials targeted the important Lancastrian honours of Richmond and Pontefract with prayers calling to mind the duke's mental and physical devotion against 'fidei inimicos et crucis hostes': *Historical Letters and Papers from the Northern Registers* ed. J. Paine, r.s. 62 (London, 1873) pp. 402–3; *Wykeham's Register* vol. II p. 430; Paravicini, *Die Preussenreisen* vol. II p. 121.

Perhaps just as self-regarding was the practice of returning home with a trophy convert. To 'raise a pagan prince from the font' was a sign of highest chic, acted out most famously by the Emperor Charles IV who maintained a noble convert at Prague and invested him with an imperial title as a sign of traditional Caroline jurisdiction. Thomas Beauchamp paraded a number of Christian converts at the 1366 parliament, including one Lithuanian youth who was purportedly a prince. Beauchamp tradition had the earl ceremoniously baptising the child in London, giving him the name Thomas, and schooling him in English verbs. Gathered about noble chambers or packing military affinities, pagan converts were visible reminders of recent crusading achievements, and they appealed to cosmopolitan tastes. The vogue was not restricted to the richest knights; pooling the rents of his London properties in 1393, Paul Salisbury struggled to provide a small annuity to support 'Peter Prus', his convert of *Pruce*. Such preoccupations fed Philippe de Mézières's suspicion that the *reyse* was a platform for knightly 'vanity', in contrast to the chastening work of attacking the Ottomans or harassing the Mamluk Sultanate.[87]

With all of its secular trappings and glamour, what of the crusade's devotional framework? Despite Mézières's sniping there can be little doubt that many disciples of the Baltic crusade identified their actions with tightly held religious ideals. The enemy were infidels, their lands *hethenesse*, and the object of every campaign was the extension of Christendom. It was popularly feared that in 'every coost of þe marches, Cristen mens lordeshippes descreases…and þe lordeshippes of hethen men groweþ vpward and in-creaseþ'. This was why Thomas Woodstock prepared a coat of mail with a brass cross riveted to it.[88] Because it lacked the full apparatus of traditional crusading – there were no preaching campaigns (outside of the Order's lands), minimal papal interference, little evidence of vows, and no church taxation or subsidies – questions arise over the precise character of the Order's seasonal wars. The contrast with the crusade bulls granted to Catholic Poland against pagan Lithuania and the Rus', for instance, is striking.[89] Nonetheless, the penitential context of decisions to join the *reyse* is also conspicuous. Unsurprisingly, chroniclers and apologists associated with the Teutonic Knights are clearest about the devotional purposes and effects. According to the Order's herald, in 1348 Sir Thomas Ufford and his English expedition arrived in the 'service of the Virgin, looking for remission of their sins'. Henry of Hervod describes Henry Grosmont as embarking on a 'pilgrimage for the expansion of the Christian faith, for the glory of Christ's name, and to destroy the pagans'. Guests

[87] Rowell, 'Unexpected Contacts' pp. 567–9; John of Reading, p. 172; John Rous, *Johanni Rossi antiquarii Warwicensis Historia regum …* (Oxford, 1745) p. 204; *Pageants of Richard Beauchamp*, plate XXII; *CPR 1391–1396* p. 323; cf. *Expeditions* pp. 52, 65, 67–8 for Lithuanian prisoners. In 1363 King Peter of Cyprus reportedly brought a Lithuanian prince to London from (confusingly) Turkey for baptism: *Eulogium* vol. III p. 238; Iorga, *Philippe de Mézières* p. 303 n. 8.

[88] *Middle English Sermons* p. 256 (c.1380); *Testamenta Vetusta* vol. I pp. 146ff.

[89] Housley, *Later Crusades* pp. 344–8; e.g. *Acta Urbani VI, Bonifacii IX, Innocentii VII* ed. A. L. Tăutu (Rome, 1970) pp. 135–6.

of the Order were almost invariably termed 'pilgrims'.[90] Arguments advanced at the Council of Constance simultaneously portrayed the Teutonic Knights as guardians of a papal fief, the harbingers of mass conversion, and the assailants of apostasy and heresy in Samogitia – all canonical grounds for a crusade.[91] Dedicated to the figure of the Virgin Mary, the Order's territorial conquests were deemed analogous to the Holy Lands of Palestine, or the patrimonies of St Peter in Italy or St James in Spain. Loosely, English commentators echoed the theme, equating the northern wars with crusades elsewhere. For Henry Knighton, Grosmont's expedition was a 'pilgrimage against the enemies of Christ'. Geoffrey le Baker thought the duke of Lancaster was fighting the 'Turks' in the service of the king of 'Cracow and Poland'. English sermon teachings reiterated the point, conflating the crusade against pagans with a larger global and spiritual struggle. War in the *hethenesse* confronted enemies no less dangerous than the carnal world itself, which was skulking with demons and other sinners. For this reason papal indulgences were granted, even if the actual violence was quite perfunctory.[92] This emphasis could serve critical as well as sympathetic agendas: in 1391 one Wycliffite preacher railed against the 'pope's lawe' that grants men 'pardone to [for] waren ageyn hethen men and sleu hem' – a pointless argument unless it was commonly believed that knights received a papal pardon, or indulgence, for fighting in the *hethenesse*.[93]

Some campaigners did take the cross, like the earl of Warwick, whose vow was regarded as transferable between Prussia and the east. Urban V praised the earl's commitment to the crusade, despite his retreat from the Cypriot expedition, holding up instead the alternative *viam laudabilem* in the north – though he apparently discriminated between peaceful pagans and those actively fighting Christians (November 1364). English pontificals reflected the practice, with cross-taking ceremonies for penitents going to fight in the heathen territories as well as for those wishing to fulfil vows in the east.[94] Men armed themselves with the usual range of spiritual and practical safeguards. The papal chancery issued licences for portable altars, personal confessors and individual grants of plenary indulgence, supplementing the thirteenth-century privileges that established the Teutonic Order's 'perpetual' or autonomous crusade, though only the wealthiest knights directly petitioned the church authorities. After

[90]　Wigands von Marburg, pp. 479, 514, 523, 544; Henry of Hervod, pp. 741–2.

[91]　Christiansen, *Northern Crusades* pp. 221–2, 231–41; Tyerman, *God's War* pp. 681–9.

[92]　Knighton, p. 113; Baker, *Chronicon* p. 119; John of Bromyard, 'Opus Trivium' (c.1330), Oxford Bod. MS New College 223 fols 19ʳ–20ʳ ('indulgentias pene et culpe romani pontifices solebant dare pugnantibus tempore parvo contra paganos').

[93]　*The Register of John Trefnant, Bishop of Hereford, 1389–1404* ed. W. W. Capes, Cantilupe Society, and Canterbury and York Society (London, 1914–1916) p. 272 (William Swinderby).

[94]　ASV, reg. vat. 248 fol. 9ʳ–9ᵛ ('contra paganos illarum partium Christianos impetentes hostiliter'); see above p. 45; e.g. the Coventry Pontifical (c.1347), rubric for blessing 'Benedictio crucis dande ituris in sanctam terram vel ituris in aliam terram ad expugnandum inimicos crucis'. See also Brundage, 'Cruce Signari' pp. 294–5 n. 18, pp. 306–7 esp. 307.

the 1360s demand tailed off.[95] Instead, the Order's varied catalogue of spiritual inducements sufficed. In April 1362, for instance, encamped before the pagan stronghold of
Kaunas, the bishop of Samland celebrated Easter Mass before an army of English and
other foreign fighters. After the sermon, the 'indulgences of the Order' were proclaimed, the remainder of mass sung and the congregation marked with the blessing.
The act of private confession completed the canonical requirements, validating the
grant of indulgences. Such ritual was probably routine on the eve of battle or at the
outset of a march. A summary of the Order's indulgences composed at Trier in 1372
referred to a remission of a third of all penance granted to those who aided the Knights
with alms, weapons and horses 'against the Saracens in support of the Holy Land',
apparently based on a commission of Honorius III. This was the minimum expected
by supporters of the *reyse*. Some blandished money as an extra measure. Hereford's
competitor, John of Blois, spent money on a certificate that guaranteed 'the indulgence of the Prussian *Reyse*', presumably bestowing a plenary remission. It is likely
that hundreds of these dockets were produced by the secretariat at Marienburg.[96]

Confidence that the *reyse* was a salvific activity extended beyond the formal
mechanisms of vows, indulgences and papal doctrine. Old Testament and patristic
teachings on fighting for the love of God, the vogue for ascetic religion and emphasis
upon bodily sacrifice – to be a 'good lyver' – conditioned knightly attitudes, occupying significant space within aristocratic spiritual life.[97] That foreign recruits dried
up after the battle of Tannenberg (1410) is perhaps the strongest argument for the
religious ethos of war on the northern frontier. Depopulated of *miscreans* or infidels, enemy lands were now officially under the protection of the cross. Such was
their political success that by 1418 the convert-rulers of Poland and Lithuania were
appointed vicar-generals in a proposed crusade against the schismatic Rus'. Even the
most spirited supporters of *hethenesse* crusading were now forced to accept that the
Order's raids into Lithuania were wrong.[98]

[95]   E.g. ASV, reg. vat. 211 fol. 190; ASV, reg. supp. 23 fol. 47ʳ pt. II (Grosmont); *CPL* vol. II p. 557
(Cobham).
[96]   Wigands von Marburg, p. 537; A. Ehlers, 'The Crusade against Lithuania Reconsidered' *Crusade
and Conversion* pp. 35–40; Paravicini, 'Die Preussenreisen des Europäischen Adels' p. 30.
[97]   Cf. P. J. Horner 'A Sermon on the Anniversary of the Death of Thomas Beauchamp, Earl of Warwick'
Traditio 34 (1978) pp. 381–401, esp. 388–9.
[98]   Walsingham, *Chronica Maiora* p. 380; Tyerman, *God's War* p. 710.

5

Constantinople and Eastern Europe

Writing in 1402, the Regent of Constantinople, John VII, addressed the English court, and narrated the grim situation of the eastern Empire. Overrun by the Ottoman Turks, the tiny and disjointed state of Byzantium was on its knees, crippled by the costs of war and the destructive raiding of Sultan Bayezid I (r. 1389–1403). The yoke of the infidels was firmly about the Christians' necks.[1] Hope of salvation rested with the west, and John VII sought to emphasise the precedent of English military aid, paying tribute to certain of Henry IV's noblemen who had already contributed to the defence of Constantinople. Striving as 'the very best of men', English knights were currently in the city, the 'House of God', populating the defences and distinguishing themselves with deeds of heroism. 'It is nothing new,' John claimed, 'for illustrious England to produce such fruit.' In the same vein, the Greek Emperor Manuel II spoke of the 'British' as the expected saviour of eastern Christendom. His famous visit to the Lancastrian court at Christmas 1401 sought to deepen diplomatic connections, and fire support for the anti-Turkish crusade. The emperor's references to 'axe-wielding warriors of British race' recalled much older associations, invoking memories of Anglo-Saxon and Celtic soldiers in Byzantine armies of the tenth and eleventh centuries, as well as the faithfulness of English knights in more recent years.[2] Aimed at cultivating sympathy, the historical allusions were not lost upon Henry IV's court. Many of the king's subjects had experienced the empire's struggle for survival

---

[1]   *Royal and Historical Letters of Henry IV* no. 42 pp. 101–3. For contemporary comment see 'Annales Ricardi Secundi et Henrici Quarti' *Chronica et Annales* ed. H. T. Riley, r.s. 28 (London, 1866) p. 231; J. W. Barker, *Manuel II Palaeologus* (New Brunswick, 1969) pp. 213–15, 500–3. In general see Setton, *Papacy and the Levant* vol. I pp. 285–326; Atiya, *Crusade in the Later Middle Ages* pp. 379–97; C. Imber, *The Ottoman Empire, 1300–1650* (2nd edn, Basingstoke, 2009); C. Kafadar, *Between Two Worlds: The Construction of the Ottoman State* (Los Angeles and London, 1995); D. M. Nicol, *The Last Centuries of Byzantium* (2nd edn, Cambridge, 1993); the early chapters of J. McCarthy, *The Ottoman Turks* (London, 1997); Lock, *The Franks in the Aegean*; Balard, *Les latins en Orient*, esp. the final three chapters.
[2]   Particularly perhaps the royal household of the 1390s – Richard II's Cheshire bodyguard famously carried axes: Saul, *Richard II* p. 394.

at first hand. At the beginning of the fifteenth century, the war in the Balkans had displaced the eastern Mediterranean as the most precarious and dangerous of Christian frontiers.

'The matter of Greece'

It is easy to exaggerate the slowness of the west to react to the threat of the Ottoman Turks. Having risen quickly from a clutch of competing emirates, by 1371 the descendants of Osman Bey and his son Orkhan (r. 1326–1362) had established themselves as the main threat to Christian power in the Balkans, building influence and power in the interior of Europe. Slipping across the Dardenelles during the Byzantine civil wars of the 1340s and 1350s, and first installed at Adrianople around 1361, the Ottomans prosecuted war at a brisk pace, annexing the last possessions of the eastern Empire and invading large swathes of Serbia, Bosnia and Albania. Victories at the battles of Kosovo (1389) and Nicopolis (1396) marked the full extent of the Ottoman advance in the fourteenth century, but Turkish dominion now stretched across the Balkans, to the lands drained by the Danube, annexing most of Bulgaria and jeopardising Hungary.[3] Alarm at the Ottoman advance in the late 1350s led to the first crusade coalitions to stop them. Pierre Thomas's multi-national raid upon Lampsacus opposite Gallipoli in 1359 (see above pp. 39–40) opened a sequence of papal schemes to bring lasting relief to Byzantium. Longer term success was elusive, but a stock of knightly enthusiasm apparently existed, particularly within French chivalry, where the houses of Valois and Anjou possessed a respected heritage of fighting in Latin Greece. English knighthood shared the preoccupation, again notably during periods of relative quiet in the Anglo-French conflict, although traffic failed to reach the same levels seen in Prussia or in other parts of the Mediterranean. Familiarity with Byzantium's struggle was widely assumed, not least because 'the matter of Greece' was a recognised setting of English romance. Here, the heroes of *Guy of Warwick*, *Sir Ferumbras*, *Beves of Hamtoun* and other chivalric romances were transported across its landscape, and found fighting within the 'Grekes sea', or at the fringes of 'Turkeye'.[4]

In practice, political fragmentation across the Balkans and the Greek successor states did not constitute fertile ground for new mass crusades. Areas such as Athens and

---

[3]   See Tyerman, *God's War* pp. 843–74; Housley, *Later Crusades* pp. 49–117; Atiya, *Crusade in the Later Middle Ages* pp. 379–97; I. Metin Kunt, 'The Rise of the Ottomans' *New Cambridge Medieval History* vol. VI ed. M. Jones (Cambridge, 2000) pp. 839–63.

[4]   Guy of Warwick killed 40,000 Saracens at the 'battle of Constantinople': *The Romance of Guy of Warwick*, ed. J. Zupitza, EETS e.s. 42, 49, 59 (London, 1883–1891) vol. II p. 111; cf. *The Romance of Beves of Hamtoun*, ed. E. Kölbing, EETS e.s. 46, 48, 65 (London, 1885–1894); *Sir Ferumbras*, ed. S. J. H. Herrtage, EETS e.s. 34 (London, 1966); 'Sir Isumbras' *Middle English Romances* pp. 125–47. 'Walakye' (Walachia), a former province of Byzantium, is listed among the knightly destinations admired by noble-born ladies in Chaucer's 'Book of the Duchesse': *The Complete Works of Geoffrey Chaucer* ed. W. W. Skeat (Oxford, 1894) vol. I p. 312.

Thebes, where a dense patchwork of competing Catalan, Greek and Turkish interests existed, exemplified the problem.[5] As a rule, local territorial and political advantage won out, at the cost of higher religious, ethnic or cultural callings. Similarly, difficult political relations among the neighbouring Latin powers meant that Byzantine alliance with the Serbs, Albanians, Bulgarians and Hungarians – potential Christian bulwarks to the north and east – failed to take lasting hold. This, more than western indifference or military inferiority, condemned Constantinople to a tenuous existence. The question of union between the Greek and Latin churches was another continuing distraction. Greek emperors flitted between appeasement of the Turks on the one hand, and the pursuit of a military alliance with the pope and the launching of a relief crusade on the other. Papal indulgences issued in the 1360s and in the 1390s, during Sultan Bayezid's siege of Constantinople (1394–1402), marked the high points of western intervention, bearing fruit with the spirited crusade of Amadeo of Savoy (1366–1367), and the infamous Franco-Burgundian expedition of 1396, destroyed at Nicopolis.[6] Less well documented were the journeys made by independent gentlemen, such as the Northamptonshire knight William de la Pole, drawn to Byzantium in search of adventure, profit or religious renewal, or for other reasons. As a destination of chivalry, the Ottoman war probably carried the most risk. Yet given this, and its inaccessibility, English chivalry maintained surprisingly strong links. The poverty of Byzantine sources and the complexity of political conditions on the ground make it possible to form only a sketchy picture.

Perhaps typical of the private crusade initiatives of the 1360s was the expedition recruited in 1367–1368 by John, Lord Mowbray, whose heroism *contra turchos* was later revered at Richard II's court. Born into an illustrious baronial dynasty, Mowbray shared the usual martial aspirations of his class, but by 1367 an eminent career in royal service had so far eluded him.[7] Enlisting a compact grouping of some twenty fellow campaigners with their retainers and servants, mainly from areas adjoining his Yorkshire and Cambridgeshire estates, Mowbray petitioned the crown for a licence to embark to the east in October 1367.[8] His following included men of significant standing in the county, such as the royal commissioner and future sheriff of Lincolnshire, John Hode of Fleet, the Yorkshire knight John Byron, and the distinguished Sir Roger Trumpeton of Girton (Cambs.). The party took passage from Dover sometime around the middle of November. To help pay his way, Mowbray borrowed money from his friend, the crusade enthusiast Humphrey Bohun, and embarked with a bill

[5]   See *Correspondance de Pierre Ameilh* pp. 366–9.

[6]   See below pp. 102–7, 110–13.

[7]   R. E. Archer, 'The Mowbrays, Earls of Nottingham and Dukes of Norfolk to 1432' DPhil thesis (Oxford, 1984). For the family's twelfth-century crusading pedigree see S. D. Lloyd, *English Society and the Crusade* p. 99.

[8]   *CPR 1367–1370* pp. 22, 53–4, 158. A fifteenth-century genealogy describes Mowbray's trip to the east as a pilgrimage: *The Coucher Book of Furness Abbey* eds J. C. Atkinson and J. Brownhill, Chetham Society (Manchester, 1886–1919) vol. II pt. 2 pp. 289–92.

of exchange for 800 marks and £100 in cash.[9] Allowing time for the arduous sea journey across the eastern Mediterranean towards the Dardenelles, he probably arrived during spring 1368, possibly with other western reinforcements.

The mood in Constantinople was unusually expectant. A brief revival of Greek military fortunes in Thessaly and parts of Thrace in 1366–1367 promised to curb the rate of Turkish expansion, and Emperor John V was conducting talks with Urban V over the possibility of Church union in return for Latin aid.[10] Lord Mowbray's movements are hard to reconstruct, but his war-party apparently joined a minor offensive against the Ottomans, launched along one of the narrow land corridors still open to Christian forces. Sallying out from the protection of Constantinople's walls, the English crusaders apparently lingered in no-man's-land too long and became trapped in a Turkish ambush somewhere in the vicinity of the city walls. Mowbray and several others in his party were killed. A later report mentions only that he was slain by 'treacherous Saracens' in a skirmish between Muslims and Christians. This was thought to have occurred sometime between June and October 1368. Retrieved from the battlefield, Mowbray's body was interred at the Dominican church at Pera, the Latin suburb of Constantinople, in a cemetery fast filling up with the remains of western knights either killed in battle with the Ottomans, or victims of recurrent outbreaks of plague.[11] It was from here that three decades later, servants of his son Thomas Mowbray, earl of Nottingham, arranged for its exhumation and return to England (1397). Other victims of the 1368 expedition included Roger Trumpeton, reportedly dead by 29 August, probably caught in the same skirmish, and Sir Alexander Mowbray, a member of the junior branch of the family.[12]

More detail can be salvaged from the dealings over Mowbray's bones in the 1390s, by which time a tradition of special worship seems to have grown up around the soldier. In exchange for a fee of 250 ducats, the Dominican custodians agreed to open Lord Mowbray's tomb and gather up the contents in a jar for shipping home with an agent of Nottingham. Describing Mowbray as *vir catholicus*, as if he were the object of a religious cult, the Dominicans insisted that his bones be placed in a western convent of their own order. To guard against the scandal of pillaging local military shrines, the exhumation of the Englishman's bones took place under a cloak of secrecy. Reflecting high esteem for foreign campaigners, and perhaps a favoured place for English chivalry, attitudes at Pera suggest that Mowbray had won lasting fame for the manner of his death. Evidently, local inhabitants felt a measure of protection in having the tombs of noted defenders of the city in their midst.[13] Perceived as a 'pilgrim' (rather

---

[9]   *CCR 1364–1368* pp. 53–4, 295; NA, C81/733/114–115 (Mowbray's military retinue).
[10] J. W. Barker, *Manuel II* pp. 1–79 esp. 10, 16–17 n. 38.
[11] NA, E326/9376; *CIPM* vol. XII no. 397.
[12] *CIPM* vol. XXII no. 420 p. 405; *CPR 1367–1370* pp. 8, 421.
[13] NA, E326/9376; S. Düll et al. 'Faithful unto Death: The Tomb Slab of Sir William Neville and Sir John Clanvowe, Constantinople 1391' *Antiquities Journal* 71 (1991) pp. 179–83.

than a *crucesignatus*) in later family tradition, it is not known whether Lord Mowbray took the cross, made a crusade vow or received papal indulgences. His royal licence omits any mention of his intended purpose or destination, though permission was granted to travel with full military harness.[14] In light of Mowbray's death what mattered most was the martial and heroic context of his journey east.

Amadeo of Savoy's crusade 1366–1367

Of more lasting significance was the well-documented Constantinople campaign of Amadeo VI of Savoy in 1366–1367. Originally an outgrowth of Peter of Cyprus's Alexandria expedition (1365), it actually surpassed the Cypriot enterprise in ambition. Vested with a range of traditional crusade privileges, including clerical tenths (in Savoy and neighbouring imperial appanages), papal indulgences and the reissue of a recent crusade bull against the Anatolian emirates, it planned for military alliance between Amadeo, Louis I (the Angevin king of Hungary) and the western emperor Charles IV.[15] Amadeo's kinship with the Byzantine ruler John V (they were cousins) perhaps narrowed the risk of treachery against the eastern empire. After a series of delays and false starts, by December 1365 at the latest, the objective of the sea of Marmara and relief of embattled Constantinople was established.[16] The platform for a strong English presence was already in place, thanks both to the earl of Warwick's prominence in the Cypriot crusade plans of 1363–1364, and to enthusiasm within the duchy of Gascony, where cultural and political ties to the house of Savoy were strong. Chief among English crusaders was Ralph, Lord Basset of Drayton (Staffs.), a rising figure of the Black Prince's court. A veteran of Poitiers (and every major campaign in France until 1387), Basset came to full prominence in 1368, winning promotion to the Order of the Garter and making an excellent marriage to the sister of Jean IV, duke of Brittany (a remarkable match, even for a man of Basset's military rank).[17] Both were prizes received soon after his return from eastern waters, a signal of his new-found standing. Besides Basset's long list of French commands, a pilgrimage to the Holy Land between 1360 and 1362 and a bequest of £200 to Canwell priory (Staffs.) are other notable biographical details. Basset's role on the Savoyard crusade has been mistakenly ascribed to a Gascon nobleman of the same name, and, more recently,

[14]   *CPR 1367–1370* p. 53; *Coucher Book of Furness* vol. II pt. 2 pp. 289–92; W. Dugdale, *Monasticon Anglicanum* eds J. Caley et al. (London, 1817–1830) vol. VI p. 320.
[15]   Setton, *Papacy and the Levant* vol. I pp. 285–326; Atiya, *Crusade in the Later Middle Ages* pp. 379–97; E. L. Cox. *The Green Count of Savoy* (Princeton, 1967) pp. 177–239; Iorga, *Philippe de Mézières* pp. 163–175; Housley, *Later Crusades* pp. 67–9.
[16]   Atiya, *Crusade in the Later Middle Ages* p. 382; Setton, *Papacy and the Levant* vol. I p. 292.
[17]   Knighton, pp. 406–7; G. F. Beltz, *Memorials of the Order of the Garter* (London, 1841) pp. 159–60; *Peerage* vol. II pp. 2–6; *Scrope and Grosvenor* vol. I p. 158, vol. II p. 206.

to the earl of Warwick's companion knight Ralph Basset of Sapcote (Lincs.).[18] His participation, and the participation of others at the Black Prince's court, is further evidence of the vogue for active crusading which seemed to sweep through Anglo-Gascon circles during the mid 1360s.

Evidence of English recruitment first emerges in petitions at the curia in April 1366, eight weeks before the bulk of Amadeo's fleet embarked from Venice. Together with members of his entourage, Ralph Basset applied for the usual papal safeguards and privileges, including portable altars and plenary indulgences *in articulo mortis*. His household clerk, William Wolaston, and treasurer, John Dikes, successfully petitioned for licences to hold multiple benefices in England. Applications for similar devices from other English knights clogged the apostolic chamber, relating mainly to the Black Prince's impending invasion of Castile, and the expected dangers to body and soul there.[19] But Lord Basset gravitated directly towards the crusade, arriving in Venice in the first weeks of June to make final preparations. His introduction to Count Amadeo of Savoy probably lay through the hot-tempered Gascon lord Florimond de Lesparre, newly returned from service with Peter of Cyprus, and repeatedly associated with Lord Basset in the Savoyard sources. Both men had attended on the Black Prince in Gascony. Another eminent companion, William de Grandson of St Croix in Burgundy, 'beloved by all the captains, men-at-arms and companies in Aquitaine', also possessed a distinguished record under English arms.[20] It is likely that Lord Basset was present on 27 May 1366 when Lesparre sealed a contract with Amadeo VI to serve with thirty gentlemen for twelve months *outre le mer*, and the Englishman almost certainly entered into a similar agreement. At the end of the appointed one-year term he took payment of 2,600 gold *parperi* (the currency of Pera) – a sum large enough to remunerate his sizeable company of around one hundred men, including ten men-at-arms, his esquire, William of London, and thirty-five arbalesters and archers.[21]

Predictably, Lord Basset's participation attracted other English recruits. Maurice le Bruyn added his complement of fifteen men-at-arms, taking passage in the same war galley as Basset. The men remained close associates in the years following the campaign.[22] Other independent gentlemen were also quick to enlist, probably at Venice, hop-scotching from Peter of Cyprus's Alexandria crusade or military service

[18] *CPR 1361–1364* p. 124; *CPR 1358–1361* p. 479; Dugdale, *Monasticon Anglicanum* vol. IV p. 104; cf. Atiya, *Crusade in the Later Middle Ages* p. 358; Luttrell, 'English Levantine Crusaders' pp. 145–6.
[19] *Urbain V: Lettres communes* nos 15868, 17093–5; *CPP* vol. I pp. 523, 526, 531; ASV, reg. aven. 162 fols 464ʳ–476ʳ.
[20] Jean Servion, 'Chroniques de Savoy' *Monumenta Historiae Patriae* eds C. Albert et al. (Turin, 1836–1855) vol. III *Scriptores* 1, cols 297–8, 302, 306, 308, 311. Officially, Basset and his retinue were in the service of the Black Prince 'in partibus Vasconi': NA, C61/78 m. 5; NA, C61/79 mm. 9, 13.
[21] Atiya, *Crusade in the Later Middle Ages* p. 385, quoting Turin State Archives, *Viaggio di Levante*, Mazzo Jº, vol. I no. 1; Barberi, nos 479, 726, doc. III pp. 336–7, doc. IV pp. 338–9.
[22] Barberi, no. 215. Basset enfeoffed Bruyn with his manor of Shawe-by-Newbury (Berks.), held in chief, sometime before February 1369: *CPR 1367–1370* p. 210.

elsewhere. The exotically named Andrew Lancerel ('Lanczo' in Amadeo's expeditionary accounts), is probably the knight of Hooton Pagnell (Yorks.) who received
Urban V's commendation in 1364 for traversing the east and fighting *viriliter* against
the enemies of Christ. A Scottish knight named only as Lord Alexander (Alexander
Lindsay?) also attached his military retinue. His campaign fee of 400 ducats, awarded
at the close of fighting, suggests high-rank. There was also success in attracting the
mercenary companies. An English military contractor recorded only as 'William'
chartered his company of archers; another captain, John Clerk (possibly a clergy-
man), served with one hundred hand-picked 'brigands'.[23]

Departing from Venice on 19 June, the crusade fleet consisted of over twenty galleys
and numerous transports and other vessels (*conducta, naves, ligna, panfili*), carrying a
not inconsiderable 4,500 men, including the rowers and crewmen aboard the supply
ships and transports. Additional strength was gathered at the Latin trading station at
Coron, July 1366, where galleys carrying soldiers from Genoa and Marseilles joined
the fleet.[24] Lord Basset and his *gens* were given a prominent position in the first of
three *batailles*, the order of sailing making the Englishman captain of the squadron on
the right flank. Companies of archers were dispersed about the galley fleet, but Basset,
like Amadeo of Savoy, was allowed to deploy his archers as he wanted, probably in
light of the Englishman's better experience of the weapon.[25] Landlocked at home, the
count of Savoy took special care with the methods of naval warfare, issuing detailed
orders on how the fleet should be deployed at sea. Techniques of formation and signalling – using coloured lanterns at night and a system of pennons in daylight hours
– kept the fleet in contact. For fighting at sea, chains lashed the main battle group
together, constituting a large defensible platform with which to engage the enemy.[26]
The fleet was able to proceed unmolested along the approaches to Constantinople,
through the Bosphorus and up the Black Sea coast as far as Varna. Turkish pirates
were a danger, but the threat at sea was more likely to originate from quarters closer to
home – from Genoese enclaves in the northern Aegean, fearful of losing their regular
custom with the Ottoman emirate, or from dissident Byzantine groupings. Nowhere
in Amadeo's naval ordinances is the enemy explicitly identified as Turkish or Muslim
shipping.[27]

The count of Savoy proved a gifted commander, landing his forces in good order
on the western shore of the Dardenelles and launching a determined assault against

[23]   *Scrope and Grosvenor* vol. I p. 125, vol. II p. 323, *Urbain V: Lettres communes* no. 8885; Barberi, nos
256, 276, 488, 624. Sir Alexander Lindsay received a royal safe conduct to pass from England on 'pilgrimage', with ten men-at-arms, October 1365: *Foedera* vol. III pt. 1 p. 102; Setton, *Papacy and the Levant*
vol. I pp. 292–3.
[24]   Ibid. pp. 294–8; Servion, cols 302–3.
[25]   Barberi, doc. IV pp. 338–9, doc. V pp. 340–3.
[26]   Ibid. doc. IV pp. 338–9, doc. V pp. 340–3, esp. p. 341.
[27]   E.g. in 1347 a Genoese fleet stole part of Humbert of Vienne's war-chest and annexed the island of
Chios, wresting a potential base away from the Holy League.

the Ottoman beachhead at Gallipoli. Lord Basset and Florimond de Lesparre joined the marshal of the host, Gaspard Montmayeur, in the first assault, reportedly fighting 'like lions'. According to the Savoyard chronicler, the Christians performed wondrous feats of arms, 'for it seemed to them that in dying they went straight to heaven'.[28] Carrying the count's banner, a group of *anglici* charged a barricade of Turkish troops defending a breach in the garrison walls, and was followed hotly by the rest of the vanguard. Suffering three days of land attacks and a blockade by sea, the Turkish soldiers eventually melted away, leaving the town's Greek inhabitants to welcome the western knights as liberators (23 August 1366). Noblemen killed in the fighting were later carried to Pera and interred with honour in its Latin cemeteries.[29] The next step was to install a Christian garrison, which would remain in place for twelve months before Amadeo returned the outpost to Byzantine control in 1367. The potential military rewards were great. Conquest of Gallipoli (and capture of the sultan's custom houses there) demonstrated what could be achieved with western sea power, and exposed an essential weakness of the expanding Ottoman state. Ottoman control over the town was vital, not only in fuelling expansion into the Balkans (supplying fresh waves of Muslim settlers and troops), but also in limiting the independence of potential rivals on the western frontier. It could be used to starve rival emirs of recruits or deny them access to the Anatolian markets for sale of their booty. Expansion of the Ottoman state on both sides of the Bosphorus rested upon it.[30]

With Gallipoli secure, Amadeo next steered the expedition away from the Turks, past Constantinople and into the Black Sea. News that the Bulgarians had blocked John V's return to Byzantium in the aftermath of a court visit with Louis of Hungary prompted Amadeo to launch an attack along the Euxine coast, taking Sozopolis, Messembria and eventually laying siege to Varna – the principal Bulgarian city on the Black Sea. The sources make no mention of any dissent among the crusaders at the targeting of fellow Christians.[31] The battle for Messembria was particularly hard fought. Lord Basset and his men were again in the thick of things, taking command of the first wave of attackers with Florimond de Lesparre, the Gascon nobleman Jean de Grolée, and William de Grandson – all former associates of the Black Prince. The weight of Christian numbers, backed by siege artillery, proved overpowering, though the Bulgarians fought hard. The defending garrison was put to the sword and the town

[28]   '... la firent les cristiens merueilliez darmes...car les gens nacontoyent riens de leurs viez et leur sembloit que en morant ilz alloyent en paradys...' (Servion, cols 306–8).
[29]   Ibid. cols 308–9; Barberi, no. 255.
[30]   Kafadar, *Between Two Worlds* pp. 127–42 esp. 142; Metin Kunt, 'Rise of the Ottomans' pp. 858–63. Gallipoli's central strategic importance was clearly recognised in Constantinople. See the courtier Demetrius Cydones's pamphlet *Oratio de non reddenda Callipoli* (c.1371); J. W. Barker, *Manuel II* pp. 16–17.
[31]   See the vow put in Amadeo's mouth, 'En nom Dieu...nous ne laisserons pas a besonger a lencontre des infidels et ennemys de la cristiennete et de lempereur' (Servion, col. 305).

sacked.[32] The most notable of the English casualties was William Scrope, a brother of Stephen Scrope, the young recruit to the Cypriot crusade. He was probably killed in the melee that followed the initial assault. With the town in the crusaders' hands, his tomb was set up in a church in Messembria with an emblazon of the Scrope arms painted on an interior wall.[33] Although Amadeo's treasury was close to exhaustion, the count next positioned his fleet outside Varna, posing enough of a threat to persuade the Bulgarian ruler, Tsar Šišman, to allow John V free passage across his lands. The emperor's party met the crusade armada at Sozopolis at the end of January 1367, and returned to Constantinople several weeks later. The western fleet followed in due course, reaching its moorings amidst scenes of thanksgiving and joy among the city's populace. John V thanked the crusaders for the favour they had done not only to the empire, but also to the whole of Christendom, remarking that without their aid he would have certainly perished in exile, since there were no Christian knights remaining in Greece or 'Romania' whom the Turks and Bulgarians had not overawed.[34]

Amadeo's crusade suffers from comparison to the more spectacular Alexandria expedition.[35] With the exception of the Italian chroniclers, it made little impact upon western opinion, probably because it lacked a high-profile conquest or battle. The matter of church union, which occupied Amadeo's proctors in Sozopolis and Constantinople, and for some time appeared to hold the count's interest, opened few doors to practical aid, despite high-flown expectations. John V's personal repudiation of 'Greek errors' at Rome (1369) merely invited a further humiliation, when on his journey home the emperor was prevented from leaving Venice because of debts to the Republic (1370–1371).[36] More questionable was Amadeo's haggling over finance, which ultimately saddled John V and his Greek subjects with a significant portion of the crusade's expense. Amadeo sought to recover some of his costs by exacting tribute from Greek inhabitants in Sozopolis, Messembria and other towns along the Black Sea coast, raising around a tenth of his costs, but greatly reducing the towns' wealth when they were returned to the empire in 1367. Byzantium took control of the great prize of Gallipoli in the same year, but only after John V agreed a fee of 15,000 florins in subsidy of the crusaders' galleys, and granted a loan of 20,000 florins for his cousin's *passagium* back to Italy.[37] On the other hand, however, re-equipped with Constantinopolitan money, Savoy did not forget the crusade's official objective of defending the eastern empire and opposing the infidel. In spring 1367 the western fleet

---

[32]   Ibid. cols 311–12.

[33]   *Scrope and Grosvenor* vol. I p. 125, vol. II pp. 323–5; Keen, 'Chaucer's Knight' esp. p. 52.

[34]   Setton, *Papacy and the Levant* pp. 300–6; Servion, col. 314.

[35]   Iorga regarded Amadeo's expedition not as a crusade, but as an escapade ('une équippé'): Iorga, *Philippe de Mézières* pp. 336–7.

[36]   O. Halecki, *Un Empereur de Byzance à Rome, Vingt ans de travail pour l'Union des églises et pour la défence de l'empire d'orient, 1355–1373* (Warsaw, 1930) pp. 213–22.

[37]   Setton, *Papacy and the Levant* vol. I pp. 304–9; Barberi, nos XIII–XVI, XL–XLII, XLVII–XLIX, LXXIII (receipts given in Roman numerals).

undertook a sequence of rapid assaults against Turkish strongholds on both shores of the sea of Marmara. Little decisive could be achieved, but the exposed Ottoman shoreline presented an attractive target. This was precisely the tactic required to disrupt Ottoman power, forcing the enemy to commit troops to fortified outcrops on headlands and beaches and away from interior estates and land routes.[38]

Once more, the English evidence provides additional insights. Although substantially outnumbered by Gascon and Savoyard elements, Lord Basset and his countrymen enjoyed special prominence. For navigating the narrows of the Bosphorus – the most dangerous sailing of his voyage – Amadeo chose a guard of fifty English archers and a company of one hundred English men-at-arms to defend his galley, apparently impressed by their action during the fighting at Gallipoli. Again, on his return from the Black Sea, Amadeo selected a mixed complement of English and German knights to escort him through the Straits.[39] Analysis of the English ranks shows the usual composition of recruits, including knights and esquires, archers, men-at-arms, *routier* captains and other hangers-on. Some took employment in Amadeo's garrisons at Gallipoli and Sozopolis, though the monotony of the work could be trying. The record of English knight Henry Spegul (*milite*), who served as an officer at Gallipoli from September 1366, is instructive. Contracted at a monthly rate of ten florins, Henry was content to stay at Gallipoli for little more than four and a half months before absenting himself and going in search of greater adventure, possibly travelling northwards to join the main army currently quartered at Sozopolis. He had returned to Gallipoli by June 1367, when a Byzantine garrison was installed, whereupon he received the balance of his wages. The Yorkshire knight Andrew Lancerel stayed at his post for around six months, before cropping up in Constantinople in February at the time of John V's joyous return. Such patterns perhaps reflected a system of troop rotation, with good communication and supply lines permitting the passage of men between the various encampments of the main army.[40] A high degree of organisation is evident in other respects. The English convention of infantry companies travelling with an appointed chaplain and barber-surgeon was observed. In 1366–1367 several such auxiliaries travelled with Basset and his contingents, the traditional deployment apparently keeping to shape. One of them, a clerk ('William'), received a gift of 20 gold *parperi* from Amadeo on his departure from Pera. Casualties generally appear to have been light, despite the armour-piercing bolts of Turkish archers and an outbreak of influenza across camp when the army was wintered at Messembria.[41] Besides William Scrope, the only other high-ranking casualty in the English group was the Cambridgeshire soldier Sir Philip Limbury. Details of his participation are vague,

[38]   Ibid. nos 515, 523.
[39]   Ibid. nos 256, 490; cf. Servion, col. 316.
[40]   Barberi, nos 488, 623–4; Setton, *Papacy and the Levant* pp. 298–306, passim.
[41]   Servion, col. 306: 'fayettes barbeless, les quellez frappoyent aux pies des cristiens'; Barberi, nos 377, 407, 575, 605, 762–3.

but after embarking from England sometime after October 1365, Limbury made his way east, almost certainly in tandem with Ralph Basset. In September 1367 a royal inquiry established that he had died 'in parts of Constantyn Noble' on 6 July. He probably numbered among the unfortunate sick and dying left at Pera in the aftermath of Amadeo's campaign.[42]

Keeping strictly to its twelve-month timetable, there was no question of the crusade surviving beyond the expiration of men's contracts. Lord Basset took his fee and returned to English service by autumn 1367, receiving a commission to stay in the king's service 'beyond the seas' for a further year in January 1368. Other Englishmen apparently returned home by September.[43] Some crusaders made promises to revisit Constantinople as part of a general *passagium*, but there were more pressing targets and obligations waiting at home. Nonetheless, the Savoyard crusade was not merely a matter of contracts, wages and lucrative campaign bonuses. At Avignon knights took out personalised papal indulgences in preparation for the expedition, and an atmosphere of heightened anticipation persisted there. A few weeks after Amadeo sailed from Venice, Edward III's envoy to Urban V, Sir Bartholomew Burghersh the younger, announced his intention to join the *viagium* 'against the enemies of the faith', vowing to take forty knights into his pay. Soliciting a papal safe conduct and a grant of plenary indulgence, his intention was probably to combine with a small crusade armada currently assembling at Aigues Mortes and Marseilles for rendezvous with Amadeo at the Aegean outpost of Coron.[44] The expedition's religious dimension was not forgotten by the Savoyard chronicler, even if reserved mainly for moments of pathos or dramatic tension, such as Amadeo's remonstrations with John V at his Orthodox religion, or at the assault upon Gallipoli when the crusade's churchmen prayed as the ranks lined up for the attack.[45] A distinctive camaraderie evidently existed between some participants, particularly Florimond de Lesparre, at least one Scrope, the ubiquitous Nicholas Sabraham and others, who took leave of Amadeo in June 1367 to take part in Peter of Cyprus's post-Alexandria raids along the shoreline of eastern Anatolia and Mamluk Syria. The earl of Hereford's following at Tripoli was partly swollen with men returning from Constantinople and Gallipoli.[46] Between the large Cypriot *passagium* of 1365, Amadeo's crusade and King Peter's naval expeditions of 1367, it was possible for some crusaders to string together nearly three years' continual service

---

[42] *CPR 1364–1367* p. 180; *CIPM* vol. XII pp. 128–9; Barberi, nos 504–5, 510, 576. Limbury was a noted servant of Henry Grosmont, assisting in the duke's administration of Brittany (1355–1358) and serving in several of his commands: Fowler, *King's Lieutenant* p. 183.

[43] *CPR 1367–1370* p. 76; see below n. 50.

[44] *CPP* vol. I p. 531; the relevant passages are not in the printed calendar. See ASV, reg. supp. 46 fol. 266ʳ; 'l'armee de Marseille et l'armee d'Ayguesmortes' joined Amadeo of Savoy at Coron towards the end of July 1366 (Servion, col. 303).

[45] Ibid. cols 307, 316, 318.

[46] Ibid. col. 319; *Scrope and Grosvenor,* vol. I p. 125, vol. II pp. 323–5; Machaut, *Capture of Alexandria* pp. 138, 178, 193, 204.

in the Aegean and eastern Mediterranean, with Avignon, Venice and Famagusta the main recruiting centres. Moving in elite and cosmopolitan circles, dependent upon contacts made at Bordeaux and other courtly settings, it is unlikely that such men recognised significant difference between the various fronts.

At the same time, however, despite the Greek crusade's rich international flavour, the local roots of crusading remained important. The close links between three English knights active in Byzantium in the 1360s help bear this out. The first, William de la Pole of Castle Ashby, died somewhere in the Aegean around 1366, after fighting in the vicinity of Athens;[47] the second and third, Sir Philip Limbury and John, Lord Mowbray, died in the regions of Constantinople in 1367 and 1368, as seen above. Although embarking separately, the men shared extremely close-knit interests at home, centred mainly around Mowbray's orbit of clients and acquaintances. Pole made Mowbray part of his crusade plans when he nominated him as one his feoffees before sailing for the east in 1364. Limbury and Mowbray held neighbouring manors in Cambridgeshire and appointed the same attorneys-at-law to represent their interests when abroad.[48] The trio were used to functioning as a grouping as charter witnesses and county administrators. A shared heritage of crusading provided additional bonds. Mowbray and Limbury each boasted active crusaders among their ancestors. The Mowbray tradition reached back to the 1140s and the Second Crusade; more recently, three Mowbrays had accompanied the Lord Edward to Acre in 1271.[49] Beyond this, wider social and tenurial networks gave contact with other knightly groupings readying to go against the infidel. Limbury held part of his estate from Antony Lucy, the central figure of local recruitment for the Lithuanian *reyse*. Also well known to Lucy was Mowbray's fellow crusader Sir John Hode of Fleet, who acted as one of Lucy's charter witnesses and as attorney for members of his retinue. Various other documentary connections existed, binding the wider social grouping and laying down patterns of behaviour. That Mowbray's entourage was preparing to embark in the same weeks as neighbouring circles testifies to the highly charged atmosphere in the east midlands and Lincolnshire during 1367–1368. Prominent men were always watchful of their neighbours' military accomplishments, but friendship probably steered much of this. Notably, Mowbray took the final decision to embark for Greece when news of the deaths of Limbury and Pole reached the English localities in autumn 1367 (apparently carried back by elements of Amadeo's crusade).[50] The collective exertion was impressive. County society was not exactly emptied in 1367, but the deaths on crusade of important landholders from the Cambridgeshire/Lincolnshire border (e.g. Lords

[47]   See above p. 3; *CIPM* vol. XII no. 76.
[48]   See *Victoria History of Cambridge* vol. VI pp. 233–5; *CPR 1364–1367* p. 180; *CPR 1367–1370* pp. 22, 158; *CIPM* vol. XII nos 76, 152.
[49]   Lloyd, *English Society and the Crusade* pp. 99, 102; *Coucher Book of Furness* vol. II pt. 2 pp. 289–92; Dugdale *Monasticon Anglicanum* vol. VI p. 320.
[50]   *CIPM* vol. XII nos 152, 233; *CPR 1364–1367* p. 315.

Lucy and Mowbray, Sir John Multon, Sir Philip Limbury, Sir Roger Trumpeton) did open large gaps in the local polity. As such, crusading in the months from autumn 1367 to autumn 1368 likely exacted as great a toll on county community as service on any of the much higher profile fourteenth-century royal campaigns.[51]

The Nicopolis crusade and beyond

Ottoman expansion quickened in tempo in the 1380s. Sultan Murad Bey's recapturing of Gallipoli in 1377 was the first of a catalogue of Christian setbacks, followed by a relentless build-up of pressure in Albania, Macedonia and towards the Dalmatian coast. By 1387 the city of Thessalonica had fallen; the following year the remnants of Bulgarian resistance crumbled; in 1389 Christian Serbia was destroyed at the battle of Kosovo. The new Greek emperor, the spirited Manuel II, was forced first into Turkish vassalage and then to turn to the west for aid.[52] On the surface, Greek appeals for military reinforcement were well timed. Alarm at the Islamisation of the Balkans restored the idea of a general *passagium* – dormant since the 1360s – to the forefront of Anglo-French diplomacy, and the recent co-operation of the Tunis campaigners provided ample additional encouragement. Politically, conditions for a large *passagium* seemed favourable. Stagnation of the French war, following the treaty of Leulingham (1389), and the relative inaction of the fighting classes meant that there was a stock of western knights and esquires free to embark. Offering a potential replacement for the Anglo-French war, a crusade to the Balkans promised to strengthen existing links with central Europe and the imperial house of Bohemia. Important informal connections were already in place with the court of Sigismund of Hungary, Byzantium's most significant ally against the Turks. The most prominent of these ran through the household of Sigismund's elder sister, Anne of Bohemia, Richard II's queen.

Early proposals concentrated on relieving Constantinople against the Turks. Genoa sought Richard II's support for an armada to the city soon after Louis of Bourbon's crusade against Tunis, and privately the English king signalled his support, confiding in the Doge that he was intending some part not only in the Genoese expedition, but also in a crusade of his own, when the moment was ripe (April 1392).[53] Talk of joint action against Islam circulated at Anglo-French peace negotiations of 1390–1392, but little immediate aid was forthcoming, perhaps because confusion existed over the main target of the proposed crusade. Richard II sent a delegation to Constantinople in the summer of 1391, probably in exploration of royal interests as intimated to the

[51]   *Victoria History of Cambridge*, vol. VI pp. 233–5. For Lucy et al. see above pp. 80, 101, 107–8.
[52]   Metin Kunt, 'Rise of the Ottomans' pp. 849–58; Imber, *Ottoman Empire* pp. 26–37; Tyerman, *God's War* pp. 843–61; Housley, *Later Crusades* pp. 66–79; Setton, *Papacy and the Levant* vol. I pp. 341–69; J. W. Barker, *Manuel II* pp. 46–122.
[53]   *Diplomatic Correspondence* no. 145 p. 98.

Doge.[54] Embassies were also sent to Sigismund of Hungary, to Rhodes, Cyprus and other eastern powers, widening the diplomatic framework. Richard II's half-brother, John Holand, earl of Huntingdon, travelled to Hungary in 1394 equipped with papal indulgences and a military retinue. According to papal letters, his voyage was 'for the defence of the Faith against the Turks and other enemies of Christ', leaving little doubt as to the purpose of his embassy. Other royal messengers were active in the eastern Mediterranean, including Henry Bolingbroke and the prior of the English Hospitallers, John Raddington, who travelled together to Rhodes, Cyprus and Jerusalem before Bolingbroke returned to report to the Anglo-French peace conference at Amiens in 1391. Some of this diplomatic activity was co-ordinated with the French court, and the impression is of Richard II's government trying hard to protect its interest in the eastern crusade.

A possibly illusory sense of cohesion was provided by the writings of Philippe de Mézières (now advisor to Charles VI) and his band of co-enthusiasts – Robert the Hermit, Jean de Blaisy (a Burgundian nobleman), Louis de Gaic and Otto Grandson from Savoy (namesake and descendant of Edward I's famous companion-knight), a *chevalier d'honneur* of Richard II. Mézières's crusade vision was now sprawling, contained in texts such as the *Songe du vieil pèlerin* (1389) the *Oratio tragedica* (1389–1390), the *Epistre au roi Richart II* (1395), the *Nova Religio Passionis Jhesu Christi* (1367–1395), a plan for a new crusading order, and several other writings since lost. This was no simple call to arms, but a manifesto to end the papal schism, unite Christendom and open a new epoch in the east, calling upon western chivalry to undergo moral reform and atone for the ills of decades-long fratricidal war.[55] Mézières appealed directly to literary and aristocratic tastes, though his work was in essence an attack upon contemporary knighthood. Meetings between Richard II's courtiers and his messengers, and the messengers of Charles VI's court, circulated the arch-propagandist's polemic. There was the usual slowness of steps in crusade planning. The looming problems of Charles VI's ill-health, church schism and financial difficulties undoubtedly dampened expectations. Nevertheless, plans for a preliminary Anglo-French attack on the Turkish empire in the Balkans under the command of John of Gaunt, Louis of Orleans and Philip of Burgundy eventually reached a somewhat settled state in 1394, providing the outlines of the expedition to Nicopolis of 1396. Rumours that Gaunt was preparing a crusade army travelled widely, including to Aragon, where English diplomacy was scouting for a potential alliance. Richard II's

---

[54] *West. Chron.* p. 480; Düll et al. 'Faithful unto Death' pp.174–90.
[55] The classic text is Iorga's biography, *Philippe de Mézières*; cf. Mézières, *Songe du vieil pèlerin*; id. *Letter to King Richard II* ed. G. W. Coopland (Liverpool, 1975). See now the collection of essays edited by R. Blumenfeld-Kosinski and K. Petkov, *Philippe de Mézières and His Age: Politics and Piety in the Fourteenth Century* (Brill, 2011) esp. M. Hanly, 'Philippe de Mézières and the Peace Movement' pp. 61–82; A. Tarnowski, 'The Consolation of Writing Allegory: Philippe de Mézières' *Le songe du vieil pelerin*' pp. 237–54; and A. Curry, 'War or Peace? Philippe de Mézières, Richard II and Anglo-French diplomacy' pp. 295–320.

courtiers exhibited interest by associating with Mézières's proposed crusading order, the *Nova Religio Passionis Jhesu Christi* (see below pp. 171–3).[56] A second royal uncle, Thomas Woodstock, the hot-tempered duke of Gloucester, also made provisions to take part. Nine months before the crusade's departure, Woodstock began inserting terms of crusade service in his life indentures, envisioning the sailing of a ducal army against 'les enemys Dieux' (September 1395).[57]

Despite evidence of the preparations and ceremonial, it is hard to show a significant English contribution to the Nicopolis campaign. A revolt in Gascony and a temporary crisis in Anglo-French relations apparently caused John of Gaunt to relinquish personal control of his crusade to John Beaufort, his careering son. The collapse of confidence induced Louis of Orleans to pull out altogether, and Philip of Burgundy followed Gaunt's cue, ceding command of the Burgundian army to his heir, John of Nevers, resulting in much more limited recruitment than had been envisaged in 1395. Palmer has suggested that there was an English contingent of perhaps fifteen hundred men under John Beaufort, including Sir Ralph Percy, son of the earl of Northumberland, identifying the army recruited by Gaunt for his Gascon command in the autumn of 1394 as the main source of troops. Numerous English crusaders had embarked from Gascony in the past, using their royal protections and licences as cover, but for Nicopolis the detailed evidence is weak.[58] If Gaunt had intended to take this force against the Ottomans it must have remained a vague plan, especially as the finer workings of the crusade (i.e. finance, papal commissions, time span) had not been finalised by the autumn of 1394. It is not improbable that several English retinues accompanied Nevers's force, as testified by various chroniclers on the continent, possibly travelling with John Beaufort from Bordeaux to the mustering point at Dijon. One Italian writer identifies the leader of the English as 'a son of the duke of Lancaster', evidently referring to Beaufort, who crossed to Gascony with his father in 1394, and whose whereabouts are unknown for the next two and a half years.[59] His candidacy as a replacement leader accorded well with his experience in the Tunis expedition and his prominence in Anglo-Burgundian crusade talks in 1394. When John Beaufort was created earl of Somerset on his return to England, officially it was for exploits (*journees et travaulx*) 'in many kingdoms and lands overseas', which had redounded to the honour of the country – perhaps a reference to his crusade exploits

[56]   Palmer, *England, France and Christendom* pp. 180–210; Tyerman, *England and the Crusades* pp. 294–301; Iorga, *Philippe de Mézières* pp. 480, 491–2; Goodman, *John of Gaunt* p. 135; Froissart, vol. XV pp. 196ff. Mézières presented John Holand, Richard II's half-brother, with a shortened version of the Order's rules and regulations, c.1395, now Oxford Bod. MS Ashmole 813.

[57]   *Indentures* no. 85 pp. 117–18.

[58]   Palmer, *England, France and Christendom* pp. 239–40.

[59]   Palmer, *England, France and Christendom* pp. 239–40; C. Tipton, 'The English at Nicopolis' *Speculum* 37 (1962) pp. 528–40; Tyerman, *England and the Crusades* pp. 300–1.

in Hungary. His elevation to the Order of the Garter was also possibly linked to leadership at Nicopolis.[60]

Sir Ralph Percy and a number of lower-ranking soldiers did leave England early in the summer of 1396, probably bound for Hungary. The Evesham chronicler says that Percy was captured at the battle of Nicopolis in September and slain by the Turks afterwards. A royal inquiry of 1400 established that Percy had died 'in parts overseas' on 15 September 1397, and despite the lack of other news, it is conceivable that he died in Turkish captivity one year after the battle. In 1403 a rumour circulated that Sultan Bayezid had killed numerous Christian prisoners once their ransoms had been paid, instead of permitting their release. Many other western noblemen succumbed to disease after months of captivity in Anatolia.[61] A group of English crusaders may have travelled from Rhodes with the English Hospitallers, represented at Nicopolis by their prior, John Raddington. Thomas Mowbray's envoy, John Meubray *heraudus*, was present in Constantinople during the weeks that the remnants of the crusader army took refuge there. He was accompanied by English Hospitaller John Ingilby, the preceptor of *Befondi* (Battisford, co. Suffolk.), perhaps suggesting that the pair were refugees from Nicopolis. It would have been in keeping for Richard II's noblemen to despatch their heralds and ensigns to join John of Nevers's force as observers and participants. John Raddington's links at Richard's court perhaps encouraged additional investments of men and material.[62]

The disaster at Nicopolis did not create a vacuum of interest among western chivalry, though increasingly the initiative moved away from the courts of France and England and passed to the house of Burgundy. Contemporary commentators failed to predict the demise of the crusade as an aspect of western unity. Walsingham struck a bullish note, ignoring events on the Danube, but reporting a fantastical Byzantine and Hospitaller victory against Sultan Bayezid in 1395 instead.[63] Expectations were little changed, with plans for another *passagium* in aid of Byzantium touted as early as October 1397. Two years later Marshal Boucicaut installed a French garrison at Constantinople, and English participation was envisaged with Boniface IX's publication, in successive years, of indulgences for penitents going against the Turks or contributing financial aid (1398, 1399 and 1400). In English parishes the sale of indulgences apparently raised significant sums, with records fullest for the towns and villages of Lincolnshire and Leicestershire where preachers cultivated generous giving. At court, the coterie of churchmen and noblemen most closely associated with Richard II were encouraged to donate money. Special efforts were made to convince a

[60] *Rot. Parl.* vol. III p. 343; Goodman, *John of Gaunt* pp. 158–9.

[61] *Historia Vitae Ricardi Secundi* p. 147; Palmer, *England, France and Christendom* p. 240; Düll et al. 'Faithful unto Death' p. 187 n 79.

[62] Ibid. pp 181–2, 187, esp. 187 n. 88; NA, E326/9376. Raddington escorted Henry Bolingbroke on his return journey from Jerusalem (1392–1393): *Expeditions* pp. 150, 226.

[63] Walsingham, *Chronica Maiora* p. 294.

visiting Greek embassy of Richard's personal devotion to the crusade.[64] The outlook deteriorated in 1399 with Henry Bolingbroke's seizure of the English throne, and the increasing gravity of Charles VI's ill-health, yet Manuel II's personal iteration around western courts between 1399 and 1402 produced generous offers of help. The interest surrounding the emperor's visit to London allowed Henry IV to strike the traditional pose of the benevolent crusader king, a ruler, in Manuel's honeyed prose, 'overflowing with merits, and bedecked with virtues' and singularly worthy of the honour of rescuing the eastern empire. Evidently, the traffic of English knights to Constantinople had not dried up. There were reports of English knights fighting in aid of the city in 1402, probably relating to soldiers travelling to Byzantium with Marshal Boucicaut or in smaller national groupings, like the contingent from Spain, where Manuel's diplomacy was also active.[65]

In the longer term, however, despite his promises, Henry IV's court could not support such aspirations, partly because of the heightened state of alarm at home, but also because of an increasingly insular ethos within the Lancastrian regime. Buffeted by internal rebellion and external threats, Henrician politics, by necessity, fostered a military culture much more narrowly monopolised by the monarch and questions of his security than by the stipulations of continental chivalry or by the international ethic of crusading. The lapsing of ambitions at Charles VI's court further dissolved commitment, depriving the crusade of the productive, generations-old rivalry between the chivalry of England and France. If these were added steps towards the 'nationalised' chivalry of the fifteenth century, one effect was to starve Constantinople and eastern Christians of aid.[66] England's burgeoning diplomatic and military links with Burgundy failed to spark a similar competitive crusade spirit, a critical setback for the war against the Turks, and still more the traditional dream of recovering Jerusalem. Already, by the 1420s, Henry V's gesture of despatching the Burgundian Ghillebert de Lannoy on a reconnaissance mission to the east in preparation of a new general *passagium* appeared almost quaint.[67]

---

[64]   J. W. Barker, *Manuel II* pp. 156–7. In 1399 Henry Bolingbroke was reportedly interested in undertaking a Balkan crusade in alliance with Sigismund of Hungary: cf. Froissart, vol. XVI p. 132; Raynaldi, *Annales Ecclesiastici* vol. XXVII anno 1398 § lx, anno 1399 §§ i-iv, anno 1400 § viii; NA, E135/10/19 (preaching commission, 17 May 1399). Between them, fifteen towns and villages in Lincolnshire and Leicestershire donated £325: NA, E159/179 Memo Roll (1399), Michaelmas m. 33; Hilary m. 40, mm. 13–14ᵛ; Easter mm. 11-11ᵛ, 16-16ᵛ; *Wykeham's Register* vol. II pp. 483–4. The St Albans-based chronicler spoke of 'great sums' being collected: 'Annales Ricardi Secundi et Henrici Quarti' *Chronica et Annales* pp. 230–1.

[65]   J. W. Barker, *Manuel II* pp. 160, 178–80; *Royal and Historical Letters of Henry IV* pp. 101–3, 421, 423, 425, 427.

[66]   On Henry IV's military affinity see C. Given-Wilson, *The Royal Household and the King's Affinity: Service, Politics and Finance in England, 1360–1413* (New Haven, 1986) pp. 226–34.

[67]   Atiya, *Crusade in the Later Middle Ages* pp. 190–7; Paviot, *Ducs de Bourgogne* pp. 63–7.

One place, notably, where the mood was not changed, however, was in the literary realm. A post-history of English involvement in the war for Constantinople was constructed in the romance and propagandist texts collected by the newest would-be crusading power, the house of Burgundy. Here, English (and Scottish) chivalry took a leading part in rescuing the Greek emperor from his abject state, usually in partnership with French knights and the Burgundian court. Jean Molinet's *La Complainte de Grece* (1464) and (less explicitly) the romance *Les Trois fils de roi* (c.1460) harked back to an idealised fourteenth century, where co-operation between princes was always on the brink of obliterating the Ottoman *imperium*.[68] The vision was nostalgic, but the choice of English knights as protagonists felt natural enough in the fifteenth century – English recruits to Constantinople and the Balkans having carved out for themselves and their countrymen a reputation that reflected their crusade efforts with dazzling generosity.

---

[68] Ibid. pp. 201–38, esp. 221–5, 229.

PART II

As the first five chapters have shown, the English sources provide ample evidence of continuing personal commitment to fourteenth-century crusading. For many in knightly society, it could be the avenue to military prestige, public honour and spiritual gain. Not all cheated the dangers of campaigning. The humble William Toli, to give one example, had to endure the rest of his days nursing terrible wounds after escaping the battered crusade camp at Smyrna. Many others fared worse. But crusading's magnetic appeals and rewards remained forceful, despite the apparent languishing of the traditional Holy Land cause. In fact, as attested by the high levels of military investment, its prominence in English chivalry makes a case for a widening, rather than a diminishing, cultural role, at least among the upper ranks. The popularity of the theme across romance literature, in noble self-representation and knightly piety, and across many other facets of military culture enabled active participants to draw on various funds of moral support, and on the all-important respect of their peers. This very wide shadow cast by the crusade is no less significant a dimension than actual patterns of recruitment and military achievements, despite not often finding much discussion in conventional histories.[1] The second part of this book therefore explores some of the issues of culture, motivation and ethos that helped define crusading in the later middle ages, and sets the pattern of English military commitment analysed above within its proper cultural context.

The four chapters that follow pick out some of the more important themes. The diffuse nature of crusade campaigns in this period, with their shifting frontiers and sometimes informal patterns of promotion and recruitment, should not disguise the roundness of crusading's appeal in the milieu of the fighting man, both within local settings in county society and in the highest circles at court. Far from being confined to the hotter elements of chivalry, the cause was one with appeals and claims across political classes and social groups. Partly, this rested on continuities of crusade institutions, such as preaching, indulgences and papal bulls. Equally potent, however, were less tangible (but related) social pressures, including expectations of lineage, competition and public display. Some of what appears has already been introduced or touched on in earlier passages, but closer scrutiny of crusade and associated ideologies in domestic settings provides a more nuanced picture of attitudes and responses. One theme deserving special study is the concept of 'crusader kingship', and the

---

[1]   Of the seventy-six chapters that make up Setton's (ed.) six-volume *History of the Crusades* (1969–1989), for example, only three are specifically concerned with crusading's cultural footprint and roots in contemporary western society: two by Norman Daniel (on crusade propaganda and the political and legal theory of crusading), and one by Alfred Foulet (on crusade-themed epic cycles). More recently, where it attracts comment, the tendency (still) is to render enthusiasm for and participation in the later crusades as both mildly eccentric and nostalgic: e.g. Anthony Tuck's summary of Thomas, earl of Warwick's (d. 1369) crusade plans of 1364–1366 in the *DNB*: 'Thomas Beauchamp, eleventh earl of Warwick' http://www.oxforddnb.com/view/article/53085, accessed 20 Dec. 2011. Many other *DNB* entries do not know of their subject's crusading career at all (e.g. the Garter knights Nigel Loring, William Beauchamp, Reginald Cobham, John Neville).

expectations bound up in the figure of the king. How to handle the military elite's vaunting crusade ambitions (and campaign successes) was a problem each of the English kings had to face. As a focus of national knighthood and patron of English arms, crown wearers operated within relatively inelastic chivalric and political ideals. Their courts remained epicentres of military appeals and activism, and the crusade sentiment deposited there provided a vital cultural dimension to claims voiced on the political or diplomatic stage. More broadly, implicit throughout the discussion below is the question of crusader motivation and intent. Because crusading existed at the intersection of so many secular and religious cross-currents, in most instances reaching firm conclusions remains notoriously difficult. It is rarely possible to ascribe specific motives or instrumental influences. Even where the content of crusade vows reflected oath-takers' narrow concerns, e.g. the advent of illness, death of a spouse, lucky escape from battle, etc., decisions to take the cross and/or fight in the *hethenesse* functioned within a public context where matters of Christian piety, lay prestige and social ambition coalesced, serving multiple purposes and effects.[2] What the following chapters make clear is that an ethos of active crusade militancy did not operate in a vacuum, separate from wider social and cultural norms.

In some instances, individuals were obliged to take the cross, the church still regarding the imposition of the cross as appropriate punishment for a variety of sins. The case of the clerk John Lawrence is one such example. For his part in the scandalous murder of the bishop of Exeter at St Paul's in 1326, Lawrence was condemned to live out the rest of his life in penitential labour, undertaking pilgrimages to Santiago, Canterbury, Our Lady of Puy (Auvergne), and Boulogne-sur-mer. The capstone was to be his participation in the next general *passagium*, which, 'if he is still alive', would atone for his putting a bread-knife to the throat of a cleric.[3] Crusading as moral rehabilitation reached its boldest fourteenth-century formulation in Urban V's plans to make crusaders out of the outlaw *routiers* in the mid 1360s, turning the 'heathenish tormentors', as the pope called them (echoing the phraseology of Urban II), into 'defenders and prize fighters of the mother church'.[4] Of course, to carry any force, injunctions to take the cross depended upon the foreseeable departure of large-scale general crusades and were vulnerable to fading expectations. The patchiness of episcopal records makes it difficult to assess the pattern accurately, though survival of legal instruments from Despenser's anti-schismatic crusade hints at wide-scale application in the 1380s.[5] More heterogeneous factors held sway. Sir John St John took a sudden interest in embarking after accidentally eviscerating the earl of Pembroke at a royal

² E.g. see for vows: *CChW 1224–1326* p. 462; *CPL* vol. II p. 382; *Jean XXII: Lettres Communes* no. 60843; *Urbain V: Lettres communes* nos 11870–1.
³ *Reg. Hethe* vol. I p. 387. See Housley, *Avignon Papacy* pp. 156–7 for continental examples.
⁴ Housley, 'Mercenary Companies' p. 270 n. 77.
⁵ Churchmen from Oxfordshire were among those undergoing 'penitential labour' for various canonical irregularities: *Reg. Wakefield* p. 678.

tournament during Christmas 1389. He took ship with those crossing from England in the early months of 1390, preparatory to the duke of Bourbon's Tunis crusade.[6] Crusading continued to attract its share of fugitives, outcasts and men with spoilt reputations: Richard II's half-brother, John Holand, may have joined John of Gaunt's Castile crusade partly as penance for killing the earl of Stafford's eldest son, Ralph; and one of Bolingbroke's companions on the *reyse*, the crusade 'evangelist' Otto Grandson, took passage while under suspicion of the poisoning of Count Amadeo VIII in his native Savoy (1391). Absence in Lithuania failed to save his estates from confiscation. Men wanted by the county courts were attracted to the Hospitaller *passagium* of 1308–1313.[7]

Yet the majority of active participants made vows and embarked voluntarily, free from any scandal or obvious duress. A wide social contact with and acceptance of crusading ideas and formulae continued to frame individual responses, particularly within the martial classes, but at other levels of late-medieval society too. Emotions sporadically called upon to support fundraising or recruitment were incubated by liturgy, literature, preaching, canon law, the sale of indulgences and taxation. Chroniclers recorded or invented accounts of Christian battles against the heathen, amplifying propagandist and didactic themes. They quarried newsletters and first-hand information gathered from returning soldiers and other travellers.[8] Crusading infiltrated the darker corners of parish life. The guardians of morality in Kent punished sex crimes with fines payable to the *terra sancta*, for instance. Those guilty of misdemeanour could choose between undertaking a public penance in their local church, or depositing indemnity money in aid of Jerusalem (1335). Many, like Elizabeth Kirby, a widow of Dartford, may have thought a monetary fine worth it in exchange for a chance of greater anonymity.[9]

By tradition, pilgrimage provided the most direct link with the east – the historic focus of crusade idealism – and the continuing lure of the Holy Places testified to lively interest. The journeys of noblemen are best documented, but just as indicative are the urban citizens and working elites who allocated all or part of their wealth to poor pilgrims embarking on their behalf.[10] Pilgrim traffic via the Mediterranean islands of Cyprus and Rhodes was well established, with points of contact stretching back to the twelfth century in the case of Cyprus. A Famagusta cemetery was set aside for English *militi*, and the lasting mark of numerous other English pilgrims, churchmen and crusaders could be seen in church names, tombstones and shrines;

[6]   NA, C81/514/61211 (February); *West. Chron.* pp. 410–11; *CPR 1388–1392* p. 215.

[7]   *West. Chron.* pp. 122, 161; G. Stretton, 'Some Aspects of Medieval Travel' *TRHS* 7 (1924) p. 90; *CPR 1307–1313* pp. 117, 194.

[8]   E.g. *West. Chron.* pp. 444–9; Walsingham, *Historia Anglicana* vol. II pp. 197–8.

[9]   *Reg. Hethe* vol. I pp. 606–7.

[10]   *CPR 1408–1413* p. 113; *Testamenta Vetusta* vol. I pp. 56–8, 68; *Calendar of Wills Proved and Enrolled in the Court of Husting, London, A. D. 1258– A. D. 1688* ed. R. R. Sharpe (London, 1889–1890) vol. I pp. 640, 657, see Walter Stokwell 'peyntour' and John Hulegh 'hosier'.

even the French spoken on the island modulated in a way pleasing to English ears.[11] As such, events on the fringes of Christendom carried material significance not just for the polemicist or armed retinue. In London in 1366 the exorbitant price of cooking spices was traced to the disruption in oriental trade following the sack of Alexandria. Earthquakes in Rhodes were felt important enough to be noted in Wiltshire.[12] In literate circles, texts of crusade history and advice were collected and copied with increasing energy, often collated with pilgrim itineraries and (in learned society) theological attacks upon Mohammedan law. At St Augustine's, Canterbury, such writings were valued for their 'entertaining, consoling and instructive qualities'.[13] Proposed university courses at Oxford were to teach oriental languages as preparation for the next general *passagium*. As stipulated by the Council of Vienne (1312), it was expected that graduates would join the offensive as missionaries and spies in the unleashing of an espionage war (a *novum bellatorum genus*), forming the vanguard of Christian recovery (canon 11).[14] As a moral and theological principle, the argument for Christian ransack and re-conquest of the *hethenesse* helped form part of men's conception of the world.

[11]   See *Biblioteca bio-bibliografica della Terra Sancta* vol. VI pp. 445–8, an English pilgrim's account of Cyprus 1344–1345 (anonymous).

[12]   Walsingham, *Historia Anglicana* vol. I pp. 301–2; *Eulogium* vol. III pp. 237–8. The Malmesbury compiler of the *Eulogium* apparently included news of a 'terrae motus' on Rhodes (1364) because it conformed with John of Rupescissa's apocalyptic prophecy 'Vade Mecum in Tribulacione', which identified earthquakes and the overturning of eastern kingdoms as the signal for Islam's imminent defeat. He, or an earlier redactor, inserted a version of Rupescissa's prophecy into his manuscript. See L. A. Coote, *Prophecy and Public Affairs in Later Medieval England* (York, 2000) p. 136.

[13]   E.g. Cambridge University Library, MS Dd I. 17; BL, MS Cotton, Otho D V; cf. F. M. Powicke, *The Medieval Books of Merton College* (Oxford, 1931) pp. 128–9; M. R. James, *The Ancient Libraries of Canterbury and Dover* (Cambridge, 1903) pp. 295–6, 372–4. For St Augustine's see W. A. Pantin, 'The Letters of John Mason: Fourteenth-Century Formulary from St. Augustine's Canterbury' *Essays in Medieval History presented to B. Wilkinson* eds T. A. Sandquist and M. R. Powicke (Toronto, 1969) pp. 216–17.

[14]   The universities at Paris, Bologna, Salamanca and the Roman Curia were also to instruct students in eastern languages. See *Reg. Clem.* no. 8634 (13 July 1312).

6

Military Service, Careerism and Crusade

Against the backdrop outlined above, participants of the crusade formulated responses urged on by a range of pressures and incentives. The structure of martial culture itself – with close contact between prominent men and strong (often temporary) demands made upon personal and local loyalties – predisposed certain groupings to military mobilisation and co-operation. Formed of large pockets of active interest, crusade idealism was primarily a function of knights' personal relationships (hierarchical or otherwise), and the gravitational pull of friendship, and service and reward. To this extent, imperatives of finance, logistics and military leadership – not unbridled zeal or personal ambition – brought expeditions to the field and sustained them over the course of a campaign. As well as being channels of idealism and social advancement, ties of affinity, formal contract, kinship, geography and friendship were the constituent parts of any fourteenth-century military retinue. How these factors coalesced in practice illustrates, then, on a more minute level, crusading's reception on the ground, in the localities and across individual social networks. This chapter seeks to outline the opportunities and interactions that could be harnessed to the crusade cause. Indeed, insofar as it involved the engaging of such key relationships, campaigning under the banner of the cross could be valued as much for its chance to enact men's military and social links as for its special moral and historical gleam. The following pages set out this 'interior' view, laying out a possible blueprint of what might be described as late-medieval crusading's sociology, picking apart the more closely packed patterns of recruitment and chivalric response. Here the focus shifts from narrating the story of expeditions, military enterprise and award of battle honours, to the material circumstances of men's decisions to fight.

Push and pull: The DNA of a crusade retinue

The first of these instrumental pressures, the ties of lordship and affinity, were of paramount importance – whether formalised in the terms of indentures and paid contracts, or through patterns of tenurial or political dependency – and their effects

have been touched upon enough times in preceding chapters for the essential pattern
to be clear. The composition of the earl of Warwick's impressive military household
conformed to type. Warwick's petitions at the papal court in May 1364 show its
shape in outline, yielding new information on the composition of the earl's personal
affinity and his links within county society. Local stalwarts of the Beauchamp family
– Sir Robert Tuchet, John Durant, John Burnell, John Wylemer, John Torrington,
Sir William Breton and Nicholas Golofre, lord of Batsford (Gloucs.) – made up the
small core of knights and men-at-arms serving as Warwick's counsellors and military aides, each almost certainly drawing pay. The grouping was a mixture of fee'd
retainers, territorial clients and the cadets of lesser noble families seeking means
for advancement and a stable income. Nearly all had tenurial links to Beauchamp,
but the dominant characteristic was experience of Warwick's campaigns in France,
most recently in Gascony and on the Rheims campaign of 1359, though in some
cases stretching back nearly twenty years to the battle of Crécy (1346) and the siege
of Calais (1347).[1] Historically, there was occasional overlap with the Black Prince's
affinity, and liberty to indent with other lords, as John Burnell did with Lionel of
Clarence in 1361, but the group was fairly well defined and active as Warwick's men
within the counties where Beauchamp possessed most influence. Durant and Tuchet
were neighbours in Rutland; Burnell acted as counsel on behalf of the Breton family
in Warwick; Golofre's father had been the earl's appointment as under-sheriff of
Worcester in 1336 when he was a young man.[2] The treasurer of the earl's army, John
Blake, was a figure on the fringes of Beauchamp's administration at home, but the
crusade provided rapid advancement. His new responsibilities brought him to the
attention of the church authorities and an award of a benefice in the gift of the bishop
of Winchester to add to livings collected elsewhere. On his return to England, Blake
was promoted to a canonry and prebend at St Mary's, Warwick, the traditional reward
of senior Beauchamp clerks.[3] A grouping of fourteen esquires, messengers and grooms

[1]   Studies of the Beauchamp earls include A. Sinclair, 'The Beauchamp Earls of the Middle Ages' Phd
thesis (London, 1986) and Gundy, 'Rule of Thomas Beauchamp'. An entry in the papal registers, 'Rotulus
Comitis Warrewici' ASV, reg. supp. 40 fols 145ʳ ff and other papal documents yield detail on the composition of Thomas Beauchamp's military household. For tenurial links see Beauchamp Cartulary, BL,
MS Add. 28024 fols 191 (Wylemer) 192ᵛ (Burnell); NA, C61/76 m. 3 (Durant). The Tuchets fought at
Poiters with the earl of Warwick: *Register of the Black Prince* vol. III p. 208; and at Crécy: *CPR 1345–
1348* p. 520.
[2]   *Register of the Black Prince* vol. II p. 196 (Durant); *CPR 1361–1364* p. 50 (Burnell); *Catalogue of
Ancient Deeds* vol. VI no. 4580 (Burnell); *A Catalogue of the Medieval Muniments at Berkeley Castle* ed.
B. Wells-Furby ([Gloucester], 2004) vol. II pp. 842, 852 (Breton, Burnell); *The Victoria History of the
County of Rutland* ed. W. Page (London, 1908–1936) vol. II pp. 108–9 (Durant, Tuchet); *The Rutland
Magazine and County Historical Record* ed. G. Phillips (Oakham, 1903–1912) vol. I p. 233 (Burnell,
Tuchet); *CIPM* vol. IX p. 373 (Burnell, Tuchet); Sinclair, 'Beauchamp Earls' p. 320 (Durant); *List of
Sheriffs* vol. IX p. 157 (Golofre).
[3]   Register of William Whittlesey, Worcestershire Record Office, b716.093-B.A.2648/4 (ii) fol. 27ʳ;
ASV, reg. supp. 42 fols 145–63 'Rotulus Comitis Warrewici' (7 May, 1364); *Reg. Wakefield* no. 481.

completed the pool of travelling household attendants. Drawn mainly from families with roots in the town of Warwick or at Beauchamp manors, they ranged in standing from Stephen de la Chambre, son of a powerful burgess, who rose to become MP for Warwick (1383–1393), to the relatively lowly John Bourhulle, a 'citizen of Warwick' whose horizons subsequently shrank to that of a prosperous yeoman: his only other mark on history was to lease a mill at the Beauchamp manor of Salwarp (1383).[4] Given its local complexion, the picture is of a cohort of military servants whose service to Beauchamp was more or less automatic. A similar continuity of service was probably the norm in other noble crusade retinues.

To this most basic unit of military organisation were added the interlacing households of Thomas Beauchamp's son William and his formidable half-brother, Sir John Beauchamp. Ralph Basset, lord of Sapcote, a soldier whose record of service with the earl of Warwick dated from at least 1346, also counted among the earl's inner circle, his military household figuring among the unnamed thirty esquires and attendants for whom the earl also reserved special papal licences.[5] The combined numbers of men-at-arms stood at around one hundred, probably representing a sizeable proportion of Warwick's full comital following. (It was well over half the total that indented to accompany Beauchamp on Edward III's Rheims campaign in 1359, for example.) Expectations that the earl should bear the bulk of the expense perhaps led him to draw up contracts with Peter of Cyprus and the crusade leadership, though this is not certain (see above p. 44. Other men of distinction associated their retinues for the purposes of the crusade. In addition to their direct dependants, crusaders quite naturally looked to their kinsmen, friends and acquaintances for support – ties of blood and friendship stirring in men sharp pressures for collaboration and mutual support.[6] As has already been seen, Beauchamp's expenditure soon became crippling, apparently far exceeding the means of his ordinary income. The pope recognised this when the earl was forced to retreat from Venice in late 1364. The loss to the Alexandria crusade was a severe blow, but his withdrawal meant escape from potentially ruinous delay while holed up waiting for King Peter's embarkation. When the crusade propagandist and chancellor of Cyprus Philippe de Mézières traced the blame for

---

[4] ASV, reg. supp. 40 fol. 179; Gundy, 'Rule of Thomas Beauchamp' p. 280; BL, MS Add. 28024 fols 13ᵛ, 72ᵛ, 76ᵛ, 98ᵛ, 146ᵛ, (Chambre family), 67ᵛ (Bourhulle). The exception was Beauchamp's messenger, Nicholas Mate of London, whose home was broken into during the earl's 1365 expedition to Prussia: *Calendar of Select Pleas* vol. I m. 19.

[5] ASV, reg. supp. 40 fols 147ᵛ (Basset), 177 (John Beauchamp), 179 (William Beauchamp); for Basset and Beauchamp see *CPR 1345–1348* p. 520; NA, C61/76 m.4; BL, MS Add. 28024 fols 104ᵛ, 149, 192ᵛ–193.

[6] Travelling to Prussia with Beauchamp in 1365 was his youngest son, William, for example. Two years later William returned to the northern frontier in the company of two elder brothers, Roger and Thomas. See above p. 77; ASV, reg. supp. 40 fols 113ᵛ (Ufford), 147 (Loring), 176 (Courtenay); Iorga, *Philippe de Mézières* p. 303.

the failure of the Cypriot crusade back to England, the setback joined a catalogue of other English dishonours that seemed to stick in his mind.[7]

Compared to the military outer core of knightly expeditions, the passage of grooms, valets, cooks, clerks, falconers, tailors, messengers, smiths and other *domestici* goes largely undetected in the official record, though they constituted a significant presence, even in slimmed-down expeditions that required shipping to the east. In 1391 those taking ship with the earl of Stafford to fight the 'enemies of the Cross' in Prussia included Matthew Souterman, Henry de Boteler, Henry Hengesinan of his domestic staff and Master John Hinkeley, the steward. The meagre wages of Souterman and Boteler reflected their relatively low standing.[8] The Scots earl James Douglas took a large number of attendants, including musicians, on crusade to Spain in the 1330s, and the earl of Hereford took minstrels to the Baltic in 1363; it is quite possible that a musical troupe accompanied him into Mediterranean waters in 1365 and 1367.[9] Given the costs and hazards of transportation, the scale of manpower could be deeply impressive. In 1352 Henry Grosmont's baggage train was seen taking two days to snake past a single point in the Silesian (south-western Poland) landscape, and Henry of Hervod thought he counted around four hundred 'pilgrims', comprising Grosmont's knightly retinue and household, which is not unlikely.[10]

As with other military enterprises, a crusade expedition could stimulate new patterns of household service and strengthen existing ones. After returning from Constantinople in late 1368, John Dodenill, a servant of Sir John Mowbray, received promotion to the post of warrener at one of his lord's larger Yorkshire manors as a reward for his loyal service on crusade. Because of Mowbray's death on campaign, it required the intervention of the king, who held the Mowbray lands in ward, and the taking of testimony from 'men of repute' (presumably the remnants of Sir John's expedition), for Dodenill to prove his case. In May 1369 he was installed at Hovingham manor with wages of 2d a day. Another of Mowbray's attendants (William Burton) was saved from similar trouble by virtue of a charter issued before embarkation (October 1367). Clearly, Mowbray was using minor estate posts to reward those serving in his company, in some cases in advance of

---

[7]   ASV, reg. vat. fol. 9ʳ–9ᵛ. In his 'Oratio tragedica', Philippe de Mézières wrote of a knight (Beauchamp?), who, having abandoned the crusade of Peter of Cyprus, went to Prussia 'for the sake of knightly vanity' ('causa vanitatis milicie Pruciam peragravit'): Iorga, *Philippe de Mézières* p. 303 n. 8.

[8]   SRO, D644/1/2/4 mm. 2, 4. For the lord's 'viagio versus Prucem' Boteler took livery of 3s 9d and Souterman one of 4s.

[9]   Froissart, vol. XVII pp. 30–1; Paravicini, *Die Preussenreisen* vol. I p. 124. When in Prussia, Henry Bolingbroke paid his minstrels 2d a day: *Expeditions* p. xcvi.

[10]   Henry of Hervod, pp. 741–2. Henry Knighton, perhaps a partial commentator, says that Grosmont travelled with 'many of the realm's greatest men': Knighton, p. 111. During a diplomatic mission to Avignon (1354–1355), Grosmont travelled with 312 men-at-arms: a regal display of power. Fowler, *King's Lieutenant* appendix 3 p. 229. Grosmont's 1350 petition for plenary indulgences puts the size of his crusade party at two hundred: ASV, reg. vat. 211 fol. 190.

departure. Adding to the group's cohesion, such measures served to instil loyalty and enhance status, as well as lighten the prospect of lengthy absence from home. Equally common was the giving of cash sums to supplement retainers' daily wages.[11] Of course, this added to the expense of joining a crusade expedition, and each retainer was expected to earn his keep. Stafford's small stock of bows, arrows and slingshots purchased from the armourers of London and Wolverhampton suggests that his servants were intended to do some fighting. In 1391 a groom of Lord Bourchier outdid his noble-born companions, being the first to plant Henry Bolingbroke's standard on the pagan battlements of Vilna.[12] An effort to limit numbers and the costs involved is reflected in the stipulation of some military indentures that, when on the *chemyn sur les enemys Dieux*, life-retainers were to travel with the smaller entourage expected in 'peacetime'. In the case of Geoffrey Walsh, an esquire of the earl of Salisbury, this meant one *chamberlyn* and a single *garsoun* (1347). Other lords put the burden of extra costs, such as shipping and ancillary wages, onto their retainers. Evidently, such measures were intended to limit the passage of other ranks.[13] Where control of passage lay in the hands of a contracting party, captains were confined to taking only those numbers fixed by mutual arrangement. The English knights making passage with the duke of Bourbon in 1390 took pains to agree the scale of their participation before embarking from Calais, for example. It was in the interests of the contracting party to restrict the size of households and the number of unskilled fighters taking passage.[14]

Localities

Cutting across and interacting with ties of both lordship and kinship, another determinant factor in chivalric recruitment was the pull of local community and knights' sense of regional identity. Knights festooned their churches with decorative windows, inscriptions and memorials, both to advertise their status and blood descent, and to place their martial achievements within the context of the local county community and the circles of influence there. Where obvious ties of affinity or family were lacking, men grouped themselves with men from their own localities, or from neighbouring areas, crusading's deep dependency on local responses existing separately from national promotional campaigns or courtly recruitment – perhaps particularly so in

[11]   *Coucher Book of Furness* vol. II pt. 2 pp. 289–92; *CPR 1367–1370* p. 242; *CIPM* vol. XII no. 397; *CPR 1367–1370* p. 240 (William Burton). For an example of a cash gift see SRO, D644/1/2/4 m.4 (gift of 7s to William de Hare, for travelling to Prussia at the lord's direction).

[12]   SRO, D644/1/2/4 m. 4; *Expeditions* p.105.

[13]   *Indentures* nos 40 (Walsh), 85, 87, 93; Walker, *Lancastrian Affinity* appendix 3 no. 1 pp. 294–5. The theorist of chivalry Geoffrey de Charny (d. 1356) warned against a lavish retinue in case excessive spending limited time spent on campaign, or caused a knight to miss out altogether: *A Knight's Own Book of Chivalry* eds R. W. Kaeuper and E. Kennedy (Philadelphia, 2005) p. 55.

[14]   Cabaret d'Orville, p. 222.

the independent campaigns of the later middle ages. It is not easy to isolate and determine the precise function of such connections, but more or less discrete groupings of this type can be identified in a number of English expeditions, helping to explain the high enthusiasm displayed in some quarters, not all regions harbouring equal pools of interest. As already noted, areas of East Anglia and Yorkshire stand out in this respect, the county elite of the East Riding, northern Lincolnshire and the lands bordering the Wash drawing upon particularly rich traditions over the course of the thirteenth and fourteenth centuries. In Yorkshire, prominent baronial and knightly families such as the Latimers, Scropes, Furnivals, Fitzhughs, Nevilles, Ros, Littlebirs and Fauconbergs could boast active crusaders within their ranks, in some cases multiple generations, and the pattern was replicated within the gentry classes, among local names such as Mauleverer, Goddard, Boynton, Dautre and Ryther, attesting to an impressive depth of participation. These areas were traditionally fertile recruiting grounds for royal armies and the greater magnates. Loyalty to the peer group and competitiveness across local social circles were twin enticements to action. An additional factor, particularly in relation to the Baltic crusade, may have been eastern England's extensive economic and cultural links with the seaboard and provinces of northern Europe. Vogue for the northern frontier travelled smoothly across such regional and commercial lines, its signature left in patterns of recruitment and trade, and even in modes of church design.[15]

Promoters of the *negotium crucis* were also sensitive to the regional complexion of the crusade. In their periodic fundraising rounds of 1320 to 1350, the Order of St Thomas of Acre repeatedly targeted the northern counties of Yorkshire and Lancashire, and judging from the trickle of clerical recruits joining the brethren at Nicosia, membership of the Order may have possessed a distinctive northern identity, much like the English Hospitallers. In 1357 two clerics of York diocese watched their companion, Richard de Tickhill, *capellanus*, being incepted as a brother of the Order in Cyprus.[16] Similarly, the indulgence sales of the 1380s and 1390s raised conspicuously large sums from Lincolnshire and southern Yorkshire. One well-trodden preacher's route in 1399 followed a circular itinerary around towns to the south-east of Boston, before passing through Boston and reaching Louth and Grimsby in the north. Passing through smaller places such as Gedney, Horncastle and Kirton, crusade

---

[15] On the nature of chivalric and military identity among the gentry see P. R. Coss, *The Origins of the English Gentry* (Cambridge, 2003); Keen, *Origins*; C. M. Barron, 'England and the Low Countries' *England and the Low Countries in the Late Middle Ages* eds C. M. Barron and N. Saul (Stroud, 1995) pp. 1–2. An example of church design is the 'English' basilica at Marienwerder (1320–1340): Rowell, 'Baltic Europe' p. 733.

[16] *Reg. Melton* p. 23; Hobhouse, 'Register of Roger de Norbury' p. 270; *Reg. Kirkby* vol. I p. 9; *The Register of Gilbert Welton, Bishop of Carlisle, 1353–1362* ed. R. L. Storey, Canterbury and York Society (Woodbridge, 1999) p. 104. The northern clergy were Robert Swillington, a canon, and Richard de Chatesby, priest: *Documents nouveaux* pp. 362–3. For northern recruitment to the Hospitallers see Luttrell, 'English Contributions to the Hospitaller Castle at Bodrum' p. 164 and references there.

preachers visited the parishes and manorial communities which had produced active crusaders in the 1360s and 1390s: this was the backyard of men such as Anthony Lucy, John Multon and Philip Limbury, likely indicating a fruitful relationship between church propaganda and local responses.[17] Another traditional source of manpower and money, the citizenry of London, could be seen acting in concert following promotion of the Hospitaller *passagium* of 1308–1313 (see below pp. 137–8), and recruits for the Smyrna crusade were optimistically sought in the capital's suburbs in 1346. Less conspicuously, London shipping took part in the Portuguese attack upon the Mahgriban port of Ceuta in 1415, despite Henry V's prohibition on English involvement. With each fresh appeal, whether of national or minor significance, the London churches, and particularly St Paul's – a primary public space of London – retained their place as centres of propaganda and fundraising.[18]

It is possible to see other considerations of geography and locality in crusaders' devotional concerns and material preparations. Thomas Beauchamp's desire to elicit individual grants of plenary indulgence for his crusade retinue and other household members went beyond obvious niceties, extending to those living under his patronage within the earl's 'country' at home, such as the womenfolk of his companion knights (in John Torrington's case, his mother), and senior estate officials such as Robert Mile, William Morton and Richard Piriton, men of high standing in governmental as well as local circles. The earl also presented a number of family clerks for preferment and canonical dispensation.[19] Magnates commonly used petitions at the curia to advance the interests of their dependants, particularly clergymen, but in his capacity as crusade captain Beauchamp sought to secure a share in spiritual privileges for other elements within the local polity as well as those closely associated with his domestic power. Thus the prominent Botetourt, Botiller and Peyto families – whose land banded Beauchamp manors in the north and west – were counted among the beneficiaries of the apostolic crusade grant, as were men of lesser substance, like Sir John Harley of Pershore, Sir Walter Shakenhurst, a former sheriff of Worcester, and the relatively obscure Thomas Stok and John Vesey, whose share in Ashorne manor (Warks.) was purchased by the earl in the late 1350s.[20]

The impression is of a blanket award across all Warwick's clients, acquaintances, allies and local agents, the purpose to stimulate local enthusiasm for the earl's crusade enterprise and to foster goodwill. It reinforced traditional hierarchical and

[17]   See above p. 114 n. 64.

[18]   'Londoniensis' p. 156; *Reg. Hethe* vol. II pp. 770–5; Walsingham, *Chronica Maiora* pp. 199–206. At Ceuta 'Mundo', a wealthy London merchant, supplied four or five ships complete with 'many archers': P. E. Russell, *Henry the Navigator: A Life* (New Haven, 2000) pp. 30–1, 377; *Reg. Baldock* pp. 134–5.

[19]   ASV, reg. supp. 40 fols 145–7, 179. Mile was the earl's steward and receiver-general, and warden of the collegiate church of St Thomas in Stratford; Morton was the countess's treasurer; Piriton, a former chamberlain of the exchequer, was Beauchamp's general-attorney. His tomb was placed next to that of John Beauchamp's in St Paul's: Gundy 'Rule of Thomas Beauchamp' pp. 280–5.

[20]   *Urbain V: Lettres communes* nos 8664, 8666–701, 8703–16; BL, MS Add. 28024 fol. 104ᵛ (Vesey).

ceremonial bonds. In the case of Sir John Botetourt it may have been an attempt to steady troubled relations. Stewarded in this way, the sympathies of local men may have helped cultivate a sense of corporate interest and mutual gain, further enhancing Beauchamp prestige within the north midlands. It possessed similar effects to the special prayers and liturgies published in their churches by other nobles embarking against the 'enemies of the cross'.[21] This local dimension appealed to men's sense of pre-eminence and patriarchy, and, as a corollary, knowledge of knights' far-flung exploits circulated within provincial society. Sir John Roches' neighbours prevented his Hampshire estates from falling into the hands of the escheator after testifying that it was generally known the knight was alive and well *in partibus transmarinas*, two years after embarking with the Hospitallers (1311). The Ely chronicler paid lavish attention to the expedition of some Cambridge knights, partly because of a miraculous sighting of St Æthelreda, but also because it involved an important gentry family whose main residence was close to Ely cathedral. Their campaign in Spain also blotted out the other local-interest story of 1348–1349, the wildfire advance of the Black Death.[22]

Loyalties

Crusade recruitment ran through other social spheres and contexts, besides those served by lordship and the ties formed in kin networks and by geography. It is possible that membership of the Coventry town guild of the Holy Trinity served to concentrate chivalric aspirations in 1390. Heavily subscribed with aristocratic influence (its patrons included John of Gaunt, Thomas Woodstock, John Holand and the earl of Northumberland), several of Richard II's knights joining the duke of Bourbon's crusade were enrolled on its register. Guild membership need not have implied active social or even ceremonial connections – though it often did – but it provided yet another focus for competition and class pride, as well as equipping would-be crusaders with useful banking and mercantile associations.[23] Contact between knights and esquires in other settings helped lay grounds for co-operation and heightened idealism. Some close-knit affiliation bound a group of forty (unnamed) English knights who, with their followers, clubbed together to build and garrison a fortified refuge for Christian converts on the Lithuanian border in 1349. It conformed to the Teutonic Order's policy of studding the frontier with defensible positions, and because the group had assigned land and rents (presumably in England) to support a chapel and Catholic mission, details of the scheme were tendered at the papal camera.

---

[21]   Although married to Beauchamp's sister, Botetourt was apparently behind a string of break-ins across the earl's Worcestershire parks and warrens between 1364 and 1366: *CPR 1364–1367*, pp. 359, 367.

[22]   *CPR 1307–1313* p. 379; NA, C54/129 m. 31; *CCR 1308–1313* p. 366 (20 August 1311); 'Continuatio Historiae Eliensis' p. 653.

[23]   *Register of the Trinity Guild* vol. I pp. 11, 27, 76, 77.

Allocation of money, the foundation of a Catholic mission, a chaplaincy to celebrate divine office, a full-time garrison, and the administration of domestic fundraising and indulgences is an indication of the scale of their ambition. While perhaps taking inspiration from Edward III's foundation of the Garter (April 1349), it reflected an outlook quite at a tangent to the crown's all-consuming war effort. The finer detail is lost, and first the knights had to blaze a trail through the Lithuanian *wildernesse* to find an appropriate site, but the pooling of resources in this way, the divisibility of responsibility, and the threshold for admission to the grouping (sponsorship of one month's salary for a garrison soldier) strongly suggest some type of sworn association between the knights, possibly the existence of a chivalric confraternity, or the genesis of one.[24] Chivalric fraternities were rare in English military life, but in the process of preparing their papal petition the knights were apparently well versed enough in chapter statutes and regulations to convince church lawyers of their foundation. It perhaps calls to mind the much more glamorous continental chivalric orders, such as the Order of the Tiercelet and the Order of the Ship, established later in the fourteenth century and espousing a strong crusading ethos.[25]

A more minute bond between military recruits is occasionally seen in the sources. The special partnerships of brotherhood-in-arms, and the swearing of oaths of mutual protection, helped to safeguard embarking crusaders against a variety of pitfalls, with binding agreements that envisioned the sharing of the costs of war, as well as its profits and dangers. It is easy to see what attraction such bonds might hold for men engaging in the crusade – especially those setting out on expeditions or pilgrimages outside the protective casing of a magnate affinity, or on particularly tenuous financial footing.[26] Such relationships, with their kin-forming and occasionally pietistic elements, could themselves be the framework for idealism. One famous pairing, Bertrand du Guesclin and Sir Hugh Calverly, conceived of their alliance with Henry Trastamara in 1366 as an attack upon Muslim Granada as well as upon Castile, for example. They went to the trouble of drawing up an indenture in order to accommodate Trastamara's promise to crown Guesclin as king of Granada, discarding their usual division of spoils (three parts to the Frenchman, one part to Calverly). If, 'by the grace of God', Granada did indeed fall, Guesclin was to take possession of the whole kingdom in his right as king, while the fortresses and ports on the southern rim of Granada, those 'que le roy de Belmarin tient per deca la mere', were to be put into Calverly's hands 'without any partition'. The Englishman was also promised a huge war indemnity from the king of

---

[24]   The knights were granted a licence to establish a perpetual chantry with five priests within their 'castrum in confinibus spurcie' (October 1349). ASV, reg. vat. 194 fol. 330ʳ; ASV, reg. supp. 21 fol. 9ʳ; *CPL* vol. II p. 331; *CPP* vol. I p. 176.

[25]   D. J. D. Boulton, *The Knights of the Crown* (2nd edn, Woodbridge, 2000) pp. 229–32, 241–2, 252–61, 306; Keen, *Chivalry* pp. 194–5; cf. N. Housley, 'Politics and Heretics in Italy: Anti-Heretical Crusades, Orders and Confraternities, 1200–1500' *Journal of Ecclesiastical History* 33 (1982) pp. 193–208.

[26]   M. H. Keen, 'Brotherhood-in-arms', *Nobles, Knights and Men-at-Arms* pp. 43–62; cf. Düll et al. 'Faithful unto Death' pp. 179–83.

Aragon. Very likely these dreams were not very sincere – though Calverly's appeal to Peter IV of Aragon for twenty galleys to go against the coasts of Granada indicates a desire to achieve something against the Moors. More important here was the knights' oath, 'on the Gospels', to uphold each other's rights to military gains and conquests against all men (save their liege-lords), and to so maintain the interests and rights of their heirs, laying a firm legal basis for military co-operation and shared liability.[27]

In practice, the division of spoils was a problem rarely encountered by fourteenth-century crusaders (though considerable riches were carried off after the sack of Alexandria in 1365 and large sums extorted from the inhabitants of al-Mahdiya in 1390). More likely was the problem of raising adequate finance in the first place, or funding ransoms in the event of capture. The agreement reached between Alexander Stewart of Swaffham and George Douglas in 1390 was probably indicative of a formal fraternal association, Stewart agreeing to compensate Douglas to the tune of 1000 marks or furnish two armed substitutes (who should be 'without reproach') in the event that he failed to muster with his companion in the Tunis expedition. The prospect of illness (mentioned here) or the occurrence of some other unforeseen obstruction was the operative factor, either party unable or unwilling to bear the cost of embarking alone. In larger military projects, such an association perhaps reflected the desire for collective liability, where the sealing of individual agreements with an expedition leader could expose knights to financial risk or penalty; equally, the design may have been a way of underwriting a solemn oath, partly as an expression of intent, but also as a measure of trust – important where promises of joint enterprise carried a fragile emotional or ceremonial charge. As already noted, the origins of the pledge may have been a tournament at Smithfield or St Inglevert, where English, French and Scots knights were at close quarters.[28]

As well as longer-term patterns of service, like that shared between companion-knights and crusaders Hugh Hastings and William Beauchamp, religious ideology could be grounds for companionship in arms. The sworn knights John Clanvow and William Neville apparently travelled together in this capacity, as sympathisers with Wyclif's teachings as well as royal envoys. Their mission was cut short with the sudden death of Clanvow near Constantinople, probably a victim of plague, and within a few days Neville died too, common report claiming that it was because of a broken heart. The unusual iconography of their joint tombstone set up in Pera, showing their coats of arms impaled, a style usually reserved for marshalling the arms of a husband and

---

[27]   Russell, *English Intervention in Spain* pp. 41–9; K. A. Fowler, 'Deux Entrepreneurs militaires au XIVe siècle: Bertrand du Guesclin et Sir Hugh Calveley' *Le Combattant au Moyen Age* (2nd edn, Paris, 1995) pp. 254–5.
[28]   BL, MS Add. 15644 fol. 3ᵛ; see above pp. 59–60, 63.

wife, commemorated the pair's loyalty.[29] The sentiment perhaps belonged more to the realm of poetic, literary romance than the world of Hugh Calverly or Alexander Stewart, but it exposes the intense bond that artificial kinship was supposed to carry. Because the crusade cause involved precisely those elements which mattered most to the chivalric mind – reputation, prowess and a prospect of Christian salvation – there was a clear premium among participants on the type of fidelity shared between the likes of Clanvow and Neville, and that diligently brokered by Calverly and Guesclin. Men wanted confidence that those about them would see to the discharge of their vows in good faith, upholding their prestige on earth and preserving the health of their souls. This was also the expectation of Sir John Dautre (d. 1313), who appointed his familial brother, Roger, to fulfil his outstanding crusade obligations, bequeathing his military wardrobe, £20 and other goods, on the understanding that, on John's death, Roger would promptly embark on campaign in the east.[30]

Of course, superseding all competing military loyalties – in theory at least – was duty to the crown, and, by convention, the king's permission was required before any of his subjects could leave the realm on campaign. A variety of factors could influence the decision to grant a chancery licence. Control seems to have been strictest in relation to the king's immediate kinsmen, especially heirs to the throne. It was probably no coincidence that none of Edward III's three adult sons ventured into the *hethenesse* during the 1360s, a period when so many of their closest associates and other leading lights of English chivalry were doing so. As a young man, John of Gaunt seemed to take interest, stipulating provision of military service against the 'enemies of God' in the contracts drawn up with his growing pool of retainers. Yet mounting pressures of government meant that, by the beginning of the 1370s, any such ambitions had to be postponed.[31] Later, 'out of religious devotion', Gaunt sent his sons, John Beaufort and Henry Bolingbroke, to join the Genoese-Bourbon expedition of 1390, possibly in expiation of an outstanding vow.[32] Similarly, considerations of government may have factored in Richard II's attitude to the crusade plans of his senior male relatives. The

---

[29] For Hastings and Beauchamp see Chandos Herald, *Life of the Black Prince* lines 2246; for Clanville and Neville see NA, C76/75 mm. 2, 3; NA, C81/1057/29; NA, C81/514/6150; *Diplomatic Correspondence* no. 145 p. 98; *West. Chron.* p. 480; Düll et al. 'Faithful unto Death' pp. 174–90.

[30] *Registrum Palatinum Dunelmense* ed. T. D. Hardy, r.s. 62 (London, 1873–1878) vol. IV p. 497.

[31] E.g. Hugh Hastings (1366): Walker, *Lancastrian Affinity* appendix 3 n. 1; John Neville (1370): *Indentures of Retinue with John of Gaunt, Duke of Lancaster* ed. N.B. Lewis, Camden Miscellany 22 (London, fourth series 1964) pp. 88–9. Both bannerets, Lord Neville and Hugh Hastings, were among Gaunt's most senior military officials. According to testimony heard in the Court of Chivalry, Hastings (d.1369) first raised his banner in a war *sur les Sarrazynes*. It is difficult to tell when this may have been. See Grey vs. Hastings, CA, MS Processus in Curia Marescalli vol. I no. 441. Neville crusaded with Gaunt's father-in-law, Henry Grosmont, in 1352, as did another banneret in Gaunt's service in the 1360s, Sir Thomas Ufford. See above p. 75 n. 8.

[32] Froissart, vol. XIV p. 156; *Chronique du Religieux de Saint-Denys* vol. I p. 635; Mirot, *Siège de Mahdia* p. 16.

duke of Gloucester at first anticipated opposition. In 1391 he waited until a session of the royal council had broken up before announcing his intention to journey to Prussia, declaiming loudly at the king in order to catch the attention of sympathetic council members.[33]

Rigid conditions could be attached to royal licences. In November 1367 among the tightly knit group of northern knights and esquires who departed *ad partes pruez*, three men – Thomas Southeworth, Richard Mauleverer and Thomas Boynton – were required to provide surety that they would depart within a month, and that they would return by the following midsummer.[34] A stern caveat was appended to their licences, warning that none of the king's hostages could be taken out of the realm by virtue of the king's licence, and, more unusually, that the men were to be vigilant against taking abroad any newsletters, transcripts 'or anything else with writing' that might damage the interests of the realm, or the interests of Edward III's subjects. A final clause stipulated that the grouping could make only one crossing during the lifetime of the licence, denying the men opportunity for preparatory excursions to Calais, the Low Countries or anywhere else.[35] Such restrictive terms were unfamiliar and can probably be linked to the government's anxiety at deteriorating relations with France. With Southeworth and friends an act of espionage was unlikely, but the danger of the group or their belongings falling prey to capture or attack while en route to the Baltic was real enough.[36] Such considerations dictated a cautious approach. Edward III's ordinance on hostages is less unusual, and was probably issued with an eye to the rich gains recently taken by the Black Prince's men at the battle of Nájera (April 1367). The wealth washing about from the prince's capture of two thousand ransomable prisoners perhaps explains the ease with which Mauleverer, a younger son (and not yet a knight), managed to raise a lavish £40, and equip a retinue of five.[37]

Above all, the king required the services of his subjects for his wars, and, as has been seen, at various points in the fourteenth century the demands of campaigning at home weighed against larger participation in a crusade. The internal military emergencies of Edward II and Henry IV ruled out the giving of large-scale support to crusading. The dilemma evoked by the writer of *Annales Henrici Quarti* in the early 1400s, for instance, as the king withdrew an offer of English crusaders for the ruler of

---

[33]   *Eulogium* vol. III p. 419; *CPL* vol. VI p. 170; *West. Chron.* p. 479.

[34]   From Yorkshire: John Dautre, Richard Mauleverer, Thomas Boynton, John Goddard, Thomas Fitzhenry, William Dalleson. From Lancashire: Robert Urswyck, Thomas Southeworth, William Scrope of Bolton. From Lincolnshire: John Multon, Richard Welby, Antony Lucy. From Staffordshire/ Derbyshire: William Furnival. See above p. 80.

[35]   *CPR 1367–1370* pp. 64–5; but following MS roll NA, C66/276 m. 10[d].

[36]   In 1352 Henry Grosmont's baggage train was sacked by a gang of Westphalian knights: Henry of Hervod, pp. 741–2. Forty years later John of Gaunt wrote to Wladyslaw II of Poland to seek the release of two knights (Thomas Rempston and John Clifton) seized in Poland on their return from Prussia (March 1391): *Diplomatic Correspondence* p. 218.

[37]   Russell, *English Intervention* pp. 105–6; *CPR 1367–1370* p. 64.

Byzantium, chimed closely with Henry III's well-known protests at crusade preaching reported by Matthew Paris (which in the chronicle tradition of St Albans it was probably supposed to). Hemmed in on every side, with insurgents in Scotland on the one front and enemies in Wales and Ireland on the other, the authorities could not afford the departure of even a single company of archers. Far-fetched or not, the stereotype of a kingdom emptied because of the crusade still carried force.[38] The needs of king and realm at such times caused the government to impose tight restrictions upon the movement of knights and men-at-arms. The writ issued by Edward II in October 1309, prohibiting 'all earls, barons, knights and other notable persons' from leaving the realm, was typical. Announced on the eve of his first expedition to Scotland, it served (unsuccessfully) to limit desertion and the problem of absenteeism. It also disrupted baronial efforts to join the Hospitaller *passagium*, despite earlier assurances of free passage. Without strict enforcement, however, such measures possessed minimal effect. The constraints of secular conflict apparently meant little to the English knights who journeyed to the Baltic in 1346–1347 (flouting a ban issued by Edward III at Calais), or to Sir Thomas Ufford, who repeatedly distinguished himself in wars of the cross but took no noted part in the struggle against France.[39] Harsher steps were taken in 1349, when Edward III ordered all his subjects to return home upon pain of imprisonment and forfeiture (how this was to work in practice is not clear). Whereas the port authorities had been lackadaisical in the past, chancery letters conceded, adventures *transmarinas* were now permitted only by royal licence.[40]

Formally, of course, the crown shared the aspirations of its subjects, cultivating an image of service to the cross as part of its martial identity (see below pp. 168–73 and 193–9). Thus in 1366 the Black Prince embroidered his alliance with Pedro I of Castile with the extravagant demand that the English, 'before all other Christian nations', should have the privilege of commanding the Christian forces in the event that Castile restart its historic war with the Moors.[41] As has already been seen, the court was, by habit, generous towards the private crusade enterprises of favoured knights. The illustrious Sir Jean Boucicaut (father of Charles VI's marshal), a prisoner of the French war, persuaded Edward III to give him parole to take a retinue against the 'enemies of the cross' in the Mediterranean in 1354. Granted a safe conduct for twelve months, Boucicaut was also authorised to import six hundred barrels of wine from the Languedoc to help offset his expenses.[42] Royal letters to the Doge and council of Venice, the Christian powers of the Baltic region and the Hospitallers at Rhodes

---

[38] 'Annales Ricardi Secundi et Henrici Quarti' *Chronica et Annales* p. 336; Matthew Paris, *Chronicon Majora* ed. H. R. Luard, r.s. 57 (London, 1872–1883) vol. IV p. 489.

[39] Paravicini, *Die Preussenreisen* vol. I p. 124. Ufford was made a Garter knight in 1360. For his crusade career see above pp. 43, 74–6, 88, 95.

[40] *CPR 1307–1313* p. 205; NA, C70/2 m. 4; *CCR 1343–1346* p. 351; Knighton, p. 107.

[41] *Foedera* vol. III pt. 2 pp. 122–3; Russell, *English Intervention* pp. 36, 39, 49, 63–9; and above p. 56.

[42] *Foedera* vol. IV pt. 1 p. 93. Captured at Agen (1352), Jean Boucicaut was Marshal of France (1356–1368).

smoothed the way for English crusaders. Messengers of the earl of Warwick petitioned the Venetians for the lease of war galleys, 'ob reverenciam domini regis Angliae' (July 1364).[43] Wards of court were permitted to enhance their reputations on crusade. Early in 1362 Humphrey Bohun, the young earl of Hereford, took the king's leave to go to Prussia, flanked by a group of Bohun retainers and trusted royal servants, including Sir Miles Stapleton, already a veteran of the northern crusade and a Garter knight.[44] There could be equal flexibility for knights in royal service. A few weeks after contracting to accompany Prince Lionel to Italy, for example, Sir Henry Beaumont was given leave to join his friends Lord Fitzwalter and Lord Hugh Despenser on campaign with the Teutonic Knights (March 1368) instead. The circumstances are unclear, but the opportunity was obviously unexpected; Beaumont had to borrow hurriedly from his patron, the earl of Arundel, to cover the cost of his bill of exchange, a banker's draft for use in foreign cities. Struggling for liquidity, Beaumont also shipped his private collection of gemstones and gold plate.[45]

Perhaps the single most significant factor in channelling chivalric crusade interest was experience of fighting in royal armies, and the sort of contact that came with service in various theatres of war. The vast range of English military experience and the abundance of related unpublished sources makes it difficult to be exact, but a strong sense of group camaraderie and continuity of service appears to underlie much of the crusade's ongoing vitality. The majority of known English crusade recruits were already seasoned warriors. Typically, they counted among the proportion of knights and esquires most actively involved in the crown's wars. Those planning to embark with Robert Fitzpayn in 1309 were veterans of Edward I's gruelling wars in Gascony and Scotland, as well as wardens of important royal castles and garrisons. The picture was not fundamentally different in later decades. A high proportion of recruits to the duke of Bourbon's expedition had established respectable military careers in the crown's large expeditions of the 1370s and 1380s. Thomas, Lord Camoys, served on at least six foreign expeditions in the years 1378–1392. When Froissart talked of men winning their spurs on crusade in the 1360s and 1390s, it corresponded with no general rule, unless referring to the belief that displaying prowess in the *hethenesse* was the proper way to prove one's true worth. Even in the case of Despenser's crusade, when the large numbers of clerical participants (making up as much as a fifth of the bishop's army) contravened military wisdom, a steady stream of noble and knightly recruits assured the expedition's status as a focus of authentic chivalry.[46] The point needing stress is that, almost without exception, the crusade war was a way of continuing active service, pursued for a blend of reasons: for its own sake, for wages or

[43]   Iorga, *Philippe de Mézières* p. 206 n. 8.
[44]   *CPR 1361–1364* p. 173; see above p. 77.
[45]   NA, C76/51 m. 8; *CPR 1367–1368* p. 132; *CCR 1364–1368* p. 473; Wigands von Marburg, p. 558.
[46]   Froissart, vol. VII p.145, vol. XIV pp. 154–5, 222–3; C. Paine, 'The Bishop of Norwich's Crusade: Its Origins and Participants' MLitt. thesis (Oxford, 1995) pp. 182, 326ff.

with some higher purpose in mind, but also as a habitual function of military society. Besides its patent religious and chivalric casing, its heavy cost – not who was doing the fighting – was the major qualitative difference.

Blurred lines, charmed circles

There was, however, another view. Discrepancies between the cultural milieu of the fighting man and the all-embracing social appeals of the crusade, with its general call for Christian repentance and self-sacrifice, could expose tensions at the heart of the whole enterprise. How to limit the massed involvement of participants unfit for war was a traditional concern for planners of the eastern crusade.[47] In practice, the rising costs of war and the increasing specialisation of military forces imposed their own limitations, but in the first decades of the fourteenth century, considerable numbers of low-born English supporters, possibly several thousand, nonetheless left for the east amidst scenes reminiscent of the popular disturbances of the twelfth and thirteenth century. The so-called 'Crusade of the Poor' of 1309 attracted the largest number of English recruits, stimulated by wide church appeals and indulgence sales. The epicentre may have been Germany, where chroniclers described a mass-movement taking shape in the wake of indulgences published for the Hospitaller *passagium*. But in England (and Ireland as well) enthusiasm spilled over when groups of urban dwellers began signing themselves with the cross and sought passage to the Mediterranean. Here it was hoped the church authorities would provide passage with the official western fleet.[48] In June 1309 a formidable multitude converged upon the curia. The continental chroniclers were largely unsympathetic, emphasising the violence visited upon Jewish quarters and town treasuries, yet pope Clement V took a more benign view, granting partial indulgences to all those who could not fulfil their vows because of a lack of ships.[49] Observers in London were impressed by the popular desire to rescue the Holy Land, though the haste with which burgesses and citizens were ready to abandon their homes and material possessions, and the fact that they embarked without electing a leader, struck some as improvident. The added psycho-

---

[47]   See, for instance, Marino Sanudo Torsello 'Liber secretorum fidelium crucis' in *Gesta Dei per Francos ... ed. J. Bongars (Hanover, 1611) vol. II pp. 74, 81, 90; Prince Hayton, 'Flors Historiarum Terre Orientis' *Recueil de historiens des croisades: Historiens arméniens* (Paris, 1869–1906) vol. II pp. 355–7.

[48]   S. Schein, *Fideles Crucis: The Papacy, the West, and the Recovery of the Holy Land* (Oxford, 1991) pp. 233–8; Housley, *Avignon Papacy* pp. 144–6; Ptolemy of Lucca, 'Vita Clementis V' *Vitae paparum* vol. I p. 34; 'Continuatio Sancrucensis Tertia' *Monumenta Germaniae Historica: Scriptores* ed. G. H. Pertz et al. (Hanover, 1826–1934) vol. IX p. 734; 'Continuatio Florianensis' ibid. pp. 752–3; 'Chronicon Elwacense' ibid. vol. X p. 39; 'Gestorum Abbatum Trudonensium' ibid. p. 412; 'Annales Gandenses' ibid. vol. XVI p. 596; 'Annales Cisterciensium in Heinrichow' ibid. vol. XIX p. 545; 'Annales Tielenses' ibid. vol. XXIV p. 26; 'Paulini' p. 266; 'Londonienses' p. 156; *Chartularies of St. Mary's Dublin* ed. J. T. Gilbert, r.s. 80 (London, 1884) vol. II p. 293.

[49]   *Reg. Clem.* no. 4400.

logical pressures of famine and an achingly cold winter may have contributed to the excitement. Talk of portents and aerial apparitions passed through the ranks.[50]

A more muted reaction met the so-called 'pastoureaux' uprising of 1320 in France, though assorted groups of low-born *anglici* apparently found passage across to Avignon and the embarkation points for the east, their aims, according to the chronicler Adam Murimuth (who was there), to recover Jerusalem and to murder the enemies of Christ. Perhaps fomented by elements at the French court, but roundly condemned by the church, the movement broke apart with the same violence and disenchantment that marked the 1309 demonstration. Wealthy laity and clergy were attacked and Jews massacred before the 'pastoureaux' were eventually dispersed by the secular authorities. The disruption caused not only to civil society, but also to the crusade plans of Philip V, made the zeal of low-born *crucesignati* look deeply suspect. To privileged outsiders, the episode was a double scandal: it devastated the countryside and upset the normal rule of lordship and secular authority. However, Murimuth's description of the English element as 'a multitude of herdsmen and middle-aged women' probably accorded more with his stiff view of criminality than with the social background of the participants, which although non-noble was likely to have been mixed.[51]

Indeed, beneath the literary veneer of religious excitement or moral distaste, the line between combatants officially welcomed by the authorities and wealthier elements of the urban and rural classes was probably thin. It is telling that many of the 'poor' in 1309 arrived at Avignon in time for the Hospitallers' official embarkation date (24 June), their supposedly slipshod organisation not hampering the ability to muster according to Clement V's timetable.[52] In England popular momentum gathered over the spring months, in tandem with crusade preparations made in baronial circles, lending the appearance of wider coherence. Respectability was cast over proceedings by the presence of churchmen readying to embark. In the south-east, senior clergy were instructed to take possession of benefices left vacant by clerics gone with the Hospitallers (1310), and those with rich livings held a realistic chance of gaining a crusade berth. The rector of Ellingham (Norwich diocese), for instance, vowing to set out 'personaliter in Terrae Sanctae subsidium', stood to gain the impressive sum of £100 after mortgaging his tithe lands, enough to equip himself with a

---

[50] 'Londoniensis' p.156; 'Paulini' p. 266. Shades of social revolt are evident in eyewitness accounts of preaching in the Low Countries: resistance against the church authorities was preached, property was held up as a communal gift of God, and martyrdom was promised to those dying on the crusade. Similar messages were probably bandied about in English cities, not least in London, where the activities of rogue crusade preachers caused significant alarm. See 'Continuatio Florianensis' *Monumenta Germaniae Historica* pp. 752–3; *Reg. Baldock* p. 134. On the frost of 1309 see *Chronicon de Lanercost* ed. J. Stevenson (Edinburgh, 1839) pp. 213–14.

[51] Murimuth, *Continuatio* p. 31; M. Barber, 'The *Pastoureaux* of 1320' *Journal of Ecclesiastical History* 32 (1981) pp. 143–66; C. J. Tyerman, 'Philip V of France, the Assemblies of 1319–1320 and the Crusade' *BIHR* 57 (1984) pp. 15–34.

[52] Schein, *Fideles Crucis* pp. 236–7; *Reg. Clem.* no. 4400.

respectable military entourage. In another example, the incumbent of Monks Colum (London diocese) received a lump sum (undisclosed) from a fellow churchman to vacate his vicarage and set out for the east, using special papal dispensation to avoid any taint of simony. Similar transactions and vows are recorded in other dioceses.[53] Licence for travel to the east was also granted to a number of individuals, such as Geoffrey Saleby, a 'surgeon' going 'in the service of God', and John Pynnok, a citizen of Salisbury, bound *ad terram Jerosolamitanam*, who, as men able to afford chancery protections, were probably wealthier representatives of the *vulgares* seen streaming towards the Mediterranean. Similarly, one Londoner's account of the 1320 'pastoureaux' has it that many participants donned rustic clothing merely as a disguise, and that they sprung *ex diversis patriis* as if by some prior command, actions fitting more with the well-organised and politically equipped than with the economically rootless or soft-minded.[54]

Such responses show the sort of obstacles which poorer elements might face if they wished to participate in a crusade. Despite what was popularly preached about God's plenty for *crucesignati*, for those who could afford passage across the channel, but no further, the crusade was a dead end.[55] A more ambiguous role seems to have characterised the involvement of women. Like their menfolk, aristocratic *crucesignatae* remained potentially valuable targets of propaganda and activism. In the fourteenth century the church could look back on the royal exemplars of Eleanor of Montfort (1240), Margaret of Provence (1248) and Eleanor of Castile (1270), who accompanied their husbands to the east, or at least part of the way, making various diplomatic and military contributions by virtue of their kin networks and political influence. The crusade zeal of Edward I's wife, Eleanor of Castile, stayed proverbial long after her death (1290).[56] When Queen Isabella and the women of Edward II's court took the cross in 1313, their conditional vows helped commit to the crusade a sizeable knightly following and considerable financial resources. Partly for this reason, the matter of her unfulfilled crusade oath remained a cause for public speculation deep into Edward III's reign.[57] Some canonists held that women might make crusading vows

[53]   Ibid. nos 2997, 4089; *CPL* vol. II pp. 43, 54; *Reg. Halton* vol. I p. 322.

[54]   NA, C66/131 m. 17 (Saleby); NA, C66/131 m. 5 (Pynnok); *CPR 1307–1313* pp. 96, 102, 163, 114, 117, 121, 180–1, 194, 224, 233–4. 'Paulini' pp. 288–9.

[55]   For examples of crusade sermons see John of Bromyard, 'Crux' (c.1340) *Summa Praedicantium*, BL, MS Royal 7 E IV and below pp. 146–53.

[56]   Margaret of Provence dissuaded the Italian fleet from abandoning Damietta after the disaster at Mansourah (1250). See John of Joinville, *Life of Louis* tr. M. R. B. Shaw *Chronicles of the Crusades* (Harmondsworth, 1963) p. 263; B. Hamilton, 'Eleanor of Castile and the Crusading Movement' *Intercultural Contacts in the Medieval Mediterranean* ed. B. Arbel (London, 1996) pp. 92–103.

[57]   NA, E30/1422 (notorial certificate of Isabella's vow); John of Saint-Victor, 'Memoriale' ed. M. Bouquet et al. *Recueil des Historiens des Gaules et de la France* (Paris, 1737–1904) vol. XXI pp. 656–7. In 1359 the bishop of London was obliged to publish a copy of Isabella's absolution from her crusade vow: *CPP* vol. I p. 605.

without the consent of their husbands or guardians, but the constraints facing female crusaders remained significant, particularly within aristocratic circles. Fourteenth-century papal bulls stipulated that discretion should be used in judging the suitability of female participants. Writing in 1389, and wanting to appear pragmatic, Philippe de Mézières expected high-born women to join the *holy passage* to Jerusalem, but worried about their vulnerability to the desert heat.[58] In reality, more pertinent outside the context of proposed royal crusading was the striking symbolism of female involvement, either as would-be military participants, or as a focus for chivalric and courtly display. In the jubilee year of 1300, for example, the noblewomen of Genoa tried to cement enthusiasm for an eastern crusade by pawning their jewellery and commissioning specially adapted suits of armour for their use in the east. Shaming the city's menfolk into action, the public display was partly motivated towards healing Ghibelline and Guelf divisions. Such associations were probably mainly limited to the sphere of courtly performance. They may also have been the root for the literary scenario of the knightly hero drawing blood with the aid of his armour-clad wife, a recognised motif of contemporary English romance. Certainly the mixed chemistry of the longed-for lady, knightly questing and male prowess was a commonplace in the world of chivalric fantasy. As will be seen, it could easily be overlaid with more overt crusading themes.[59] Of course, the most obvious direct experience of crusading for noblewomen was the absence of their menfolk on campaign. In many cases, special fortitude might be required to cope with the inherent emotional and financial strains. Time might be spent attending to religious devotions, maintaining the noble household, and ensuring that royal protections and other legal safeguards providing for the lord's absence on crusade were observed. The guardianship of male kinsmen was a common precautionary measure. Given the nature of the sources these aspects are difficult to reconstruct. Otherwise, noblewomen in England converted their devotional vows into cash for the crusade and remembered the captive Jerusalem in their wills. Lower down the social order, crusade vow redemptions continued to be made.[60] In the absence of a general *passagium*, the baronial campaigns in the *hethenesse* were inhospitable to female crusaders. The example of Lucy, an English sister of the Trinitarian Order who fought at the heroic defence of Rhodes in 1480, was exceptional, both by the standards of her day and those of a hundred years earlier.[61]

[58]   J. A. Brundage, 'The Crusader's Wife: A Canonistic Quandary' *Studia Gratiana* 12 (1967) pp. 425–42; 'Exurgat Deus' *Reg. Clem.* no. 2988; 'Ad commemorandum' *Register of Simon de Montacute, Bishop of Worcester, 1334–1337* ed. R. M. Haines, Worcestershire Historical Society (Worcester, 1996) no. 984; 'Salvatoris Omnium' *Reg. Langley* vol. III pp. 136–45; Mézières, *Songe du vieil pèlerin* vol. II p. 101.

[59]   T. S. R. Boase, *Boniface III* (London, 1933) p. 261. For a crusading example see Isumbras's wife, 'Sir Isumbras' *Middle English Romances* pp. 146–7.

[60]   E.g. *CPL* vol. II p. 383; *Testamenta Vetusta* vol. I pp. 56–9, esp. p. 57; *Accounts Rendered by Papal Collectors in England, 1317–1378* ed. W. E. Lunt (Philadelphia, 1968) p. 48.

[61]   HMC, *Third report* (London, 1872) p. 274.

When the call to action fell on richer soil, however, it is possible to trace the seams of crusade interest and recruitment that could radiate out from a single military household or individual nobleman. A common point of contact for several crusaders in 1309, for instance, was service in the retinue of the late Gilbert de Clare, earl of Gloucester, twice *crucesignatus* (1268, 1290) and a leading exponent of Edward I's chivalry. The military culture of his household incubated expectations of full-blooded involvement. Gilbert de Clare and his wife, Joan of Acre, Edward I's daughter, took the cross together in 1290 as part of a courtly grouping in partnership with the Savoyard Otto Grandson. Clare's daughter inherited similar sensibilities, leaving enough money for five armed men to fight in the east, 'for the destruction of God's enemies' (1363).[62] For knights moving in such circles, commitment reached beyond the normal ties of affinity and lordship. It reflected the specific martial ethos of a close ring of contacts and dependants. Various examples are available, including the formidable Henry Grosmont, Thomas Beauchamp, the Ufford earls of Suffolk and the Scropes of East Riding, whose crusade habits filtered across clients and retainers. The short career of Humphrey Bohun, ninth earl of Hereford (d. 1373), is perhaps the most illuminating. The core of his military household – men such as John Burley, Richard Waldegrave, Walter Devereux and William Lucy – performed multiple tours of duty in Hereford's crusade retinues, in Prussia, Egypt and along the shores of Syria, as well as acting as a cohesive grouping in Essex and Hereford, as the earl's feofees, charter witnesses and annuitants. Other crusade companions included noted regulars in Bohun retinues such as the Scropes of Masham and the Stapleton family.[63] Overlap with the personnel of court and the households of Edward III and the Black Prince meant that many of the earl's pool of servants and acquaintances already rubbed shoulders with the leading lights of English chivalry, but the particular brand of idealism espoused by Bohun, including disaffection with the state of affairs created by the treaty of Brétigny and zealous worship of chivalric war, struck high within his inner circle and across his social network.

A number of Bohun's friends followed him out of court on crusade. The eminent Sir Richard Pembridge took Humphrey's cue in 1368–1369, embarking for the northern crusade with a party of twenty-five knights. Already a highly decorated soldier, his recent elevation to the Garter – where experience of the *hethenesse* was commonplace – may have been an additional spur. With him travelled Bohun's annuitant Walter Devereux.[64] Bohun encouraged others, like John, Lord Mowbray, to make crusade vows, lending money on the eve of their embarkation, and there is evidence

[62] E.g. John Elsfield and Payn Turberville, above pp. 24–6; Lloyd, *English Society and the Crusade* pp. 59, 114; *Testamenta Vetusta* vol. I pp. 56–9, esp. p. 57 (Elizabeth de Burgh).
[63] For Bohun's retinue in 1362–1363 at Thorn and Könisberg see NA, DL25/1989; NA, DL25/1638; NA, DL25/1639; NA, DL34/1/27; cf. the earl's retinue roll for Edward III's final (abortive) 1372 expedition, NA, E101/32/20.
[64] NA, C76/51 m. 5; Paravicini, *Die Preussenreisen* vol. I p. 123.

that experience of Hereford's campaigns helped instil underlying attitudes. In 1383 Sir John Burley made clear his continued commitment to the *negotium crucis*, writing the Hospitallers into his will, 'for the saving of his soul, and the soul of his brother'. Mention of the prior's hall on Rhodes (the *Maison d'Honneur*) called to mind his own visitation to the island in the company of Hereford thirteen years earlier. Ties with the Order were strengthened through Burley's kinship with John Raddington, prior of the English Hospitallers for much of Richard II's reign.[65] Sir John Clanvow was another apprentice of Bohun and a native of Herefordshire. His high standing in the Bohun affinity by the time of the earl's death raises the strong possibility of an active role in Humphrey's expeditions of the 1360s. He (with William Neville) was among the first of Richard II's chamber-knights to plan a new foray into the *hethenesse* after the signing of the Anglo-French truce.[66] Similarly, in their own military households, Bohun's men added a fresh tier of crusade activism. Veterans of the Burley household joined John Beaufort in his campaign with the Teutonic Knights in 1394, for example. While the milieu was inescapably one where military records and fighting qualities were held up to intense scrutiny, the honour accorded to the headstrong Humphrey marked out the earl's affinity as a beacon of English chivalry. This was reflected in the remarkable success of many of Bohun's former associates in the households of Edward III, the Black Prince and Richard II, as well as the competitive acquisition of Bohun books and tapestries – some bearing crusade and romance themes – by royal brothers, the Black Prince and Thomas Woodstock.[67]

Hereford's identification with the crusade war was celebrated in more abstruse circles, in the output of John Erghome, reviser of the Bridlington prophecy, a figure with very strong Bohun connections. Commentating upon what he believed to be the concerns of his intended patron, Erghome assumed that the earl shared his and the Bridlington prophecy's view that peace was the ultimate purpose of the war with France, and that the ideals of Christian knighthood were best turned against the infidel. This was a message open to wider consumption, and may have been partly stock convention, but it was almost certainly trained specifically on Bohun's unfolding ambitions in the *hethenesse*, as well as the earl's supposed desire for moral and spiritual reform at home. Erghome threaded the theme into other writings produced under Bohun influence.[68] How closely this related to the sometimes fractious noble whose

[65]   *Registrum Johannis Gilbert, Episcopi Herefordensis, 1375–1389* ed. J. H. Parry, Canterbury and York Society (London, 1915) pp. 34–6; cf. N. B. Lewis, 'Simon Burley and Baldwin of Raddington' *EHR* 52 (1937) pp. 662–9.
[66]   Given-Wilson, *Royal Household* p. 162; NA, E403/531 m. 7.
[67]   E.g. Richard Eton, see above p. 85 n. 51. Devereux, Burley, Clanvow and Waldegrave entered Richard II's service as chamber-knights or life-retainers: Given-Wilson, *Royal Household* pp. 217–19; *Register of the Black Prince* vol. IV p. 476. For the dissemination of Bohun's library and hangings see Goodman, *Loyal Conspiracy* pp. 80–2.
[68]   *Political Songs of England* vol. I pp. 179–208, esp. 184, 197; Coote, *Prophecy and Public Affairs* pp. 139–44. On Bohun's literary patronage see B. Cottle, *The Triumph of English, 1350–1400* (London, 1969)

retinue caused obvious annoyance at Königsberg, and who itched for renewal of the French war, is hard to tell, but it accorded with the earl's general interest in chivalric and contemplative literature, and caught squarely the themes which would surface at Richard II's court in the 1390s. The same continuity was signalled in the activities of other royal knights drawn from Hereford's charmed circle. Sir Thomas Peytevyn was one such figure. He took leave of the teenage Richard II and a post as a chamber-knight to embark for Prussia sometime towards the end of 1384.[69]

pp. 41, 44 and the references cited there; also T. Turville-Petre, 'Humphrey de Bohun and *William de Palerne' Neuphilologische Mitteilungen* 75 (1974) pp. 250–2.

[69] Paravicini, *Die Preussenreisen* vol. I p. 125.

7

'All are truly blessed who are martyred in battle': Crusading and Salvation

While the competitive pressures of military society provided the platform for material action, and urged would-be crusaders on, a range of other incentives retained
important dynamic force. Predictably, church sources formed an unequivocal view of
crusader motivation and ethos, identifying exceptional piety as the primary characteristic in military recruitment. Papal letters described crusader devotion in visceral
terms: men's bodies were aflame with fervour; hearts fell sick at the gathering forces
of paganism; compassion for the Redeemer and love of the church flooded mental-
ities. Urban V referred to the mood descended upon English crusaders in 1364 as
cruciatum mentis, an agonised state of mind, or possibly a serene state of devotion. At
the curia such sentiment was more or less automatic.[1] Of course, there was another
view. Surveying the ranks gathered at Rhodes for Peter of Cyprus's crusade, Philippe
de Mézières diagnosed only vanity, avarice and guile. (Writing after the sack of
Alexandria, Mézières wanted to denigrate the crusade's western element.) Outwardly,
in crusade armies there may have been diminishing emphasis upon formal religion
and piety. The sumptuary legislation and other devotional regulations of twelfth- and
thirteenth-century crusades, for example, appear to have fallen out of favour in the
later period. Requirements of sober dress, abstinence and religious observance that
made a show of penitential purpose in the crusade bulls of Eugenius III, Innocent
III and Gregory X are generally missing in fourteenth-century crusade bulls, and
the leadership of churchmen in the *hethenesse* appears increasingly marginal, though
numerous lesser clergy accompanied baronial households on campaign. Noblemen
put their full finery on display for camp in Prussia and squabbled openly for the sake
of battle honours. Perhaps partly for these reasons, the piety of the later crusades is
sometimes cast in doubt. On the other hand, the language of pilgrimage remained
intact, and combatants knew what was expected of pilgrims. In her book of chivalry,

---

[1]   *Vitae paparum* vol. III pp. 87–90; *Urbain V: Lettres closes* nos 890, 898; ASV, reg. vat. 246 fol. 9ʳ;
ASV, reg. lat. 34 fol. 191ʳ. On the slipperiness of *cruciata* and other 'crusade language' see Tyerman,
Invention pp. 49–55.

Christine de Pisan (1410) reiterated crusading's penitential intent: 'the man of armes that deyeth in the were against them of evyl byleve ... soo that he be repentyng & sory for his sinnes: he goeth straygthe as a martyyr unto heven'. If there were changes in the corporate religious discipline of crusade armies, this probably reflected changing tastes in religious practice at large.[2]

Sometimes chivalric careers veered close to achieving the loftiest Christian ideals. In addition to his celebrated *aventures* in Egypt, Syria and Anatolia, the Gloucestershire knight John de la Ryvere was renowned for his exceptional personal piety. He converted the family church at Tormarton into a shrine for his impressive collection of relics, including a fragment of the True Cross and a vesicula of the Virgin's milk, probably bought on his travels through the Holy Land. His careful choice of chapel furnishings and specified cycle of masses and collects reflected an unusually sophisticated taste in liturgy and church decoration.[3] In spite of his military vocation, and his holding of various royal commands in the 1330s and 1340s, a great unease at the spiritual dangers of war reportedly stopped him from killing or maiming while on campaign. By his own account, he abstained altogether from fighting that seemed morally unjust. Instead, as seen above, as a 'pugil Christi', Ryvere put his sword to the service of the church, unfurling his war banner against the Turks and Mamluks in 1346 and 1347. Ryvere's acute sense of spiritual purpose again surfaced when he surrendered his worldly belongings and sought sanctuary as a confrère of the Dominican order, receiving papal dispensation to take holy orders in the 1360s. It epitomised the symbiosis between perfected knighthood and vocational life as vaunted by the church and in imaginative literature.[4] Others also perceived a thin line between pious knighthood and mendicant religion. Geoffrey le Baker, an avid reporter of Edward III's wars, knew initiates of the English Carmelites who had been among the crusaders present at Alfonso XI's siege of Muslim-held Teba (1330) for example. Higher up the social scale Humbert of Vienne substituted public rank for the Dominican habit after leading the Holy League of 1345–1347, and the zealous Mézières (another veteran of Smyrna) retreated to the Celestine convent in Paris after reaching middle age.[5]

Few practising knights shared Ryvere's moral vigilance, but crusaders of all ranks moved within an environment thick with outward signs of lay devotion. It was more than a matter of blandishing alms or beautifying family chapels. Reminded of the need to 'tranquillise the conscience', knights were shadowed by personal confessors and instructed in a regular diet of observances: vows, fasts, processions, expiatory

[2]   Mézières, *Life of St. Peter Thomas* p. 126; Christine de Pisan, *The book of fayttes of armes and of chivalry* ed. A. T. P. Byles, EETS o.s. 189 (London, 1932) pp. 282–3.

[3]   *Reg. Bransford* pp. 84–6; *CPL* vol. III p. 300. Ryvere was evidently an early enthusiast of the cults of St Anne and St Joachim, parents of the Virgin Mary.

[4]   For details on Ryvere's life see 'John de la Ryvere' *DNB* http://www.oxforddnb.com/view/article/92453, accessed 20 Dec. 2011; cf. *Clément VI: Lettres rapportant à la France* no. 1605; *Urbain V: Lettres communes* nos 11870–1.

[5]   Baker, *Chronicon* p. 41; Housley, *Avignon Papacy* pp. 34–5; Iorga, *Philippe de Mézières* p. 422.

masses, prayer, meditation, pilgrimage and modest dress. The sheaf of special religious privileges sought by English knights embarking on crusade reflected the formal preoccupations of aristocratic religion and provides a sense of their social influence as well. Next to the right to carry portable altars and appoint household confessors, petitioners sought licence to hear a first mass of the day before sunrise and in places under interdict, to host the religious at their tables, to prorogue or commute works of penance, and to adjudicate in a variety of ecclesiastical matters (presentations, rebuildings, enlargements, etc.) in their local parishes.[6] A great expansion of the penitential system, with increasing availability of full and partial remissions, was the background to fourteenth-century crusading. Grants of plenary indulgence at the hour of death (*in articulo mortis*) became particularly abundant after the pontificate of John XXII, awarded to Christians who received confession from a licensed chaplain when near death. It is difficult to agree with Housley that the church distributed these in a systematic way to facilitate crusade recruitment, though there was a high demand for such 'confession letters' among knights embarking against the infidel.[7] Rather, it reflected the premium increasingly placed upon personal religious instruction within knightly households, the wealthy classes entrusting their private confessors to confer spiritual grace and remit sins in the vicinity of the battlefield as well as in their inner chambers, a privilege traditionally reserved to crusaders but now spread widely across other military ranks. Generous terms for the Black Prince's army embarking against Henry of Trastamara in 1367 meant indulgences *in articulo mortis* were reserved even in cases where soldiers were involved in violent criminality, such as rapine and larceny. Whether salaried warrior, *crucesignatus* or both, raiders of the *hethenesse* probably saw such measures as a form of extra indemnity, in addition to the indulgences published in crusade bulls, and easily worth the cost of a private petition. Sceptics, on the other hand, wondered about the value of personalised pardon letters if they became lost or nibbled by vermin.[8]

Pulpit and cross

Despite the shifts towards a more diverse system of remissions and penance, as one of crusading's oldest institutions the charismatic preacher before a knightly audience remained central to perceptions of church organisation and devotional response.[9] It was one of the continuities associated with the age of the massed crusades. For most

---

[6]   E.g. *Urbain V: Lettres communes* nos 8861, 8875, 8881, 8885, 10869–72; *CPL* vol. III pp. 142, 560, 572, vol. IV p. 396.

[7]   Lunt, *Financial Relations* vol. II pp. 447–66 esp. 487; Housley, *Avignon Papacy* pp. 132–4.

[8]   SV, reg. avin. 162 fols 464ʳ ff 'non ex justo bello sed in comitivus ad publicam praedam existens vel alium violeanter aliena'; *Reg. Trefnant* p. 247.

[9]   See in general Cole, *Preaching of the Crusades*; Maier, *Preaching the Crusades*; id. *Crusade Propaganda and Ideology: Model Sermons for the Preaching of the Cross* (Cambridge, 2000).

contemporaries, the relationship between sermonising and religious fervour did not need much testing. Just as all successful battles seemed to turn on rousing words given before the assembled ranks prior to combat, so the call of the cross to the faithful was considered instrumental in galvanising military and chivalric responses. Emotionally charged, ritualised events, crusade sermons belonged to that category of public speaking credited with transforming an individual's moral outlook, altering the course of men's lives. Yet, as in earlier periods, English (and non-English) evidence of crusade preaching in practice is patchy. Preaching in aid of Despenser's crusade (1382–1383), John of Gaunt's expedition to Castile (1386) and the relief of Constantinople (1398–1400) won the wider attention of English chroniclers and other observers, but in the first half of the fourteenth century several large-scale promotional campaigns were also launched across the English parishes (1308–1313, 1333–1337 and 1345–1347), leaving a significant imprint on diocesan registers. Here the long-term shift in emphasis from the recruitment of men to the raising of money was supported by bureaucratic procedures designed to achieve cash donations and vow redemptions, eliciting mainly charitable responses. It was to tap into this trade that bogus preachers and collectors could be regularly tempted into the market.[10]

Even so, the milieu was not restricted to local mendicants or parish alms-collectors. Exhortatory sermons were still heard in the vicinity of battlefields. English and French knights were the targets of legate Pierre Thomas's sermonising in 1365. His words moved all camp-followers to tears, cleansed minds, and made the crusaders ready for bodily sacrifice on behalf of Christ, according to one appreciative eyewitness. His unyielding emphasis upon confession and the act of repentance caused men-at-arms who had (reportedly) not confessed for years to seek out their chaplains' graces. (It was even thought to have melted the hearts of Turkish mercenaries, their tents sited within view of the legate's preaching platform.) To his disciples, the preaching tour-de-force was confirmation of Thomas's saintliness.[11] In 1383 sermons encouraged Despenser's crusaders during their successful assault upon Gravelines in Flanders. Battlefield reports attributed the English victory to the preachers' promises of martyrdom to all *crucesignati* killed on the town defences, which instilled the necessary courage among those attacking enemy gates and walls.[12] Crusade sermons were also aired in courtly settings, before the assemblies of church and state. In 1313 Clement V's legate, Cardinal Freuville, developed the sermon theme of spiritual and physical renewal in his call to the cross before Edward II and Philip IV at Paris. The

---

[10]   See Chapter 2, n. 7 for 1308–1313. For 1333–1337 see *Reg. Melton* vol. III pp. 142, 144, 149, 152; *Reg. Montacute* nos 984–90. Transcripts of John XXII's crusade bulls (reissued by Benedict XII) are also found in Canterbury, Winchester, Lincoln, Salisbury, Bath and Wells, and York registers. See Haines, *Archbishop Stratford* p. 456. For 1345–1347 see *Reg. Hethe* vol. II pp. 770–5; Lunt, *Financial Relations* vol. II pp. 478, 559; John Purvey, *Remonstrance against Romish Corruptions in the Church* ed. J. Forshall (London, 1851) p. 57–66 esp. 59 (exploitative preachers).

[11]   Mézières, *Life of St Peter Thomas* p. 126.

[12]   Walsingham, *Chronica Maiora* pp. 88–9.

archbishop of Canterbury and the bishop of Winchester both preached on Edward III's crusade intentions during the spring parliament of 1332, commending the king's military and spiritual ambition. Sermons were almost certainly preached at the important Anglo-French peace conferences at Amiens in 1391 and 1392, where space was made for the charismatic crusade preacher and 'evangelist' Robert the Hermit.[13]

What preachers actually said in their sermons, and the sort of religious appeals made to the military classes generally, remains elusive. Literary accounts sometimes offer didactic reports of preaching's emotional force, or of the scale of indulgences available, but they reveal very little about the act of preaching itself or the content of sermons.[14] Possibly one reason for this is that preachers were normally expected to reserve their main strength for reciting crusade bulls. (In 1335 these amounted to over six thousand words – filling approximately one hour – and a faithful recitation probably left little space for embellishment.)[15] Crusade sermons were also academic confections, bound by conventions of genre and form, and valued as much for their scholastic, didactic and entertaining qualities as for their practical worth in firing emotional responses. By the fourteenth century a large market in preaching treatises, exempla collections and *florilegia* existed to supply a range of additional illustrative material.[16] So-called 'model' crusade sermons, contained in the collections of preachers such as James of Vitry, Humbert of Romans and Gilbert of Tournai, were the best known, supplying ready-made sermons which the working preacher could use as the basic structure for his own propaganda, and there was demand for such aids in England. Model sermons 'ad crucesignatos et crucesignandos' circulated within Worcester diocese in the 1330s, for example, perhaps in tandem with crusade bulls advertising Edward III's grand intended crusade. Also useful were the sermon anecdotes, collected in preaching handbooks and exempla collections, bearing the folkloric and moralist patterning of much contemporary preaching.[17] The audience

---

[13]   *Reg. Clem.* no. 9941; *Rot. Parl.* vol. II pp. 64–5; 'Rochester Chronicle' BL, Cotton Faustina B V fol. 60ᵛ; Murimuth, *Continuatio* p. 73; Palmer, *England, France and Christendom* pp. 180–210.

[14]   As the chronicler of St Paul's put it, to those contributing to the Hospitaller crusade publicised in 1309, Clement V 'concessit indulgentias culparum et poenarum quales a saeculo non errant auditae': 'Paulini' p. 266.

[15]   'Non absque grandi' (1333) *Reg. Montacute* no. 984; cf. the prolegomena of 'Exurgat Deus' (1308) and 'Redeor Noster' (1313) *Reg. Clem.* nos 2989, 9983.

[16]   E.g. the crusade-themed exempla contained in the widely used *Le Speculum laicorum: édition d'une collection d'exempla, composée en Angleterre à la fin du XIIIe siècle* ed. J. Welter (Paris, 1914) esp. pp. 33–6, 66–7; also the *Gesta Romanorum* ed. C. Swan (London, [1824] 1964) pp. 197–208, 224–6, 354–61; Stephen of Bourbon (d. 1261), *Anecdotes historiques, légendes et apologues,* ed. R. A. Lecoy de la Marche (Paris, 1877) nos 29–30, 99, 197; and, in the vernacular, John Mirk (c.1382–1414) *Mirk's Festial. A Collection of Homilies* ed. T. Erbe, EETS e.s. 96 (London, 1905) pp. 135, 142–6, 249–52. One of the most widely known English preaching-aids of the period, Robert Holcot's commentary on the Book of Wisdom, included a *lectio* on the crusade war (c.1335): K. V. Jensen, 'Robert Holkot's *Questio* on Killing Infidels' *Archivum Fratrum Praedicatorum* 63 (1993) pp. 207–28.

[17]   For 'ad status' sermons see Maier, *Crusade Propaganda* pp. 83–242. For Gilbert of Tournai 'sermones

for these, though, was probably largely limited to local parish congregations and the public vicinities of cathedral and abbey churches.

It is not possible to say this about the work of the celebrated English Dominican preacher John of Bromyard, however, whose spiky social commentaries and popular moralist style possessed an enormous influence over English preaching during the period, finding audiences amongst the lay and clerical elite. Bromyard's model crusade sermon 'Crux', in the author's widely circulated alphabetical compendium *Summa Praedicantium* (c.1348), has been strangely neglected by crusade historians.[18] First intended for crusade preaching, but also adaptable to feast days of the cross, it is not a strict record of what crusade preachers actually said, but its central concepts, images and arguments show what was expected to hold appeal for lay audiences and the military classes. Insofar as it opens a window on English chivalry's religious and secular tastes, Bromyard's text provides a valuable basic template for late-medieval crusading's devotional mentality. Formed of three expository sections – 'why the Cross must be handed out', 'the power of the Cross's defence' and 'the virtues required to receive the Cross's protection' – unity was achieved in the sermon's dominant purpose, which was to transition audiences from sentiments of anger, grief and awe to a state of emotional release and the impulse to act. The general purpose, as will be seen below, was to draw on entrenched religious and moral convictions, invoking a sense of knightly duty in defence of the faith.[19]

The sermon opens with a stockpiling of legal and biblical proofs to substantiate the legitimacy of crusading, an emphasis which presupposes a well-educated lay audience. Moving from the position that the Holy Land is the heritage of Christ, a rightful possession of Christians, not the Saracens, Bromyard establishes the larger precept that the pope has authority to punish all rulers who oppress the faithful, even in those lands never part of Christendom, reinforcing papal doctrine on crusades outside of the Holy Land. The destruction of life is not the crusade's ultimate purpose, yet as an act of defence, the killing of infidels is justified. The famous struggles of Christian history, from the time of Constantine and Heraclius, are provided to give context, showing the crusade to be a historic vendetta. Stress on concepts of theft and

---

ad status' see Worcester Cathedral, MS Cath. F. 36, MS Cath. F. 77, MS Cath. Q. 57. See also CUL, MS Peterhouse 200; Maier, *Preaching the Crusades* pp. 170–1.

[18] Briefly described by G. R. Owst in his *Literature and the Pulpit* (2nd edn, Oxford, 1961) pp. 174–5, 316. Bromyard's crusade sermon is overlooked by Maier in his important collection, *Crusade Propaganda*. See P. Binkley, 'John Bromyard and the Hereford Dominicans' *Centres of Learning: Learning and Location in Pre-Modern Europe and the Near East* eds J. W. Drijvers and A. A. MacDonald (Leiden, 1995) pp. 255–64; L. E. Boyle, 'The Date of the *Summa Praedicantium* of John Bromyard' *Speculum* 48 (1978) pp. 533–7. On alphabetical preaching aids see C. von Nolcken, 'Some Alphabetical Compendia and How Preachers Used them in Fourteenth-Century England' *Viator* 12 (1981) pp. 271–9. For manuscripts see T. Kaeppeli, *Scriptores Ordinis Praedicatorum Medii Aevi* (Rome, 1970–1993) vol. II p. 394.

[19] John of Bromyard, *Summa Praedicantium* (Vienna, 1484); but reading from BL, MS Royal 7 E IV fols 110ʳ–114ʳ (c.1350) and Oxford Bod. MS Oriel College 10 fols 31ᵛ–34ᵛ (1440).

trespass – Bromyard judges the whole of Islam to be in breach of Roman property law – invites psychological identification and heightens the sense of victimisation, a sentiment that breaks the surface several times.[20] Bromyard next gives a sequence of Old Testament verse with, as he puts it, proven value for preaching the cross. There is little commentary, but the effect is to demonstrate that crusades were part of the biblical framework of war ordained by God, and he is particularly concerned to show God's agency on the battleground. Chariots of fire, celestial hosts and horsemen arrayed in white are held up as evidence of the sanctity of Christian violence. Such visions, Bromyard suggests, help to fortify those soldiers fearful of the enemy's vast numbers. He also cites the well-known exemplum from crusading history, where the outnumbered First Crusaders at Antioch defeat the Saracens with the help of an angelic throng. The strident language here leads to a contemplation of the fanatic Christian martyr, and Bromyard gives short shrift to the anxieties of knights reluctant to fight, adducing St Bernard's words from *De laude novae militae*, 'All are truly blessed who are martyred in battle', and insisting that 'the fewer you are, the more glorious will be your victory, or your martyrdom!'[21]

More space is reserved for discussion of the spiritual profit attached to the crusade, in many ways the conventional centrepiece of sermon propaganda. To demonstrate the dramatic benefits of crusade indulgences, Bromyard incorporates a number of traditional sermon exempla into his text, most with military subjects. The outline of two of them are as follows. First, a ship transporting a retinue of crusaders sinks with all hands lost. Red crosses miraculously mark the crusaders' flesh when the corpses are found, showing, as Bromyard comments, the cross's salvific power after death. Second, a knight fighting on behalf of his brother completes a tour on the Albigensian crusade. He agrees to delay his departure out of love for his deceased father. A ghost of the father visits and praises the knight for freeing him from the fires of purgatory.[22] With their strong narrative lines and simple moral purpose, such preaching exempla set out the benefits of repentance, acceptance of the cross, and crusaders' protection from spiritual danger. At the same time, their negative side provides a similarly effective force; and arguing by dichotomy, Bromyard paints a grim picture of those who refuse to embrace the cross. Society is divided into two: the virtuous who support the crusade and the non-virtuous who do not. Given the massive spiritual boon awarded crusade participants, the logic runs, those refusing to commit must face great danger.

---

[20]   BL, MS Royal 7 E IV fol. 110r ; e.g. citing Justinian's Codex on property rights 'de Agricolis'.
[21]   BL, MS Royal 7 E IV fol. 110ʳ Several of the Old Testament references are added in a later hand. Bernard of Clairvaux, *Treatises III, Liber ad milites Templi: de laude novae militae*, tr. C. Greenia (Kalamazoo, 1977) p. 130.
[22]   BL, MS Royal 7 E IV fol. 111ʳ. Three of Bromyard's examples are attributed to the famous James of Vitry (d. 1240). Two may be found in the *Speculum Laicorum* ch. XXII, 'De Crucis virtute' no.148, and in Stephen of Bourbon, *Anecdotes historiques* no. 29.

The theme is as old as the crusade itself, and, alive to the effects of instilling shame and fear, Bromyard makes it the longest part of his text.

A Christo-centric view of the crusade is also present throughout the exhortation. Contrasting images of Christ are associated with the various military, penitential and devotional aspects of crusading. Here, guilt over the crucifixion and the creedal tenet that Christ died because of human sin is the operative emotion.[23] 'To not take up the cross for Christ,' the sermon warns, 'is to demonstrate enormous ingratitude.' The crusade shows who is joined to Christ and who is not. The ungrateful will be held to account at Judgement Day. The concept of the crusade as an act of imitating or 'following' Christ is a pivotal theme. Crusaders are soldiers of the militant Christ, following him into battle like Jonathan and his armour-bearer in the book of Samuel (1 Samuel 14:12–16). Crusaders are disciples of the Lord, forsaking all worldly things (Matthew 19:29). Crusaders are penitents suffering in imitation of Christ. Crusaders are martyrs, climbing, like St Andrew, onto the Lord's cross with joy in their hearts.[24]

A more meditative treatment is available with reference to the prophecies of Isaiah and Ezekiel, and a sample of non-biblical sources. Elements of a literary topos are clearly apparent. In the words of Ezekiel 9:4–6, 'Do not kill those you see bearing the sign of the Thau!', for example, Bromyard sees the anagogy of Christ's cross. At Judgement, those marked with God's spiritual badge are spared. The typology of the Passover shows the same thing. People signed with the blood and thorns of the crucifixion, as Bromyard puts it, are kept safe. Impressed on the soul through love and suffering, God sees the cross, and shelters those bearing it. Bromyard develops the metaphor with Ovid's popular story of Philomela. Just as Philomela the nightingale hid in the thicket to escape the eagle-owl, he says, penitents must hide their hearts within the cross, within the crown of thorns and Christ's wounds. Simultaneously guarded and pricked by thorns, the nightingale figure is an imaginative attempt to visualise Christ's suffering and experience his agony in conquering sin. Like Ovid's Philomela escaping from the eagle-owl, crusaders must endure a painful pressing forward and piercing of flesh in setting the cross upon their chests and fleeing from evil, the visceral language here calling to mind the corruptible nature of the corporeal world, and the concept of the crusade as an act of mental and physical self-mortification. Washed in Christ's blood, the hearts and souls of men are sacralised and repellent to the devil.[25]

Elsewhere Bromyard shows a lighter touch. He pokes fun at those knights and esquires who lounge around bragging of how many Saracens they want to kill, and the heroics they will perform, yet who, 'when it comes to the crunch', are frightened by

---

[23]   BL, MS Royal 7 E IV fol. 111.
[24]   Ibid.
[25]   'Sic fugat, ut dicitur Philomena bubonem ei de nocte insidiantem, ponendo se in arbore concava, vel inter spinas densas, ubi ille cum grosso capite intrare non potest. Sic nos ponendo cor intra crucem, et vulnera et spinas crucifixi.' Ibid. fol. 112ᵛ.

the slightest open insult. Colour is added with the use of jokes, puns and vernacular phrases.[26] The sermon culminates with a richly allusive passage on the virtues demanded of crusade participants and the crusade's place in God's plan for humanity. The intention is to prepare congregations for the rite of confession and the cere-mony of cross-taking, a final act perhaps increasingly reserved for the battlefield.[27] Combatants needed to be properly confessed and wholly penitent for indulgences to have redemptive value, and the process was supposed to be psychologically taxing. Confronted by the enormity of their sin, listeners were shepherded through the cycle of remorse, punishment, forgiveness and, in the act of confession and making vows, a return to communion with Christ. Adducing St Paul's words, 'The world is crucified unto me, and I unto the world' (Galatians 6:14), Bromyard holds up the crusade as a means of achieving partnership with Christ and the lofty ideals of apostolic life.[28] In taking the cross, body and soul are to be turned in contempt so that mankind is put at one's back. An illustration of St Paul's verse is held up. Like two men crucified upon a single tree, the world and the crusader are positioned back to back, facing away from one another. The crusade is an act of imitating Christ, and the conjoined symbols of the cross and the biblical Tree of Life simultaneously destroy sin and restore spiritual health.[29]

Like other species of sermon, 'Crux' was generously coloured for popularist appeal as well as for academic audiences and knightly elites. It clearly paid to trade on a traditional core of scripture, stories, phrases and words found among other crusade sermons and papal bulls. Examples include the common crusade refrain 'If any man will come after me, let him deny himself, and take up his Cross' (Matthew 16:24); Ezekiel's prophecy 'Sign a Thau on the foreheads of all who grieve' (Ezekiel 9:4); the canticle 'Set me like a sign in your heart, like a sign on your arm' (Canticles 8:6); the prophecy 'There shall come forth a rod out of the stem of Jesse' (Isaiah 11:1); and excerpts drawn from the Mosaic statute 'When thou goest out to battle' (Deuteronomy 20). Many of the biblical figures found in 'Crux' (e.g. Jonathan, Judas Maccabeus, St Paul and Jacob) had common use in other surviving crusade sermons, as did Bromyard's allegorical emblems of Jacob's ladder, the bronze serpent and the Tree of Life.[30] Elements more narrowly directed towards military society included use of feudal concepts as a means of justifying crusading and explaining the fighter's duties and rewards. In 'Crux' God is likened to a feudal king. The Holy Land is his patria. To be baptised is to perform homage to God, and, as Bromyard puts it, 'to be set working at His plough'.[31] Notions of military service, discipleship and *imitatio Christi* all belonged within this paradigm.

---

[26]   Ibid. fol. 111[v].
[27]   See above n. 11 (preaching at Rhodes on the eve of the Alexandrian crusade).
[28]   BL, MS Royal 7 E IV fol. 113[v]
[29]   Ibid.
[30]   Ibid fols 110[v], 111[v], 112[v], 113[r]. In general see Maier, *Crusade Propaganda* pp. 51–70.
[31]   BL, MS Royal 7 E IV fol. 112[r].

Although the impact of such sermon propaganda cannot be measured with precision, the crusade's message of renewal and salvation comprised a range of all-Christian values. Sermon meditations on the significance of Christ, the cross, the crucifixion, the miracle of life through death, the temptation of the flesh, and the spiritual rewards of holy work set the *negotium crucis* squarely within the moral and affective currents of aristocratic devotion, with its tendencies towards contemplative and ascetic observance. To take part in crusading was to participate in an active moral Christian life. As such, though he acquired a fearsome reputation for attacking the wealthy for their love of finery and riches, Bromyard's obsession with apostolic poverty and the amendment of secular living implied spiritual humility more than economic destitution and ruin of the elite classes. For the working preacher the hoarders of wealth were natural targets of vow-redemptions and sale of crusade indulgences.[32] At any rate, the central concepts were widely felt. The same atmosphere of shame, self-denial and devotion directed at the gaining of heaven, not worldly fame, characterises the crusade-themed middle-English romance, *Sir Gowther* (c.1375), for instance (see below pp. 161–2). Cadences of sermon propaganda are also audible in the popular middle-English Charlemagne romance *The Sege of Melayne*, where prayers are offered to God that opposing Saracen armies should magically swell in order to increase the honour of Christian martyrs. Finally, in 1309 a confederation of Londoners preparing to embark for the east after hearing reports of the Hospitaller *passagium* declared the goal of their journey was 'to avenge the wounds and the blood of Christ Crucified', echoing faithfully the language of pulpit and crusade bull.[33]

Sin and salvation

The crusade and associated ideologies remained widely available as an expression of faith and identity through other social rituals and religious institutions, besides sermons and preaching. Integral to this was an increasing emphasis on the individual's conscience and performance of intercessory works. In 1383 participants were encouraged to take the cross to expiate the sins of others, preachers citing the spiritual profits shared by deceased family members, and sometimes staging open-air 'miracles' where imaginary angels were summoned at their bidding to guide souls straight from earth to heaven.[34] Though never enshrined in canon law, the principle nonetheless sat squarely with the social and philanthropic function of confession and penance, becoming widely accepted. Concern for salvation of the dead was reflected in grants to the earl of Warwick's crusade companions in 1365, when they lobbied the pope for partial indulgences for those who gave masses in memory of their parents and

---

[32] 'Crux' ends with an excursus on the corrupting power of wealth and the grace available through the cross. Ibid. fols 113ᵛ–114ʳ.

[33] *Middle English Romances* pp. 42–3 ('Sege of Melayne'), 164–86 ('Gowther'); 'Paulini' p. 156.

[34] *Eulogium* vol. III pp. 356–7; Knighton, p. 325.

ancestors.[35] At a different, more routine, level, in their churches and religious foundations, the lay elite could be confronted with ritual expressions of grief at the relentless
rise of the *hethenesse*, through the performance of prayer and weekly services. As
Amnon Linder has shown, church rites for the crusade – contracting the military
and spiritual cause into a sequence of intelligible and cognate rituals (fasts, silences,
Ave Marias, psalmody and graveyard processions) – appeared in a number of liturgi-
cal categories and are widely dispersed among fourteenth-century English sources.
Commonly stipulated by crusade bulls and intimately connected with the life of
the parish and collegiate church, such long-running ritual commentary conditioned
mainstream attitudes, paving the way for material action and sales of indulgences.[36]

A common form for the weekly mass in English churches throughout the period
was, for example, a specially adapted *clamor* to invoke God's help for the Holy Land.
Inserted between the breaking of the Host and the Pax Domini before communion,
the *clamor* consisted of a group of psalms, prayers and versicles chosen for their relevance to the crisis in the east. Psalm 78 ('O God, the Heathen are come into thine
inheritance ...') retained primacy as the central text, but this could be flanked by
a flexible set of versicles and antiphons.[37] Its ceremonial effect was defined by
the dramatic interruption of the Eucharistic rite and by striking visual acts, such
as the placing of sacred objects on the ground or on coarse cloth and covering
them with thorns, embodying notions and sentiments typically associated with
the Passion and the symbolic figure of Jerusalem. Contemporary English missals stipulated its performance on all ferial masses from the second Sunday after
Epiphany to Maundy Thursday and from the first Sunday after Trinity to the
Christmas vigil, i.e. on most feast days and Sunday masses of the church calendar.[38] In special circumstances the entire apparatus of the Eucharistic mass could
be dedicated as a vehicle for the crusade. A large body of English evidence relates to
the mass setting *Contra Paganos*, refined and popularised by Clement V in aid of the
Hospitaller *passagium* of 1308–1313, where each component of the mass is coloured

---

[35]   ASV, reg. supp. 40 fols 145–7, 179; *CPP* vol. I pp. 493–501.

[36]   A. Linder, *Raising Arms: Liturgy in the Struggle to Liberate Jerusalem in the Late Middle Ages*
(Turnhout, 2003) pp. 102, 363–4. For contemporary diocesan use see *Registrum Roberti Winchelsey
Cantuariensis Archiepiscopi, 1294–1313* ed. R. Graham, Canterbury and York Society (Oxford, 1952–
1956) vol. I p. 26; *Registrum Johannis de Pontissara Episcopi Wyntoniensis, 1282–1304* ed. C. Deedes,
Canterbury and York Society (London, 1915–1924) vol. I pp. 191–3; *Chronicle of St. Mary's Abbey* pp.
46–7, 50–1.

[37]   E.g. Oxford Bod. MS Barlow 1 fol. 162; Oxford Bod. MS Laud Misc. 302 fols 119ᵛ–120ᵛ; BL, MS
Harley 4919 fols 158–160ᵛ. For other manuscripts, see Linder, *Raising Arms* pp. 50–8.

[38]   For relevant rubrics see *Missale ad usum Insignis et Praeclarae Ecclesiae Sarum* ed. F. H. Dickinson
(Burntisland 1861–1883) pp. 631–4; Oxford Bod. MS Barlow 1 fol. 162; cf. for fourteenth-century inter-
polation or 'trope' of Holy Land *clamor* in thirteenth-century manuscript (Rochester) *Missale de Lesnes*,
ed. P. Jebb (London, 1964) p. 76.

by ritual focus on the plight of the east. Derivations of this setting were widely used.[39] A more innovative use of crusade liturgy was the so-called Gregorian trentals, combining masses said for the dead with prayers for the liberation of the Holy Land. Here the anticipated release of the Holy Places from infidel hands was held to be synonymous with the coming Judgement and liberation of souls from purgatory. Popular among testators of all classes, such trentals enabled crusade ideals to be harnessed to the active drama of men's salvation without recourse to military action.[40] The expense of endowing trental masses may have diverted charity otherwise allocated to embarking combatants – perhaps stretching the connection between ideal and action to the point of implausibility – but it is doubtful whether men noticed a gulf widening between their appetite for active crusading and their acts of mental devotion. One high-ranking trental testator, Hugh, earl of Stafford, sealed his will on Rhodes after visiting the earthly Jerusalem – his ability to move among the Holy Sites in person not easing the guilt he felt about his mortal life and the fact that Christ's heritage remained in the hands of 'enemies of the Cross' (1385).[41]

In terms of propagandist impact, perhaps the most instrumental of the crusade rites were bidding prayers – vernacular intercessory prayers said in parish churches across Europe on Sundays and feast days directly after the *sermo*, and before the offertory. A typical set comprised various causes, but from the late thirteenth century they adopted the objective of the Holy Land and incorporated the ideal of the recovery crusade. The form used in Worcester diocese in 1349 is representative, inviting the faithful to join with the priest in seeking God's favour for 'the Patriarch of Jerusalem, for the holy lond, and for the holy Croys, that Jhesu Christ sendeth it out of hedne mennys honde into Christenmennys honde ... ', thus extending the short section of the service which might be given in the congregation's tongue.[42] Other bidding prayers issued injunctions against 'enemies of the cross' across all frontiers within Christendom's interior, not just at its borders or in the east. Individual knightly campaigners and crusades might receive important recognition in this way. In 1352 cathedral officials in York issued prayers on behalf of the duke of Lancaster's expedition against the 'enemies of the Cross' in the Baltic. Recited at High Mass on each Sunday and other feast days, the *orationes fidelium* called upon God to be the duke's spiritual shield and companion in battle. Circulated throughout the diocese, the supplications instructed the faithful in the soldier cult of Henry Grosmont, dubbed

---

[39]   Linder, *Raising Arms* pp. 118–20; *Orationum* ed. E. Moeller *Corpus Christianorum Series Latina* 160–1 (Turnhout, 1992–1999) no. 3873. For additional published examples see *Missale ad usum ... Herfordensis* pp. 417–18; *Missale ad usum ... Sarum* p. 824; *Missale ad usum Ecclesie Westmonasteriensis* ed. J. W. Legg (London, 1891–1897) col. 1155; *Liber ecclesiae Beati Terrenani de Arbuthnott. Missale secundum usum Ecclesiae Sancti Andreae in Scotia* ed. A. P. Forbes (Burntisland, 1864) p. 454.

[40]   For manuscripts see Linder, *Raising Arms* pp. 275–325. Printed examples include *Missale ad usum ... Sarum* pp. 883–4; *Sarum Missal* p. 460; *Missale ad usum ... Herfordensis* p. 436.

[41]   *Testamenta Vetusta* vol. I p. 118.

[42]   *Forms of Bidding Prayer* ed. H. O. Coxe (Oxford, 1840) pp. 11–25.

'protector of the mother church and of the one faith'. Because the duke's fortunes involved the honour and safety of the English realm, a strong show of solidarity was indispensable. Likewise, prayers despatched on behalf of Thomas Woodstock in 1391 focused upon God's agency upon the battlefield and the hazards encountered by the English prince against *inimicos Crucis Christi*.[43] A much wider reception of the crusade bidding prayer is attested by its migration into other social contexts. In Norfolk in 1384, for instance, the town confraternities of St Christopher's at Norwich and St Mary's at Wiggenhall on the Ouse began their meetings with prayers for the recovery of the Holy Land: at Wiggenhall, 'we shal be-seke for ye holy lond yat Jhesu crist, for is mekul mercy, brynge it in to criste powere'; and at the craft guild of St Christopher, 'for ye holy londe and ye holy crosse, yat Godd for his myght and his mercy bryng it oute of hethen power into reule of holy chirche', adopting words probably lifted directly from a missal.[44]

In such ways potentially empty liturgy, citing the fate of the Holy Land or the rise of the pagan nations, acquired special focus when set against English knightly traffic to the Baltic and Mediterranean. Not only did it help lay down military ideals, but it was also a focus for galvanising dynastic and chivalric pride. Devotion to the crusade naturally impinged directly upon this sphere of public religion, sharing the same pietistic roots as other widely felt obligations and customary good works. Action against the infidel could be the capstone to long absence on pilgrimage, and the supplement or alternative to the founding of family chantries, the giving of alms, or the taking of holy orders – all common components of aristocratic religion. Exceptional for its sacralising of bloodshed, crusading as a practical devotional work was distinctive mainly for its risk and enormous expense. Thus it was not unusual for men like William, Lord Botreaux, and Lord Bourchier in 1390 to round out long spells of pilgrimage to the east with a term fighting in Prussia, or for veterans of the *reyse* and Spanish *reconquista* to visit Jerusalem. In practice, the transition from crusader to pilgrim required no special canonical rite or divergent frame of mind. Dedication of funds and bodily effort for the sake of Christendom was crusading's oldest argument, generously lauded in church liturgy and sermons, as has been seen above. This is why fourteenth-century popes repeatedly equated praise for crusaders' 'great labour' with the amount of money they spent; it is also caught in English wills where donations and vows to the Holy Land are adjacent to bequests of social conscience and works of mercy, whether it was repairing parish bridges, building and enlarging hospitals and schools or clothing orphans.[45]

---

[43] *Historical Letters* pp. 402–3; *Wykeham's Register* vol. II p. 30.

[44] *English Gilds* ed. L. Toulim-Smith, EETS o.s. 40 (London, 1870) pp. 11, 22, 114.

[45] 'Pridem ad supplicem' *Reg. Montacute* pp. 219–21; *Reg. Dunelmense* vol. IV p. 497. For wills as sources, see *Wills of the Archdeaconry of Sudbury, 1439–1474, Wills from the Register 'Baldwyne'* Part 1 (1439–1461) ed. P. Northeast (Woodbridge, 2001) p. xxxvii. Such crusade bequests are scattered throughout the English records. Published examples include *Testamenta Vetusta* vol. I pp. 52, 56–7, 62; *Calendar of Wills*

Not all subscribed to acts of public religion in this fashion, however. An increasingly puritanical strain was becoming evident in the devotions of some nobility and gentry in the latter half of the fourteenth century, finding expression in language denigrating the physical body and earthly privilege. Emphasis upon personalised relations with Christ, the conflict between flesh and spirit, and the mystical inter-penetration of the divine and natural order characterised the more exploratory modes of contemporary piety. Crusading, despite its worldly glamour and high social prestige, could also be a mechanism for this religious temperament. The remarkable devotional treatises of Henry Grosmont (*Livre de Seyntz Medicines*) and the Lollard sympathiser Sir John Clanvow (*The Two Ways*), for example, are dominated by an acute sense of self-disgust and a sense of the spoliation of the soul by the weakness and wickedness of the flesh. Grosmont takes a more equivocal tone, but rejection of the physical world and the difficulty of attaining eternal life permeates his self-scrutiny as it does the thinking of Clanvow. For such men the crusade could offer relief, if not release, in subjecting the body to the will of God; to follow in the footsteps of Christ (the 'supreme doctor of souls'), as vigorously exhorted by crusade preachers and numerous papal bulls. Those with more refined and reflective tastes, like Henry Scrope of Masham, Sir William Beauchamp and perhaps even Richard II's uncle Thomas Woodstock, were turning to the works of mystics and manifesting an appetite for the ascetic. Here fighting for the love of God served as a purifying spiritual ideal, as well as encapsulating more arcane prophetic and soteriological seams of thinking.[46] Even where papal indulgences were met with suspicion, there remained the models of meritorious violence in patristic and Old Testament texts, where slaughter meted against the heathen nations was blessed as God's work.

However it was couched, the crusade's message remained essentially unchanged from the time of the first expeditions to the east. It was a call to repentance and an offer of salvation, which was understood by many. Preaching messages and the ideals set down in contemporary church ritual helped underpin knightly responses, providing conventional form and expression for crusade militancy, though the precise relationship between religious convictions and individual decisions to embark in

... *Court of Husting* vol. I pp. 263, 653, vol. II pp. 2, 104–5; *The Cartulary of God's House, Southampton* ed. J. M. Kaye (Southampton, 1976) p. 88; *The Cartulary of the Priory of St. Denys, Southampton*, ed. E. O. Blake (Southampton, 1981) vol. I p. 181; *Reg. Gilbert* pp. 34–5; *The Register of Ralph of Shrewsbury, Bishop of Bath and Wells, 1329–1363* ed. T. S. Holmes (London, 1896) vol. I p. 267; HMC, *Fifth Report* p. 562; HMC, *Calendar of MSS of the Dean and Chapter of Wells* (London, 1907–1914) vol. II p. 587; cf. *Accounts Rendered by Papal Collectors* pp. 34, 48–9, 83–4, 120, 224, 321.

[46]   Fowler, *King's Lieutenant* pp. 193–6; *Livre de Seyntz Medicines* ed. E. J. Arnould (Oxford, 1940); A. Hudson, *Lollards and their Books* (London, 1985) p. 54; K. B. McFarlane, *Lancastrian Kings and Lollard Knights* (Oxford, 1972) pp. 199–206; J. I. Catto 'Religion and the English Nobility in the Later Fourteenth Century' *History and Imagination. Essays in Honour of H. R. Trevor-Roper* eds H. Lloyd-Jones et al. (London, 1981) pp. 43–55. On the rich interplay between crusade and prophecy see Coote, *Prophecy and Public Affairs* pp. 121–56 and below pp. 186–92, 195–6, 200–2, 206.

most cases remains indistinct. As such it is misleading to insist on the religiosity of fighters departing for the *hethenesse* – just as it is wrong to assume the reverse. There is, however, no reason to suspect a creeping secularism or an insincerity specific to the period following the loss of the Holy Land, despite the limitations of crusade successes there in the fourteenth century. The desire for vengeance over Christ's suffering was readily transferable to the Turks, Mamluks, pagans, heretics and other enemies currently harming Christendom, although the particular allure of Jerusalem and the *imitatio Christi* remained strong. When men like Robert, Lord Fitzpayn, spoke of being ready to destroy their bodies, friends and wealth for the sake of the crusade (1309), it was supposed to invoke echoes of Christ's sacrifice, as well garner respect, financial aid and social prestige.[47]

---

[47]   *Vitae paparum* vol. III pp. 87–90.

8

Chivalry, Literature and Political Culture

Besides individual concern for the health of the soul, numerous other factors helped to sow enthusiasm for the physical contest with the infidel. According to Froissart, talk of royal crusades in the early 1330s was warmly received by warlike men because they had nothing better to do at the time. The desire to cross swords in a rewarding cause is evident throughout the period, when western soldiery, toughened by fighting in France and elsewhere, became swollen in numbers and in need of an outlet for its energy. This violent and opportunistic quality can be highlighted ample times, whether in the career of John Holand, who became implicated in crusade plans on three separate occasions, including as Captain of the Roman Church in Italy, as retinue leader on John of Gaunt's Castile expedition, and as an independent campaigner in Hungary and Bohemia, or in the more obscure careers of men like John Hampton of Mortimer, who apparently served in the Iberian crusades for pay.[1] Diversity of motive was nothing intrinsically new. What provided a large measure of cohesion among participants, however, were the various codes of behaviour and expectation held up for emulation in the tenets of chivalry, and the pressures of prestige and competition between men. Court pageantry and ceremony, imaginative literature, myth, military competition, the expectations of lineage, the decorative arts and patterns of social advancement all spoke to crusading's higher calling, instilling in knights an ethos of admiration and material response.

Those engaged in promoting the crusade sought to press such active influences into service. It was a commonplace of crusade preaching that histories of the crusade and chivalric romance were utilised as an aid to recruitment, for instance. The influential thirteenth-century preacher Humbert of Romans recommended that crusade propagandists quarry the stories of Charlemagne, Godfrey de Bouillon and other

---

[1] Froissart, vol. XVII pp. 43–4. According to the author of the 'Annales Ricardi' Holand fought out of ambition and avarice: *Chronica et Annales* p. 201. See also *CPL* vol. IV pp. 294–6; Romano, 'Un Inglés en la Guerra contro el Morro' pp. 457–9; Tyerman, *England and the Crusades* pp. 260–3.

figures of the First Crusade. John of Bromyard patterned his sermonising with references to Richard I, the Nine Worthies and other martial figures from Christian history. The paradigm of the crusader knight was part of the preacher's canon across a range of other moral subjects, taken as shorthand for the Christian virtues of fidelity, sacrifice and repentance.[2] Similarly, Roger Stanegrave invoked Tristram, Lancelot, Charlemagne and Arthur in his theoretical scheme for attacking the east, his tone chiming with the revival of Arthurianism at Edward III's court in the early 1330s. Another apologist for the Mediterranean crusade, Hugh of Liege (writing c.1343), drew on an even wider panoply of military heroes, from Norse mythology to Archbishop Turpin, in his pamphlet of crusade *excitatoria* addressed to Philip VI and Edward III.[3] The arguments of romance and myth were further underlined by the many pertinent observations in chivalric treatises. Ramon Lull considered that the first duty of a knight was to defend the faith against the infidel. Christine de Pisan echoed the sentiment, citing the immutability of the church's patrimony; and for Geoffrey de Charny, crusading appears as a form of quasi-martyrdom, exalted not only as a function of religious piety, but also because it served his mantra of 'living by force of arms and by good works'. The author of the *Tree of Battles* formulates a similar view, although emphasised in a different way. For him, the crusade was one war where flight from the battlefield was all but ruled out, since the knight knows that if he remains in the fight 'he will die for the faith and be saved'.[4] Such treatises are mainly concerned with knightly conduct in domestic settings and service to the lay lord, but the basic assumption about the crusade's sovereign virtue is patently clear. Knights engaged in this form of war are, following Charny's typology, enacting something which is righteous, holy and sure. Their bodies will be honoured in a saintly fashion and their souls will, in a short space of time, be borne in holiness and without pain into paradise. 'This war is good, for one can lose in it neither one's reputation in this world, nor one's soul.'[5]

Literary ideals

Throughout the middle ages, a significant proportion of the literature composed for knights' entertainment was concerned with the deeds of Christian warriors confronting the infidel. The struggle lay at the heart of the Charlemagne cycle and provided the crucial focus of the *chansons de croisade*, including compositions which celebrated later crusading icons such as Richard I. Arthurian romance held up the ideal in a different fashion, but works such as *Perlesvaus* and the *Queste del Saint Graal* served

---

[2]   Maier, *Preaching the Crusades* pp. 114–16; BL, MS Royal 7 E IV fols 110[r]–114[r].

[3]   BL, MS Cotton Otho D V fols 6[v]–7[r], 13[r]; Mézières, *Songe du vieil pèlerin* vol. II p. 222; Hugo von Lüttich, *Peregrinarius* eds F. Unterkircher and P. G. Schmidt (Leiden, 1991).

[4]   Ramon Lull, *The Book of the Ordre of Chyvalry* ed. A. T. P. Byles, EETS o.s. 168 (London, 1926) pp. 24–5, 76–7; Geoffrey de Charny, *Book of Chivalry*, pp. 88–9; Pisan, *Book of fayttes of armes and of chivalry* p.12; Bonet, *Tree of Battles* p. 122.

[5]   Geoffrey de Charny, *Book of Chivalry* pp. 88–9.

equally to instil the notion that the knight should wield his sword in a sacred cause.[6] A distinctive group of English texts possesses particular relevance to the ideals of knight-errantry and crusading, partly because of their popularity, but also because of their contemporary comment on the doctrine of penance and violence. Drawn from the world of fiction and fantasy, such stereotypes help to suggest the frame of mind which coaxed men into their costly exertions; or (in a different view) it shows the contemporary instinct to deploy romantic arguments as a means of glamorising unpalatable, cruel realities.

In this regard, the most important texts were the Middle English romances *Guy of Warwick* (c.1300x1330), *Sir Isumbras* (c.1320) and *Sir Gowther* (c.1375). Each featured what has been characterised as a penitential pattern, with central characters who are transported from a stable condition of worldly nobility and high honour to a sudden and catastrophic revelation of sin, followed by repentance and a determination to make atonement.[7] What is striking is the dominant position of holy war and the crusade as mechanisms of plot and character development. Conscious of doing penance and acting according to God's will, the knights are each pressed into performing service against the pagans, either as part of a sequence of martial challenges or as a pivotal demonstration of valour and contrition. In all three poems, plenary indulgence – in the limited and specific sense of remission of penance for warfare against the enemies of the church – can be seen in operation. Gowther's wholesale slaughter of Saracens is an integral part of his expiation as instructed by the pope. His donning of armour of different colours expresses symbolically the cleansing of sin and his metamorphosis from devil incarnate to knight-penitent. The fairy tale ending of *Sir Isumbras* shows its hero as the instrument of God chastising the pagan hordes, the cross gashed into Isumbras's shoulder at the beginning of the romance anticipating his reception into heaven; and *Guy of Warwick* has its hero preparing to atone for his former life as a boastful and murderous knight with more killing – but this time as an instrument of God. He is credited with forty thousand Saracen deaths at the 'battle of Constantinople'.[8]

Of central significance in these texts, apart from their contemporaneity, is the deliberate rejection of conventional penitential practice, namely that of making gifts of money to religious foundations or employing the services of a churchman to pray on the penitent's behalf in lieu of other more exacting forms of penance. With the

---

[6] The classic study is Keen, *Chivalry* pp. 44–63. For what follows cf. D. Mehl, *The Middle English Romances of the Thirteenth and Fourteenth Centuries* (London, 1969) esp. pp. 10–13, 17–21, 253–4; Barron, *English Medieval Romance* pp. 89–105, 182–6; H. J. Nicholson, *Love, War and the Grail: Templars Hospitaller and Teutonic Knights* (Leiden, 2004) pp. 211–15.

[7] *Romance of Guy of Warwick*; *Sir Ferumbras*; 'Sir Isumbras' and 'Gowther' *Middle English Romances* pp. 125–47, 148–68; A. Hopkins, *The Sinful Knights: A Study of Middle English Penitential Romance* (Oxford, 1990).

[8] *Middle English Romances* pp. 164–8 ('Gowther'), 129, 145–57 ('Sir Isumbras'); *Romance of Guy of Warwick* vol. II p. 111; Hopkins, *Sinful Knights* p. 57 and passim.

heroes' bodily exertions, access to indulgences at the direction of a confessor is dismissed in preference of a 'true' penitential process and a fundamental restitution of the relationship between God and man. Guy's objection to the suggestion that he can expiate his sins simply by founding an abbey or a church – 'Þat ich haue wiþ mi bodi wrouȝt/ Wiþ mi bodi it schalde bouȝt/ To bote me of þat bale' ('That what have with my body wrought/ With my body it shall be bought/ To cure me of that misery') – embodies the sentiment neatly, conveying an unflinching concept of physical culpability. In the romances, the impossibility of atonement through means other than bodily sacrifice and self-abnegation is accepted as a consequence of the protagonists' wealth and their military vocation, the parallelism functioning both on poetic and moral grounds, and reaching for special resonance with the noble classes.[9] Awoken to their sin, the protagonists are flooded with self-loathing, and the penances undertaken are shockingly harsh. Each hero is reduced to poverty. Isumbras and Gowther nearly perish of starvation. Divine interventions include the miraculous provision of food and weapons and, in some manuscripts, the appearance of celestial reinforcements (both favourite themes of crusade preachers). Significantly, the forgiveness of the heroes does not take place until after the military penance is complete.[10] Such doubts over the efficacy of lesser penances than that of fighting for the faith were expected to carry weight, impressing upon knightly audiences the devotional context of their decisions to embark. None of this detracts from other romance motifs. The violence makes a loud clatter – brains are spilt down hauberks and limbs hacked off. The inner tensions between romantic love and knightly independence are tested.

Imaginative literature held up numerous other exemplary careers, many associated with the crusade, others serving wider themes of patriotism, fealty, *courtoisie*, prowess, questing or the qualities of human and divine love. But the archetype of a nobly born sinner who repents, and, abandoning his wealth and power, wanders through the world warring with the infidel and undergoing trials of hardship, seems to have been particularly deeply impressed.[11] Set against the real-life careers of men like John de la Ryvere, Giles d'Argentein ('the third best knight in Christendom') and Sir Francis Villiers (who lost all his wealth in the east), the fictional protagonists of *Guy of Warwick* and other romances look somewhat less like figures cut from pasteboard fantasy or confined to a distant golden age. In the 1380s there was common report of knights who had vowed not to eat or turn home until they had crossed swords with the infidel. Before sailing to Alexandria in 1365, Peter of Cyprus vowed not to set foot

---

[9]   *Romance of Guy of Warwick* vol. II p. 29 lines 10–12; cf. pertinent comments in E. Fowler, 'The Romance Hypothetical: Lordship and the Saracens in *Sir Isumbras' The Spirit of Medieval English Popular Romance* eds A. Rutter and J. Gilbert (Harlow, 2000), pp. 97–121.

[10]   E.g. 'Gowther' *Middle English Romances* p. 166. lines 655–60.

[11]   Hopkins, *Sinful Knights* pp. 67, 198; R. A. Rouse, 'An Exemplary Life: Guy of Warwick as Medieval Culture Hero' *Guy of Warwick: Icon and Ancestor* eds A. Wiggins and R. Field (Cambridge, 2007), pp. 94–109.

again in his kingdom until he had landed his army on Muslim shores.[12] Their precise recruitment value is difficult to ascertain, but taken up with enthusiasm such models possessed strong resonance, teaching the integral tenets of Christian knighthood and mirroring the energy of contemporary chivalry.

Some of this is reflected in the patterns of manuscript ownership among the nobility. The Bohun library held copies of the *Histoire de Chivaler a Cigne*, a story steeped in crusade mythology, a *Lancelot du lac* and various exemplary religious *vitae*, such as the *voyage of St Antony in the Holy Land* and *vita sancti Eustacii*, all emblazoned with family coats of arms. Among the texts collected by the earls of Warwick were *un del Romance Iospeh ab Arimathie e deu Seint Graal*, the *romance del William de Orenges*, a *volum de a mort ly Arthur* and *un del Romance e de Ferebras*, as well as numerous redactions of *Guy of Warwick* – all narratives with an applicable crusading motif.[13] More broadly, well-stocked libraries like the one owned by Joan Beaufort included copies of *les cronikels de Jerusalem* and *le viage de Godefray de Bouillon* and works other than romances on the Holy Land, such as travelogues, treatises and pilgrim itineraries. Thomas Woodstock thumbed a large decorative *livre de Godefray de Bouillon* complete with enamel and silver clasps. Of course, ownership was not the same as readership, and the general subject matter of knightly endeavour against the infidel was so commonplace that analysis of its influence must lie in terms of broad appeal rather than pocketed interest, but occasionally texts were used in a more specific way. Robert the Bruce famously recited the story of *Ferumbras* – a romance of Oliver's defeat of Islam – to stir up chivalric feeling at his court. Similarly, the Beauchamp earls of Warwick adopted the mythologised Guy of Warwick as their dynastic and territorial ancestor, with the aim of instilling a sympathetic ethos among their political clients. Belief in the romance's historicity helped to cultivate family celebrity and wider interest in the careers of three earls of Warwick in the fourteenth and fifteenth centuries. Reinforcement of this was found among family artefacts and local tradition. Relics of the fictional Guy, including his battle-standard, sword and drinking cup, were 'discovered' at Warwick and passed down the Beauchamp line. Likewise, in the 1360s at least one redaction of *Beves of Hamtoun* – an adventure story divided between Southampton and Muslim Armenia – was commissioned by the earl of Hereford for consumption by his retinue, possibly fanning interest among the earl's circle.[14] In the case of the Beauchamp family and Humphrey Bohun, if not for scores of others, it is tempting to suppose a close productive relationship between

---

[12]   Keen, *Chivalry* p. 213; Mézières, *Life of St. Peter Thomas* p. 124.

[13]   S. Cavanaugh, *A Study of Books Privately Owned in England 1300–1450* (Ann Arbor, 1985) vol. I p. 26, vol. II pp. 606, 847; *Testamenta Vetusta* vol. I p. 147. On the genesis of the Swan cycle see A. R. Wagner, 'The Swan Badge and the Swan Knight' *Archaeologia* 97 (1959) pp. 127–38.

[14]   *Bruce of John Barbour* vol. III p. 436; E. Mason, 'Legends of the Beauchamps' Ancestors: The Use of Baronial Propaganda in Medieval England' *Journal of Medieval History* 10 (1984) pp. 25–40; A. I. Doyle, 'The Manuscripts' *Middle English Alliterative Poetry* ed. D. A. Lawton (Cambridge, 1982) p. 93; *Romance of Beves of Hamtoun* vol. I p. vii.

literary exemplars and their own crusade ambition. So widely known was the crusade heroism of *Guy of Warwick* that accounts of his bravery in the Holy Land and
Prussia were adopted by preachers as stirring sermon exempla. Images drawn from
the romance were scattered across fourteenth-century religious and secular manuscripts, and carved onto furniture and other household items. To many, then, the
crusade may have represented both a Christian gesture of concern for the defence of
the faith and an enterprise in which the crusader was simultaneously *miles Christi* and
knight-errant: eager for adventures, desirous of displaying his martial prowess and
other chivalric qualities, and seeking to win worldly prestige whilst laying up merit in
heaven. According to the poets Chaucer, Gower and Guillaume Machaut it was also
the route to a lady's heart.[15]

Court and crusade

Crusading's diffuse literary and didactic influences received perhaps their sharpest
focus in the ceremonial settings and chivalric practices at court, the context in which
aristocratic enthusiasm was often most expectantly sought. Edward I's famous vow at
the Feast of Swans (May 1306) – to first destroy Robert the Bruce and then fight the
infidels in the Holy Land – used the backdrop of the crusade romance *Chevalier au
Cygne* for its pageantry, for instance, speaking directly to crusade plans at the curia
and the recent receipt of papal tenths, ostensibly for the Jerusalem expedition but
also to defray the costs of war in Scotland. The reciprocal vows of the baronage, and
the ceremonial context of Prince Edward's knighting served to accentuate the point.[16]
A few years later, when taking the cross with Edward II and the assembled ranks of
the Capetian court in Paris, English courtiers were party to one of the most elaborate civic festivals of the period. A sequence of urban processions, staged tableaux
and banquets occupied proceedings for over a week.[17] Similar theatrical feats were
repeated in Paris in 1378 and 1390 with lavish productions of the First Crusaders'
siege of Jerusalem and scenes from the Third Crusade. On one level ludic and nostalgic, these displays also possessed a practical resonance, narrowing the gap in time
and circumstance, prompting men to strive to maintain or revive traditional values.
Religious ceremonial at court provided another possible model. Wars of the cross
featured squarely in the language and ritual of the new *ordo* employed at Edward II's
coronation in 1308, for example, reflecting the heightened expectations of a general

[15]   *Gesta Romanorum* pp. 354–61; V. B. Richmond, *The Legend of Guy of Warwick* (New York, 1996)
pp. 90–106; T. Jones, *Chaucer's Knight* (London, 1980) pp. 38, 52 and references there to the *Confessio
Amantis, Dit d'ou Lion, Le confort d'Ami* and *The Book of the Duchess*.
[16]   Nicholas Trivet, *Annales* ed. T. Hog (London, 1845) pp. 408–9; Murimuth, *Continuatio* p. 9;
Wagner, 'Swan Badge and the Swan Knight' pp. 127–38.
[17]   E. A. R. Brown and N. F. Regalado, '*La grant feste:* Philip the Fair's Celebration of the Knighting of
His Sons in Paris at Pentecost of 1313' *City and Spectacle in Medieval Europe* eds B. A. Hanawalt and K.
L. Reyerson (Minneapolis, 1994) pp. 56–86.

passagium at the beginning of his reign, as well as pressure to show continuity with Edward I. Joined in prayer for the new king's rule, the political community asked God to pour down his blessings over the king, to uphold his rule against enemies, to conserve the English church and people, and to direct him in arms against the infidel. Blessings over the royal regalia underlined the crusade priority, consecrating it as a princely duty. The *curtana* (the sword of state) and the ring of faith, symbols of the monarch's secular and religious power, were talismans against the *paganos nationes* and *barbara gentes*, as well as preservers of the realm's powerless – orphans, widows and the destitute. Prayers were sought so that Edward II could break the devil's grip and the infidel's tyranny, which 'by virtue of the cross' the Almighty destroys. If only temporarily, such ritual made it hard to avoid crusading's moral and public claims.[18] In 1326, in another church ceremony, the future Edward III witnessed the laying of the foundation stone of the new church of the Paris *confrarie* of the Holy Sepulchre, a society of noble-born and wealthy urban crusaders sponsored by the count of Clermont. Accompanied by his mother, a *crucesignata* of 1313, and other foreign dignitaries, the English prince-in-exile played spectator to Capetian claims of religious and political leadership. It was part of the thirteen-year-old's formative experience of the milieu of the French court.[19]

The performance of court drama closer to home could provide an additional backdrop for crusading's diverse forms and appeals. With the use of military relics to lend authenticity, costumed processions and tournaments responded to the visual and historic cues of English crusading.[20] Thus Edward III's wardrobe inherited a helmet that was purportedly Saladin's, described in the household accounts as 'one round hat of steel lately of the Sultan Saladin, with a silver-gilt circle, with tressures and with babewyns [baboons/monkeys]' – apparently an example of the wide-brimmed *chapel-de-fer* helmets favoured by the Mamluks. The antique piece was in circulation close to the first major feast of Edward's reign (Easter 1327), raising the strong possibility of its appearance in some dramatic celebration or military display. The obvious place was an enactment of the legendary joust between Richard I and the Sultan (as evoked in royal tapestries and murals), possibly with the young king himself debuting as one of the champions.[21] There was opportunity for similar topical comment in the appearance of costumed 'Saracen' teams or groupings at Garter celebrations, marked out by the Saracen-head crests sported by famous knights such as Miles Stapleton

---

[18] *Liber Pontificalis of Edmund Lacy, Bishop of Exeter* ed. R. Barnes (Exeter, 1847) pp. 137–52.

[19] For full references see Tyerman, 'The French and the Crusade' pp. 138–41.

[20] For commemoration of the crusade within the royal buildings of Henry III see Lloyd, *English Society and the Crusade* pp. 199–200. For tapestried crusade iconography at Edward I's and Richard II's courts see S. McKendrick, 'Tapestries from the Low Countries in England during the Fifteenth Century' *England and the Low Countries in the Late Middle Ages* pp. 43–60.

[21] J. Vale, 'Image and Identity in the Pre-History of the Order of the Garter' *St. George's Chapel Windsor in the Fourteenth Century* ed. N. Saul (Woodbridge, 2005) p. 36. A connection with Richard I's anniversary (6 April) is likely. Easter fell on 12 April in 1327.

and Thomas Ufford, or in the tunics specially designed for Edward III's use, decorated with a silvered Saracen motif.[22] That such ceremonial tallied with the crusade
enthusiasm of Edward III's knights may or may not have been incidental, but it was
comparable to the didactic theatre valued by the likes of Philippe de Mézières, evoking
men's obligations in defence of the faith along with the multiplicity of other elements
in the *ludi domini regis*. The presence at courtly gatherings of real-life 'Saracens', such
as the children ('Sigo' and 'Nakok') dressed by the Black Prince's wardrobe clerk in
1351, or Christian knights from Armenia and Cyprus in the 1360s, almost certainly
heightened the dramatic effect.[23]

The jousting at Cheapside in 1331, a few days before the autumn parliament, was
probably the most elaborate of this sort of staging, combining idealism with military drama and competition. The key component (as recorded by eyewitnesses) was
a procession featuring a train of noblewomen (*pulcrioribus regni*) dressed in coloured
tunics and led on silvered chains by knights costumed in the manner of Tartars (*ad
similitudinem Tartarum*), wearing face masks and head-dresses. An escort of squires
and minstrels narrated the sequence. Three days of tourneying followed, in which the
king and his household knights challenged all comers. Full Tartar costumes may or
may not have implied exoticism, but the female procession made the chivalric and psychological scheme clear, involving elements of erotic charge, ethnic difference and the
jeopardy of male honour.[24] Most important was the dress code. Despite their remoteness and pagan religion, the Tartars (i.e. the Mongols of the il-Khanate of Persia) were
relatively well known in England, owing mainly to embassies in the reigns of Edward
I and Edward II, and the widely circulated manuscript descriptions of writers like
Odoricus de Pordenone, William de Rubruquis and Marco Polo. Seen as potential
allies in the war against Islam, the Tartars' success in occupying parts of Syria at the
turn of the fourteenth century raised expectations of a new grand offensive in the east.
In tandem with royal diplomacy, English chroniclers and poets expanded upon the
notion enthusiastically, incorporating it in narrative and fictional accounts, probably
reaching their widest audience in the tail-rhyme *King of Tars* (London, c.1320x1330),
a popular story based upon contemporary rumours of a marriage between a Christian
princess of Armenia and the brother of an il-Khan.[25]

Significantly, in the romance, a tournament is the scene of the heroine's ritual
humiliation. The princess looks down from a perch in her captor's castle, as a day-

---

[22]   Ibid. p. 47; Vale, *Edward III and Chivalry* pp. 70–1.

[23]   *Register of the Black Prince* vol. IV p. 10; Walsingham, *Historia Anglicana* vol. 1 p. 269; John of
Reading, pp. 152–3.

[24]   'Paulini' p. 354; Murimuth, *Continuatio* p. 63; Vale, *Edward III and Chivalry* pp. 62–3.

[25]   L. H. Hornstein, 'The Historical Background of the *King of Tars*' *Speculum* 16 (1941) pp. 404–11;
King of Tars ed. J. Perryman (Heidelberg, 1980). On the image of Tartar peoples and lands in the west
see P. Biller, *The Measure of Multitude: Population in Medieval Thought* (Oxford, 2000) pp. 228–35. For
English manuscripts of Odoricus de Pordenone and William de Rubruquis see Cavenaugh, *Study of
Books* vol. I p. 121.

long combat involving thirty thousand pagan knights is held in her honour. Earlier, Christ has appeared wearing white armour, but the competition concludes without a Christian champion, and the pagan prince proceeds with his marriage. Key scenes include a caravan of Tartar knights leading the heroine into captivity, the prince's miraculous conversion to the cross and, in closing, a triumphant military alliance against the entire pagan world.[26] Such strong narrative lines make it tempting to see motifs from the *King of Tars* in Edward III's September tournament. The court's staging of two dramatic sequences – the Tartar procession and the tourneying – apparently functioned as theatrical tableaux, compressing the story to its core didactic components: a wrong to be avenged and a martial reckoning with the heathen. Spice was perhaps added because of the chance to subvert an established storyline – displays of valour among Edward III's knights doubtless winning freedom for the ceremonially paraded noblewomen. It is impossible to be categorical (in the manuscript tradition the Tartar King can also appear as the 'Suodan of Damascus'), but the symbolic thread was obvious. Comparison of eastern Christendom's plight to that of an abused or captive maiden was a staple of crusade propaganda.[27] Set against Edward III's public proclamations of crusade devotion in parliament a few days later, the spectacle expressed, in arch chivalric mode, crusading's literary and romantic claims, and sought to conjure enthusiasm and political support.

The sifting of such ephemera needs to be set within the proper documentary context of cultural life at court, but behind the recourse to old emblems of Plantagenet prestige and the use of ornate dramatic schemes, there clearly lay sensitivity to the crusade's traditional political and emotional appeals. As seen in previous chapters, tournaments were commonly focal points for enthusiasm and military responses, assisting recruitment for the Hospitaller crusade in 1309, the diplomacy of the Cypriot campaigns in the 1360s and Anglo-French preparations for Louis of Bourbon's 1390 crusade. It was against this backdrop that Roger Stanegrave presented his recovery treatise *Li Charboclois* to the king, and that members of Edward III's household made vows to fight in the east.[28] Although expectations of a royal crusade were intermittent, historical knowledge was assumed and consciously elaborated. Richard I's crusade was the subject of discussion during Edward III's feasting of Peter of Cyprus, for instance, Edward teasing his guest that if Peter managed to recover Jerusalem, Cyprus, 'which my ancestor Richard restored to your predecessors for safekeeping', should be restored to the English king. Peter was perhaps ambushed after trying to recommend the example of the Lionheart himself. In light of Peter's visit, commentators close to

[26] *King of Tars* lines 370–80, 505–20, 965–70, 1555–2000.

[27] E.g. 'Non absque grandi' (1333) where the Old Testament prophetic image of Jerusalem as the captive daughter of Zion features in the prolegomena: *Reg. Montacute* no. 984. Cf. Isaiah 52:2 and Lamentations 2: 1–18. The daughter of Zion becomes the Bride of Christ in the book of Revelation (Revelation 3:12; 21:2, 9–10).

[28] BL, MS Cotton Otho D V fol. 9ᵛ; *Foedera* vol. II pt. 3 p. 162 (Bartholomew Burghersh).

court speculated that an English king would very shortly again be visiting Cyprus and Syria to convert Islam, notwithstanding Edward III's decidedly lukewarm attitude in the 1360s. Elsewhere at court, contact with crusading's fund of stories and historic forms remained close. A casual entry in an exchequer inventory of 1341 lists an old dagger as 'un cultell dount le roi Edward esroit nafry en la terre seinte'. This was evidently the assassin's knife used during the attempt on Edward I's life at Acre, now a relic of the royal household. Because it had entered popular folklore, with wide coverage in chronicles and church propaganda, the exchequer clerk assumed details of the episode to be everywhere familiar, which they almost were.[29]

Courtiers and crusade

Royal commemoration of the crusade raises broader questions about the military culture fostered by Edward I and his successors, particularly Edward III, whose own martial interests after 1337 focused almost entirely on the war he was waging against the French. This will be considered in greater detail in the final chapter, but insofar as it represented a prominent focal point of chivalric ambition it deserves mention here. Indeed, as previous chapters have shown, the overlapping circles of royal household, court and the aristocratic elite were often a special hub of crusade idealism and recruitment. In the 1340s, for example, the court was heavily represented in the *hethenesse*, bounded by the crusading adventurism of royal chamber-knights and *familiares*. Such close friends and important servants as the Burghersh and Bradestone families, Reginald Cobham, Henry Grosmont, William Montagu, Thomas Holand, and William Kilsby were quick to identify themselves with the crusade, and it was, as just described, a context in which the mimetic qualities of crusade literature and drama enjoyed a sympathetic audience. Other influential figures about the court in the 1340s, like John Fauconberg, Ralph Cromwell and William Clinton, made vows in the midst of full careers in Scotland and France, or while administering royal interests at home. Enthusiasm took a variety of guises, but the vogue possessed a firm institutional grip, incorporating lesser officials and household servants along with the more prominent names. Robert Littlebirs and John Bond, both recruits to the Smyrna campaign (1345), counted among the former, for instance, as did Thomas Usflete (d. 1355), dean of St Martins, an old clerk of Edward II, who bequeathed part of his estate to the church's Holy Land subsidy.[30] In terms of inculcating wide enthusiasm and material responses, it is not hard to see how patterns of behaviour at court provided a benchmark for knights keen to make a name for themselves, and for English

[29]   *Chronique Valois* p. 128; 'Alliterative Becket' *Bernadus de cura rei familiaris* ed. J. R. Lumby, EETS o.s. 42 (London, 1870) pp. 23–31. esp. 29; cf. Coote, *Prophecy and Public Affairs* pp. 130–1; Vale, *Edward III and Chivalry* p. 93. For the story of Edward's scrape with death see *Chronicle of Pierre de Langtoft* ed. T. Wright, r.s. 47 (London, 1866–1886) vol. II pp. 152–60.

[30]   *Calendar of Wills ... Court of Husting* vol. II p. 6.

chivalry as a whole. The outlook was the same in the 1360s, with royal knights and courtiers again assuming highly visible roles. Edward apparently spoke specifically of the royal chamber when he told Peter of Cyprus that he could expect the assistance of his knights and esquires against the Mamluks – at least two of his household squires were allocated to the Cypriot king. Enthusiasm touched the court hierarchy in various other ways. In the 1360s, for example, the faction dominated by Edward III's mistress, Alice Perrers, did brisk business lending money to cash-strapped knights trying to embark on the Lithuanian crusade.[31]

To some extent this reflected the king's desire to share in the glow of his knights' distant achievements, as might King Arthur. On the other hand it suggests a sufficiently elastic expectation of independence, whereby royal sanction was customarily (though not always) sought, and quite regularly given (as with pilgrimage) as a matter of aristocratic privilege. For long periods absorption in the French war naturally took centre stage – great efforts were expended by Edward III and the Black Prince to create a chivalry wedded tightly to the crown, culminating in the period's outstanding expression of chivalric fidelity, the Order of the Garter. But the special prestige of fighting the infidel remained plain to men such as Robert Morley, Bartholomew Burghersh and John Fauconberg, who, for different reasons, publicly threatened to withdraw from Edward III's wars, and all other wars against Christians, in order to devote their arms to the classic *cursus honorum* of crusading.[32] Such gestures could contain elements of political theatre, yet they also illustrate what passed in many quarters as respectable martial ideology: that the ultimate objective of knighthood was service to God, and one's own salvation, not defence of a secular ruler – ideas carefully weighed in the works of Geoffrey de Charny and Christine de Pisan. The high enthusiasm in the royal chamber merely added substance to the sentiment, as did the steady stream of knights venturing north to fight in the Baltic, or petitioning the curia for safe conducts to embark for the east. It did not matter that, unlike competing continental chivalric orders, the Garter's statutes omitted any mention of the crusade goal for brethren knights. On the contrary, it underlines the priority independently awarded the *hethenesse* by Edward III's knights.[33]

A special case may be made out of the 1390s when, despite his underwhelming military record, Richard II found himself presiding over an impressive revival of courtly crusading. The royal household was a main focus of ambition and crusader prestige. It is indicative that, as a grouping, the dozen or so courtiers and intimates appointed to the royal chamber from the mid 1380s showed particularly strong loyalty to the wars of the cross, amassing a breadth of experience in the years following the Anglo-French truce in 1389. Older knights, such as Lewis Clifford, John Harleston, John Clanvow

[31]   *CCR 1364–1368* p. 396; *CPR 1367–1370* p. 57.
[32]   For Morley, see Keen, *Origins* p. 58; *Foedera* vol. II pt. 3 p. 162; ASV, reg. supp. 22 fol. 53ʳ (new foliation) (Burghersh); *CPR 1343–1345* p. 6 (Fauconberg).
[33]   Boulton, *Knights of the Crown* pp. 229–32, 241–2, 252–61, 306. For Prussia see above pp. 74–80.

and William Neville, planned and participated in campaigns in Prussia, the Balkans and the eastern Mediterranean as well as Tunis. Younger men, like Richard's contemporaries and most trusted servants, Thomas, Lord Clifford, Sir John Russell, Sir Simon Felbrigg, Sir Thomas Percy, Richard Breton and Sir Stephen Scrope, also vacated the chamber to undertake crusade campaigns between 1390 and 1395. In 1390 Clifford's party of knights and esquires in the Tunis expedition provided a main plank of English participation, apparently underlining royal commitment. As under-chamberlain, Thomas Percy represented the household on Henry Bolingbroke's glamorous Baltic expedition.[34] Experience of the crusade was also generously represented in Richard's wider military affinity among the larger, more heterogeneous network of knights and esquires that aided the king's recovery of personal authority after 1389. Crusade militants in this bracket included prominent lords and knights such as Thomas, Lord Botiller, John Cornwall, Thomas Peytevyn junior, Bernard Brocas junior, John St John, Otho Grandson, Henry Percy 'Hotspur', Walter Bitterly, John Beaufort, John Paveley and Henry Scrope. The concentration of experience lay with the Prussian crusade during the early 1390s, and several knights were retained by the king shortly after their return to home shores.[35] There was obvious cachet in attracting veteran knights and esquires, men with international reputations, but the general effect was an argument of crusading's higher prestige, a message generously received and amplified in the independent actions of other English nobles and knights, though winning only limited applause from chroniclers. Key appointments to the chamber underlined the point. The most senior, the chamberlain John Holand, led a retinue against the Turks in 1394 and acted in the diplomacy surrounding the Nicopolis crusade, his appetite for dangerous campaigning as well as his high birth (he was half-brother to Richard II) recommending him to foreign powers. John Russell, the veteran of Tunis, was installed as Master of the King's Horse (1391–1397) and Simon Felbrigg, who fought in Prussia between 1391 and 1392, was named the king's Standard Bearer in 1394, both posts considered to hold special chivalric bearing. An influential figure in west midlands society, Russell's expertise in the joust and his widely reported exploits on crusade paved the way for his promotion. The prestigious post had been previously occupied by Thomas, Lord Clifford, who died in Prussia in 1391.[36]

If its topicality made the crusade a tempting emblem for Richard II's household, underpinning this was a genuine worship of knightly deeds. Indeed, as Christopher Fletcher has argued, although denied the battlefield adulation of his father and grandfather, Richard II nonetheless remained in thrall to martial achievement and sensitive to the legitimising qualities of active involvement in honourable war.[37] Among the

[34]   For these knights and campaigns see above Chapters 3 and 4.
[35]   See Given-Wilson, *Royal Household* pp. 212–22.
[36]   *West. Chron.* pp. 475, 481.
[37]   C. D. Fletcher, 'Manhood and Politics in the Reign of Richard II' *Past and Present* 189 (2005) pp. 3–39. Fletcher's ideas are expanded in his monograph *Richard II*, though with little attention to

knights high in Richard's esteem was Sir John Raddington, the royal diplomat and prior of the English Hospitallers. Royal letters singled out his impressive physical bearing and personal bravery. As a knight of St John, his was a form of higher chivalry, tested by uncommon hardship and the accumulation of great honours.[38] In terms of fostering a particular military culture, it may be no coincidence that Raddington's 'strenuous' (*strenuitas*) demeanour, which caught the king's eye, was a quality picked out by other commentators as a stamp of superior knighthood at court. The Westminster chronicler used the same term to describe three of Richard II's knights – John Clanvow, William Neville and John Paveley – individuals who had achieved great virtue and fame, having fought in pagan lands. The Ely chronicler (writing in 1388) used the adjective when recounting the story of the Hinton brothers and their exploits against Muslim Granada in the late 1340s. Similarly, Richard Fotheringhay was posthumously honoured for fighting 'manfully' (*viriliter*) against enemies of the faith. Language such as this built a case for crusading's superior calling.[39] Courtly events, including the reception of Lord Mowbray's bones at the Carmelite house in London in 1397, and the 1390 Smithfield tournament, helped reinforce the message at a time when Richard's martial leadership was under close scrutiny. The iconography of the celebrated Wilton Diptych, that sumptuously illuminated altarpiece of Richard II's court, may well have signalled similar idealism (see below pp. 202–3).

Insofar as part of crusading's attraction lay in its rich ceremonial forms, the most alluring symbol of enthusiasm in the 1390s was Philippe de Mézières's Order of the Passion, a potentially rich mixture of pageantry, diplomacy and aristocratic religion. This was the group that would precede the general *passagium*, clearing a path deep into Islam so that a second and greater Christian army could set out for Jerusalem.[40] On paper, at least, the foundation enjoyed impressive success. Between 1390 and 1395 over eighty knights, lords and peers pledged themselves to the Order either as brethren or promising to give patronage and supply funds. Some were from Scotland, Germany, Italy or Spain, but by far the greater number were English and French,

---

Richard's courtly connections to crusading. See too J. L. Gillespie 'Richard II: Chivalry and Kingship' and 'Richard II: King of Battles?' both in *The Age of Richard II* ed. J. L. Gillespie (Stroud, 1997) pp. 115–38, 139–64.

[38] *Diplomatic Correspondence* pp. 114–15.

[39] *West. Chron.* pp. 433, 481, 510 (Clanvow, Neville, Paveley); *CPR 1388–1392* p. 368, detail in NA, C66/332 m. 37 (Fotheringhay); cf. Froissart, vol. XIV p. 254; 'Continuatio Historiae Eliensis' p. 653 (Hinton); Raddington was appointed admiral of the Western Fleet in 1385. It seems most likely that he was a close relative of Baldwin Raddington, controller of Richard II's household (1381–1397). See Lewis, 'Simon Burley and Baldwin of Raddington' pp. 662–9. Luttrell makes a forceful case for Raddington's presence at Nicopolis, where he seems to have been killed: Düll et al. 'Faithful unto Death' pp. 181–2, 187, esp. 187 n 88.

[40] L. Staley, in *Languages of Power in the Age of Richard II* (University Park, 2005), holds an interesting discussion, pp. 131–7; see also A. Bell, 'English Members of the Order of the Passion: Their Political, Diplomatic and Military Significance' *Philippe de Mézières and his Age: Politics and Piety in the Fourteenth Century* eds R. Blumenfeld-Kosinski and K. Petkov (Leiden, 2011) pp. 321–48.

who enlisted in roughly equal proportions, according to Mézières's ordinances. They included the most powerful and influential figures from both realms: the dukes of Berry, Bourbon and Orleans, the admiral, the constable, and the renowned Marshal Boucicaut of France; the dukes of Lancaster, Gloucester and York, and the earls of Huntingdon, Rutland, Nottingham and Northumberland from England.[41] The twenty-eight English members represented a cross-section of Richard II's government, including household servants, courtiers, magnates and churchmen. Most were closely involved in the peace negotiations with France, as messengers, diplomats and attendants, and a number were close associates of John of Gaunt, including Otto Grandson, Sir Richard Abberbury, Thomas Erpingham and John Gilbert, the bishop of St David's. From the royal chamber there counted John Holand, Lewis Clifford, Simon Felbrigg and the veteran campaigner Sir John Harleston, who was also a retainer of the duke of Gloucester. Other notable affiliates included chamber knights and courtiers Hugh Despenser, the young Thomas Despenser (future earl of Gloucester) Ralph Percy, Henry Percy 'Hotspur', Sir Thomas West (a partisan of the earl of Rutland), the eminent Thomas, Lord Morley, and possibly Sir William Elmham. Of lesser rank was the esquire Richard Chelmswick, whose services were shared by Gaunt, Henry Bolingbroke and Richard II. In the Order's ordinances he is listed as *escuier du roy*. With the exception of the earls of Arundel and Warwick, who remained disaffected with Richard II's regime, the most prominent members of the English aristocracy were represented.[42]

The cosmopolitan framework of Mézières's Order was alluring, giving expression to key concepts of group loyalty and alliance. Most courtiers were conversant in such forms, familiar to the grand secular orders of chivalry. Of the twenty-eight Englishmen associated with the Passion, fourteen were current or future knights of the Garter, for example, and well used to the overlapping demands of group loyalty, competition and military honour. Courtiers regarded the creation of such bonds – used to chivalrously display and cement mutual interests – seriously.[43] In the event, however, beyond its diplomatic function – which is hard to pick out from the numerous ceremonial exchanges during the peace talks in the 1390s – the Order failed to make any significant military impact against heathendom. While the absence of knights from

---

[41]   A. Molinier, ' Description de deux manuscrits contenant la règle de la "Militia Passionis Jhesu Christi"' *Archives de l'Orient Latin* 1 (1881) pp. 335–64, 719; M. V. Clarke, *Fourteenth Century Studies* (Oxford, 1937) pp. 286–8. John Holand was presented with a copy of the Order's ordinances in 1395: Oxford Bod. MS Ashmole 865.

[42]   Clarke, *Fourteenth Century Studies* pp. 286–8. For Chelmswick's career see Walker, *Lancastrian Affinity* pp. 30, 82, 225. Richard's *familiares*, Rutland, Huntingdon and Nottingham, the nobility promoted by the king, would soon eclipse the royal uncles as main representatives of court – signalled by their supervision of marriage talks in 1395 and diplomacy to the imperial diet in 1397.

[43]   They were John of Gaunt; Edmund of York; Henry Percy, earl of Northumberland; Lewis Clifford; Thomas Woodstock; John Holand; Thomas Mowbray; Edward, earl of Rutland; Henry Percy 'Hotspur'; Thomas Despenser; Simon Felbrigg; Thomas Rempston; Henry Fitzhugh; Thomas, Lord Morley.

eastern powers reflected an essentially inward-looking emphasis, Mézières's stipulation that his knights should not fight anywhere outside of the Holy Land raises doubts over its practical application and objectives. Following the destruction of the Christian army at Nicopolis in 1396, it was obvious to contemporaries that the gravest threat to Christendom lay not in the Middle East, but in the Balkans. Even so, the list of English patrons and affiliates possessed strong cohesion when experience of fighting in the *hethenesse* is taken into account. Before the end of the 1390s at least fifteen had participated in crusade campaigns. Prussia was the most heavily represented, but other fronts such as Hungary, the eastern Mediterranean and north Africa widened the scope. As such, the fraternity represented an impressive concentration of idealism.[44]

In some cases, contact with the Order sparked fresh enthusiasm. It was shortly after meeting Mézières's evangelist Robert the Hermit that Thomas Woodstock began making provisions for a second crusade (1395), for example. A colleague in Mézières's Order (and in the Garter), Thomas, Lord Despenser, made similar preparations in 1396, placing his household retainers on notice of his crusade ambitions as the English and French courts prepared to meet near Calais. Another affiliate, Sir Ralph Percy, almost certainly mustered with the largely Burgundian Nicopolis crusade, and Thomas Mowbray, the earl of Nottingham, sent along members of his household. When exiled in 1398, Mowbray's instinct (with Richard II's approval) was to try to salvage his honour by visiting the Mediterranean and the northern frontier, embarking with a large military wardrobe and forty armed companions, possibly in execution of a crusade vow.[45]

Reputations and honour

For many knights, not just those implicated in royal diplomacy, rich social and cultural contact between the courts of northern Europe was the background to continued fascination with crusading. Genoa held up the prospect of *bone compaignie et bone chere* to English knights and squires travelling with the Tunis crusade, catching chivalry's elitist ethos, but also promising the essential ingredient of solidarity and fraternity between participants.[46] The influence of high-ranking foreign exponents of the *reyse*, such as the duke of Guelders in 1390 and William IV, count of Jülich, of the Low Countries in the 1360s, has already been suggested; numerous other 'stranger-knights' helped shape the milieu. Men such as Robert, count of Namur, Enguerrand de Coucy, Soudic de la Touc, Jean Boucicaut, Giles d'Argentein, Leo IV of Armenia and Otto Grandson in one capacity or another – as members of the

---

[44] See appendix for details.

[45] *Indentures* no. 85 pp. 117–18 (Woodstock), no. 87 pp. 119–20 (Despenser); Düll et al. 'Faithful unto Death' pp. 181–2, 187 (Percy); *Foedera* vol. III pt. 4 p. 141 (Mowbray).

[46] NA, SC1/51/37.

Order of Garter, knights of the royal chamber, members of noble affinities, or as prisoners – enjoyed close interaction with English nobles and knights, stretching social horizons and sowing enthusiasm for the crusade. Froissart's readership knew that knights acted upon a platform that extended from the southern uplands of Andalusia and Extremadura to the freezing shores of the Baltic.[47] It is difficult to reconstruct the fame of figures such as Adam von Moppertingen, Henry II, count of Holstein, and Sanchet d'Aubréticourt, all men well known at Edward III's court, but reputations hewn out of crusading automatically gained currency. Moppertingen, 'a true knight of Lady Honour', who fought for Edward III against the Scots 'like a very Roland', was equally renowned for his exploits against the tribes of Lithuania. His career was cast in fashionable literary mode by the famous poet Claes Haenen, Gerles herald.[48] To be much spoken of in the way of Yveres Jovere, a Frieslander who had covered himself in glory in Prussia, Hungary, Turkey, Rhodes and Cyprus, or the valorous Marshal Boucicaut, was the motivation of many going against the enemies of God, according to Froissart. Literary reports, minstrelsy, and contact at tournaments kept English knights schooled in the latest chivalrous names, and kept men eager to partake in crusading's prestige.[49] Nor was the traffic all one-way. As already seen, English knights would regularly carry the torch of crusade zeal on behalf of their continental counterparts. The Black Prince's court at Bordeaux was a prime focus of recruitment in the 1360s, and individual crusaders such as John Grey, lord of Codnor, who fought in the bodyguard of Pierre Thomas (1365), and John Bond, a veteran of Smyrna (1344), established international reputations on crusade, winning high praise for their deeds in royal and papal letters. On his part, Henry Grosmont used his 1352 expedition to Prussia to confirm his high standing on the continent and to foster support for Edward III's wars among German and northern knights. That with him travelled many of the victors of Crécy, where the German king John of Bohemia had been killed (fighting for the French), may have added special notoriety. In the same way, when it came to appointing his military advisors, Hugh IV of Cyprus chose an English knight, William Gaston, as the official responsible for gathering foreign recruits against the Turks. Not much is known of Gaston's career, but his nationality and fighting record clearly recommended itself to a Mediterranean power seeking greater contact with the west.[50]

Threaded throughout, and of particular importance, was the question of family honour and prestige. Because little outshone crusading as an outward marker of noble lineage and knightly virtue, the cult of arms, the family's stature and a record of crusading were closely associated in the contemporary aristocratic mind. A strong

---

[47]   Even at Henry IV's court, the most insular of the period, twenty of his household knights were foreigners: Given-Wilson, *Royal Household* pp. 287–90.
[48]   Keen, *Chivalry* p. 140.
[49]   Froissart, vol. XIII p. 132.
[50]   *De Visione Sancti Simonis Stock* pp. 245–95, 306; *Documents nouveaux* pp. 362–3.

sense of dynastic honour, what Hoccleve described as the 'prickk of duetee', continu-
ally broke the surface. Traditions of crusading found expression in numerous family
churches and residences, in funerary muniments, stained glass windows and inscriptions, and in the plastic arts. Window memorials similar to that erected for Lord
Morley, who was killed in Prussia, helped advertise the special honour of crusading
and other notable deeds among local knightly families and clients, signalling dynastic
pride and Christian devotion. The Scrope family had one made in the church of St
Michael, Heydour (Lincs.), to commemorate Geoffrey Scrope's Lithuanian crusade.[51]
It followed that for many fourteenth-century knights and their families the crusade
war offered potential for historical speculation and the creation of a gilded past. The
elaborate claims of Sir William Carrington, a Cheshire knight of no particular distinction, alleging that his ancestor Michael had been Richard I's standard-bearer in the
Holy Land, epitomised the impulse. The story has no foundation, but its social aspiration was mirrored in the claims of numerous other families, such as the Moultons
and D'Oillys of Lincolnshire, where supposed ancestral involvement in the Third
Crusade was the stamp of true chivalry.[52] Genealogists of the Cobhams, Furnivals,
Willoughbys, Cliffords, Beaumonts and Mowbrays were on much firmer ground,
emphasising the genuine crusade achievements found within their pedigrees. The
Beaumonts, for instance, three generations of whom undertook crusades in the fourteenth century, could trace their direct descent from John Brienne, king of Jerusalem
and emperor of Constantinople (d. 1237), leader of the Fifth Crusade, and they often
displayed the arms of Jerusalem quartered with their own. A variety of connections
– dynastic, emulatory and mythical – existed between several English noble houses
and Godfrey de Bouillon, the crusade hero *par excellence*.[53] The strongest claims were
held by the Bohun earls of Hereford, who could trace their line to the eleventh-cen-
tury counts of Boulogne. They signalled their descent with the emblem of the swan
in their livery, the animal device traditionally associated with Godfrey and the myth
of the *Chevalier au cigne*.[54] Others laid a like claim. The Tosney swan badge was well
attested at the beginning of the fourteenth century, worn, it was said, by virtue of their
descent from the Swan Knight. Historians of the Beauchamp family also made busy
with the legend, incorporating a variation of the story into their historical mythology,
alongside *Guy of Warwick*. The Courtenay earls of Devon, Stafford earls of Stafford,

[51] Thomas Hoccleve, *Minor Poems* ed. F. J. Furnivall, rev. J. Mitchell and A. I. Doyle, EETS e.s. 61,
73 (London, 1970) no. 42 lines 37–40. For Morley see above p. 84; P. Hebgin-Barnes, 'A Triumphant
Image: Henry Scrope's Window in Heydour Church' *Medieval Life* 4 (1996) pp. 26–8.
[52] Oxford Bod. MS Dugdale 15 fol. 281 (Carrington); J. Finlayson, '*Richard, Coer de lyon*: Romance,
History or Something in Between?' *Studies in Philology* 87 (1990) p. 166 (Moulton, D'Oilly).
[53] J. G. Waller, 'The Lords of Cobham, their Monuments and the Church' *Archaeologia Cantiana* 11
(1877) p. 53; *Peerage* vol. II p. 59; Keen, *Chivalry* p. 139; Gough, vol. I pt. 1 p. 181; Dugdale, *Monasticon
Anglicanum* vol. VI p. 320; W. Dugdale, *Baronage of England* (London, 1675–1676) vol. II pp. 85–6.
[54] For the crusader Walter of Hereford (d. 1159) see Evans 'Crusade and Society' pp. 91–2; Wagner,
'Swan Badge and the Swan Knight' p. 127.

and Luttrell family absorbed similar traditions.[55] It is easy to see how this fitted with men's consciousness of pedigree and knightly quality. Thomas Woodstock, setting great store by his marriage to Eleanor Bohun, liberally adopted her father's glamorous crusading mantle. On the eve of his departure for Prussia, he presented the prior of Westminster with a decorative golden cope, embroidered with the letters T. A. in monogram and interspersed with his livery badge of the swan made out in pearls. Synonymous with the duke's military and dynastic ambitions, the swan design and the initial letters of Thomas and Eleanor (Alianora) invoked both Woodstock's marriage into the Bohun family and his burgeoning crusade intent. Meanwhile, the earl of Stafford, taking his cue from his father-in-law, sent a jewelled badge bearing Woodstock's swan livery to the prominent London goldsmith Nicholas Twyford for repair, and had a second one of a heavier weight newly produced as part of preparations for their joint *reyse*.[56]

Clearly, more than nostalgia was involved in the search for an ancestral origin-myth or antique crusade heritage. Woodstock's tight grasp of the symbols and heritage of Bohun's knighthood, including the crusade, possibly served a narrower political agenda – one angled against his nephew Henry Bolingbroke, whose marriage to Humphrey Bohun's co-heir in 1381 established a rival claimant to the Hereford/Essex inheritance. Yet the desire to emulate the deeds of previous generations reached out beyond simple convention or political expedience to reflect a whole cultural outlook, in which the proving of hereditary worth and knightly identity was of very treasured significance. The obligations imposed by lineage were held up conspicuously in crusade bulls and sermons, where it was customarily taught that cross-takers followed not only in the path of Christ, but also in the footsteps of their forefathers. Canon law and noble wills provided reinforcement, making the heirs of *vovens* responsible for outstanding or defaulted crusade oaths, though in most circumstances this could be relaxed without action or with payment of a vow redemption.[57] The injunction of Psalm 116, 'I will pay my vows to the Lord in the presence of all his people' (v.14), could load the public proving of one's worth, and the worth of one's dynasty, with

[55]   Mason, 'Legends of the Beauchamps' Ancestors' pp. 25–40; Wagner, 'Swan Badge and the Swan Knight' p.127.

[56]   *West. Chron.* p. 479. A pictorial record of another gift, this time to St Albans in 1388, shows Woodstock holding a swan with open wings in his left hand. The accompanying inscription states that the duke had donated a cloth of gold and a circular collar with a white swan with open wings as though about to fly. 'Catalogus Benefactorum Monasteri S. Albani', BL, MS Cotton Nero D V II fol. 110. Amongst a number of crusade-themed texts collected at Gloucester's Essex and London residences was the Anglo-Norman *Histoire de Chivaler a cigne*. Goodman, *Loyal Conspiracy* p. 80; SRO, D644/1/2/4 m. 4.

[57]   E.g. 'Non absque grandi', 'Ad commemorandum', *Reg. Montacute* nos 984–90. William Marchia, the bishop of Bath and Wells (d. 1302), bequeathed 100 marks for the crusade expenses of his brother, or in the event of his death, the bishop's nephew: *Reg. Droxford*, vol. I p. 43. For other published examples see *Reg. Shrewsbury* vol. I p. 267; *Testamenta Vetusta* vol. I pp. 62, 103; J. A. Brundage, 'The Votive Obligations of Crusaders' *Traditio* 24 (1968) pp. 77–118.

religious intensity. Here, demonstrations of worldly fame and knightly prestige were spiritual ends in themselves, enabling proponents of the crusade to designate the prize of military celebrity as the workings of pious devotion.

Closer analysis shows that a large proportion – possibly the majority – of known English crusaders in this period were possessed of family traditions that extended back to the twelfth and thirteenth centuries. Some, like the Ferrers of Groby and Percies of Northumberland, could trace their heritage back to the First Crusade, with ancestors travelling in the train of Robert, duke of Normandy. In both cases the habit survived three centuries. More recent traditions could also take strong hold: four generations of the Fitzwarin family completed expeditions between 1270 and 1370, two fighting in the east, two campaigning with the Teutonic Knights. Four generations of the Montagu family undertook to go against the 'enemies of the faith' between 1310 and 1390. Like other crusaders of the 1340s, John de la Ryvere's father took the cross with Edward II in Paris.[58] Hardening barriers of class and hereditary office may have concentrated the effect, encouraging a view that true chivalry was confined to those who built significantly upon the deeds of their ancestors. The Tunis edict – that only soldiers of gentle birth were to be embarked – tallied with the entry prohibitions of knightly confraternities and the customary law books of the age that defined nobility and its privileges.[59] Ambivalence towards the *routiers*, the rising costs of war, and a perceived decline in knightly standards during the reigns of Edward II and Richard II sharpened the debate, giving eminence to the wars of the cross as a function of 'old' chivalry (what Mézières terms 'true chivalry'), notwithstanding that most social groups were open to the crusade's emotional, spiritual and material pressures. This gave families at all levels of military society reason to exhaust their history of crusading no less than their record of service to the crown.[60]

Points of conflict

Not all approved of the synthesis between chivalric display, social esteem, literary invention and *negotium crucis*. The crusade was certain to be controversial so long as it remained alive in politics and religion. Prominent targets of criticism in this period were crusades against Christians and the bad behaviour of the military elite, either because they fought with dubious intent or because they failed to take up arms at all. The revulsion at killing pagans articulated in John Gower's *Confessio Amantis* (c.1390),

---

[58]   For Ferrers and Percy see Evans, 'Crusade and Society' pp. 105–7. For Fitzwarin see Lloyd, *English Society and the Crusade* appendix 4; *Brut* pp. 277–8; Paravicini, *Die Preussenreisen* vol. I p. 123; *CPR 1367–1370* p. 57. For Montagu see *Reg. Droxford,* vol. I p. 65; *CCR 1308–1313* p. 389; Villani, *Cronica* vol. IV pp. 57–8; *Cronica Alfonso* vol. I pp. 360–70; Paravicini, *Die Preussenreisen* vol. I pp. 123, 127, 180, vol. II p. 216. For Ryvere see *CPR 1307–1313* p. 581.

[59]   Froissart, vol. XIV pp. 154–5.

[60]   Oxford Bod. MS Ashmole 865.

although to be read partly as literary convention, reflects the ambivalence towards the knightly code which seemed to take hold in some quarters during the second half of the period, fed by the stagnation of the Hundred Years War and papal schism. Chaucer's *Book of the Duchesse* poked fun at noblewomen who sent knights out to Christendom's ends (to 'Walakye, Pruyse, Tartarye,' to 'Alisaundre' and 'Turkye') on errands of love and chivalry, calling instead for more reflective displays of *gentillesse* (c.1365). Some higher purpose was expected of knightly questing. The contrast with the Knight of the *Canterbury Tales* who fights in the *hethenesse* out of regard for his own soul and for the sake of 'trouthe, honour, fredom' and 'curteisie' is telling.[61] The opulence and rivalry sometimes attached to chivalric crusading in the Baltic attracted the ire of Mézières in the 1360s and 1390s. It was a counterpoint to the vision of a Holy Land crusade formed of soldiers as committed to the priestly and contemplative life as he. To some extent, Walsingham's well-known attack upon the knights of Richard II's court echoed this commentary. Alleging their preference for the bed chamber over the battlefield and ignoring their strong record in the *hethenesse*, the chronicler bemoaned (writing after 1399) the decline in royal chivalry. Disapproval at Richard II's abandonment of the French war, rather than a sudden collapse of martial values, seems to have been at work.[62]

Much of this was familiar ground, the crusade long being a ripe target for moralists and social critics. Since the twelfth century, failure to relive the victories of Godfrey de Bouillon had been put down to the various pathologies of body and soul.[63] Even the national crusade hero Richard I was vulnerable to forensic criticism. John of Bromyard singled out the king's lapse into vanity and pride as a reason for the destruction of the Third Crusade. Treachery, jealousy and loose-living had invaded the ranks of Richard I's army, according to the preacher. The crusade, and particularly the events of the First Crusade, presented an opportunity to lecture on vainglory as well as spiritual regeneration. The fact of its prominence at court during the fourteenth century in itself invited such comment.[64] Occasionally, factors other than clerical ambivalence towards chivalry seem to be at play. Despite his daubing of the Nájera campaign (1367) with a quasi-crusade mantle, the well-informed author of the *Vie du Prince Noir* is curiously quiet on the subject of crusade enthusiasm at the Black Prince's court in Gascony, for example, with the recruitment and passage

---

[61]   Gower, *The English Works* vol. I pp. 293–4, pp. 345–7; Chaucer, *The Complete Works* vol. I p. 312; Keen, 'Chaucer's Knight' pp. 45–63. The Knight's service in the Muslim armies of the 'lord of Palatye', against the onslaught of the Ottomans, may be seen as pragmatic defence of local Christians. See Pratt, *Chaucer and War* pp. 124–5.

[62]   Mézières, *Songe du vieil pèlerin* vol. I p. 264; Walsingham, *Chronica Maiora* p. 375.

[63]   See Peter of Blois's (c.1130–c.1203) carping (sentences from his *Epistolae*) interpolated into an early fourteenth-century sermon handbook compiled by Thomas of Ireland (c.1270–1340): *Manipulus Florum* (Venice, 1483) 'Militia'; and in the vernacular sermon (c.1380, anonymous) *Middle English Sermons* pp. 254–5.

[64]   Bromyard, *Summa Praedicantium* 'Bellum' §50.

of Peter of Cyprus's crusade and Amadeo of Savoy's Constantinople expedition in the 1360s meriting no mention at all. Interested in high chivalry and eulogising the 'most valiant prince in the world', the author follows a sympathetic agenda, making a case for the prestige of Plantagenet wars, while apparently dissembling over the competing claims of the Mediterranean crusade. He tells nothing of divergent ambition within the prince's retinue, including the famous argument between the prince and the Gascon lord Albret over the thwarted crusade plans of the Gascon feudatory. When Albret found out that the Black Prince had needlessly raised – and then disbanded – eight hundred of his soldiers, he was furious, reportedly scolding the prince for keeping his men from passing the sea to Jerusalem, Constantinople or Prussia (1366).[65] Partly, this was about affirming the special standing of dynastic and royal wars, as opposed to other noble causes. An ethos of justice, amity and knightliness was what explained the Black Prince's participation in foreign war, according to the poet, as well as a prophecy that the Plantagenet leopard would spread into foreign lands. Shutting out news of the capture of Alexandria and recent fighting in Prussia and the Black Sea, expeditions which attracted the support of the Black Prince's clients and dependants, the poet instead deployed recognisable 'crusade' motifs to help underline the special standing of the Prince's Iberian campaign.

Thus, against Henry Trastamara, Englishmen outdid even the paragons of Christian chivalry Oliver and Roland in acts of heroism, and the embarking Prince is shown as a pious warrior setting out despite the tearful remonstrations of his wife and household, a stock scene of wars of the cross.[66] As seen many times above, such sensitivity over the rival claims of national and crusade war was rare among the English nobility, although it probably reflected attitudes among the ranks of the royal family. Possibly, it marked the hardening of debate over the crown's monopoly of military power. One effect was to protect the reputations of those who refrained from taking the cross or making vows. Another factor may have been the English government's growing suspicion towards the church's award of crusade monies to the *routiers* and others implicated in papally-blessed campaigning during the 1360s.

A similar silence or omission among English (but not continental) chronicle accounts perhaps explains why the crusade enthusiasm among Richard II's household and inner circle of friends went largely unreported in the early 1390s. Instead, emphasis upon household abuses conjured the image of an unchivalric king and a dandyish royal chamber, a picture pressed most forcefully by Walsingham after Richard's deposition, but present in other accounts too. By contrast, aided by Lancastrian newsletters, Bolingbroke's exploits in Lithuania and the eastern Mediterranean received generous applause, his crusade activities – along with his bloodless invasion of England in 1399 – helping to establish the future Henry IV as a figure of higher nobility and energetic knighthood. It is doubtful that this amounted to wider collusion in the

[65] Froissart, vol. VII p. 145.
[66] Chandos Herald, *Life of the Black Prince* lines 45, 1641, 2030, 2049–103, 2783.

construction of an image of king and court, and the expunging of all references to Richard II's knightly interests and patronage of the crusade. But given the stir caused by campaigning in Prussia between 1390 and 1394, and Tunis in 1390, the lack of commentary is conspicuous. It would seem that the need to account for the king's increasingly divisive policies and erratic behaviour encouraged something of an ellipsis – ecclesiastical chroniclers and other critics finding it hard to square the crusade's positive dimensions and its usual associations of power and honour with what was considered Richard II's increasingly arbitrary and unpopular rule.[67]

Finally, a more radical attitude towards the crusade was formed in the writings of arch-heresiarch John Wyclif and some of his Lollard disciples. Incensed at the passage of Despenser's Flanders crusade and the sale of indulgences in 1382–1383, Wyclif condemned the institution in his *De Cruciata* (1383), which portrayed the exercise as a corrupt and deceitful ploy, among other things, to raise money. Other heterodox texts, such as the *Opus Arduus*, a treatise on the Apocalypse, corroborated the view, the Flanders crusade attracting some of Lollardy's most violent polemic. Famous as a diatribe against schism crusades, Wyclif's denial of papal jurisdiction, sacramental theology and other salient beliefs amounted to a wholescale attack upon crusading's function as a penitential exercise, stripping all crusade wars of their historic, formal identity.[68]

Despite their rhetorical force, however, it is hard to see how widely the influence of such views travelled, particularly as they converged with less radical anti-clerical and pacifist dissent. Even among suspected Wyclifite disciples, such convictions were not uniformly held. Sir William Beauchamp, a nobleman reputedly sympathetic to Wyclif, considered fighting as a captain on Despenser's crusade, for example (he withdrew in a dispute over pay).[69] Other supposed sympathisers of Wyclif found ways to reconcile knightly endeavour with their unorthodox positions on doctrine, or to otherwise temporarily hold their religious convictions and military life apart, regardless of the dubious trappings of the campaign trail. It is significant that the Lollard manifesto pinned up in parliament in 1395 singled out chivalric crusading as a symptom of the moral torpor instilled by the institutional church. This attested to its vogue. But as a response to burgeoning crusade enthusiasm among Richard II's nobility, its chief criticism was not the poisonous corruption of papal indulgences, but that knights merely attacked the infidel as a way of making a name for themselves, with temporal fame in mind: 'knythtis that rennen to hethnesse to geten hem a name in sleigne

[67] For Bolingbroke's image as a crusader hero see L. Staley, 'Gower, Richard II, Henry of Derby, and the Business of Making Culture' *Speculum* 75 (2000) pp. 68–96.

[68] John Wyclif, *Polemical Works in Latin* ed. R. Buddensieg (London, 1883) vol. II pp. 592, 595, 603, 610–24. For the *Opus Arduus* and comment see A. Hudson, *The Premature Reformation: Wycliffite Texts and Lollard History* (Oxford, 1988) pp. 368–9.

[69] 'William Beauchamp, first Baron Bergavenny' *DNB* http://www.oxforddnb.com/view/article/50236, accessed 11 Dec. 2011.

of men'. Far from vilifying all devotees of the *hethenesse*, rhetoric of this type was intended to limit offence given to the political classes, including those knights sympathetic to Wyclif's other teachings, leaving intact the ideal of fighting for the love of God as a positive virtue. Shorn of its radical content, emphasis upon old sermon themes of vanity and flamboyance instead added to the debate about puritanical religion, knightly endeavour and legitimate violence unfolding in other parts of political society.[70]

---

[70] 'Twelve Conclusions' *Selections from English Wycliffite Writings* ed. A. Hudson (Cambridge, 1978) pp. 24–9.

9

The Chivalric Nation and Images of the Crusader King

Central to this emergent debate over the preferred outlet for arms in the 1380s and 1390s lay the relationship between national patriotic interests and faithful prosecution of the crusade ideal, tensions prominent throughout the pages above. Knightly constituents of the later crusades may, or may not, have been well placed to reconcile such competing ideals, but their presence raises some important final questions. As many knights found, going against the infidel offered a route to social advancement, promotion in county community and at court, as well as an opportunity to escape the backwaters of domesticity. It has been seen how crusading's various appeals and forms could spill over into military behaviours at court, not only when talk of a royal crusade was in the air. It has also been seen how the wide reach of English crusading on the fringes of Christendom was mirrored by a generous reception for its participants within the value system of contemporary chivalry. Supporting this, as previous chapters have tried to make clear, was a raft of sidewards cultural pressures and incentives, affirming the role of the itinerant knight-penitent. Yet also bearing down on aspirant crusaders was an increasingly rich vision of chivalric honour, national destiny and Christian salvation, centred on the figure of the warrior king and the much-prophesised recovery crusade. Importantly, although largely overlooked in modern accounts, this image of royal and chivalric power, bound up in the crusade, helped nourish and affirm military society's commitment to the cause, fusing with other messages and pressures associated with loyalty to the crown. Aspects of this have been sketched out already, but because it added a vital symbolic reference point for chivalric society, fuller study of its various forms and appeals may help us to begin to draw together conclusions about the behaviour and outlook of those pledging arms against the infidel. At the meeting point of noble religion, military loyalty, group identity and political fidelity, it helped instil underlying ideas of honourable war and what constituted good kingship, good politics and good chivalry.

Partly this was because by the late middle ages the office of kingship and the ideals of knighthood had reached a state of near-symbiosis, the warlike needs of the state and the growth of the cult of arms promoting successfully a code of 'chivalric kingship'.[1] Such a royal style has often been identified as the primary vehicle of an increasingly national or insular-minded chivalry. Yet, as practising knights, kings were themselves inseparable from the chivalric milieu, including the crusade. Here, too, they were held to personally epitomise national knighthood, its spirit, vigour and military ambition. Famously, the French royal house could draw on the traditions of St Louis, Charlemagne, and Clovis, revered for their religious dedication and the parts they had played in identifiably holy war. The squaring of the crusade with the history and destiny of English monarchs was perhaps a greater creative challenge, given the energy expended by kings of England and English chivalry in wars of a different nature, along the contested fringes of Britain and France. Edward II was, after all, the last king of England to take the cross. Yet support for the crusade idea (here meaning Christian hegemony over the east and destruction of the *hethenesse* in the west) drew from the rich compound of historical, literary and mythological influences that helped inform English kingship in this period. Besides the Old Testament models of Prudence, Justice, Temperance and Fortitude, emphasised by instructional texts, focus on the sacral qualities of royal power encouraged at coronation and other rituals stressed the sanctity of monarchs and their holy destiny in leading their people to pre-eminence in Christendom.[2] Evidence of the looked-for English crusader king may be found across a range of literary and non-literary sources, including treatises on the nature of kingship, political prophecy and royal ceremonial. It offered a mode of political thought, amongst a range of other entrenched influences, and served to reinforce both crusading's higher calling and English chivalry's privileged place as rescuers of Christendom. To the extent that it coloured wider perceptions, proper insight into the political, ethical and symbolic dimensions of the late-medieval crusade can only be found by exploring this context. Framed against this ideological background, and meshed with ideas about personal religion, national honour and public duty, a series of fresh perspectives may be opened on the actions and motivations of would-be knightly crusaders.

Crusading and the fabric of royal power

Chivalric society's attachment to the concept of royal power as an instrument of holy war was deep. In 1307 a striking image of the English king as *rex crucesignatus* was

---

[1]   M. H. Keen, 'Chivalry and English Kingship in the Later Middle Ages', *War, Government and Aristocracy in the British Isles, c.1150–1500* eds C. Given-Wilson, A. Kettle and L. Scales (Woodbridge, 2008) pp. 250–66; Saul, *For Honour and Fame* pp. 76–93; see also A. B. Ferguson, *The Indian Summer of English Chivalry* (Durham, N.C., 1960). For an anatomy of late-medieval English kingship see J. L. Watt, *Henry VI* (Cambridge, 1996) pp. 13–39.
[2]   For literary constructions of English sovereign power see D. Matthews, *Writing to the King: Nation, Kingship and Literature in England, 1250–1350* (Cambridge, 2010); cf. Watt, *Henry VI* pp. 13–39.

coined in the days and weeks following the death of Edward I. In an unprecedented spurting of panegyric, the former king, 'Edward the old and hoary', was held up as the lost hope of Jerusalem, 'the flower of her chivalry' and devoted servant of her 'lordship'. Loosened from Edward's hands, the banner of the Holy Church, which was to be 'reared up full high', was now cast down low. The show of grief, formulaic and masking a measure of relief at the promise of new beginnings, was nonetheless an unusual departure in royal obsequies, drawing heavily on French and continental traditions.[3] A powerful echo was sounded at the papal court, where Clement V presided over masses for Edward I, again mourning the loss of a champion of the church and the setback for the crusade. Papal encomium of this nature was also a new development (as was noticed at other courts), reflecting Edward's status as chief custodian of Christian hopes.[4] Such statements were capable of being read various ways. The formulae of *Commendatio lamentabilis* (c. 1307), a narrative meditation on Edward's death, for example, was analogous to the instructional genre of 'mirrors for princes', and in its focus on crusade, elements of a manifesto for kingship are clear. As God's vehicle of national glory and public salvation, the late king 'had taken in hand all England to rule and teach to go to the Holy Land to win us heaven's bliss', the roles of high priest and warrior king concentrated in his hands. A messianic strain ('very long we may cry and call before we have found such a king') called to mind the deliverance of the nations of Israel, and the claims of special sanctity bound up in crusading.[5] Beneath the florid prose, a key purpose was to lay down new markers of English royal and chivalric power. Political expectations were intended to run seamlessly between generations, beyond Edward I. One English lament singles out his heir for special hope: 'May it please God in Trinity that your son may effect conquest of Jerusalem the noble city and pass into the Holy Land.'[6] Messages of this type joined a range of literary strands and other mediums intended to instruct new kings in their office, marking out the sphere of the crown. As has already been seen, the coronation ceremony ritualised similar sentiment, coupling conquest of the pagan world with other core responsibilities of anointed rulers.

Stanegrave's *Li Charboclois*, referencing the well-known *Secreta Secretorum*, with its injunction to all crowned princes to chastise enemies of the church, establishes the scope of the vision at play. Here crusading was set central to the king's anointed task of ministering to the health of body politic, alongside the other mystical and practical

---

[3] 'Commendatio lamentabilis' *Chronicles of the Reigns of Edward I and Edward II* vol. I pp. 3–21; *Political Songs of England* pp. 241–50, and especially the prayer for Edward I's soul, romantically attributed to Clement V (E dist per grant humilité:/a place à Dieu en Trinité/ Qe vostre fiz en post conquere/Jerusalem la digne citié/ E passer en la seinte tere!) p. 245.

[4] D. L. D'Avray, *Death and the Prince* (Oxford, 1994) pp. 70–9, 168–71.

[5] Commendatio lamentabilis' *Chronicles of the Reigns of Edward I and Edward II* vol. I pp. 3–21; see B. Weiler 'The *Commendatio Lamentabilis* for Edward I and Plantagenet Kingship' *War, Government and Aristocracy in the British Isles, c. 1150–1500* pp. 114–30.

[6] *Political Songs of England* p. 250.

functions of monarchy. John XXII drew on the same themes in his letters to Edward II and later to his son.[7] This was special pleading of course, but the core message was widely diffused. Addressing practitioners of chivalry, Bonet's *Tree of Battles* identifies the crusade war as a priority for all 'virtuous, wise and discreet' kings. It was central to their safe custody of the church, and dispensation of their God-given duties. Similarly, Christine de Pisan describes defence of Christian patrimony as incumbent upon Catholic princes, following Bonet outside the normal confines of the chivalric treatise to discuss issues of royal political and social obligation.[8] Sermon texts and moralist stories helped amplify associated themes. An English vernacular sermon composed c.1380x1390 draws on the structure and invective of protest poetry and 'estates satire' to single out the connection between just and prudent kingship and the successful defence of Christendom. Inverting the image of the righteous crusader king, the preacher points instead to the depravity of Christian princes as an explanation for the growing power of the heathen. It was because of their sinful abuses and tyrannical rule that God saw fit to inflict ever more powerful heathen rulers on Christian domains.[9] Popular sermon exempla adopted similar edifying story lines. The case of the emperor who repented of his wayward rule by leading a crusade was featured in the most widely used sermon collection for mendicant preachers. His reward for rectifying his government was reconciliation with God and martyrdom in the east. Another well-worn story was the tale of the righteous king who risked all to save his patrimony and people from an onrush of Saracens, only to be abandoned in battle by his son and heir. Battered and bloody from the fight, the king, having defeated the invaders, seized away his son's princely crown and condemned him to perpetual imprisonment. It was impossible to overlook the triple crime of ignoring a feudal summons, denying a father and failing to make a stand against the infidel. On counsel from his barons, the king judged the prince to lack the necessary qualities of a Christian ruler and made an heir of his younger son instead.[10] These stock portraits, arguing for a particular vision of kingly and noble power, were not fringe ideas. Such archetypes wormed their way into popular consciousness, complementing and building upon other established models of kingly and knightly behaviour. Old Testament templates of holy war involved similar core principles, their evident historicity rendering the wars *in hethenesse* as part of a timeless bending to God's will. The struggles of Saul, David, Judas Maccabeus and their anointed successors against the heathen enemies of Israel laid up a vision of legitimate warfare pursued for the deliverance of God's inheritance and the salvation of his people. The Old Testament kings enacted several 'regal' functions simultaneously: fulfilling prophetic discourse as saviour-

[7]   BL, Cotton Otho D V fol. 11ᵛ. For the *Secreta* chapter 'How a king should be religious' see *Lydgate and Burgh's Secrees of Old Philisoffres* ed. R. Steele, EETS e.s. 66 (London 1894) p. 34 lines 1072–9. *CPL* vol. II pp. 427, 434, 500.

[8]   Bonet, *Tree of Battles* p. 211; Pisan, *Book of fayttes of armes and of chivalry* p. 11.

[9]   *Middle English Sermons* pp. 255–6.

[10]   *Gesta Romanorum* pp. 197–208; Bourbon, *Anecdotes historiques* no. 197.

rulers, they were also law-givers, temple-builders, conduits of God's grace and indomitable instruments of divine wrath, slaying the heathen tribes, annihilating all tainted by sin.

It was probably within the tradition of formal 'princely' counsel that evidence of an operating crusade ethos at Edward II's court is first seen. A few days before his father's funeral, Edward II received an embassy sent by Öljeitü, the il-khan of Mongolia (16 October 1307), bearing letters reminding the court of the historic alliance against the Mamluks of Syria, which the il-khan proposed to maintain. Edward's letters of reply, issued some weeks later, contain various strands of political thought associated with crusading. From the royal manor of King's Langley he urged the Mongols to carry through the plan to extirpate the whole of Islam; the king was not yet able to mount an armed expedition – amongst other things, the costly matter of his marriage and coronation kept him from doing so – but with the Lord's favour he would soon be in the east. The diplomacy was largely redundant, western hopes for a Mongol alliance already having started to fade, but the bullish language was typical of Edward I's chancery, royal advisors apparently sticking to a conventional stance. Edward II went further, however, adducing in his letters the biblical theme of *tempus ad hoc adest acceptibile* (2 Corinthians 6:2), as well as the evidence of prophecies found in 'certain books', to air his confidence that the time was imminent when the 'sect of Mohammed' would be cut off and destroyed. Rumours that Islam was about to collapse, inflated by prophetic texts, gave the king certainty that a new Christian epoch was dawning. More detail was presumably to be conveyed in confidence via the il-khan's representatives, the conjuring of Christian eschatology and speculative thought helping to illuminate the bonds and purposes of formal diplomacy. In this context it is telling that a blueprint of Christian kingship was also supplied. Rulers should govern with equanimity and justice, according to their divinely appointed office, going always hard against the infidel, and upholding the ranks of the faithful, the novice king preached. Thus temporal kings and princes acquire great celestial glory in the judgement of the Lord King, shielding Christendom from perfidy. The sentiment is hardly recognisable in Edward's calamitous rule in the coming months and years, but his court's weakness for crusading's prophetic and mystical themes, and the political corollary of crusader kingship is instructive. It reflects patterns of thought moving through royal circles in the weeks before Edward II's marriage and coronation. A more familiar subject was taken up in a second letter. Here the quietening power of peace, which Edward hears is freshly seeded in the il-khan's lands will, 'God permitting', be brought to the shores of Syria. The smothering of discord and controversy in the west is virtually complete, the way almost open to material alliance with the Mongols. Internal harmony and the passage of a Christian army were intertwined expectations. A just peace guaranteed by kingly power, the proper condition of Christian society, was synonymous with the crusade and rescue of the Holy Places.[11]

---

[11] *Foedera* vol. I pt. 4 pp. 93, 100–1.

What was intended as an authoritative image of the *rex crucesignatus* could be found in the papal bulls issued in support of English kings and their crusading colleagues. Emphasis was placed on the special luminescence awarded crusader kings and their peoples in the eyes of God. Here they were the 'most Christian of princes' (an epithet most commonly reserved to the kings of France) alive to the debt owed to Christ the King who raises all princes up. Papal letters set the crusade within the framework of theocratic royal power, as *negotium Dei*. To crusader kings was promised heavenly patrimony as well as generous expansion of their ancestral lands. To take up the cross was the apogee of sovereign power: snapping the brittle bonds of temporal rule, Clement VI argued, crusader kings earned their crowns in perpetuity, to be king-saints among the heavenly host.[12] Wedded to this was the earthly fame available to all warriors of the church, a consideration repeatedly laid out by papal appeals. Nothing rivalled the crusade as a magnifier of prestige and power, devotion to the cross sustaining the memory of princes and reflecting glory upon their anointed successors, verifying their holy majesty. Tallying with the crusade pride of noble dynasties, Edward II and Edward III were directed to follow the footsteps of their illustrious ancestors in the Holy Land, sustaining the honour and legacy of their blood-line – as well as shadowing the labours of Christ the King. By this equation, even the most junior of princes could attain grandiose power, as Gregory XI explained to the English and French courts in 1375, while trying to broker a lasting European peace. Scripture had a heavy bearing in such representations. Papal letters claimed that God had fitted Edward III and his knights with a special aptitude for war, as might be attested by their famed victories over the French, conquests comparable to that of Old Testament heroes. Against the enemies of the faith he could fulfil his appointed function as might a David or Saul. Concepts of crusader kingship were also overlaid with appeals to biblical prophecy. Like Charles V (and the Black Prince), Edward III was invited to envision himself as a latter-day Joshua or Gideon, privy to God's will and hardened against the heathen swarms. Burdened, like the warrior leaders of Israel, with the deliverance of God's inheritance, the crowned heads of Christendom were to act as intercessors of God's majesty, awake to the purposes of his might and the ordained recovery of the Holy Sites.[13]

What appears across these first sample representations amounts to more than just a theological or literary model. Taken together, the view is of a special form of *imperium* available in the crusade, enabling kings, and their nations, to act on a supreme moral and political plane. In fact, viewed from the papal and royal chanceries, this was exactly what was on offer. As an apotheosis of royal power, captaincy of a general *passagium* entitled would-be crusader kings, and their knights, to a raft of privileges

---

[12] E.g. *Reg. Clem.* no. 9941; *Clément VI: Lettres rapportant à la France* nos 1582, 1844; *Reg. Montacute* no. 984.

[13] *Lettres secrètes et curiales du pape Grégoire XI ... relatives à la France* eds L. Mirot et al. (Paris. 1935–1957) no. 1896.

and rights, bridging the gap between lay and religious authority, anchoring the most vaunted of literary or didactic claims. Because of this, it was incumbent upon Philip VI of France to act as an arbiter between Edward III and the Scots in the 1330s, canon lawyers and French diplomats argued. In 1335 confirmation of his extensive privileges as 'Rector and Captain of the Crusade' was intended to equip Philip with the necessary political standing to adjudicate over English actions in Gascony and Scotland, comprising a wide range of papal protections and church penalties. Instead, it served to raise alarm. A sequence of chancery memos, circulated to the English royal council between 1335 and 1337, warned that Philip VI was plotting against Edward at the curia, accusing the English king of being a hindrance to the general *passagium*.[14] It was alleged that Philip kept an army of churchmen in the wings ready to issue sentences of excommunication and other canonical sanctions. Because of the French king's status as rector of the Christian army, counterclaims were unlikely to succeed. Philip's immunities and privileges were 'greater' than those granted to all other crusaders, including the king of England, never officially a *crucesignatus* but apparently in receipt of papal assurances in expectation of his participation. John XXII's letters appointing Philip captain of the crusade prescribed excommunication to all who troubled, invaded or disturbed Philip's lands, rights or property, here plainly understood to mean Gascony.[15] History provided Edward III with an additional warning. A chancery memo dated to 1336 cited Edward I's struggle against Philip IV between 1294 and 1303. Here, royal advisors argued, the English king's rank as *rex crucesignatus* had attracted significant papal support, including the threat of excommunication and 'other penalties of the crusade' against the French for their impediment of an international *passagium*. Such admonitions were deemed to have eventually persuaded Philip IV to reach terms and restore Gascon towns and *bastides* according to the treaty secretly negotiated by Edmund of Lancaster in 1293–1294. This was an idiosyncratic interpretation of Boniface VIII's role in settling Gascony (1298–1300), but the central emphasis upon papal immunities and protections exposed the political leverage thought to accompany the crusade.[16]

Political prophecy and the crusader king

Perhaps the most imaginative treatment of the crusader king is found in the rich seams of contemporary English political prophecy, a category of thought gaining wide circulation in the fourteenth century. As Lesley Coote has shown, an important sequence of prophetic ideas connected the crusade to the various cross-currents

[14] Tyerman, 'Philip VI and the Recovery of the Holy Land' pp. 25–52; NA, C47/30/4/10; C47/30/21; C47/28/2/44–5; C47/28/3/15; C47/28/4/24–5; C47/28/8/39.

[15] NA, C47/30/4/10; C47/28/8/39; and especially C47/28/4/24; cf. *Diplomatic Documents, 1101–1272* ed. P. Chaplais (London, 1964–) vol. I pp.178–9, 268.

[16] NA, C47/30/4/21; C47/28/4/24.

of national mythology, folklore and political complaint, with the figure of king-as-saviour-of-Christendom the device providing recurrent narrative form.[17] Present in numerous prophecies, ranging from the obscure to the very widely known, the crusader king strikes a pervasive image. He haunts the figurative landscape, if not actually making a personal appearance or achieving a rescue of the Holy Places. Nor was this a passive literary form. The function of prophecy amounted to a dialogue, inviting comment and further invention according to changing circumstances and revelation of God's will. Its central relevance was twofold: its accessibility – with audiences spanning various groups in society, including the arms-bearing elite – and its malleability in the hands of the politically informed, including supporters of the royal dynasty. Alongside numerous other influences, its associated forms could be worked into royal ceremonial and self-representation. This heavy dependency on the crusade idea attests to the sort of yearning present within the political community, notwithstanding the other abundant political and propagandist priorities and messages shared and communicated with the crown.

Part of the attraction of political prophecy was its capacity for neutralising the problems of misfortune and for encouraging counter-intuitive thought – premium qualities given the numerous obstacles in the path of traditional massed crusades. The successes and failures of royal authority could be plotted as revelation of divine will, with the crusade goal drawing ever nearer. Following Edward I's death, expectations close to court were transposed in the form of the prophecy 'Adam Davy's Five Dreams', a text in twelve-line stanzas of English verse. First appearing about the time of Edward II's coronation, and apparently with strong connections to Westminster, the prophetic sequence shows the English king undertaking a pilgrimage in arms, receiving the imperial diadem from the pope in Rome, and enlisting the crucified Christ himself as a campaign partner.[18] An expression of goodwill and encouragement to the new king, the companionship of Christ communicates suffering and penance, the king seen as a sacrificial figure riding against heathendom. A magical light leaps out from the king's ears, showing Edward to possess sanctity, identifying him with God's salvation of his people. Dated to 1307–1308, the text's crusade claims and mystical imagery may well have drawn from the sort of language and ritual employed at Edward II's coronation.

Two later prophecies, the 'Verses of Gildas' (c.1318) and 'Lilium regnans' (c.1320x1327) drew inspiration from the political setbacks and turbulence of Edward's later reign. They show the king of England emerging triumphant after a period of crisis, achieving hegemony with subjugation of Ireland, Scotland and France, before defeating the rulers of Africa and Egypt, and driving the infidel from the Holy Land.

---

[17]   Coote, *Prophecy and Public Affairs* pp. 13–42 and passim.
[18]   *Adam Davy's Dreams about Edward the Second* ed. F. J. Furnivall, EETS o.s. 69 (London, 1878) pp. 11–17; V. J. Scattergood, 'Adam Davy's Dreams and Edward II' *Archiv für das Studium der Neuren Sprachen und Literaturen* 206 (1970) pp. 253–60.

Shades of the story of Arthur and the old prophecy of the Last Emperor are evident, but the political claims of Edward *rex crucesignatus* clearly show through. Defeat of the Irish and Scots is capped with his pacifying of the realm and the exile of English rebels. Edward's vow to embark *ad terram sanctam* is enacted with enormous success, leading the king to defeat the Byzantine emperor, recover the Holy Land and win the imperial crown. This was a partly defensive psychology. It showed how the exhausting war against the Scots might be turned into an attractive narrative of royal power. It helped to satisfy expectancies stirred up by talk of the crusade and to rationalise successive disappointments. The Arthurian 'Prophecies of the Six Kings' possessed similar dimensions, positing that the path to Jerusalem lay in the fringes of Britain, with the destruction of Ireland and unification of the Isles. Only then would Islam be laid low. It encompassed the larger speculative issues of redemption, judgement and the Final Coming, and reminded audiences that peace could break out just as suddenly as war. In each of these, the outlines of royal propaganda (as formulated by Edward II's repeated protests that Scots and Irish rebels, not royal back-pedalling, were obstacles to the crusade) are transparent, confirming the productive relationship between courtly messages and competing political commentaries.[19] Thus the allegorical 'Lilium regnans' matched events as they gathered pace in the 1320s, narrating how the king would first fight for Flanders against the French before embarking for the east – an explicit reference to Anglo-Flemish relations on the eve of the St Sardos crisis (most likely dating the 'Lilium' to the middle of 1323).[20] What transpires across each of these narratives is a vision of material prosperity, salvation and universal power, bound up in the crusade. It was a summation of Christian kingship and Christian politics, ushering in a new historical epoch.

That crusading's speculative themes might resonate personally with those around Edward II is attested in one of the more celebrated exchanges in his reign. Sometime between 1317 and 1318, Edward secretly petitioned the pope for advice on his use of a mysterious oil, allegedly given by the Virgin Mary to Thomas Becket with the prophecy that if the fifth king to succeed Henry II (i.e. Edward II) was anointed with the unction he would rescue the Holy Land. Perhaps independently, a textual tradition passed into currency describing the oil's potential in fuller detail, engaging a wider audience. Its blessing would give the king mastery of his ancestral lands in France, Normandy and Aquitaine, and help him to overrun the Middle and Near East. After chasing away the pagans of Egypt, this ruler was expected to reconstitute the Church of God in the places where it has been destroyed, both spiritually and physically. He will be *maximus inter reges*.[21] John XXII's reply to Edward II's letter was a study of

---

[19]   Texts in Coote, *Prophecy and Public Affairs* pp. 83–100; cf. J. R. S. Phillips, 'Edward II and the Prophets' *England in the Fourteenth Century* ed. W. M. Ormrod (Woodbridge, 1986) pp. 189–201.

[20]   See Coote, *Prophecy and Public Affairs* p. 96 for the problem of dating the 'Lilium'.

[21]   *CPL* vol. II pp. 436–7; T.A. Sandquist, 'The Holy Oil of St Thomas of Canterbury' *Essays in Medieval History presented to B. Wilkinson* eds T. A. Sandquist and M. R. Powicke (Toronto, 1969)

caution: if Edward believed in the oil and would receive it in a faithful frame of mind, committed to crusading against the infidel, then no harm would come of it, and it would not jeopardise the king's first anointing. But this should be carried out in secret so as to avoid possible scandal. John held back from endorsing the sentiments of the prophecy or advising the king on what to do, not unwise to the potential diplomatic embarrassment. Clearly, the prophecy's message of English hegemony over France required tact. If this was Edward clutching at straws, enthusiasm for Becket's chrism also filled the recesses of the royal household. It originated with Nicholas Wisbech, the king's confessor and papal clerk. Wisbech was the first to argue the legend's plausibility with the king, and he carried Edward's letters on the subject to Avignon.[22] At an apparent turning point in Edward's fortunes, this was to be less an antidote to the realm's troubles than a manifesto of new beginnings. There was acknowledgement that his rule had failed – indeed, the prophecy required the onset of 'evil times', and a tyranny to reverse for it to become operative. The Virgin bequeathed the oil to a salvator king, a healer of social and religious ills. Edward II's reanointment would reinstall the sacral qualities of his kingship and magnify the promises of his first coronation, including the crusade. As such, the story (and Edward's letter to John XXII) contrived to justify much more than receipt of crusade monies – which was the business simultaneously being advanced by royal proctors at the papal court. It sought to repair the king's sacral identity and personal authority, badly bruised by the destruction of his army at Bannockburn and by his opponents' incessant and dangerous sniping.[23]

How such prophetic strands might reach into functional politics is vividly caught in two manuscripts presented at the 1313 Paris cross-taking festival. The first, received by Philip IV, contained six colour miniatures with subjects ranging from Edward II's knighting of Louis of Navarre, to a projected vision of the English and French monarchs embarking a crusade host. Here, with trumpets preceding them, the royal armies carry the banner of the 'heavenly angel', one of the seven messengers sent to prefigure the Last Judgement. The pictures formed part of the text of *Kalila and Dimma* – a collection of tales embodying moral lessons for princes. What was probably a companion piece commissioned for Edward II's queen (also presented at the ceremony) took the form of a richly illuminated apocalypse, again carrying a clear crusade theme. One illustration shows the French monarch and English prince as agents of cosmic justice leading kings of the east gathered together for the battle of Armageddon (cf. Revelation 16:16). Philip IV and Edward are shown armour-clad, followed by the

---

pp. 330–44; Tyerman, *England and the Crusades* pp. 245–6; Coote, *Prophecy and Public Affairs* pp. 94–6.

[22]   *CPL* vol. II pp. 436–7. For Wisbech and his career at Avignon see Phillips, 'Edward II and the Prophets' pp. 189–201 and J. R. Wright, *The Church and the English Crown, 1305–1334* (Toronto, 1980) p. 102.

[23]   NA, SC7/25/22; SC7/25/15; *Foedera* vol. II pt. 1 pp. 117–18; *CPL* vol. II pp. 414–16.

rulers of Castile and the German Empire as they face the enemy in the apocalyptic guise of dragon, beast and false prophet, the instruments of Satan. The over-riding vision in both manuscripts (other high-born cross-takers may have been issued with parallel texts) was to connect the politics of Philip IV's crusade and the rescue of the Holy Land to the supreme prophetic platform of God's Revelation. Amidst the rounds of religious observance, feasting and diplomacy, what might otherwise have appeared as a riskily grandiose decorative scheme helped seal the associated politics, encouraging participants, and their national chivalries, to adopt this understanding of their anointed roles and princely obligations. It tallied with the devotional atmosphere fostered by the attendant clergy and much of the rhetoric attaching itself to Philip IV's kingship and the memory of St Louis.[24]

It is impossible to state exactly how such a backdrop impacted on men's political and military perceptions. The agency of prophetic discourse probably lay primarily with its national and regional audience, less with courtly centres of action (Coote terms it 'a living language'). Yet given the intimate access afforded to devout forecasters of the crusade, such as Roger Stanegrave and Nicholas Wisbech (surfacing at court within a few months of each other), the steady traffic of household servants despatched to the Holy Land 'for the health of the king's soul', and the various speculative currents eddying around Edward II, it is tempting to ascribe to the king a far greater sensitivity to the call of the cross than has been previously thought.[25] A similar dynamic can be seen throughout Edward III's reign, despite later efforts to distance the king from serious crusade expectations. A variety of prophetic voices stuck stubbornly to the traditional crusade agenda, mirroring the adventurism of many of Edward III's knights. 'Anglia transmittet' (n.d. but c.1330), for example, inverted the traditional bonds of the political nation with the monarch, casting the hero-king as an actor prompted not by God, or by his own office, but by the wishes of his knights. It is they ('Anglia') that send him on the path to prophetic fulfilment. A sequence of conquests in Europe and a cleansing of the church in his native lands lead the king inexorably to command of a Christian army and the freeing of the Holy Places. Acre and Jerusalem are redeemed from the enemies of the Cross, and Christendom is reconstituted under his imperial power. The ultimate expression of national and royal destiny is attained. The binding of common national interests with royal claims possesses similar prophetic results in 'The Last Kings of the English', a text detailing Edward III's attaining of Jerusalem and worldly glory after the successive setbacks and disappointments of his father's and grandfather's reigns.[26]

---

[24]   N. F. Regaldo, 'Kalila et Dimma, liber regius' *Satura: Studies in Medieval Literature* eds N. M. Reale and R. E. Sternglantz (Donington, 2001) pp. 103–23; S. Lewis, 'The Apocalypse of Isabella of France: Paris; Bibl. Nat. Ms. Fr. 13096' *Art Bulletin* 72 (1990) pp. 224–60.

[25]   For some of those speculative currents see Coote, *Prophecy and Public Affairs* pp. 83–105 esp. 96. His most recent biographer finds mainly evidence of 'gullibility' in Edward's religious tastes: J. R. S. Phillips, *Edward II* (New Haven, 2010) pp. 66, 327.

[26]   For texts see Coote, *Prophecy and Public Affairs* pp. 112–15.

Crusader king, chivalric king: A relationship tested

Unsurprisingly, vigorous kingship and the successful prosecution of war invited this currency of traditional expectations and ideals onto centre stage. During the first phase of the Hundred Years War, for example, Edward III was sensitive to what the crusade cause symbolised in his struggle against Philip of Valois, and the moral legitimacy it bestowed. Stanegrave recommended the path to Jerusalem as Edward's best chance of proving his *noble ligniage*, and trading upon Philip VI's questionable succession and his perceived failures and abuses, including treachery towards English crusade aims, royal propaganda articulated a form of kingship that sought to hijack the crusade ideal, alongside other prized symbols of French monarchy. Repeatedly, Edward III cast his cause in France as a remedy to injuries against his sovereign rights and as a restoration of the natural political order. The crusade goal was instrumental among Edward's claims to be the true heir of St Louis. Central to the 'good customs' pledged when he adopted the title and arms of King of France in 1340 was the formation of a lasting peace so that an army could speed to the Holy Land and deliver it from 'the hands of wicked men'. Along with Edward's promise to maintain honest council, preserve the currency, refrain from excessive tax and protect the liberties of the church, the crusade objective was a moral underpinning of his 'alternative government', a basis of his war aims. It was identified with his just cause in France and the promise to restore the customs 'of the time of the good St Louis'. Edward's manifesto (pinned to church doors in places where the English army passed) constituted a comprehensible political and ethical programme, pressing his claim as a legitimate heir, and labelling Valois an impostor.[27] For this there was clearly a general audience, besides harassed local populaces. In the 1340s, according to Benedict XII, Philip VI remained the target of widespread abuse for the collapse of the Holy Land crusade. Refugees from the east reportedly journeyed to France in order to remonstrate with him personally for cheating the church and worsening the situation of Christians in Syria. While Edward repeatedly protested innocence in the collapse of the recovery crusade, he sought to make a moral case out of Philip's reluctance to reach compromise. On the specifics of Anglo-French tension in Gascony, the old sticking point, English talk of crusade resonated with over a half-century of abortive settlements and (in the English view) French duplicity, telescoping arguments about bad faith and thwarted ambitions. There was further support for this sentiment outside England. French misfortunes up to the battle of Poitiers, the Florentine chronicler Matteo Villani claimed, were a divine judgement on Philip VI's desertion of the crusade. This

---

[27]   BL, Cotton Otho D V fols 1ʳ, 6ᵛ–7ᵛ. For competition with the 'royale religion' of France see J. W. McKenna, 'How God Became an Englishman' *Tudor Rule and Revolution, Essays for G.R. Elton* eds D. J. Guth and J. W. McKenna (Cambridge, 1982) pp. 25–43; *Foedera* vol. II pt. 4 pp. 76–7, 80; cf. J. le Patourel, 'Edward III and the Kingdom of France' *The Wars of Edward III: Sources and Interpretations* ed. C. J. Rogers (Woodbridge, 1999) pp. 254–7.

casuistical reading of history remained current in the 1390s, Mézières diagnosing French iniquity and sin as an explanation of Edward III's early triumphs.[28]

The emblem of the crusade also corresponded with an emerging argument about Edward III's superior chivalric standing, as part of a doctrine that fused knightly and royal honour and helped sacralise his cause. Having taken the title King of France in 1340, Edward offered single combat to Philip in order to submit their dispute to 'the will of our Lord Jesus Christ God'. This was so peace might thrive, the enemies of God be resisted and Christendom made free. Philip refused to be goaded into such a risky trial of strength, but it chimed with common assumptions about the proper function of Christian peace. Cast as the flip-side to war, peace (and the consequent crusade) fitted into Edward's providential view of battle and the workings of moral agency. It was contingent on God's restoration of proper rights. Synonymous with crusade, a just peace would usher in the era of Christian recovery in the east. Such talk was perhaps as likely to sustain expectations as induce cynicism.[29] Edward III revisited the theme on the eve of the famous Crécy campaign, with the war about to enter a transitional phase. To his subjects he proclaimed that all avenues for negotiated settlement had been exhausted, including suggestions for a marriage, war reparations and a joint crusade to the *terra sancta*. Arguing the impossibility of lasting peace without overcoming his foe, it followed that the *negotium crucis* now rested upon Edward's successful prosecution of war (March 1346).[30] Such precepts, not easy to contest, permitted the king to pose as a disciple of the crusade while focused upon the political goals in France. Not until 1346, Edward III's 'year of miracles', did diplomacy and war enter into a different phase, the sack of Caen, defeat of Philip VI's army at Crécy and besieging of Calais changing fundamentally the character of the Anglo-French conflict. The rivals now confronted each other knowing that more was likely to be gained in choosing to fight than in reaching terms. While Philip VI was honour-bound to avenge French disgrace at Crécy, Edward III knew he had to press ahead to capitalise on his apparently divinely delivered success.

Yet, if the cult of the crusader king conjured the necessary moral associations and chivalric impulses for opening a just war against the house of Valois, it offered limited

---

[28]   *Lettres closes, patentes et curiales du pape Benoît XII se rapportant à la France* ed. G. Daumet (Paris, 1899–1920) no. 713; Matteo Villani, *Cronica* vol. II pp. 6–10; Mézières, *Letter to King Richard II* p. 14.

[29]   *Foedera* vol. II pt 4 p. 80; Robert of Avesbury, *De Gestis Mirabilibus regis Edwardi Tertii* ed. E. M. Thompson, r.s. 93 (London, 1889) pp. 309–10, and for Philip's response pp. 315–16. For Edward III's belief in the providential nature of kingship see Ormrod, *Edward III* pp. 97–8, 261–2; Patourel, 'Edward III and the Kingdom of France' *The Wars of Edward III* pp. 250–7. On the conventions and theatre of single combat see M. Strickland, 'Provoking or Avoiding Battle? Challenge, Duel and Single Combat in Warfare of the High Middle Ages' *Armies, Chivalry and Warfare in Medieval Britain and France* ed. M Strickland (Stamford, 1998) pp. 317–43.

[30]   *CCR 1346–1349* p. 57; *CPL* vol. II p. 584. In the challenge sent to Philip VI the week before Crécy, Edward stated his readiness to join battle at any place and hour, 'for the common good of Christendom': *CPR 1345–1348* pp. 516–17.

appeal in royal efforts to turn English chivalry to the arduous business of garrisoning Gascony and imposing the terms of Brétigny in the years after the heady victories of Crécy and Poitiers. Instead, in the aftermath of Crécy, increasingly emboldened as a military and chivalric figure, Edward began to move steadily out of the shadow of St Louis, his dynastic claims and public style of kingship seemingly better fitted to the tradition of King Arthur and the vision of a unified Britain, dominant across all her continental possessions. This was to be a signal transformation, abandoning the crusade policy and *royale religion* of the French monarchy in favour of Arthurian imperialism. Fostered by lavish pageantry and invigorated English military power, emphasis on Edward as Arthur *redivivus* conjured enthusiasm for his military ventures and confirmed the values of knightly fraternity and service to the crown. The leader of the Britons had been an enemy of pagan elements threatening neighbouring lands, but he was most celebrated for creating an empire of continental dominions. A royal cult of arms, epitomised by the Order of the Garter, communicated the image of the chivalric king and knight with round tables and demonstrations of fidelity and valour, shading out earlier visions of St Louis and Capetian-style crusade devotion. Proven worth in battle and tournament, and devotion to a panoply of chivalric heroes, including St George, the Nine Worthies, Lancelot, Roland, Oliver and Richard I, qualified men for entry to the chivalric world orbiting Edward III's court at Windsor. This was a vision of royal destiny which was realm-centred, built of unity of purpose between king and knightly community, and an ethic of defence of crown and commonweal (the image most flavourfully evoked in modern studies of Edward III's kingship and chivalry).[31]

Nonetheless, if the intention was to bind English chivalry more narrowly to the royal house and service of the crown, and divert it from other outlets, it was, as has been seen, only partially successful. Concepts of nation and national identity emerged tentatively, requiring constant reiteration.[32] Edward III's attempt to dominate visions of royal destiny would inevitably remain contested by wider politics, as well as by many practitioners of English chivalry. The prophetic vision of the northern text 'Alliterative Becket' (n.d. but after 1356), for example, remains fixed on the sacral and dynastic claims of Edward III against the Valois, including the supreme mantle of the crusade. Thus, subverting traditional Capetian claims, the English king, and *not* the French, is David and is entitled to the headship of Christendom. He is also the rightful keeper of the relics of the Passion ('Þe crowne, and the thre nalles, & A spere') installed at St Denis by St Louis, now wrongly held by the impostor rulers

---

[31]   Vale, *Edward III and Chivalry* passim; J. Bengtson, 'St George and the Formation of English Nationalism' *Journal of Medieval and Early Modern Studies* 27 (1997) pp. 314–40; J. Barnie, *War in Medieval Society: Social Values and the Hundred Years War* (London, 1974) pp. 65–88; and, most recently, Saul, *For Honour and Fame* pp. 76–93. For a possible parallel movement in French monarchy see D. Delogu, *Theorising the Ideal Sovereign: The Rise of the French Vernacular Royal Biography* (Toronto, 2008) pp. 92–123.

[32]   On so-called 'nationalist' literature and writings see Matthews, *Writing to the King* pp. 152–5.

of France. The English are deserving of this special honour because they have been selected by God as his Chosen People. After subduing the French and winning the imperial crown, Edward will then resurrect the heroics of an earlier English hero-king, Richard I, by sailing to Cyprus and embarking an army at 'Ryche Jaffe', the site famed for the Lionheart's exploits of Christian chivalry. Holding up an English saint-king and an elect nation cast of unique virtue, the 'Alliterative Becket', with its blending of hybrid historical and symbolic influences, sought to both assimilate and surpass the tradition of St Louis. It also sought to keep the political and moral horizons of the king at full stretch after the miraculous success at the battle of Poitiers, when the final completion of French conquest, and therefore the first achievement of the prophecy, seemed within grasp.[33] More acerbic voices could also be heard. Critical of the peace settled by Edward III in 1360, for instance, John Erghome's treatment of the popular Bridlington prophecy identified the crusade war as the ultimate objective of dealings with France. Given that Christian knighthood was best turned to service of the cross, Edward III's failure to win the French throne was self-evidently the fault of bad counsel and the king's own sinfulness. War between Christian men was the work of Satan. By contrast, Erghome claims, anyone who dies in battle against the Saracens, who are God's enemies, will go straight to heaven and win eternal life.[34] The insular-minded and widely read chronicle *Brut* helped gloss over the matter of Edward III's shifting royal and chivalric personas by dubbing him a patron saint of English arms, whose courtly projections of knighthood had made the name of England known 'in heathenesse and Barbary'. In the manner of an aging Arthur, arbiter of chivalry and dispenser of youthful prowess, Edward sets forth his knights to prove the king's 'worthynese and manhode' against the infidel in lands along the fringes of Christendom, the knights' exploits serving as vehicles of national and royal pride, but also as compensation for frustrated national crusade ambitions.[35]

Chivalry perfected?

It is within this context of shifting political identities that the impulse to affirm the values of crusader kingship was played out, widening its cultural force. As has been seen, when themed with Muslim dress and narrative lines pitching Christian heroes against pagan warriors, royal tournaments could be a fertile environment for this sort of elaboration. An opportunity to spice displays of royal power with exoticism and glamour, diplomacy could be framed by such events. In the 1350s and 1360s the presence of Armenian and Cypriot knights as spectators and participants in the joust spoke to the cosmopolitan draw of Edward III's court. It also underlined the pressures

---

[33] 'Alliterative Becket' *Bernadus de cura rei familiaris* pp. 23–31; Coote, *Prophecy and Public Affairs* pp. 130–3.
[34] *Political Poems and Songs* pp. 182–4, 203.
[35] *Brut* vol. II p. 334.

to pay lip-service to the roles of the looked-for saviour-king and his pious military following, themes regularly breaking the surface, independent of courtly and political
realities. It is possible to read tournaments hosted by the Black Prince and Richard
II in this way (see above p. 42, 60, 69). The hoarding of relics associated with royal
crusading helped enlarge the ethos, providing tangible links to the honoured heritage.[36] Of course, among kings specially venerated for their chivalry, the reputation
of Richard I offered the most fertile ground. Numerous murals, tiles, manuscripts,
carvings, tapestries and roof bosses were decorated with scenes of Richard's crusade,
particularly his legendary joust with Saladin, spawning what became a central vision
of royal chivalry and English heroism. So established was the key figurative device
of Richard knocking Saladin from his steed, Saracen horse and warrior crumpled by
the force of impact, that it is possible to talk of its influence as an archetypal image
of chivalric war against Islam.[37] To this extent, Richard's personal knightly encounter
with Saladin became a motif synonymous with broader categories of Christian and
crusade heroism, in addition to that of the champion *rex crucesignatus*. Across the
broad canvas of chivalric tableaux only images of Arthur and St George could rival its
influence as formative statements of English prowess and royal valour. Entwined with
a budding literary tradition, including the *Pas Saladyn* (a Flemish poem apparently
first rooted on Richard's exploits at Jaffa), the scene featured in numerous tapestries
and murals adorning noble and royal residences across northern Europe. The count
of Hainault and Holland had it painted in rooms at Valenciennes castle (1376), the
Black Prince bequeathed to his son Richard 'une sale darras du pas Saladyn', and an
inventory of the possessions of the Dauphin in 1416 lists two 'tappis de Roy Richart',
for example. Wall hangings carrying the scene distinguished a number of English aristocratic halls. In less grand settings, it was inked onto family psalters, and portrayed
on household furniture.[38]

Yet, by the fourteenth century, the image of Richard I's encounter with Saladin, and
its associated meanings, contrived to do more than amplify purely chivalric themes.
Amidst the interplay between legend, history and chivalric discourse, an argument
about the sort of kingly behaviour vaunted on crusade was framed. Depicted at full
tilt, bearing a forty-foot lance (reputedly a hastily felled tree), Richard as *rex crucesignatus* lands a blow of such ferocity that it rips his Muslim opponent from his seat,
tearing the harness and stirrups of his horse.[39] This is not the transcendent saint-king
of the French crusade tradition – shaded by papal banners and girded with holy relics,
invulnerable at the epicentre of miracle conquests – but selfless, adrenaline-fuelled

[36] See above pp. 165, 168 and references gathered there.
[37] See R. S. Loomis, '*Richard Cœur de Lion* and the *Pas Saladin* in Medieval Art' *Publications of the
Modern Language Association* 30 (1915) pp. 509–28, esp. 515, 518.
[38] Ibid. pp. 516–18, 525, 528. For tapestries possessed by Thomas Woodstock and Humphrey Bohun see
Goodman, *Loyal Conspiracy* pp. 80–2.
[39] The story is elaborated in the Middle English romance *Richard Coeur de Lion*. See *Der mittelenglische Versroman über Richard Löwenherz* ed. K. Brunner (Vienna and Leipzig, 1913) lines 5481–797.

heroism in the charge. The king's wince-making, yet non-fatal, blow belongs to the pages of romance and the tournament field. It is a moment of pathos, a humiliating schooling for the Saracen knight and patent wish-fulfilment for the Christian audience; yet it is a necessary function of royal majesty that the testing of military honour and moral worth is ultimately settled between princes.[40] Christendom's champion, and the physical embodiment of collected, national hopes, Richard was destined to shoulder the burden of salvation on behalf of his subjects and shield the Mother Church. As a supreme representative of his faith, it is inevitable, in the world of heroic fiction at least, that the king is the chief actor in armed reckonings with Saladin. The values celebrated by the episode were enlarged in the historical romance *Richard Coeur de Lion*, the popular tail-rhyme poem of the 1330s, the origins and transmission of which went hand in hand with the artistic traditions outlined above. Here, King Richard is a warrior leader bonded to his men through feudal codes of loyalty, honesty, adventure, pious violence and a shared distrust of the French. Meshed with the historical events of the Third Crusade, openly heroic and epic themes heighten the personal aura of Richard, crusader king. The poem's deliberate unmanning of French crusaders and their king (depicted as saboteurs of the Third Crusade) acquired particular pertinence in the first decade of Edward III's reign, creating a message as much to do with English martial identity and loyalty to the liege-lord, as with the duty of princes and knights against Islam. But the fight against the heathen is always the necessary backdrop. Only on this frontier, the most exalted of causes, are revelations of genuine knightly and princely character possible. The vigorous personal chivalry of Richard, *rex Christianissimus*, is set against the boastful claims and empty chivalry of the French king and his followers who are in league with the Greeks (and thus placed outside the Christian value-system).[41] The temptation here, as with the famous image of the jousting king, is to see something of an argument about a distinctive English crusader kingship, and efforts to present a portrait of a Christian warrior prince of the old, heroic, less ethereal sort. In surviving manuscripts the poem is found alongside other texts carrying roughly congruent themes, seeming to bear this out. Partnered with heroic and pseudo-historical works, such as the *Brut*, Robert of Gloucester's *Chronicle*, *Beves of Hamtoun* and *The Siege of Jerusalem*, on the one hand, and satires on contemporary corruption, such as *Simonie* and *The Parlement of the Three Ages*, on the other, the vision of national crusade heroism was supposed to be edifying. Possibly the effect was to comment on a perceived decline of national chivalry, as John

---

[40]   The unseating of Saladin is given with relish in Walter of Guisborough's chronicle (c.1305): 'obviantem ei Saladinum militem quidem strenuissimum et congressu militari cum lancea exceptum, etiam cum assessore in terram prostravit'. *The Chronicle of Walter Guisborough* ed. H. Rothwell, Camden Society 89 (London, third series 1967) p. 116.

[41]   *Der mittelenglische Versroman über Richard Löwenherz*, lines 1677–82, 1771–2, 3849–62, 6706–10. Cf. Finlayson, '*Richard, Coer de lyon*' pp. 170–1, 176–7.

Finlayson has suggested.[42] Side-lit by core narratives of national history and romance, the central image of the English *rex crucesignatus* promised to remedy political and social ills, and deliver a glorious military future.

Godly warrior, godly prince: A problem of identity

If this amounted to a debate about the substance of crusader kingship, it was also testament to its plasticity in the hands of lay and clerical audiences. The business of making Richard I a 'culture-hero' involved a synthesis of ideals and characteristics. It was a source of crusading's enduring appeal that there could be natural interplay with other fundamental aspects of monarchical and lordly identity. The image of the crusader king could provide topical comment on princely *prudentia*, endurance in the melee, and the decorum of dynastic and feudal leadership, as well as serve a providential view on the crown's mysterious religious functions. By the same token, of course, precisely because of such deep-rooted idealism, there were also risks in maintaining faithfulness to the imagery and ideals of crusader kingship – of protesting enthusiasm too loudly – particularly when not tempered by other noted military and chivalric achievements. In the 1390s Richard II ultimately failed to narrow the gap between self-image and wider expectations and realities, finding it hard to translate his role as patron of chivalric endeavour into a broader political ethos, or to make it a focus of lasting unity. This was not without sustained efforts by those close to court to cultivate the image of *rex crucesignatus* in his name, encouraged by Richard's desire to reaffirm the crown's sacral and hegemonic qualities. It was at least auspicious that the king carried the same name as the historic hero-king, and was the first Richard to ascend the throne after the Lionheart's death.[43] As has been seen, in some quarters the image of Richard II as a patron of crusading, and other noble causes, succeeded in taking hold, leaving its imprint upon various writings, texts and ritual events. In this context, the crusade can be viewed as fundamental to the king's attempts to triangulate his personal knighthood with chivalric kingship and political action. It was also an additional means of instilling reverence for the supreme agency of royal blood.[44]

---

[42]   E.g. BL, MS Add. 31042; BL, MS Harley 4960. For other manuscripts and comment see Finlayson, 'Richard, Coer de lyon' pp. 160–3.

[43]   In addition to the inherited martial template was the added poignancy that the name had been selected partly in honour of the prince's main baptismal sponsor at Bordeaux in 1367, King 'Richard' of Armenia, a refugee from Muslim aggression. For Richard's baptismal arrangements see Saul, *Richard II* p. 12. For Constantine IV of Armenia (r. 1362–1373) ('Richard' in western sources) see J. G. Ghazarian, *The Armenian Kingdom in Cilicia during the Crusades* (Richmond, 2000) pp. 161–2.

[44]   For a fuller exploration of the character of Richard's kingship see S. Walker, 'Richard's Views on Kingship' *Rulers and Ruled in Late Medieval England* eds R. Archer and S. Walker (London, 1995) pp. 49–63; N. Saul, 'The Kingship of Richard II' *Richard II: The Art of Kingship* pp. 37–58; id. *Richard II* pp. 439ff.; Fletcher, *Richard II* passim.

One of the most interesting manuscripts of Richard's reign, a lavish volume produced in East Anglia, seems to bear this out, carrying important salient crusade and
nationalist themes. Made for Henry Despenser, bishop of Norwich, the main contents were documents of English, ecclesiastical and imperial history, including the
Flores Historiarium and Murimuth's *Chronicle*. The selection is idiosyncratic. There
are descriptions of England and Rome, historical accounts of Scotland and Ireland,
and the claims of the English crown over the Celtic nation. Also included are letters
of kings and popes, correspondence between Saladin and Frederick Barbarossa, and
other material on the crusade.[45] Perhaps most significant, as Coote has pointed out,
is the fact that this manuscript does not begin with a chronicle or a romance as most
historical manuscripts do, but with three crusade-related prophecies. These are the
'Lilium regnans', 'The Holy Oil of St Thomas', and the thirteenth-century 'Catulus
Linxeis'. In a text specially conceived as a luxury manuscript for its sponsor, a man
known as much for his love of fighting as for his stewarding of souls, this was not
unintentional. As a prefatory comment (placed on the verso of the first folio), the
prophecies communicate the thinking behind the rest of the writings. They immor-
talise the English king as a crusading, world-healing ruler who is also an Arthurian
hero who will restore Britain and be consecrated via the exploits of his crown. This
figure is Richard II, the focus of the bishop's political loyalties and personal ambition. In arch chivalric style, Despenser's arms feature throughout the manuscript,
but his portrait, with that of the king, appears on the first folio, confirming the purpose of the writings and the nature of the bond between the two men that the text is
supposed to convey.[46] The text immediately below is 'Catulus Linxeis', an argument
for British hegemony over western nations, envisioning royal triumph against the
Islamic powers and ultimately global dominance. This achieved, 'Catulus' proposes,
the British ruler will attain the favour of the Most High and be taken up to heaven.[47]
This was a message echoed outside the realm, where literary voices also identified
Richard II as a notable martial figure. A tribute penned by Christine de Pisan after
Richard's fall, when there were no rewards to be gained by flattery, described the king
as a 'chevalier wearing a crown'. She had heard French knights heap praise on the king
for his readiness to take up arms. When it came to matters of war, Richard was 'a
preux, a true Lancelot'.[48]

   An appetite for similar themes is reflected in other contemporary manuscripts. It
is from Richard II's reign that the sole manuscript of 'Adam Davy's Dreams' survives,
the mystical argument for the redemption of the Holy Land, among other things,

[45]   BL, MS Cotton Vespasian E VIII; Coote, *Prophecy and Public Affairs* pp. 151–3.
[46]   Despenser collected texts with a chivalric theme, including a chanson on the First Crusade, romances
on the 'Matter of Greece' and an unidentified order of chivalry. The latter also had his arms emblazoned
on the margins: Cavanaugh, *Study of Books* vol. II p. 801.
[47]   Coote, *Prophecy and Public Affairs* pp. 152–3.
[48]   Cited by Gillespie, 'Richard II: Chivalry and Kingship' p. 118, referencing *Oeuvres Poetiques de
Christine de Pisan* ed. M. Roy 3 vols. (Paris, 1863–1864), volume and page number not given.

centred upon the figure of Edward II.[49] Similar prophecies surfaced at Charles VI's court, casting the French king as the saviour of Jerusalem, and there was opportunity for cross-fertilisation. In his famous letter to Richard II, Philippe de Mézières refers to a revelation that both kings had received, foretelling the making of peace, the end of the schism and the passage of a joint Franco-English crusade to the Holy Land.[50] A version of the prophecy of Merlin (alluded to several times in the *Epistre*) is perhaps what Mézières had in mind, or a newly divined prophecy relayed by Mézières's co-evangelist Robert the Hermit. Richard was thought to enjoy scrutinising prophetic strands of thought. More pointed comment was available in Mézières's allegorical *Songe du vieil pèlerin* (c.1389). Here animal and heraldic imagery associated with the Merlin prophecy concealed an ad hominem attack upon the earl of Arundel, cast as the Black Boar, and roundly condemned for his opposition to Anglo-French peace. A well-informed Mézières sought to exploit other currents at the English and French courts, including interest in astrology and the practice of geomancy.[51] Closer to home, loyalty to the image of the crusader king was verified in an anonymous letter-book or formulary (c.1395) which associated Richard II's household with holy war in Egypt. An apocryphal text reported that one of the king's relatives was currently 'in parts of Babylon' with a very fine company. The army had torched the land around Alexandria and won a great victory in an open field near Cairo. Many Saracens had been slain, and the sultan of Babylon had been taken prisoner, 'to the great honour of our liege lord the king' and 'all the chivalry of England'. An admixture of speculation and fantasy, the letter was apparently modelled upon other newsletters that spoke of authentic English crusade achievements. Interested in themes of national honour and military enterprise, its author anticipated a future occasion when it could be placed with chroniclers and other sources.[52]

As has already been seen, such staple images were ripe for migration into ceremonial demonstrations of kingship, and could be allowed to help articulate a particular polit-ical agenda. At the Whitefriars feast in honour of the crusade martyr John Mowbray, Richard exercised the ceremonial distance so important to this courtly style by sitting on an elevated platform under a magnificent starred canopy, the repose of an imperial God-like ruler. The ceremony was to set a seal upon a particularly contentious asser-tion of regal power. Taking place immediately after the infamous 1397 parliament, in which Richard successfully laid charges of treason against three leading peers of the

[49]   Oxford Bod. MS Laud Misc. 622; Coote, *Prophecy and Public Affairs* p. 277; Scattergood, 'Adam Davy's Dreams' pp. 253–60; Phillips, 'Edward II and the Prophets' pp. 189–201.

[50]   M. M. Chaume, 'Une prophétie relative à Charles VI' *Revue du moyen âge latin* 3 (1947) pp. 27–42; Mézières, *Letter to King Richard II* p. 45. For a fresh interpretation of the *Epistre* and Mézières's 'peace aims' see A. Curry, 'War or Peace? Philip de Mézières, Richard II and Anglo-French Diplomacy' *Philippe de Mézières and His Age* pp. 295–320.

[51]   Mézières, *Songe du vieil pèlerin* vol. I pp. 395–403; id. *Letter to King Richard II* p. 14.

[52]   BL, MS Harley 3988 fols 39–41; cf. for newsletter reports *West. Chron.* pp. 444–9; Walsingham, *Chronica Maiora* pp. 278–9; id. *Historia Anglicana* vol. II pp. 197–8.

realm (including his uncle Thomas Woodstock), the feast was supposed to signal the king's unfettered authority and fresh unity within politics. With the elevated Richard at its hub, a distinctive political and chivalric ethic, drawing on cosmopolitan tastes and a puritanical concept of Christian duty and knighthood, was evidently being proposed.[53] Parallel messages could be formed in other crusade-themed events. In 1392 Richard's famous reception into London saw the capital decorated as a new Jerusalem, complete with a mannequin John the Baptist in the wilderness, 'floating' castle-turrets and citizens dressed as angels and disbursing wine. Staged as a political reconciliation between the 'Christ-like' Richard II and the Londoners, the iconography of the king's triumphal entry caught an echo with the prophetic visions of a liberator king entering Jerusalem. Inspiration may have been drawn from Queen Isabella's formal entry into Paris in 1390, a 'joyeuse entrée', where pageantry featured scenes from crusading and biblical history, including a joust between Saladin and the Christians, the Nativity scene, and a representation of the heavenly kingdom. The theatre bestowed a certain religious glow upon London itself, but it was a chance to publicly affirm and enact the ideal order of political and spiritual life, with Christ's patrimony restored to the centre, part of terrestrial Christianity. Insight into Richard's mood is offered in a letter to Charles VI written on the day after the London procession, where he welcomed overtures for peace and co-operation, and spoke warmly of an audience he had held with the crusade 'evangelist' Robert the Hermit. The urban ceremonial also corroborated the king's self-image as a merciful prince, returning to his inheritance in peace, David-like, after the inhabitants had broken their faith with him. Taking up the analogy in his *Epistre* to Richard, Mézières later compared David's forgiveness of the Jerusalemites and restoration of power to the king of England's projected royal crusade to the Holy City.[54]

The best-known – and perhaps most misleading – expression of Richard II's crusade intent is the celebrated Wilton Diptych, that sumptuously illuminated altarpiece of Richard II's court, made for the king in the mid 1390s. May McKisack first identified the image with the idealism of the period. The king is depicted as a youth supported by saints and martyrs, being presented to the Virgin and Child, who appears to be blessing a banner of the Redemption. The iconography of the cross and symbols of the Passion are perhaps reminiscent of the manuscripts of Mézières's *Epistre* and the abridged ordinances of the crusading Order of the Passion. Not only are the Crown of Thorns and the Nails of the Cross depicted on the halo of the Christ Child, but a lamb, another common symbol of the Passion, is carried under the arm of John the Baptist. Use of these devices and the bestowal of the banner upon the king may

[53]   N. Saul, *The Three Richards* (London, 2005) p. 120.
[54]   Described by Richard Maidstone (d.1396) in elegiac couplets. See G. Kipling, 'Richard II's "Sumptuous Pageants" and the Idea of Civic Triumph' in *Pageantry in the Shakespearean Theater* ed. D. M. Bergeron (Athens, GA, 1985) pp. 83–103; *Diplomatic Correspondence* nos 150–1; Mézières, *Letter to King Richard II* p. 28.

have suggested a crusading context to contemporaries, for the Holy Land was Christ's bequest to the Christian world, won for it with his blood, and it was the duty of Christian kings to win it back. The king and angels who surround the Virgin and Child are shown wearing the liveries of both Richard II and Charles, the White Hart and the Broom-pods. It can be read as an icon of common devotion to the Holy Land and the task of redeeming the patrimony of Christ. More recent interpretations focus on the diptych's Marian imagery and the submission of Richard's kingship into her hands, the English realm dedicated to the Virgin as her dowry, just as Jerusalem was the property of her son. Richard's youthful portraiture may also symbolise a renewal of the 'crown of his youth' and restoration of his sovereign rights. Whether an argument over England's special sanctity, or a mandate for rescuing the east – the readings are not mutually exclusive.[55]

Finally, crusading's capacity to express royal power could reach far into the inner patterns of royal piety. Awareness of the mystical qualities of crusade kingship temporarily drew Edward II to the legend of the Holy Oil. A more expansive understanding of royal religion and crusade seems to have appealed to Richard II, fitting his interest in the English saints of the pre-Conquest period, particularly those saints of royal stock. Prominent here were the cults of St Edmund, the East Anglian king widely regarded in the fourteenth century as an English patron saint, and St Edward the Martyr. Mézières, tapping into Richard's deep devotion for the progenitors of English monarchy, sought to press their example into his argument for Christian reform and a royal crusade, praising the bodily sacrifices of English kings who had suffered martyrdom on behalf of the Catholic faith. The example of St Edmund was suitably evocative. His death came at the hands of attacking pagan hordes in c.870, his readiness for martyrdom emphasising the impossibility of Christian compromise with Heathendom. Marked out as a national hero of the faith, Edmund became a focus of special devotion among English crusaders in the twelfth and thirteenth centuries. It was probably in this context that his image was featured so prominently in the Wilton Dyptch.[56] St Edward the martyr, like Richard, was a boy king, and was canonised following his murder at the hands of assassins in 978. He was also venerated for his defence of the church.[57] Crusade connections could also be drawn with the life of St Edward the Confessor (also portrayed attending on Richard II in the Wilton Diptych), Mézières alluding to the Confessor's chastity and 'glorious peace' as an argument for Richard's acceptance of a chaste marriage (that is, of the French princess Isabel, a child-bride) and the mantle of *rex pacificus*. Knightly glamour was

---

[55] Palmer, *England, France and Christendom* pp. 242–4, 384–5; Saul, *Richard II* pp. 304–8 and references there; E. Scheifele, 'Richard II and the Visual Arts' *Richard II: The Art of Kingship* pp. 265–71; Fletcher, *Richard II* pp. 258–62; N. Morgan, 'The Signification of the Banner in the Wilton Diptych' *The Regal Image of Richard II* eds D. Gordon, C. Monnas and C. Elam (London, 1997) pp. 178–88.

[56] For Richard's veneration of the saints see Saul, *Richard* II pp. 311–16; Tyerman, *England and the Crusade* pp. 73, 98 (cult of St Edmund).

[57] Mézières, *Letter to King Richard II* pp. 29, 46.

added with the exemplar of the crusade hero Godfrey de Bouillon, whose chastity (i.e. lack of a direct heir) was the sacral quality that enabled him to cut through the infidel army at Antioch.[58] Identification with the principles of sacramental kingship, as exemplified by the first Latin ruler of Jerusalem, the English royal saints, and Richard's own (pre-visioned) sainthood was thought to sit central to the king's piety. This connection between the royal saints and the crusade was not new. The notoriously pious Henry III, the first great late-medieval patron of the Confessor's cult, looked to the Confessor to help legitimise his kingship when planning his crusade. He announced his intention to use a service of rededication at the Confessor's shrine at Westminster as the backdrop for his departure on crusade. The date was to be St Edward's Day 1255, when he would wear his crown. The Westminster shrine remained a focus of chivalric devotion. Richard II deposited his war standard there in 1385. Six years later the duke of Gloucester made an offering before embarking his army for Prussia.[59]

In the event, of course, Richard's exalted form of kingship, including the crusade, folded in on itself, unable to sustain its vision of uninhibited regal authority and power. The currents of crusade idealism at court and in other sections of the political community, including those harnessed by Mézières, helped to reinforce royal claims, but they also drew attention to Richard's inability to prosecute his higher aspirations, or the aspirations of the body-politic, to lasting effect. What seemed an increasingly partisan and vindictive rule exposed the gulf between Richard's vision of a unified realm and pre-eminence in Christendom, and growing disillusion among many of his subjects. Richard II's conception of monarchy ultimately proved chimerical.[60] This was brought into strong relief at the September parliament of 1399, when he was charged with various crimes against his subjects. Here, significantly, the most vociferous critics of Richard's rule, Lords Morley, Fitzwalter and Bergavenny, were reacting to Richard II's shortcomings as a warrior leader as much as his perceived 'tyrannies', though to historians of Richard's reign the latter now seem more obviously sensational.[61] All three were veterans of the Prussian crusade – Bergavenny first campaigned there as a young man (in 1365) – and like many other active knights they were possessors of proud chivalric pedigrees. While the trio attacked Richard II and his councillors mainly for their destruction of the duke of Gloucester, the exchange also served to highlight contrasting knightly and political values. A vigorous career under arms and close links to Gloucester made Lord Morley a suitable symbol of esteemed chivalry. As has already been seen, his movement in elite circles drew him close to the diplomacy of the Nicopolis crusade and into the ranks Mézières's Order of the Passion, along with several other of Gloucester's associates. For Morley, loyalty

[58] Ibid. p. 36.
[59] Lloyd, *English Society and the Crusade* pp 202, 204–5, 207; Knighton, pp. 336–9. For Woodstock see above p. 176.
[60] Saul, *Richard II* pp. 405–34, 439ff.; Fletcher, *Richard II* pp. 262–74.
[61] 'Annales Ricardi Secundi et Henrici Quarti' *Chronica et Annales* pp. 310–14.

to the crusade ideal was a means of achieving political influence at court, but also a matter of personal pride. He could trace a family tradition of crusading back to the mid thirteenth century. Similarly, Fitzwalter belonged to a prominent line of active knights and crusaders. He fought in Prussia in 1391 and accompanied the king to Ireland four years later. He was last reported alive adventuring in the Mediterranean. As a template of chivalry, his career contained much that Richard had outwardly admired.[62] The more senior Bergavenny, son of the fearsome Thomas Beauchamp, earl of Warwick (d. 1369), had campaigned extensively in the 1370s and 1380s, accumulating wide respect for his soldiery, most notably as Captain of Calais (1383–1389). He was the last of Edward III's promotions to the Order of the Garter (excepting child-knights Prince Richard and Henry Bolingbroke).[63]

The grouping was a strong platform, and their indictment of Richard II's regime acquired a menacing inquisitorial tone. Yet implicit in the personal attacks was a broader protest at ignoble, non-chivalric kingship, and an argument for military renewal, including the crusade. This was expressed by traditional ritual means against Richard's favourites, with Fitzwalter challenging the earl of Rutland (Aumale), and Morley throwing down his gauntlet against the earl of Salisbury.[64] More explicit comment was available in the speech of Lord Cobham. Lamenting the dishonour and disappointment recently visited upon the realm, he lingered over the subject of Christian fidelity, casting unfavourable comparisons between Richard II's associates (his 'foster-children') and the heathen enemies of Christendom. He reminded the assembly how Richard II's friends had revelled 'in the evils of the time' and argued that 'with such a king, such dukes, and such rulers, the condition of the English people had sunk lower even than that of the heathen peoples'. Whereas the Christians are now downtrodden and 'never dare to speak or act according to the truth under such rulers ... those who are infidels to the Christian faith and thus erroneous in their belief, nevertheless speak the truth, acknowledge the truth and act according to the truth'. Richard II's deceit was a common refrain, and the paradox of the honest heathen a well-known preaching exemplum, but the jibe was a calculated blow, hijacking the language of the court and speaking sardonically about what had been an intermittent focus of Ricardian politics. The recent crusade preaching against the Turks imparted strong topicality, as did Richard II's public protests of crusade enthusiasm nine months before at Christmas 1398.[65] That Cobham grieved at the condition of England in contrast to the heathen nations clearly magnified the scale of Richard II's criminality, the speaker's main charge, but it also cut away the king's moral ground as patron of religious war. This was bitterness towards a ruler whose actions were

[62]   See above pp. 49, 82–4, 172 for Morley and Fitzwalter.

[63]   For Beauchamp in Prussia see above pp. 76–7, 80.

[64]   'Annales Ricardi Secundi et Henrici Quarti' *Chronica et Annales* p. 310.

[65]   Ibid. pp. 306–7. See above pp. 113–14 for crusade agitation of 1398. Cf. *Chronicles of the Revolution, 1397–1400: The Reign of Richard II* ed. C. Given-Wilson (Manchester, 1993) pp. 204–5.

now deemed dangerous and whose intentions appeared inscrutable. His subjects and knights envisioned a fruitful relationship between ruler and realm, one forged through military greatness and God's favour. On the appointed day they would take part in his final crusade, the saving of the Holy Land, and the dawn of a new epoch; but now Richard II's kingship was exposed as specious.

Richard II's downfall revealed the brittleness of his personal rule, but something more could be said for the public image of kingship his court tried to cultivate during the later 1390s, including the self-imposed role of captain and arbiter of Christendom. Indeed, it was an ongoing strength of the institution that many considered the image of the crusader king to stand integral to world affairs and issues of politics and moral leadership, not separate from them. Of course, much else besides the crusade was to animate the relationship, but it spoke to the idealised function of knight and liege-lord within that world that the vision of national chivalry and English king conjoined against the pagan nations was allowed so prominent a place. That the English and their rulers were primary candidates to lead the defence of Christendom was a message not cut adrift from the centre or allowed to slip undirected into the mainstream, despite the absence of royal vows to embark on crusade. Not all crusaders may have seen their actions in so fine a light – as part-fulfilment of an ordained political order, or as fidelity to an authentic vision of royal and princely power. But it was a reflection of its wider resonance that Henry Bolingbroke and later his son Henry V gravitated towards the traditional vision of a royal crusade to help bolster their moral and political standing, attracted to the conservative political and chivalric values stored up in the ideal. In 1399 Bolingbroke made a point of using the Oil of St Thomas Becket in his coronation, chiming with various prophetic strands and inviting speculation about his possible future as a saviour of Christendom. It showed God's rejection of Richard II and his acceptance of Henry IV as rightful king. The usurper was another Judas Maccabeus come into God's inheritance as an instrument of God's justice and as hero of the English nation. He was destined to restore health to the crown and wrest back ancestral lands in France that were his, and his country's, right. Bolingbroke's impeccable crusade chivalry, reputed across the courts of Europe, could be presented as another transcending quality. Indeed, the core message in the special anointing (and in other prophetic texts seeking to legitimise Henry IV's usurpation) was that the full destiny of prince and realm lay outside the confines of the nation and indeed outside of the west. Set over the English race by the momentous events of 1399, Bolingbroke was to be greeted as the warrior king whose career would culminate in a new Christian epoch across continents and the salvaging of Jerusalem. Preferred by God, it was the fate of the restored nation to direct Christendom against the *heth-enesse*: this was to be the ultimate objective of English politics, chivalry and kingship, all other ideological pressures and constraints notwithstanding.[66]

---

[66] Sandquist, 'The Holy Oil of St Thomas of Canterbury' pp. 330–44. In his letters Henry identified himself as Mattathias, the patriarch of the Maccabees: M. J. Bennett, 'Henry Bolingbroke and the

Revolution of 1399' *Henry IV: The Establishment of a Regime* eds G. Dodd and D. Biggs (York, 2003) p. 17; *Royal and Historical Letters of Henry IV* no. 88. For other prophetic voices and the crusade during Henry IV's reign see Coote, *Prophecy and Public Affairs* pp. 157–69.

Conclusion

This book has documented the various ways in which active experience of fighting in the *hethenesse* remained a central characteristic of fourteenth-century chivalric society. Evidence of attitudes and behaviour among the military elite show a rich culture of distant campaigning and crusader militancy, unstifled by the demands of the Hundred Years War, the collapse of Jerusalem crusading and the onset of the papal schism. There was no general decline in enthusiasm for war in the *hethenesse*, despite the various obstacles that lay in the path of embarking captains and retinues. We have seen, moreover, that English knights and esquires did not move in a backwater of idealism or play the junior partner to continental nobility, as traditionally depicted in histories of the later crusades. On the contrary, in the period following Richard the Lionheart's famous crusade of the 1190s, it is likely that English knights enjoyed their greatest degree of independence and opportunity in the years between 1307 and 1399, the range of war-frontiers and shorter terms of crusade service encouraging a response which rivalled, if not eclipsed, the late twelfth and early thirteenth centuries, the 'heyday' of crusading, for its wide distribution of experience among arms-bearing families. Prussia and the coastal marches of the eastern Mediterranean displaced Syria and Palestine as primary frontiers, but it is right to think of the fourteenth century as a golden age of English crusading. Failure to organise a grand international *passagium* involving all the crowned heads of Europe can be put down to more complex factors of government and politics, not the coolness of western knights or the excesses of English armies in Scotland and France.

Taken together, the book's nine chapters suggest a more analytical approach to the study of the late-medieval crusade and the cultural contexts in which it was fostered. One of the most important themes to emerge is the relationship between the martial ethos of the knightly and elite classes, and the influence of much broader underlying cultural experiences and expectations. Continuities of propaganda, fundraising, ideology, logistics and military tactics ensured that the wars of the cross remained, in various ways, an aspect of mainstream society and domestic life, not caught in the half-light between perceived chivalric ideals and military realities. With a cultural impact somewhat larger than the military campaigns themselves, it was too early in the fourteenth century to talk of romantic idealism or old-fashioned institutions. Preaching messages, prayers, alms-giving and propaganda provided important shared focal points. Compared to earlier periods, it is difficult to identify similar levels of pressure brought about by embarking crusaders on the land market, finance or government and church bureaucracies, partly because, in the absence of a royal expedition, there lacked a centrally organised system of finance and recruitment. But the general picture emerging from the evidence is that decisions to take the cross and fight in the *hethenesse* possessed domestic and material implications of no lesser significance, involving a host of humdrum considerations to occupy participants' energy and time.

Crusaders undertook immense personal gambles, alienating land to raise money, taking out loans and vacating good positions at court or in county society. Preparations could involve the lavishing of gifts upon religious establishments, the suing out of royal and papal licences and protections, military provisioning, the charter of shipping, pooling of resources and even the siring of heirs before sailing, men's duty to lineage requiring action before new campaigning.[1] So long as crusading was as likely a route to bankruptcy, captivity and a disrupted or extinguished political career as it was to personal honour, armed adventure and prestige, it is unfair to think of an increasingly hollow or vainglorious ideal. Nothing in the evidence uncovered above suggests that decisions to embark could be taken lightly, free of concerns about family, household finances, the safeguarding of inheritances and the various other associated problems of prolonged absence from home. It was not hollow literary convention that how to negotiate for the release of knights from Turkish prisons was one of the shared concerns of chivalric treatises.[2]

Limitations of space have prevented fuller discussion of some of the broader issues and sub-themes arising in the text. The wider diplomatic pressures and purposes animating Anglo-papal relations in the fourteenth century have clear implications for a study of this nature, for example. The sometimes tense, long-term drift towards greater church exceptionalism – characterised by Edward III's strained relations with Urban V, the failure of papal meditation in the Anglo-French war, and recurrent struggles over church revenues – opened up distance between the English episcopate and the Holy See, muddying the issue of crusade response and control. With the onset of the Great Schism in 1378, the papacy ceased to be an arbiter of Christendom, as each pope became tied to and dependent upon national support. Similarly, the association of royal crusading with the formation of a state of Christian peace, a core principle of much crusade talk in this period, opens up perspectives on the values of a political theology that understood the crusade and holy war to be a restorer of divine order in

---

[1]   In 1368 John Multon and Lord Lucy left infant children as heirs before leaving for Prussia; John, Lord Mowbray, waited for the birth of a second son (Thomas, 1366) before embarking for Constantinople (1367). For Multon and Lucy see above p. 79.

[2]   Bonet, *Tree of Battles* p. 191; Pisan, *Book of fayttes of armes and of chivalry* pp. 249–50.

the west, a soother of troubled polities. Equally, where the wars of the cross provided a platform for the workings of courtly love and knightly questing, much more could be said about the image of the Holy Land and crusader heroism in the literary and intellectual realms. Some of the material gathered above provides a starting point for a more focused discussion of the transmission of values and ideals across such related contexts and settings.[3] Additionally, diocesan registers and other ecclesiastical sources shed light on various aspects of church organisation, including patterns of preaching, indulgence sales, alms-giving, vow-redemptions, crusade taxation and numerous special subsidies. I have tried to indicate how such sources relate to the outlook of the military and other classes, examining the promotional activity that still accompanied papal crusade appeals, but there remains room for further study. As for patterns of knightly participation, further evidence of English preparations and related activity is likely to be found in local source collections for Calais, Avignon, Rhodes, Venice, Castile and Gascony, each at various times the centres of supply and recruitment for crusade expeditions.

As a comment upon chivalry in the era of the Hundred Years War, it is difficult to argue that crusading attracted any more controversy or criticism than before. Paradigms of pride, display, individual prowess and martial ambition, while prominent in chivalry's value system and roundly condemned by its critics, had little to do with western failure to provide a military solution against the Turks, nor do they adequately account for crusading's ongoing popularity. Equally, western knighthood did not suddenly shed the qualities of discipline, bravery and skill repeatedly demonstrated on battlefields across Europe when encountering enemies on the borders of Christendom. Unfamiliar terrain, problems of logistics and conflicting local interests – rather than cultural and psychological flaws – dictated the outcome of wars and campaigns. As for the tension between national war in the service of princes and the ethic of knightly crusading, increasingly it appears to have possessed positive rather than negative dynamics. A culture of international chivalry and contact fostered by the diplomatic, courtly and campaign experiences of the Anglo-French war helped energise the knightly classes in spirited crusade emulation. While proving disruptive of efforts to launch a general *passagium*, the stop-start pattern of royal campaigning may regularly have caused contemporaries to think that a lasting peace and massed crusade was a good deal closer than it proved. As with earlier periods, the question of crusader motivation resists any convenient grading or typology. That campaigns in the *hethenesse* in themselves carried little or no prospect of material profit, plunder or power, may perhaps distinguish the participants of later crusades from those embarking on the first, more famous, expeditions. Possibly knights were increasingly sensitive to the standards of high chivalry as idealised in literature and

---

[3]   Nicholson's *Love, War and the Grail* lays out some of the relevant themes; see also L. Manion, 'The Loss of the Holy Land and *Sir Isumbras*: Literary Contributions to Fourteenth-Century Crusade Discourse' *Speculum* 85 (2010) pp. 65–90.

court ceremonial, particularly in the years when the piratical activities of the Free companies dismayed observers, and when English armies began to suffer military reverses in France.[4] But crusading's allure was always that it offered something not easily available elsewhere, permitting knights and esquires to distinguish themselves and their actions from less worthy rivals or classes. The rewards of high military prestige, with its often overtly religious as well as secular sheen, carried the promise of material and social promotion in county and courtly circles, storing up opportunities for future advancement and dynastic display. Many noble-born participants such as the Beauchamp family made their crusade heritage the outward face of their knighthood, and sceptical voices such as Gower were capable of romanticising the crusade as praiseworthy warfare, providing a necessary outlet for knights' (regrettable) need to 'wexe wrothe'.[5]

The great 'secretary of chivalry' Froissart was equally well versed in this moral dimension. Interested in deeds of arms and scales of honour, the chronicler constructed a larger didactic argument around crusading's higher calling. In his treatment of the Tunis crusade of 1390, for example, he created space for a counter-narrative of corruption and treachery in the career of the robber baron and celebrated anti-hero Méricot Marchès, governor of Aloise in the Auvergne. Whereas many of France's best knights vacated their lands to go into *Barbarie* for the exaltation of the Christian faith, the most ignoble set their hearts to mischief. Placed against the telling of the Tunis expedition, Marchès's violent career takes up rather more space in Froissart's account, causing the author to interrupt and deviate at length from the story of the crusade. But that did not lessen the crusade's dramatic narrative impact, the chronicler taking care to build tension and returning to Tunis and the honourable reputations established there as a showcase of purified chivalry. The plotlines converge, with Méricot receiving his comeuppance on the scaffold, and the crusaders returning to rapturous applause at Charles VI's court. If not for its own sake, but as the antithesis to brigandage and criminality, fighting in the *hethenesse* was an entry-point to reputable Christian society.[6] This was not necessarily a static view (Froissart was capable of questioning the wisdom of crusading when it caused unnecessary danger at home), but it reflected mainstream sentiments and values.

Against this backdrop, the relationship between crusade ideology and late-medieval concepts of kingship and royal duties and rights may be set within its proper cultural and political context. Formed of numerous divergent strands and influences, an over-arching argument about crusading, holy war and virtuous monarchy emerges from the sources. Prominent among a number of overlapping kingly and

---

[4] Saul, *For Honour and Fame* pp. 128–34, 193–6.
[5] Gower, 'In Praise of Peace' *The English Works* vol. II p. 227.
[6] Froissart, vol. XIV p. 154. For Marchès's career see M. H. Keen, *The Laws of War in the Late Middle Ages* (London, 1965) pp. 97–100. See P. F. Ainsworth, *Jean Froissart and the Fabric of History* (Oxford, 1990) for Froissart's historical technique.

knightly personas, the image of the crusader king provided the English monarchy with a language of aspiration and power, equipping national politics with a framework for interpreting past, current and future events. For this reason Edward II, Edward III, Richard II and Henry IV made use of related iconography and language as part of a legitimising discourse. Attitudes were partly shaped by the pressures and appeals of the Hundred Years War, a conflict bestowed with its own quasi-religious status, and by suspicion of French claims of leadership over the general *passagium* and Christendom as a whole. But what guaranteed the crusader king image force beyond the abstract and theoretical was crusading's ongoing function in chivalric and military life. Here the cult of the knight-errant, far from being a play-thing of poets, remained in active tension with evolving claims of the political centre, helping to shape the relationship between liege-lord and fighting men. As has been seen, against the rising tide of national or patriotic feeling demanded by the wars of Edward III, loyalty to the international ethic of crusading lay down a potential counterargument to the military priorities of the crown. It is wrong to see this as a well-defined or hotly-fought debate. Knights themselves, kings were bound to observe the fundamental tenets of chivalry, including the crusade, as well as to cast some influence over them. Instead, knighthood's slowness to abandon the *hethenesse* compelled the crown to operate within fairly narrow moral and political parameters. Not starved of access to the highest courts, then, or the prestige of kings, talk of the cross was unavoidably integrated into political thinking and, from time to time, political action. Even as prospects of royal crusading declined, the mantle of *rex crucesignandus* held persistent allure, its silhouette taking up large cultural and political space. When Henry V temporarily revived the dream of marching on Jerusalem in 1421, it was in conjunction with his Burgundian allies, and as conqueror of France, striking emotional parallels with the post-1389 period as well as with the recurrent crusade-and-peace talk of earlier decades.[7] As such, it may be possible to approach the crusade theme in royal diplomacy in a more sympathetic way. It spoke less of empty or formalised modes of address, and more of the collected values and outlook of the wider political community. Numerous other currents and influences besides the *negotium crucis* operated at court, of course, dictating fashions and events, and it is important to keep balance. The reputations of English kings after Edward I, as generally passive in the international crusade, remain intact. But what this book has tried to show is that the crusade war remained an important part of the synthesis of values that made up the English monarchy in this period.

Finally, if the stereotype of the crusading knight-errant is now better documented against the context of fourteenth-century political and religious life, what of later decades and the period after the flowering of interest in the 1390s? Almost as striking as the ethos of crusade militancy among the contemporaries of the Black Prince and

---

[7]   *Proceedings of the Privy Council* ed. N. H. Nicolas (London, 1834–1837) vol. III pp. 117–18; Paviot, *Ducs de Bourgogne* pp. 63–7; Atiya, *Crusade in the Later Middle Ages* pp. 190–7.

Richard II is the tailing off of commitment after 1399. Although English knightly traffic to Rhodes and other outposts of Christianity in the east and elsewhere persisted, their military impact and numbers remained, by comparison, minimal, and by the end of the Hundred of Years War the audience for which Chaucer, Mézières, Christine de Pisan and other sympathisers of crusading wrote had largely disappeared. Partly this was down to the domestic political crises of the late 1390s and the increased demands of war in the reigns of Henry IV and Henry V. More significant than obstacles of politics, however, the idea of chivalry as a value system – of a united order of Christian soldiers pledged to the armed defence of justice and faith – was coming under increased pressure in the contemporary world of emergent nation states. Concepts of sovereign authority, legitimate war-making and the guiding principles of profit and loss helped shape military expectations, and from the very beginning of the Hundred Years War signs of the pressure of standards quite other than those on which chivalry was founded had been apparent, if not yet ready to come to the fore. Little of this was obvious to contemporaries, even to the knights of Edward III, the most vigorous promoter of national chivalry. Indeed, Henry V's victory at Agincourt in 1415 at first gave fresh impetus to the image of the apocalyptic ruler and champion of Christendom, with possibly great implications for English chivalry and the crusade. A variety of expectation identified the king with the context of the Holy Land. Gossip at the Council of Constance recycled the fanciful story of Islam's internal collapse, an event once more thought to be in the offing. One of the English delegates wrote to the court about it, sharing details of an eastern prophecy that Islam would either be conquered or converted within five years, plainly thinking that Henry V would be interested in it too. The writer of the *Gesta Henrici Quinti*, a member of the chapel royal, made clear his hope that the king would eventually fight the Saracens and free the Holy Land as an epilogue to the Agincourt campaign. Elsewhere, to help make sense of Henry's deliverance from the French, the legend of the Holy Oil resurfaced in connection with this latest king, ignoring its first public use in 1399.[8] This was a poor substitute for the regular contact kept up with eastern powers throughout most of the fourteenth century, but the court still clearly saw the need for a higher moral framework. It was in this context that crusade talk helped cement a delicate military alliance with Burgundy. According to Burgundian chroniclers, the young duke and Henry V exchanged crusade vows on the eve of their joint offensive against the Dauphin in the autumn of 1420. The conquest of *Sainte-Terre* was Henry's 'final aspiration', supposedly within touching distance once resistance in northern France had been crushed.[9]

[8]   *Gesta Henrici Quinti* eds F. Taylor and J. F. Roskell (Oxford, 1975) pp. 101–13; *Letters of Margaret of Anjou* ed. C. Munro, Camden Society 86 (London, first series 1863) p. 10; Eton College MS 191, quoted by Coote, *Prophecy and Public Affairs* p. 172.
[9]   Paviot, *Ducs de Bourgogne* pp. 63–7; Atiya, *Crusade in the Later Middle Ages* pp. 190–7.

While conventional ideology and rhetoric remained in place, however, in the first decades of the fifteenth century, decisive changes in the character of contemporary chivalry and national politics were coming to light. Movement away from the dynastic or entrepreneurial wars of the fourteenth century towards what was formulated as a struggle for the *respublica* and the well-being of the realm had the effect of bestowing upon the chivalric classes a superseding set of obligations, distinct from the old idea of knightly Christendom pledged to the defence of the faith. This more inhibited outlook would take hold at the very top of military society. Probably the most significant breach with traditional chivalry occurred in 1399, when the greatly enlarged Lancastrian affinity imposed itself at court. Called upon to deal with successive rebellions and internal crises between 1400 and 1406, Henry IV's retainers practised circumscribed chivalry, fighting skirmishes and launching emergency marches across the interior. When not protecting the king, their function was to defend his interests in county society, imposing the political settlement of 1399. In contrast to Henry IV's carefully cultivated reputation for knighthood, and his public preference for traditional chivalry epitomised by the crusade, the royal affinity exhibited an introverted martial ethic, centred upon loyalty to the Lancastrian dynasty and the duties and rewards of service-politics.[10]

The appeals of international crusading came under pressure from other directions. Closer scrutiny of the affairs of government, royal expenditure and the freedoms of royal lordship helped feed a critical debate about the king's personal aspirations and power, and his duty to exercise power for the common good. In very general terms, the ongoing centralisation of monarchy – seen in government bureaucracies, the growth of a tax state, royal ceremonial, and narrowing courtly itineraries – abetted an increasingly strong sense of the crown's physical presence, its incumbency upon the political community and its geographical confines. At war, English monarchs displayed similar conservatism, reluctant to stray far from insular interests, in contrast to many of their knightly subjects. In 1415 Henry V was the first monarch to fight at the head of an army outside the British Isles since 1359. After Henry's death, the feat was not repeated until 1513. More to the point, the last English king to undertake a continental campaign outside the confines of northern France or royal lands in Gascony was Richard I, embarking the Third Crusade in 1190.[11] Relief from this geographical fixity could be found in the activities of diplomacy and a court culture of knight-errantry, but inevitably the late-medieval community was accustomed to crown-wearers campaigning within traditional environs. To venture further afield meant unwelcome novelty and risk of stirring harmful tensions within the polity, no matter how appealing the operative vision. Henry V's abandonment of seasonal campaigns in favour of year-

---

[10]   In general see G. L. Harriss, *Shaping The Nation: England 1360–1461* (Oxford, 2005) pp. 494–7 and the references collected there.

[11]   A large English army protected the nine-year-old Henry VI's entry to Paris in 1430. Edward IV (1475) and Henry VII (1491) accompanied expeditions to France but saw no significant fighting. When in France, Edward III limited himself to campaigning in the north. He led no force south of the Loire.

round operations against the French further narrowed expectations and experiences. The intensity of royal campaigning – in the war's second phase (1417–1420) Henry held together an army for three years – discouraged the sort of opportunism that had been the hallmark of English chivalry and active crusading since the end of Edward I's reign.[12] Royal prohibitions on foreign travel may have been no more tightly enforced than before, but expanded incentives and royal inducements succeeded in narrowing much more the channels of material and social advancement, making armed service increasingly the exclusive jurisdiction of the crown. Church propaganda and patriotic feeling helped validate this monopoly of military resources, particularly in the heady years surrounding Agincourt.[13]

Meanwhile, opportunities for aspiring crusade militants began to dry up. The popular Prussian crusade suffered a near-fatal reverse in 1410 at the battle of Tannenberg, when combined Polish-Lithuanian forces routed the Teutonic Knights. Eight years later Baltic crusading struggled to win the support of the Council of Constance.[14] In the east, a hiatus in warfare against Muslims in the Balkans and Mediterranean reflected the preference among local Christian powers for conciliation and trade – factors of stability in local and regional politics that paid little heed to religious divides. Absence of strong papal leadership in the years surrounding the papal schism minimised church control. Civil war in France between 1407 and 1435 further depleted the crusade of ranks of French chivalry. The defence of Christendom became increasingly a matter for frontier-kings and states, receiving less and less stimulus and aid from western rulers and knights.

This did not spell the end of crusade enthusiasm in the English context, though its role in chivalric life was changed. While the years following Nicopolis witnessed a steep decline in courtly contact with the east – attested in decreased requests for aid and reduced traffic of knights – compensation was found in a flourishing of the sort of crusade dreaming seen throughout the fourteenth century. The infant Henry VI was identified with his father's imperial destiny, including the freeing of the Holy Places. Another recommendation was his double lineage from Louis IX, a divine quality repeatedly stressed in official propaganda. The writer of the *Tractatus de Regimine Principum* advised that the greatest good would be to achieve peace between England and France, so that Henry could then drive the infidel from the Holy Land. His theme was recycled across poetry, prophetic texts and other political commentaries, considered part of the ornamentation of kingship.[15] As with Edward II, against the

---

[12] For the scope of organisational change in war see the articles by A. Ayton, A. Curry and M. Jones in *Arms, Armies and Fortifications in the Hundred Years War* eds A. Curry and M. Hughes (Woodbridge, 1994) pp. 21–68, 103–20.

[13] A. K. McHardy, 'Liturgy and Propaganda during the Hundred Years War' *Studies in Church History* 18 (Oxford, 1982) pp. 215–27.

[14] See above p. 86.

[15] *Four English Political Tracts of the Later Middle Ages,* ed. J.-P. Genêt, Camden Society 18 (London, fourth series 1977) p. 71. In general see Coote, *Prophecy and Public Affairs* pp. 179–94.

backdrop of Henry VI's adult reign, the vision of the royal crusade was an antidote to discordant politics and a non-chivalric king. This growing divergence between image and reality was apparent elsewhere in crusading, not only in the decline of English experience of fighting in the *hethenesse*, disconnecting military achievements from political expectations at the height of society. It could be seen in the continuing round of indulgence sales and the efflorescence of Jerusalem-related prayers and masses recorded in English missals. Such continuities pointed the way for the future of the crusade in political life, and in the outlook of English chivalry. Discredited as a means of papal alliance and largely cut away from its knightly constituent, support for the crusade entered a new phase among the arms-bearing classes, incorporated much more as commemoration of prized social origins and family status than as a goal of practical and military ends. Always partly an exercise of custom and nostalgia, by the middle of the fifteenth century crusading became increasingly an aspect of ceremony and display for most noblemen and knights, resting in large part on four-teenth-century exploits, rather than (interestingly) twelfth- and thirteenth-century achievements. Vows to perform a service against the Turks or fight in the *hethenesse* were kept largely to the confines of court rooms, banqueting halls and audience chambers, unencumbered by the threat of church penalties or public chastening of preachers. Changing devotional tastes, escalating military costs and the increased political and administrative demands of the state narrowed crusading's appeal. Nor were the necessary conditions of domestic peace or foreign truce ever firmly established enough during the fifteenth century to permit the sort of knightly adventurism seen in the reigns of Edward III and Richard II.[16]

Against such a background, the role of the knight in English society was itself changing, edging towards a less martial occupation, and a period when alternative qualities, those which equipped men to be office holders and law-givers, came to be perceived as equally valuable. The right to bear arms, and claims to knightly status, would depend less and less on fighting crusades or earning honour on royal chev-auchées.[17] By the time of William Worcester's *Boke of Noblesse* (1452–1453) horizons for exotic chivalry and crusade campaigning were firmly closed in. It was, he thought, a great pity that many descended of noble blood and born to arms, 'as knightis sonnes, esquires and other of gentile bloode', now took up pursuit of the law with greater vigour than traditional martial occupations. In the absence of the prestigious 'con-questis and werris' beyond the sea, English chivalrous society was set on a much more insular and gentrified course.[18] Although not yet seen as antique, talk of the crusade was by now largely figurative and ornamental.

---

[16] For the fifteenth century and beyond see Tyerman, *England and the Crusades* pp. 302–23.
[17] Keen, *Origins* pp. 101–20.
[18] *The Boke of Noblesse* ed. J. G. Nichols (London, 1860) p. 77.

Appendix: Register of English Crusaders c.1307–1399

Many of the names listed here applied for chancery licences and papal safe conducts to travel 'against the infidel' as leaders of military retinues. In some instances there is little or no corroborative evidence to confirm that the licences were ever used and expeditions made. Licences do, however, indicate a level of interest and on occasion provide incidental information regarding size of retinue, financial contingencies and other details. Chronicle sources provide information about those who actually left, and in many cases leave a record where a licence has not survived.

# indicates member of the Order of the Garter
* indicates member of the Order of the Passion
+ indicates crusading fatality

Name/rank	Date/campaign	Expenses	Size of affinity	Retinue/association
Abberbury, Richard, the younger, knight*[1]	1390 Prussia			
Aclum, John[2]	1394 Prussia			John Beaufort
Alberton, Thomas, 'domicello' of Royal Household[3]	1365 Alexandria			associated with King Peter of Cyprus
Alneto, Nicholas[4]	1309 Rhodes			
Argent, John, knight[5]	1351 Prussia			duke of Lancaster and earl of Suffolk
	1365 Alexandria			earl of Hereford

[1]   NA, C76/74 m. 4; NA, C81/525/7233; NA, DL28/3/2 fol. 6ᵛ; Paravicini, *Die Preussenreisen* vol. I p. 125; Keen, 'Chaucer's Knight' p. 57.
[2]   Hirsch, *Danzigs Handels* pp. 234–5.
[3]   *CPP* vol. I p. 490; *Urbain V: Lettres communes* nos 8635, 11489, 17028, 17029.
[4]   *CPR 1307–1313* p. 181; NA, C66/133 m. 40.
[5]   *Anonimalle* p. 51; *CPR 1350–1354* p. 182.

Name/rank	Date/campaign	Expenses	Size of affinity	Retinue/association
Argentein, Giles, knight[6]	1311–1313 Rhodes			
Assheley, John, esquire[7]	1390/1 Prussia			earl of Derby
Astel, Thomas[8]	1391 Prussia			
Aysterby, John[9]	1367 Prussia			lords Beaumont, Fitzwalter et al.
Bagot, Walter, knight[10]	1390 Prussia	£20		earl of Derby
Bakon, Adam rector of Olton[11]	1309 (Rhodes?)			
Basset, Ralph, lord of Drayton[#12]	1366–1368 Gallipoli		c.100 men	count of Savoy and Maurice le Bruyn
Basset, Ralph, lord of Sapcote[13]	1365/6 Prussia			earl of Warwick
Beauchamp, John, of Hatch, knight[14]	1309 Rhodes			Fitzpayn et al.
Beauchamp, John, knight[15]	1365/6 Prussia		7 household	earl of Warwick
Beauchamp, Roger, knight[16]	1367/8 Prussia	1000 marks	9 esquires 20 yeomen	William and Thomas Beauchamp
Beauchamp, Thomas, earl of Warwick (d. 1401)[#17]	1367/8 Prussia	1000 marks	9 esquires 20 yeomen	William and Roger Beauchamp

[6]   *CPR 1307–1313* p. 324; *Foedera* vol. II pt. 1 p. 50 (captured by Greeks nr. Rhodes); *CCR 1308–1313* p. 251.

[7]   *Expeditions* p. xxxv.

[8]   Paravicini, *Die Preussenreisen* vol. I p. 126.

[9]   *CPR 1367–1370* p. 41.

[10]   *Victoria History of the County of Stafford* eds M. W. Greenslade et al. (London, 1908–) vol. III p. 153.

[11]   *CPL* vol. II p. 54; *Reg. Clem.* no. 4089.

[12]   *Urbain V: Lettres communes* nos 15868, 17093, 17094, 17095; Cox, *Green Count of Savoy* p. 211; Setton, *Papacy and the Levant* pp. 296, 302; Barberi, nos 110, 111, 215, 256, 479, and documents IV and V pp. 338–43; Luttrell, 'Chaucer's Knight' p. 141; *CPR 1361–1364* p. 124; *CPR 1358–1361* p. 479; NA, C61/79 mm. 9, 13.

[13]   *CPP* vol. I pp. 496, 500; *CPL* vol. IV p. 38; *Urbain V: Lettres communes* nos 8875, 8876; Luttrell, 'Chaucer's Knight' p. 141; id. 'English Levantine Crusaders' p. 145.

[14]   *CPR 1307–1313* pp. 102, 111; *Peerage* vol. II pp. 48–9.

[15]   *CPP* vol. I p. 498; *CPL* vol. IV p. 36; ASV, reg. supp. 40 fols 145ʳ–179ʳ; *Accounts Rendered by Papal Collectors* p. 84.

[16]   *CPR 1367–1370* p. 56; NA, C66/276 m. 19ᵈ.

[17]   *CPR 1367–1370* p. 56, 24; NA, C66/276 mm. 13, 19ᵈ.

Name/rank	Date/campaign	Expenses	Size of affinity	Retinue/association
Beauchamp, Thomas, earl of Warwick (d. 1369)[18]	1365/6 Prussia		7 knights 13 household 1 priest ('300 lances')	
Beauchamp, William, knight[19]	1365/6 Prussia 1367 Prussia	1000 marks	1 knight 1 priest 9 esquires 20 yeoman	earl of Warwick
Beaufo, John, esquire[20]	1390/1 Prussia	£27 6s 8d		
Beaufort, John, marquess of Dorset, marquess of Somerset (d. 1410)[21]	1390 Tunis 1391 Prussia 1394 Prussia 1396 (Nicopolis?)			John Botiller earl of Derby Stephen Scrope
Beaumont, Henry, lord[22]	1368 Prussia	£1000	23 horsemen	Walter Fitzwalter and Hugh Despenser
Beaumont, John, knight[23]	1391 Prussia			Lords Despenser, Fitzwalter, Clifford, Bourchier
Bentley, Richard[24]	1390/1 Prussia			earl of Derby
Bernak, William[25]	1351 Prussia	£40	5 horsemen	duke of Lancaster
Berwick, Hugh de, knight[26]	1391 Prussia			duke of Gloucester

[18]   John of Reading, p. 172; Wigands von Marburg, p. 549; *CPL* vol. IV pp. 5, 9, 10, 19, 39; *CPP* vol. I pp. 456, 494–500; *CCR 1364–1368* p. 143; *Urbain V: Lettres closes* nos 682, 940; *Urbain V: Lettres communes* nos 8664, 11536, 11537, 11538; ASV, reg. supp. 40 fols 145^r–179^r; *The Register of William Edington, Bishop of Winchester, 1346–1366* ed. S. F. Hockey (Winchester, 1986–1987) vol. I p. 202; 'Reg. Whittlesey' WRO, b716.093-B.A.2648/4 (ii) fol. 27^r; Setton, *Papacy and the Levant* p. 258.

[19]   *CPP* vol. I p. 500; ASV, reg. supp. 40 fols 145^r–179^r; *CPR 1367–1370* p. 56; NA, C66/276 m. 19^d; *Urbain V: Lettres communes* nos 8834, 8879.

[20]   As 'king's esquire' Beaufo received £27 6s 8d on coming out of Prussia: NA, E403/536 m. 11; *CPR 1391–1396* p. 276.

[21]   *Expeditions* p. 301; Wigands von Marburg, p. 653; Mirot, *Siège de Mahdia* p.16; Hirsch, *Danzigs Handels* p. 234.

[22]   Wigands von Marburg, p. 558; *CPR 1367–1370* p. 132; NA, C66/277 m. 30^d, 'vessels of gold and silver necessary for his household his jewels and a letter of exchange for £1000 '; *CCR 1364–1368* p. 473 (recognisance of debt to earl of Arundel for £1000).

[23]   *West. Chron.* pp. 455, 475.

[24]   Paravicini, *Die Preussenreisen* vol. I p.126.

[25]   *CPR 1350–1354* p. 171; Paravicini, *Die Preussenreisen* vol. I p. 125.

[26]   NA, C81/1059/15; Paravicini, *Die Preussenreisen* vol. I p. 126.

Name/rank	Date/campaign	Expenses	Size of affinity	Retinue/association
Bitterley, Walter, knight[27]	1390 Prussia			John Standish
Blake, John, priest, treasurer to earl of Warwick[28]	1365/6 Prussia			earl of Warwick
Bohun, Humphrey, earl of Hereford[#29]	1361 Satalia 1363 Prussia 1365 Alexandria 1365 (Prussia?) 1367 Med.			William Scrope John Argent
Boilend, Richard, knight[30]	1351 Prussia			duke of Lancaster
Bolingbroke, Henry, earl of Derby, King Henry IV (d. 1413)[#31]	1390/1 Prussia 1392 Prussia	£4,440 £4,000	150–200 approx. as 1390/1	Thomas Percy, Beaufort, Thomas Swinford
Bond, John, 'donsel'[32]	1345 Smyrna			
Botiller, Thomas, lord[33]	1390 Tunis			John Beaufort
Botreaux, William, the younger[34]	1391 Prussia		5 servants	
Botreaux, William, the elder[35]	1390 (East Med.?)			
Bourchier, John, lord[#36]	1390/1 Prussia	£300	6 esquires 23 household	Lords Despenser, Fitzwalter, Clifford, Beaumont

[27] NA, C81/515/6212; Paravicini, *Die Preussenreisen* vol. I p. 125.

[28] ASV, reg. supp. 40 fols 145ʳ–179ʳ; *CPP* vol. I p. 494; *Reg. Edington* p. 202; *Reg. Wakefield* p. 67, nos 480–1; 'Reg. Whittlesey' WRO, b716.093-B.A.2648/4 (ii) fol. 27ʳ; 'Register of John Barnet' Worcestershire Record Office b716.093-B.A. 2648/4 (i) fol. 39ʳ; *Urbain V: Lettres communes* no. 8706.

[29] Machaut, *Capture of Alexandria* p. 147; *Scrope and Grosvenor* vol. I pp. 165–6, vol. II p. 377; Fowler, 'Seals' p. 115; NA, DL25/1989; NA, DL25/1638; NA, DL25/1639; NA, DL34/1/27; *Anonimalle* p. 51; Luttrell, 'Chaucer's Knight' p. 141; *CPR 1361–1364* p. 173; *CPR 1367–1370* p. 41; Paravicini, *Die Preussenreisen* vol. I p. 124.

[30] Paravicini, *Die Preussenreisen* vol. I p. 124.

[31] *West. Chron.* pp. 433, 441, 445–9; Knighton, p. 537; Walsingham, *Historia Anglicana* vol. II pp. 197–8; Higden, *Polychronicon* vol. VIII pp. 235, 238; 'Franciscani Thorunensis Annales Prussica' *SRP* vol. III pp. 164, 168; *Expeditions passim*; NA, C76/77 m. 14; *Diplomatic Correspondence* pp. 77, 218.

[32] *CPL* vol. III pp. 15, 160; *Clément VI: Lettres rapportant à la France* no. 1462.

[33] Froissart, vol. XIV p. 225; *Reg. Wakefield* no. 671; NA, C76/74 m. 4.

[34] *Calendar of Select Pleas* vol. III pp. 182–92.

[35] 'ad ficiendem votum suum quod ipse ante hec tempora vovit in exonerationem animesue', *CPR 1388–1392* p. 324; NA, C66/331 m. 10. See too his licence to travel of June 1380, NA, C76/64 m. 6.

[36] *Peerage* vol. II p. 246; M. K. Jones, 'Fortunes of War' p. 152; *West. Chron.* p. 475; NA, C76/74 m.

Name/rank	Date/campaign	Expenses	Size of affinity	Retinue/association
Boynton, Thomas, esquire[37]	1362 Prussia 1367 Prussia	£20	2 esquires 3 household	Geoffrey Scrope, Richard Waldegrave, et al. Thomas Southeworth
Boys, Roger, knight[38]	1361/2 Satalia 1367 Prussia			Miles Stapleton
Bradestone, Robert, knight[39]	1345 Smyrna			John St Philipot and William Dachet
Breton, Richard, knight, yeoman of the Chamber[40]	1391 Prussia			duke of Gloucester et al.
Breton, William, knight[41]	1365/6 Prussia			earl of Warwick
Breux, John[42]	1385 Prussia			Robert Morley
Brocas, Bernard, knight[43]	1390 Tunis			
Bruyn (Broun), Maurice le, knight[44]	1366–1368 Gallipoli 1386 Prussia		15 men	Ralph Basset of Drayton
Bucton, Peter, knight[45]	1390/1 Prussia 1392 Prussia			earl of Derby earl of Derby
Bugge, Edmund, knight[46]	1390/1 Prussia 1392 Prussia			earl of Derby earl of Derby
Burghesh, Bartholomew, the elder, knight (d.1355)[47]	1345 (Med.?) 1349 (Med.?)		8 knights, 20 esquires 20 knights, 30 esquires	

4; NA, C81/515/6289.

[37] *Scrope and Grosvenor*, vol. I p. 117, vol. II p. 310; *CPR 1367–1370* pp. 30, 65.

[38] *CPR 1361–1364* p. 147; *CPR 1367–1370* p. 21.

[39] *Clément VI: Lettres rapportant à la France* no. 1617; *CPR 1345–1348* pp. 21, 330; *CCR 1343–1346* p. 646.

[40] *Foedera* vol. III pt. 4 p. 71; Paravicini, *Die Preussenreisen* vol. I p. 126.

[41] *CPP* vol. I pp. 497, 499; ASV, reg. supp. 40 fols 145ʳ–179ʳ.

[42] NA, C47/6/1 no. 102 m. 36.

[43] Gough, vol. I p. 160.

[44] *Scrope and Grosvenor* vol. I p. 161, vol. II p. 367; Paravicini, *Die Preussenreisen* vol. I p. 125; Barberi, no. 215; NA, C143/369/3; *CPR 1367–1370* p. 210.

[45] *Expeditions* p. xliv.

[46] Paravicini, *Die Preussenreisen* vol. I pp. 125–7.

[47] *Foedera* vol. II pt. 3 p. 162 (for first crusade vow, 1337); ibid. vol. III p. 115 (1344 licence to go on crusade); *CPL* vol. III pp. 272, 327, 359 (1349), 383, 514, 353 (1351, vow deferred for 3 years); *CPP* vol. I pp. 52 (1344), 167, 207; *CPR 1343–1345* p. 261.

Name/rank	Date/campaign	Expenses	Size of affinity	Retinue/association
Burghesh, Bartholomew, the younger, knight (d. 1369)[*48]	1354 (Med.?) 1366 (Med.?)		40 persons	Walter Paveley 'chivaler'
Burley, John, knight, elder brother of Simon Burley[*49]	1363 Prussia			earl of Hereford
Burnell, John, 'donsel' of the earl of Warwick[50]	1365/6 Prussia			earl of Warwick
Byron, John, knight[51]	1368 Greece			John Mowbray
Caltoft, John, knight[+52]	1351 (Med.?)			
Camoys, John, knight[53]	1351 Prussia			duke of Lancaster
Camoys, Thomas, lord[*54]	1390 Tunis	£400	12 retainers	
Caus, Richard, lord[55]	1391 Prussia			earl of Stafford
Chalons, Robert[56]	1390/1 Prussia 1392 Prussia			earl of Derby
Chastellayn, Richard, knight[57]	1364 Rhodes			
Chelmsyck, Richard, knight[58]	1390/1 Prussia 1392 Prussia			earl of Derby earl of Derby
Chesney, William, 'the king's cousin'[59]	1308 Med.			

[48] *CPP* vol. I p. 551; *CPR 1353–1358* p. 55; *Urbain V: Lettres communes* no. 15995.
[49] *Anonimalle* p. 51; Fowler, 'Seals' p. 115; NA, DL25/1989; NA, DL25/1638; NA, DL25/1639; *Reg. Gilbert* p. 34.
[50] *CPP* vol. I p. 500; ASV, reg. supp. 40 fols 145ʳ–179ʳ; *Urbain V: Lettres communes* no. 8678.
[51] *CCR 1364–1368* pp. 53–4, 295; NA, C81/733/114–15.
[52] *Register of the Black Prince* vol. IV p. 130; *CPR 1354–1358* p. 258; *CIPM* vol. X no. 71.
[53] Paravicini, *Die Preussenreisen* vol. I p. 124.
[54] NA, C81/515/6291; NA, C76/74 m. 4.
[55] SRO, D641/1/2/4.
[56] *Expeditions* pp. 9, 30, 31, 106; Cherry, 'Courtenay Earls of Devon' p. 93.
[57] *Eulogium* vol. III pp. 237–8.
[58] Paravicini, *Die Preussenreisen* vol. I p. 125–7.
[59] *CChW 1244–1326* p. 292.

Name/rank	Date/campaign	Expenses	Size of affinity	Retinue/association
Clanvow, John, knight[60]	1390 Tunis			John Beaufort, William Neville
Clare, John de, knight of Llandaff[61]	1364 Med.		40 'persons'	William Trussel (Fulk Pembridge)
Clifford, Lewis, knight#*[62]	1390 Tunis			John Clinton, William Neville, et al.
Clifford, Thomas lord+[63]	1391 Prussia			Lords Despenser, Fitzwalter, Beaumont, Bourchier
Clifton, John, knight[64]	1390/1 Prussia			earl of Derby
Clinton, John, lord[65]	1390 Tunis			John Beaufort
Clinton, William, earl of Huntingdon (d. 1354)[66]	1344 (Symrna?)			
Cobham, Reginald, knight#[67]	1340/5? Prussia			William Fitzwarin
Cok, Thomas, knight[68]	1343 Algeciras			earl of Derby
Colvill, Thomas, knight[69]	1343 Algeciras			earl of Derby
Cope, John, knight[70]	1390/1 Prussia			earl of Derby
Cornwall, John, knight, Lord Fanhope[71]	1390 Tunis			John Beaufort

[60] *West. Chron.* pp. 433, 481; NA, C76/75 m. 2; NA, C76/74 mm. 8, 11; NA, C81/514/6150; NA, E403/531 m.7; Higden, *Polychronicon* vol. VIII p. 234.

[61] *CPL* vol. IV p. 13; *Urbain V: Lettres closes* no. 1393.

[62] Cabaret d'Orville, pp. 222, 238, 249.

[63] *West. Chron.* pp. 455, 475, 481; *CPR 1388–1392* pp. 363, 498; NA, C66/332 m. 41; NA, C76/75 m. 5; Düll et al. 'Faithful unto Death' p. 180; *Peerage* vol. III p. 292.

[64] *Expeditions* p. xliv; *Diplomatic Correspondence* p. 218.

[65] Cabaret d'Orville, p. 222.

[66] *CPP* vol. I p. 45; ASV, reg. supp. 6 fol. 319d.

[67] Paravicini, *Die Preussenreisen* vol. I p.123; *CPL* vol. II p. 557.

[68] *CPR 1343–1345* p. 18; *CPL* vol. II p. 526.

[69] Froissart, vol. IV p. 303.

[70] *Expeditions* p. xxxv; Paravicini, *Die Preussenreisen* vol. I p. 123

[71] Cabaret d'Orville, pp. 222, 238.

Name/rank	Date/campaign	Expenses	Size of affinity	Retinue/association
Courtenay, Edward, earl of Devon (d. 1419)[72]	1390 Tunis	1,000 marks	1 priest 1 knight 16 household	William Neville, John Clanvow
Courtenay, Edward, son of earl of Devon (d. 1372)[73]	1364/5 Prussia 1368 Prussia	£130	17 household	earl of Warwick Peter and Philip Courtenay
Courtenay, Peter, knight#*[74]	1368 Prussia	£130	17 household	Edward and Philip Courtenay
Courtenay, Philip, knight[75]	1368 Prussia	£130	17 household	Edward and Peter Courtenay
Courtenay, Thomas, knight[76]	1351 Prussia			duke of Lancaster
Cromwell, Ralph, knight[77]	1345 Smyrna		7 knights	
Cross, William, knight[78]	1351 Prussia			duke of Lancaster
Curteys, Reginald, knight[79]	1390/1 Prussia			earl of Derby
Cusance, William, knight[80]	1343 Algeciras			earl of Derby
Dachet, William[81]	1345 Smyrna			John St Philipot and Robert Bradestone
Dalleson, William, esquire[82]	1367 Prussia	30 marks	1 yeoman	
Dalyngridge, John, esquire[83]	1390/1 Prussia			earl of Derby

[72] *West. Chron.* p. 433; Higden, *Polychronicon* vol. VIII p. 234; *CPR 1388–1392* pp. 195, 199; NA, C66/329 mm. 5, 7.

[73] *Peerage* vol. IV p. 325; *CPP* vol. I p. 498; *CPR 1367–1370* p. 128; NA, C66/277 m. 31; ASV, reg. supp. 40 fols 145ʳ–179ʳ.

[74] *CPR 1367–1370* p.128; NA, C66/277 m. 31ᵈ.

[75] *CPR 1367–1370* p. 128; NA, C66/277 m. 31ᵈ.

[76] Paravicini, *Die Preussenreisen* vol. I p.123.

[77] *CPP* vol. I p. 213.

[78] Paravicini, *Die Preussenreisen* vol. I p. 123.

[79] Ibid. p. 125.

[80] *CPR 1343–1345* p. 16.

[81] *CPR 1345–1348* pp. 21, 330; *CCR 1343–1346* p. 646; Setton, *Papacy and the Levant* p. 193.

[82] *CPR 1367–1370* p. 57; NA, C66/276 m. 19ᵈ.

[83] *Expeditions* p. xxxv.

Name/rank	Date/campaign	Expenses	Size of affinity	Retinue/association
Dancaster, Richard, esquire[84]	1390/1 Prussia			earl of Derby
Dautre, John[85]	1367 Prussia	£40	5 household	Richard Mauleverer
Despenser, Hugh, lord[86]	1367 Prussia	£20	3 knights 4 esquires 1 falconer	lords Beaumont, Fitzwalter
Despenser, Hugh*[87]	1383 Prussia		8 household	
Despenser, Thomas[88]	1360/1 Prussia			
Despenser, Thomas, lord**[89]	1391 Prussia		50 horse	Lords Clifford, Fitzwalter, Beaumont, Bourchier
Devereux, Walter, lord[90]	1363 Prussia			earl of Hereford
Dodenhill, John[91]	1368 Greece			John Mowbray
Donat, Andreas, 'squyer'[92]	1391 Prussia			duke of Gloucester
Dronfield, William, knight[93]	1392 Prussia			earl of Derby
Durant, John, 'donsel' of earl of Warwick[94]	1365/6 Prussia			earl of Warwick
Dyve, John[95]	1309 Med.			
Ecton, John, esquire[96]	1390/1 Prussia			earl of Derby
Elkyngton, John, lord[97]	1390/1 Prussia			earl of Derby
Elmham, William, knight[98]	1390 Tunis			

[84] Ibid.
[85] *CPR 1367–1370* p. 30; *CIPM* vol. XII p. 159.
[86] *CPR 1367–1370* pp. 34, 55, 58; NA, C66/276 m. 19ᵈ.
[87] *CPR 1381–1385* p. 274; Paravicini, *Die Preussenreisen* vol. I p. 178, vol. II p. 125.
[88] Ibid. vol. I p. 124.
[89] *West. Chron.* p. 475; *CPR 1388–1392* p. 413; NA, C66/332 m. 13; *Indentures* pp. 119–20.
[90] *Anonimalle* p. 51; Fowler, 'Seals' p. 115; NA, DL25/1989; NA, DL25/1638; NA, DL25/1639.
[91] *CPR 1367–1370* p. 242; *CIPM* vol. XII no. 397; Düll et al. 'Faithful unto Death' p. 181.
[92] NA, C76/76 m. 13; Paravicini, *Die Preussenreisen* vol. I p. 126.
[93] Ibid. p. 127.
[94] *CPP* vol. I p. 500; *Urbain V: Lettres communes* no. 8692; ASV, reg. supp. 40 fols 145ʳ–179ʳ.
[95] *CPR 1307–1313* p. 121; NA, C66/131 m. 1.
[96] Paravicini, *Die Preussenreisen* vol. I p. 125.
[97] Ibid.
[98] NA C76/74 m. 7.

Name/rank	Date/campaign	Expenses	Size of affinity	Retinue/association
Elsfield, John[99]	1309 Rhodes			
Elys, John, esquire[100]	1390/1 Prussia			earl of Derby
Erpingham, Thomas, knight#*[101]	1390/1 Prussia 1392 Prussia			earl of Derby
Eton, Richard, esquire[102]	1392 Prussia 1394 Prussia			earl of Derby John Beaufort
Evrart, William, knight[103]	1363 Prussia			
Fauconberg, John, knight[104]	1343 Smyrna	£ 100		
Felbrigg, Roger, knight+[105]	1368 Prussia			
Felbrigg, Simon, knight[106]	1391 Prussia			
Ferrers of Groby, Henry, lord[107]	1362 Prussia			Richard Musard
Finari, William[108]	1366/7 Gallipoli			
Fishlake, Robert[109]	136? East Med.			Hugh Hastings
Fitzhenry, Thomas, esquire[110]	1362 Prussia 1367 Prussia			Geoffrey Scrope et al.
Fitzhugh, Henry (Hugh), knight[111]	1408 Prussia 1409 Rhodes			
Fitzwalter, Walter, lord[112]	1391 Prussia 140? East Med.			Lords Clifford, Despenser, Beaumont, Bourghier

[99] *Foedera* vol. I pt. 4 p. 143; *CPR 1307–1313* p. 165.
[100] Paravicini, *Die Preussenreisen* vol. I p. 125.
[101] *Expeditions* p. xliv; Keen, 'Chaucer's Knight' p. 57.
[102] Paravicini, *Die Preussenreisen* vol. I p. 127; Hirsch, *Danzigs Handels* pp. 234–5.
[103] Paravicini, *Die Preussenreisen* vol. I p. 124.
[104] *CPR 1343–1345* p. 6; NA, C66/209 m. 40; *CCR 1343–1346* p. 82; *CCR 1346–1349* p. 175.
[105] *CPR 1367–1370* p. 18; NA, C66/276 m. 16; Paravicini, *Die Preussenreisen* vol. II p. 117. See memorial brass in Housley, 'The Crusading Movement, 1274–1700' p. 274.
[106] NA, E30/1515.
[107] *Scrope and Grosvenor* vol. I p. 188, vol. II p. 443; Paravicini, *Die Preussenreisen* vol. I p. 124.
[108] Barberi, no. 559.
[109] Keen, 'Chaucer's Knight' p. 51; CA, MS Processus in Curia Marescalli vol. I pp. 432–3, 462.
[110] *Scrope and Grosvenor* vol. I p. 123, vol. II pp. 323–5; Paravicini, *Die Preussenreisen* vol. I p. 125; *CPR 1367–1370* p. 71–2.
[111] *Foedera* vol. IV part I p. 161; *CCR 1409–1413* pp. 2–3.
[112] *West. Chron.* p. 475; Usk, *Chronicle* p. 163; NA, C76/75 m. 4.

Name/rank	Date/campaign	Expenses	Size of affinity	Retinue/association
Fitzwalter, Walter, lord[113]	1367 Prussia	500 marks	12 knights	Lord Beaumont, Hugh Despenser
Fitzwarin, Fulk, knight[114]	1309–1313 (Rhodes?)			
Fitzwarin, Ivo, knight[115]	1367 Prussia	£100	1 knight 5 esquires 6 household	
Fitzwarin, William, knight[116]	1340/5? Prussia			Reginald Cobham
Fletelbike, David, knight[117]	1351 Prussia			duke of Lancaster
Fotheringhay, Richard, 'esquire of the king'[+118]	1390 Tunis			
Furnival, William, knight[119]	1367/8 Prussia	£200	5 knights	
Gantelion, William, knight[120]	1351 Prussia			duke of Lancaster
Garin, John[121]	1345 Smyrna			
Gerberghe, John, knight[122]	1351 Prussia			duke of Lancaster
Gloucester, Thomas, esquire[123]	1391 Prussia 1392 Prussia			earl of Derby earl of Derby
Goddard, John, knight[124]	1361 Prussia 1365 Alexandria 1367 Prussia			William Scrope earl of Hereford
Goldingham, Alexander, knight[125]	1361 Satalia			earl of Hereford

[113] Wigands von Marburg, vol. III p. 558; *CPR 1367–1370* pp. 129, 131; NA, C66/277 m. 30^d.

[114] *Brut* pp. 277–8.

[115] *CPR 1367–1370* p. 57; NA, C66/276 m. 19^d; Paravicini *Die Preussenreisen* vol. II p. 178.

[116] Ibid. vol. I p. 123.

[117] Ibid. p. 124.

[118] Cabaret d'Orville pp. 229–30; *Chronique du Religieux de Saint-Denys* vol. I pp. 668–9; NA, C66/332 m. 37; NA, C76/74 m. 12.

[119] *CPR 1367–1370* p. 72; NA, C66/276 m. 4^d.

[120] Paravicini, *Die Preussenreisen* vol. I p. 124.

[121] *CPL* vol. III p. 18; ASV, reg. supp. 40 fols 145^r–179^r.

[122] Paravicini, *Die Preussenreisen* vol. I p. 124.

[123] *Expeditions* p. xxxv; Paravicini, *Die Preussenreisen* vol. I p. 127.

[124] *Scrope and Grosvenor* vol. I pp. 171–2, vol. II p. 377; Paravicini, *Die Preussenreisen* vol. I p. 125.

[125] *Scrope and Grosvenor* vol. I p. 70, vol. II p. 272.

Name/rank	Date/campaign	Expenses	Size of affinity	Retinue/association
Goldsburgh, Richard, knight[126]	1391 Prussia			earl of Derby
Golofre, Nicholas, lord of Batsford, 'donsel' and steward of earl of Warwick's household[127]	1365 Prussia			earl of Warwick
Goter, Thomas, knight[128]	1390/1 Prussia 1392 Prussia			earl of Derby earl of Derby
Gourney, Matthew, knight[129]	1343 Algeciras 1365 Alexandria			earl of Hereford
Goys, Thomas, knight[130]	1367 Prussia			lords Beaumont, Fitzwalter et al.
Greenwich, Sampson, knight[131]	1391 Prussia			duke of Gloucester
Grey, John, of Codnor, 'Standard Bearer of the church'[132]	1365 Alexandria			Nicholas Sabraham et al.
Grey, John, of Rotherfield[133]	1366 East Med.			count of Savoy?
Greystoke, William, lord[134]	1351 Prussia			duke of Lancaster
Grosmont, Henry, duke of Lancaster (d. 1361)[135]	1343/4 Algeciras 1351/2 Prussia			earl of Salisbury 'with many of the greatest men of the realm'
Gritton, William[136]	1309 Rhodes			Giles Trumpeton

[126]   *Expeditions* p. xliv.
[127]   *CPP* vol. I pp. 498–500; ASV, reg. supp. 40 fols 145ʳ–179ʳ; *Urbain V: Lettres communes* no. 8680.
[128]   Paravicini, *Die Preussenreisen* vol. I pp.126–7.
[129]   Gough, vol. II p. 20; Luttrell, 'Chaucer's Knight' p. 136.
[130]   *CPR 1367–1370* p. 43.
[131]   NA, C76/76 m. 13; Paravicini, *Die Preussenreisen* vol. I p. 126.
[132]   *De Visione Sancti Simonis Stock* pp. 294–5, 306; *CPP* vol. I p. 45; *CPL* vol. III p. 67.
[133]   *CPP* vol. I p. 531.
[134]   Paravicini, *Die Preussenreisen* vol. I p.123; *CPR 1350–1354* p. 172.
[135]   Knighton, pp. 47, 111; Baker, *Chronicon* p. 119; *SRP* vol. III pp. 452, 741–4 (1351); John Capgrave, *Liber de Illustribus Henricis* ed. F. C. Hingeston, r.s. 7 (London, 1858) p. 188; *CPL* vol. III p. 459; *CPP* vol. I pp. 214, 225; *CPR 1350–1354* p. 191; NA, C66/235 m. 6; NA, C81/ 291/15587; *Historical Letters* pp. 402–3; *Foedera* vol. III pt 1 p. 80.
[136]   *CPR 1307–1313* p. 122; NA, C66/131 m. 1.

Name/rank	Date/campaign	Expenses	Size of affinity	Retinue/association
Gybbethorpe, John, knight[137]	1390/1 Prussia			earl of Derby
Gyse, William, knight[138]	1392 Prussia			earl of Derby
Haket, Walter, knight[139]	1309 Granada			Robert de Tony
Hales, Robert, provincial prior, Order of St John[140]	1365 Alexandria			earl of Hereford
Hampton of Mortimer, John[141]	1319 Vega, Spain			
Harleston, John, knight*[142]	1392/3 Prussia			
Harpendon, John, knight[143]	1390 Tunis			John Russell
Haseldon, Thomas, knight[144]	1390/1 Prussia 1392 Prussia			earl of Derby earl of Derby
Hastings, Edmund, knight[145]	1390/1 Prussia			earl of Derby
Hastings, Hugh, knight[146]	136? Rhodes			
Hastings, William, lord[147]	1349 Prussia			
Hemendale, Ralph, knight[148]	1351 Prussia			duke of Lancaster
Heveningham, John, knight[149]	1390 Tunis			
Hessy, Hugh, knight[150]	1351 Prussia			duke of Lancaster

[137] Paravicini, *Die Preussenreisen* vol. I p. 125.
[138] Ibid. p. 127.
[139] *CPR 1307–1313* p. 117.
[140] Luttrell, 'English Levantine Crusaders' p. 144.
[141] Romano, 'Un Inglés en la Guerra contro el Moro' pp. 457–9.
[142] *West. Chron.* p. 515.
[143] Froissart, vol. XIV p. 225.
[144] Paravicini, *Die Preussenreisen* vol. I pp. 125–7.
[145] Ibid. p. 125.
[146] Keen, 'Chaucer's Knight' p. 51; CA, MS Processus in Curia Marescalli vol. I pp. 432–3, 462.
[147] *CIPM* vol. VI pp. 229, 479; Paravicini, *Die Preussenreisen* vol. I p. 123; *CPL* vol. III p. 288.
[148] Paravicini, *Die Preussenreisen* vol. I p. 123; *CPR 1350–1354* p. 188.
[149] NA, C81/515/268; NA, C76/73 m.4.
[150] Paravicini, *Die Preussenreisen* vol. I p. 123.

Name/rank	Date/campaign	Expenses	Size of affinity	Retinue/association
Hinkely, John, knight[151]	1390/1 Prussia			duke of Gloucester
Hinton, Hugh, knight[152]	c.1349 Spain			
Hinton, William, knight[153]	c.1349 Spain			
Hode of Fleet, John[154]	1368 Greece			John Mowbray
Hogge, Richard, knight[155]	1391 Prussia			
Hoghton, Henry, knight[156]	1390/1 Prussia 1394 Prussia			earl of Derby
Holand, John, earl of Huntingdon, duke of Exeter (d. 1400)**[157]	1394 Hungary 1397 Italy			
Holand, Thomas, earl of Kent (d. 1360)#[158]	1341 Prussia 1343 Algeciras			
Howard, Robert, knight[159]	1362 Prussia			Thomas Ufford
Jeke, Ive, knight[160]	1390/1 Prussia			
Kerdeston, William, knight[161]	1350/1 Prussia	£600		earl of Derby
Kilsby, William[162]	1344 East Med.			
Kingsmeade, Walter, knight[163]	1309 Granada			Robert Tony

[151]   SRO, D641/2/4 mm. 4, 6.
[152]   'Continuatio Historiae Eliensis' p. 563.
[153]   Ibid.
[154]   *CCR 1364–1368* pp. 53–4, 295; NA, C81/733/114–15.
[155]   NA, C81/1059/41.
[156]   Hirsch, *Danzigs Handels* pp. 234–5.
[157]   *West. Chron.* p. 161; *Diplomatic Correspondence* pp. 144–5, 244; *CPL* vol. IV pp. 294–5, 300, 489; 'Annales Ricardi Secundi et Henrici Quarti' *Chronica et Annales* pp. 230–1; *Foedera* vol. III pt. 4 p. 93.
[158]   Froissart, vol. IV p. 303; Parvicini, *Die Preussenreisen* vol. I p. 123.
[159]   *CPR 1361–1364* p 251; NA, C66/266 m. 25.
[160]   Paravicini, *Die Preussenreisen* vol. I p. 126.
[161]   Ibid. vol. I p. 123, vol. II p 214; *CPL* vol. II pp. 142, 144.
[162]   *CCR 1343–1346* pp. 106–7; *Foedera* vol. II pt. 4 pp. 141–2.
[163]   *CChW 1244–1326* p. 287.

Name/rank	Date/campaign	Expenses	Size of affinity	Retinue/association
Lalford, Robert, knight[164]	1362–1365 East Med.			William de Pole the younger (of Ashby)
Lancerel, Andrew, knight[165]	c.1364/5 East Med.			
Langford, Roger, knight[166]	1390/1 Prussia			earl of Derby
Latimer, William, lord of Corby[#167]	1351 Prussia			duke of Lancaster
Laton, Simon, rector[168]	1309 Rhodes			
Limbury, Philip, knight[169]	1367 Gallipoli			count of Savoy
Littlebirs, Robert, knight[170]	1343 East Med.			
London, William, esquire[171]	1366/7 Gallipoli			Ralph Basset of Drayton
Loring, Nigel, knight, chamberlain to Prince of Wales[#172]	1351 Prussia 1365 Prussia		20 men-at-arms	duke of Lancaster earl of Warwick
Loudham, John knight[+173]	1390/1 Prussia			earl of Derby
'Louza', Robert de, knight[174]	1361 Cilicia			
Lovell, John, lord[175]	1371 East Med. 1385 Prussia			John Breaux, Robert Morley
Loveyn, John, knight[176]	1390/1 Prussia			earl of Derby

[164] *CPR 1361–1364* p. 249; NA, C66/266 m 26; *Urbain V: Lettres communes* no. 8631.

[165] Ibid. no. 8885.

[166] *Expeditions* p. xxxv.

[167] Paravicini, *Die Preussenreisen* vol. I p. 123; *CPR 1350–1354* p. 170.

[168] *Reg. Halton* p. 322.

[169] *CIPM* vol. XII pp.128–9; *CPR 1364–1367* p. 180.

[170] *CPP* vol. I p. 14.

[171] Barberi, no. 726.

[172] *CPR 1350–1354* p. 179; Paravicini, *Die Preussenreisen* vol. I p. 123; *Urbain V: Lettres communes* nos 8880, 8881, 11544, 11546; *CPP* vol. I pp. 495, 496.

[173] *West. Chron.* p. 447; Higden, *Polychronicon* vol. VIII p. 244; Wigands von Marburg, p. 643; *Expeditions* p. xliv; *CIPM* vol. XVI p. 411.

[174] Luttrell, 'Chaucer's Knight' p. 140.

[175] Paravicini, *Die Preussenreisen* vol. I. p. 125; NA, C47/6/1 no. 102 m. 36.

[176] *Expeditions* p. xxxv.

Name/rank	Date/campaign	Expenses	Size of affinity	Retinue/association
Lucy, Antony, knight[+][177]	1368 Prussia	£500	15 horsemen	Mauleverer, Boynton and Southeworthe?
Lucy, William, knight[178]	1362/3 Prussia 1365 Alexandria			earl of Hereford earl of Hereford
Ludergarshale, Richard, the younger[179]	1311 (Rhodes?)			
Ludham, John, priest[180]	1361 (Satalia?)			Miles Stapleton
Malbis, Walter, knight[181]	1366 Med.			
Malet, John, knight[182]	1390/1 Prussia			earl of Derby
Martel, William[183]	1384/5 Prussia			Thomas Peytevyn
Mauleverer, Richard, knight[184]	1367 Prussia	£40	5 yeoman 6 household	John Dautre et al.?
Mauvesin, Robert, knight[185]	1391 Prussia			duke of Gloucester
Melbourne, Peter, knight[186]	1392 Prussia			earl of Derby
Montagu, John, earl of Salisbury (d. 1400)[187]	1391/2 Prussia	£800	31 household	
Montagu, Simon, knight[188]	1310 Rhodes			
Montagu, William, earl of Salisbury (d. 1344)[189]	1343/4 Algeciras			earl of Lancaster

[177]   *CPR 1367–1370* pp. 34, 57; *CCR 1364–1368* p. 396; *CIPM* vol. XIV no. 169.
[178]   *Scrope and Grosvenor* vol. I pp. 77–8, vol. II p. 261; NA, DL34/1/27.
[179]   *CPR 1307–1313* p. 358; NA, C66/135 m. 4.
[180]   *CPR 1361–1364* p. 36.
[181]   Gough, vol. I pt. 2 p. 122.
[182]   *Expeditions* p. xlvi.
[183]   Paravicini, *Die Preussenreisen* vol. I p. 125.
[184]   *CPR 1367–1370* pp. 30, 64; NA, C66/276 m. 10[d]; Paravicini, *Die Preussenreisen* vol. II p. 178.
[185]   SRO, D644/1/2/4 m. 4.
[186]   Paravicini, *Die Preussenreisen* vol. I p. 127.
[187]   NA, C76/76 m. 12; NA, C81/528/7578; NA, E30/1515; *Peerage* vol. XI p. 394; NA, C76/76 m. 12; Paravicini, *Die Preussenreisen* vol. I pp. 127, 180, vol. II p. 216.
[188]   *Reg. Droxford* vol. I p. 65; *Peerage* vol. IX pp. 78–9.
[189]   Giovanni Villani, *Cronica* vol. IV pp. 57–8; *Cronica Alfonso* vol. I pp. 360–70; *Peerage* vol. IX p. 388; *CPL* vol. III p. 109.

Name/rank	Date/campaign	Expenses	Size of affinity	Retinue/association
Montagu, William, earl of Salisbury (d. 1397)[190]	1351 Prussia			earl of Lancaster
Morley, Robert, knight[191]	1385 Prussia			John Breaux, Lord Lovell
Morley, Thomas, lord, Marshal of Ireland[192]	1391 Prussia			duke of Gloucester
Mowbray, Alexander[193]	1368 Greece			John Mowbray
Mowbray, John, lord[+194]	1368 Greece	500 marks and £100	20 horsemen	
Multon, John, knight[+195]	1367 Prussia	£40	4 yeoman	Richard Welby
Musard, Richard, knight of the Order of the Collar[196]	1366 Gallipoli			Ralph Basset, lord of Drayton
Neville, John, knight[#197]	1351 Prussia			duke of Lancaster
Neville, William, lord[198]	1390 Tunis			lord Clanvow
Noble, John, priest[199]	1346/7 East Med.			John de la Ryvere, John Wayfor
Norbury, John, knight[200]	1390/1 Prussia			earl of Derby
Pagan, Robert 'nobilis'[201]	1309 Rhodes			

[190] *CPR 1350–1354* p. 187; Paravicini, *Die Preussenreisen* vol. I p. 123.

[191] NA, C47/6/7/1 no. 152 m. 26; Keen, 'Chaucer's Knight' p. 50.

[192] NA, C76/76 m. 13; NA, C81/1059/4; *Foedera* vol. III pt 4 p. 71.

[193] *CIPM* vol. XXII no. 420 p. 405; *CPR 1367–1370* pp. 8, 421.

[194] NA, E326/9376; Düll et al. 'Faithful unto Death' p. 181; *CIPM* vol. XII no. 397; NA, C66/276 m. 14; *CPR 1367–1379* pp. 22, 53, 54, 158, 242; *Peerage* vol. IX p. 384.

[195] *CPR 1367–1370* pp. 57, 58; NA, C66/276 m. 19[d]; Paravicini, *Die Preussenreisen* vol. I p. 117; *CCR 1364–1368* p. 396.

[196] Barberi, nos 316, 479, 559, 676, 929, 1161.

[197] Paravicini, *Die Preussenreisen* vol. I p. 123.

[198] *West. Chron.* pp. 433, 481; Higden, *Polychronicon* vol. VIII p. 234; NA, C76/75 m. 3; NA, C76/74 mm. 10–11; NA, C81/514/6150; NA, E403/531 m.7; Cabaret d'Orville, p. 222; *Issues of the Exchequer* p. 250.

[199] *CPP* vol. I p. 119; *CPL* vol. III p. 28; *Urbain V: Lettres closes* nos 1155, 1156; *Reg. Bransford* p. 186.

[200] *Expeditions* p. xliv; NA, C76/74 m. 4.

[201] *Reg. Clem.* no. 3054; *Vitae paparum* vol. III pp. 87–90.

Name/rank	Date/campaign	Expenses	Size of affinity	Retinue/association
Paris of Castle Homby, William[202]	1309 Rhodes			
Paveley, John, the younger, knight of Wiltshire[+203]	1390 Tunis 1391/2 Prussia			
Paveley, Walter, knight of Kent[#204]	1351 Prussia			duke of Lancaster
Payne, John, knight[205]	1390/1 Prussia 1392 Prussia			earl of Derby earl of Derby
Pembridge, Fulk[206]	1364 East Med.			William Trussel
Pembridge, Richard, knight[#207]	1368 Prussia			
Percy, Henry, lord[#208]	1351 Prussia			duke of Lancaster
Percy, Henry 'Hotspur'[**209]	1383 Prussia 1383 Asia Minor 1390/1 Prussia			Beaumont et al.
Percy, Ralph, knight[*210]	1396 Nicopolis			
Percy, Thomas, lord[211]	1383 Prussia			Henry Percy?
Percy, Thomas, earl of Worcester (d. 1403)[#212]	1391/2 Prussia			earl of Derby
Peytevyn, Thomas, knight[213]	1384/5 Prussia			Thomas Martel
Pole, Michael de la, earl of Suffolk (d. 1415)[214]	1391 Prussia			duke of Gloucester, earl of Stafford

[202]   *CPR 1307–1313* p. 114; NA, C66/131 m. 6.

[203]   NA, C76/76 m. 10; NA, C76/75 m. 3; NA, C76/74 m. 8; *West. Chron.* p. 511; NA, E403/533; NA, E403/531 m.7; NA, E404/14/96; *Issues of the Exchequer* p. 250.

[204]   Paravicini, *Die Preussenreisen* vol. I p. 123; *CPR 1350–1354* pp. 55, 187.

[205]   Paravicini, *Die Preussenreisen* vol. I pp. 126–7.

[206]   *CPP* vol. I p. 490; *CPR 1361–1364* pp. 331, 472; *CIPM* vol. XI no. 533.

[207]   Ibid. p. 125.

[208]   Paravicini, *Die Preussenreisen* vol. I p. 124.

[209]   Ibid. pp. 124–5; *CPR 1388–1392* pp. 367, 368; NA, C66/332 m. 39; NA, E403/536 m. 22; NA, C76/75 m. 12; *West. Chron.* p. 455.

[210]   Iorga, *Philippe de Mézières* p. 491.

[211]   Froissart, vol. X p. 243.

[212]   Wigands von Marburg, pp. 645–6; *Expeditions* p. 100.

[213]   Paravicini, *Die Preussenreisen* vol. I p. 125.

[214]   *Foedera* vol. III pt 4 p.71; *Peerage* vol. XII p. 441.

Name/rank	Date/campaign	Expenses	Size of affinity	Retinue/association
Pole, William de la, lord of Castle Ashby[+215]	1365 Alexandria			Robert Lalford
Pympe, Reginald, knight[216]	1391 Prussia			duke of Gloucester
Pynnok of Sarum, John[217]	1309 Rhodes			
Rempston, Thomas, knight[#218]	1390/1 Prussia			earl of Derby
Rigmaiden, Richard, knight[219]	1390/1 Prussia			earl of Derby
Rigmaiden, William, knight[220]	1390/1 Prussia 1392 Prussia			earl of Derby earl of Derby
Roches, John[221]	1309 Rhodes			
Rochford, Ralph, esquire[222]	1390/1 Prussia 1392 Prussia			earl of Derby earl of Derby
Ros, Robert, le, knight[223]	1367 Greece			
Ros, William le, lord[+224]	1351 Prussia			duke of Lancaster
Russell, John, knight[225]	1390 Tunis			
Rye, John, esquire[226]	1362 Prussia			Geoffrey Scrope et al.
Rye, Nigel, knight[227]	1351 Prussia			duke of Lancaster

[215]   *CPR 1361–1364* pp. 249, 250; *CCR 1364–1368* p. 172; *Correspondance de Pierre Ameilh*, pp. 366–9; NA, C66/266 mm. 25–6; *CPL* vol. IV p. 15; *CIPM* vol. XII no. 76; *Urbain V: Lettres closes* nos 890, 892; *Urbain V: Lettres communes* nos 10869, 10870 10871, 10872.

[216]   NA, C76/76 m. 13; Paravicini, *Die Preussenreisen* vol. I p.126.

[217]   *CPR 1307–1313* pp.117, 194; NA, C66/131 m. 5.

[218]   *Expeditions* p. xliv.

[219]   Paravicini, *Die Preussenreisen* vol. I p.126.

[220]   Ibid. pp. 126–7.

[221]   *CPR 1307–1313* pp. 115, 121; NA, C66/131 m. 5; *CCR 1308–1313* p. 366; NA, C54/129 m. 31; *CIPM* vol. V no. 298.

[222]   *Expeditions* p. xxxv; Paravicini, *Die Preussenreisen* vol. I p.127.

[223]   *Urbain V: Lettres communes* no. 22967; Machaut, *Capture of Alexandria* pp. 138, 178, 193, 204; NA, C61/79 mm. 7, 13.

[224]   Knighton, p.111; *CIPM* vol. X p. 32; Paravicini, *Die Preussenreisen* vol. I p. 123.

[225]   NA, C76/74 m. 7; NA, C81/515/269; Cabaret d'Orville, pp. 229–30; Froissart, vol. XIV p. 254.

[226]   *Scrope and Grosvenor*, vol. I p. 144, vol. II p. 352.

[227]   Paravicini, *Die Preussenreisen* vol. I p. 124.

Name/rank	Date/campaign	Expenses	Size of affinity	Retinue/association
Ryther, John, esquire[228]	1362/1367 Prussia			Geoffrey Scrope et al.
Ryvere (Rivere), John de la, knight[229]	1346 Egypt/Syria		1 priest 1 esquire	John Noble, John Wayfor
Sabraham, Nicholas[230]	1365 Alexandria 1366 Gallipoli pre-1386 Prussia			Stephen Scrope et al. count of Savoy
Saleby, Geoffrey[231]	1308 (Rhodes?)			
Salisbury, Paul, knight[232]	1391 Prussia			
Scales, Roger lord[233]	1367 Prussia			lords Beaumont, Fitzwalter et al.
Scrope, Geoffrey, of Masham, knight[+234]	1362 Prussia			Thomas Fitzhenry
Scrope, Henry, 3rd Lord Masham[#235]	1390 Tunis			
Scrope, Stephen, of Bolton, knight[236]	1394 Prussia			John Beaufort
Scrope, Stephen, of Masham[237]	1365 Alexandria			Sabraham et al.
Scrope, William, of Bolton, earl of Wiltshire, chamberlain of Ireland (d. 1399)[#238]	1362 Prussia			
Scrope, William, of Masham[+239]	1366 Gallipoli			count of Savoy

[228]   *Scrope and Grosvenor*, vol. I p. 144, vol. II p. 352.
[229]   *CPL* vol. III pp. 28, 33, 209; *CPP* vol. I p. 118–19; *Urbain V: Lettres closes* nos 1605, 1155, 1156; *CPR 1345–1348* p. 128; NA, C66/217 m. 27; *CCR 1346–1349* p. 488; *Urbain V: Lettres communes* nos 11870, 11871.
[230]   *Scrope and Grosvenor* vol. I p. 125, vol. II p. 323.
[231]   *CPR 1307–1313* p. 96; NA, C66/131 m. 17.
[232]   NA, C76/75 m. 4; *CPR 1391–1396* p. 323.
[233]   *CPR 1367–1370* p. 27.
[234]   *Scrope and Grosvenor* vol. I pp. 117, 188, vol. II pp. 310, 443; Paravicini, *Die Preussenreisen* vol. I p. 125.
[235]   NA, E403/533 m. 14; *Issues of the Exchequer* p. 245; NA, C81/515/6267.
[236]   Wigands von Marburg, p. 653; Hirsch, *Danzigs Handels* pp. 234–5.
[237]   *Scrope and Grosvenor* vol. I pp. 124–5, vol. II pp. 323–5.
[238]   Ibid. vol. I pp. 171–2, vol. II pp. 389–90.
[239]   Ibid. vol. I pp. 124–5, vol. II pp. 323–5.

Name/rank	Date/campaign	Expenses	Size of affinity	Retinue/association
Seint-George, Baldwin, knight[240]	1390 Tunis			John Beaufort et al.
Sekford, John, knight[241]	1367 Prussia			lords Beaumont, Fitzwalter et al.
Sewardby, William, esquire[242]	1390/1 Prussia			earl of Derby
Southeworth, Thomas, esquire[243]	1367 Prussia	£20	2 yeoman 3 household	Thomas Boynton
Spegul, Henry, knight[244]	1366/7 Gallipoli			count of Savoy
St Philipot, John, knight[245]	1345 Smyrna			Robert Bradestone, William Dachet
Stafford, Thomas, earl of Stafford[246]	1391 Prussia			duke of Gloucester
Standish, John, knight[247]	1390 Prussia		3 household	
Stapleton, Miles of Bedale#[248]	1351 Prussia 1357/8 Prussia 1361 Satalia 1363 Prussia			duke of Lancaster earl of Hereford earl of Hereford
Stapleton, Miles the younger, of Haddlesey[249]	1365 Alexandria 1367 Med.			Lords Grey, Scrope et al.
Staveley, Ralph, esquire[250]	1390/1 Prussia 1392 Prussia			earl of Derby earl of Derby
Stewart, Alexander, knight[251]	1390 Tunis			

[240] NA, C76/74 m. 4; Cabaret d'Orville, pp. 222, 238, 257.
[241] *CPR 1367–1370* pp. 25, 54.
[242] *Expeditions* p. xxxv.
[243] *CPR 1367–1370* pp. 30, 65; Paravicini, *Die Preussenreisen* vol. II p. 178.
[244] Barberi, no. 623.
[245] *Clément VI: Lettres rapportant à la France* no. 1617; *CPR 1344–1348* pp. 21, 330; *CPL* vol. III p. 160; *CCR 1343–1346* p. 646.
[246] SRO, D641/1/2/4; *West. Chron.* p. 481; NA, C76/76 m. 12.
[247] NA, C81/515/6212.
[248] *Anonimalle* p. 51; Fowler, 'Seals' p. 115; NA, DL25/1989; NA, DL25/1638; NA, DL25/1639; *CPR 1361–1364* p. 24; *CPR 1350–1354* p. 170.
[249] Luttrell, 'English Levantine Crusaders' p. 149; *De Visione Sancti Simonis Stock* pp. 294–5, 306.
[250] *Expeditions* p. xxxv.
[251] BL, MS Add. 15644 fol. 3ᵛ.

Name/rank	Date/campaign	Expenses	Size of affinity	Retinue/association
Sturmy (Stromin), Henry, knight[252]	1364 East Med.			
Sutton, Ralph knight[253]	1367 Prussia			lords Beaumont, Fitzwalter et al.
Swinford, Thomas[254]	1390/1 Prussia			earl of Derby
Tautheby, John knight[255]	1367 Prussia			lords Beaumont, Fitzwalter et al.
Toli, William, of Dunmowe, priest[256]	1345 Smyrna			
Tony, Robert, knight[257]	1309 Granada			Walter Kingsmeade
Torrington, John, 'donsel' of the earl of Warwick[258]	1365/6 Prussia			earl of Warwick
Totesham, Robert, knight[259]	1351 Prussia			duke of Lancaster
Toty, Thomas, esquire[260]	1392 Prussia			earl of Derby
Trewin, Thomas, esquire[261]	1390 Tunis		1 servant 2 horse	John Beaufort
Trumpeton, Giles, knight[262]	1309 Rhodes			William Grytton
Trumpeton, Roger, knight[263]	1368 Greece			John Mowbray
Trussel, William, knight[264]	1364 Med.		40 persons	John de Clare
Tuchet, Robert, knight[265]	1365 Prussia			earl of Warwick

[252] *Calendar of State Papers: Venice* vol. VI pt. 3 pp. 1578–80.

[253] *CPR 1367–1370* p. 57.

[254] *Expeditions* p. 301.

[255] *CPR 1367–1370* p. 41.

[256] *CPL* vol. III p. 186.

[257] *CChW 1244–1326* p. 287.

[258] ASV, reg. supp. 40 fols 145ʳ–179ʳ; *CPP* vol. I p. 500; *Urbain V: Lettres communes* nos 8869, 8670.

[259] Paravicini, *Die Preussenreisen* vol. I p. 124.

[260] *Expeditions* p. xxxv.

[261] NA, C81/515/6266.

[262] *CPR 1307–1313* p. 122; NA, C66/131 m. 1.

[263] *CPR 13677–1370* p. 54.

[264] *CPL* vol. IV p. 13; *Urbain V: Lettres closes* no.1393; *CPR 1364–1367* p. 331; *CIPM* vol. XI no. 533; cf. NA, C61/76 m. 3.

[265] ASV, reg. supp. 40 fols 145ʳ–179ʳ; *CPP* vol. I p. 500; *Peerage* vol. XIII p. 56; *Urbain V: Lettres*

Name/rank	Date/campaign	Expenses	Size of affinity	Retinue/association
Turberville, Payn, knight[166]	1309 Rhodes	£300		
Turk, Robert, knight[167]	1391 Prussia			earl of Gloucester
Ufford, Robert, 1st earl of Suffolk (d. 1369)[#268]	1351 Prussia			Miles Stapleton, John Argent, duke of Lancaster
Ufford, Thomas[269]	1331 Prussia		100 'lances'	
Ufford, Thomas, knight[#270]	1348 Prussia 1351 Prussia 1362 Prussia 1365 Prussia			duke of Lancaster Robert Howard earl of Warwick
Ufford, William, 2nd earl of Suffolk[#271]	1367 Prussia			Thomas Beauchamp, Roger and William Beauchamp
Urswyck, Robert, esquire of earl of Cambridge[272]	1367 Prussia	100 marks	6 yeoman 7 horsemen	
Villiers, Francis, knight[273]	1309 Rhodes			
Waldegrave, Richard, knight[274]	1361 Satalia 1363 Prussia 1365 Med.			earl of Hereford et al. earl of Hereford et al.
Wale, Thomas, knight[275]	1343 Algeciras			earl of Derby
Warre, Roger de, lord[276]	1351 Prussia			duke of Lancaster

communes no. 8687.

[166] *CPR 1307–1313* p. 102; NA, C66/131 m. 14; *CCR 1307–1313* p. 122; NA, C54/125 m. 22ᵈ.

[167] *Foedera* vol. III pt.4 p. 71; NA, C76/74 m. 18.

[168] Paravicini, *Die Preussenreisen* vol. I p. 123; *CPR 1350–1354* pp. 179, 182, 185.

[169] Wigands von Marburg, p. 479; Paravicini, *Die Preussenreisen* vol. I p. 123.

[270] *Peerage* vol. XII p. 151; Capgrave, *Liber de Illustribus Henricis* p. 188 (1352); Wigands von Marburg, pp. 514, 549; *CPL* vol. IV p. 15; *CPP* vol. I p. 490; *CPR 1361–1364* pp. 251, 472; NA, C66/266 m. 25; Paravicini, *Die Preussenreisen* vol. I p. 124; *Urbain V: Lettres communes* nos 8861, 8862, 11463, 11464, 11488; *Urbain V: Lettres closes* nos 890, 891, 898.

[271] *CPR 1367–1370* pp. 10, 21, 54.

[272] *CPR 1367–1370* p. 127; NA, C66/277 m. 31ᵈ.

[273] *CPL* vol. II p. 55; *CPR 1307–1313* p. 107; NA, C66/131 m. 11; *Rot. Parl.* vol. II p. 381; *Reg. Clem.* no. 4118.

[274] *Scrope and Grosvenor* vol. I pp. 165–6, vol. II pp. 171–2; Fowler, 'Seals' p. 115; NA, DL25/1989; NA, DL25/1638; NA, DL25/1639.

[275] NA, C81/291/15587; *CPR 1343–1346* p. 159.

[276] Paravicini, *Die Preussenreisen* vol. I p. 124.

Name/rank	Date/campaign	Expenses	Size of affinity	Retinue/association
Waterton, Hugh, knight[277]	1390/1 Prussia 1392 Prussia			earl of Derby
Waterton, John, esquire[278]	1390/1 Prussia 1392 Prussia			earl of Derby earl of Derby
Waterton, Robert, knight[279]	1392 Prussia			earl of Derby
Wayfor, John, esquire[280]	1346 East Med.			John de la Ryvere John Noble, priest
Welby, Richard[281]	1367 Prussia	£40	4 yeoman	John Multon
Welles, John, lord[282]	1390 Tunis			
Willoughby, William, lord[#283]	1390/1 Prussia 1392 Prussia			earl of Derby earl of Derby
Woodhouse, Robert[284]	1364 East Med.			company of 'anglici'
Woodstock, Thomas, duke of Gloucester (d. 1397)[##285]	1391 Prussia		multi moerentibus	earls of Stafford and Suffolk, Thomas Morley, Richard Breton, Robert Turk
Wylemer, John, 'donsel' of earl of Warwick[286]	1365/6 Prussia			earl of Warwick
Ypre, Thomas, knight[287]	1391 Prussia			duke of Gloucester
Zouche, William, of Haringworth, knight[288]	1362 Med.			

[277] *Expeditions* p. xliv; NA, C76/77 m. 14.

[278] *Expeditions* p. xxxv.

[279] NA, C76/77 m. 14.

[280] *CPL* vol. IV pp. 28, 33.

[281] *CPR 1367–1370* pp. 34, 57.

[282] BL, MS Royal 20 D IX fol. 190ᵛ.

[283] *Expeditions* pp. xliv, 158.

[284] *Urbain V: Lettres closes* no. 886; *CPL* vol. IV p. 8.

[285] *West. Chron.* pp. 479, 481, 483–5; Walsingham, *Historia Anglicana* p. 202; Higden, *Polychronicon* vol. VIII pp. 76–8; *CPR 1388–1392* pp. 477, 482; NA, C66/333 m. 23; *Wykeham's Register* vol. II. p. 430; *CPL* vol. IV p. 396; NA, C76/76 mm. 13,15; NA, E403/536 m. 22; *Foedera* vol. III pt. 4 p. 71.

[286] ASV, reg. supp. 40 fols 145ʳ–179ʳ; *CPP* vol. I p. 500; *Urbain V: Lettres communes* no. 8969.

[287] NA, C81/1059/14.

[288] *CPR 1361–1364* p. 249; NA, C66/266 m. 26.

Select Bibliography

Manuscript Sources

Cambridge
Cambridge University Library
MS Dd I. 17
MS Peterhouse 200

London
British Library
MS Add. 15644
MS Add. 28024
MS Add. 31042
MS Add. 40859
MS Add. Ch. 7487
MS Cotton Faustina B V
MS Cotton Nero D V II
MS Cotton Otho D V
MS Cotton Vespasian E VIII
MS Harley 3775
MS Harley 3988
MS Harley 4304
MS Harley 4690
MS Harley 4919
MS Royal 7 E IV
MS Royal 20 D IX

College of Arms
MS Processus in Curia Marescalli

The National Archives
C 46   E 30

C47
C54
C61
C66
C70
C76
C81
DL25
DL28
DL34

E36
E101
E135
E159
E326
E403
E404
SC1
SC7

Oxford

Bodleian Library
MS Ashmole 813
MS Ashmole 865
MS Barlow 1
MS Dugdale 15
MS Laud Misc. 302
MS Laud Misc. 622
MS New College 223
MS Oriel College 10

Stafford

Staffordshire Record Office
D641/1/2/4
D641/1/2/40 A
D644/1/2/4

Worcester

Worcester Cathedral
MS Cath. F. 36
MS Cath. F. 77
MS Cath. Q. 57

Worcestershire Record Office
b716.093-B.A.2648/4 (i)
b716.093-B.A.2648/4 (ii)

Rome

Vatican Secret Archive (Archivio Segreto Vaticano)
Registra Avinionensia
Registra Lateran
Registra Supplicationem
Registra Vaticana

Printed Primary Sources

Accounts Rendered by Papal Collectors in England 1317–1378 ed. W. E. Lunt (Philadelphia, 1968)

Acta Aragonensia ed. H. Finke (Berlin-Leipzig, 1908–1922)

Acta Urbani VI, Bonifacii IX, Innocentii ed. A. L. Tăutu (Rome, 1970)

Adam Davy's Dreams about Edward the Second ed. F. J. Furnivall, EETS o.s. 69 (London, 1878)

The Anonimalle Chronicle 1333 to 1381 ed. V. H. Galbraith (Manchester, 1970)

Avesbury, Robert of, *De Gestis Mirabilibus regis Edwardi Tertii* ed. E. M. Thompson, r.s. 93 (London, 1889)

Baker, Geoffrey le, *Chronicon Galfridi le Baker de Swynebroke* ed. E. M. Thompson (Oxford, 1889)

Barberi, A. *Illustrazioni della spedizione in oriente di Amedeo VI* ed. F. E. Bollati di Saint-Pierre (Turin, 1900)

Bernadus de cura rei familiaris ed. J. R. Lumby, EETS o.s. 42 (London, 1870)

Biblioteca bio-bibliografica della Terra Sancta e dell' Oriente francescano ed. G. Golubovich (Quaracchi, 1906–1954)

The Boke of Noblesse ed. J. G. Nichols (London, 1860)

Bonet, Honoré, *The Tree of Battles* ed. G. W. Coopland (Liverpool, 1949)

Bourbon, Stephen of, *Anecdotes historiques, légendes et apologues* ed. R. A. Lecoy de la Marche (Paris, 1877)

Bracton, Henry de, De legibus et consuetudinibus Angliae ed. T. Twiss, r.s. 70 (London, 1878–1883)

Bromyard, John of, *Opus Trivium* (Cologne, 1474)

——, *Summa Praedicantium* (Vienna, 1484)

The Bruce of John Barbour ed. W. W. Skeat, EETS e.s. 21, 29, 55 (London, 1870–1889)

The Brut ed. F. W. D. Brie, EETS o.s. 131, 136 (London, 1906–1908)

Calendar of Chancery Warrants

Calendar of Entries on the Close Rolls

Calendar of Inquisitions Post Mortem

Calendar of Papal Letters

Calendar of Papal Petitions

Calendar of Entries on the Patent Rolls

Calendar of Select Pleas and Memoranda of the City of London, 1381–1412 ed. A. H. Thomas (Cambridge, 1926–1961)

Calendar of State Papers and Manuscripts relating to English Affairs: Venice eds R. Brown et al. HMSO (London, 1864–1947)

Calendar of Wills Proved and Enrolled in the Court of Husting, London, A.D. 1258–A.D. 1688 ed. R. R. Sharpe (London, 1889–1890)

Capgrave, John, *Liber de Illustribus Henricis* ed. F. C. Hingeston, r.s. 7 (London, 1858)

Cartulary of God's House, Southampton ed. J. M. Kaye (Southampton, 1976)

Cartulary of the Priory of St. Denys, Southampton ed. E. O. Blake (Southampton, 1981)

Catalogue of Ancient Deeds

A Catalogue of the Medieval Muniments at Berkeley Castle ed. B. Wells-Furby ([Gloucester], 2004)

Chandos Herald, *Life of the Black Prince* eds M. K. Pope and E. C. Lodge (Oxford, 1910)

Charny, Geoffrey de, *The Book of Chivalry of Geoffroi de Charny* eds R. W. Kaeuper and E. Kennedy (Philadelphia, 1996)

——, *A Knight's Own Book of Chivalry* eds R. W. Kaeuper and E. Kennedy (Philadelphia, 2005)

Chartularies of St. Mary's, Dublin ed. J. T. Gilbert, r.s. 80 (London, 1884)

Chaucer, Geoffrey, *The Complete Works of Geoffrey Chaucer* ed. W. W. Skeat (Oxford, 1894)

——, *The Riverside Chaucer* ed. L. Benson (3rd edn, Boston, 1987)

Chronica et Annales ed. H. T. Riley, r.s. 28 (London, 1866)

Chronicle of Pierre de Langtoft ed. T. Wright, r.s. 47 (London, 1866–1886)

Chronicle of St. Mary's Abbey, York eds H. H. E. Craster and M. E. Thornton, Surtees Society (Durham, 1934)

The Chronicle of Walter Guisborough ed. H. Rothwell, Camden Society 89 (London, third series 1967)

Chronicles and Memorials of the Reign of Richard I ed. W. Stubbs, r.s. 38 (London, 1864–1865)

Chronicles of the Reigns of Edward I and Edward II ed. W. Stubbs, r.s. 76 (London, 1882–1883)

Chronicles of the Revolution, 1397–1400: The Reign of Richard II ed. C. Given-Wilson (Manchester, 1993)

Chronicon de Lanercost ed. J. Stevenson (Edinburgh, 1839)

Chronicon Moguntinum ed. C. Hegel (Hanover, 1885)

Chronique des quatre premiers Valois ed. S. Luce (Paris, 1862)

Chronique du Religieux de Saint-Denys ed. L. F. Bellaguet (Paris, 1839–1852)

Clairvaux, Bernard of, *Treatises III, Liber ad milites Templi: de laude novae militae*, tr. C. Greenia (Kalamazoo, 1977)

Codex diplomaticus Prussicus ed. J. Voigt (Königsberg, 1836–1861)

Complete Peerage ed. G. E. Cokayne (London, 1910–1957)

'Continuatio Historiae Eliensis' *Anglia Sacra, sive Collectio Historiarum* ed. H. Wharton (London, 1691)

Controversy Between Sir Richard Scrope and Sir Robert Grosvenor in the Court of Chivalry ed. N. H. Nicolas (London, 1832)

Corpus Iuris Civilis eds P. Kreuger et al. (Berlin, 1954)

Correspondance de Pierre Ameilh, archevêque de Naples puis d'Embrun 1363–1369 ed. H. Bresc (Paris, 1972)

Coucher Book of Furness Abbey eds J. C. Atkinson and J. Brownhill, Chetham Society (Manchester, 1886–1919)

Court Baron: Being precedents set for use in seignorial and other local courts, together with select pleas from the Bishop of Ely's Court of Littleport eds F. W. Maitland and W. P. Baildon, Seldon Society 4 (London, 1891)

Cronica del Roy Don Alfonso el Onceno. Cronicas de los Reyes de Castilla ed. C. Rosell (Madrid, 1875, 1877)

Diplomatic Correspondence of Richard II ed. E. Perroy, Camden Society 48 (London, third series 1933)

Diplomatic Documents, 1101–1272 ed. P. Chaplais (London, 1964–)

Documents nouveaux servant de Preuves à l'Histoire de l'Ile de Chypre sous le Reigne de la Maison de Lusignan ed. M. L. de Mas Latrie (Paris, 1882)

Dugdale, W. *Baronage of England* (London, 1675–1676)

——, *Monasticon Anglicanum* eds J. Caley et al. (London, 1817–1830)

English Gilds ed. L. Toulmin-Smith, EETS (London, 1870)

English Suits before the Paris Parlement, 1420–1436 eds C. T. Allmand and C. A. J. Armstrong, Camden Society 26 (London, fourth series 1982)

Epistolario di Coluccio Salutati ed. F. Novati (Rome, 1891–1911)

Eulogium Historiarum … ed. F. S. Haydon, r.s. 9 (London, 1858–1863)

Expeditions to Prussia and the Holy Land made by Henry, Earl of Derby ed. L. Toulmin-Smith, Camden Society 52 (London, new series 1894)

Fleta eds H. G. Richardson and G. O. Sayles, Seldon Society 72, 89, 99 (London 1955–1983)

Foedera, conventiones, literae etc. ed. T. Rymer (3rd edn, Hague, 1739–1749 [facsimile, Farnborough, 1967])

Foglietta, Uberti, *Historia Genuensium libri XII* (Genoa, 1585)

Forms of Bidding Prayer ed. H. O. Coxe (Oxford, 1840)

Four English Political Tracts of the Later Middle Ages ed. J.-P. Genêt, Camden Society 18 (London, fourth series 1977)

Froissart, Jean, *Oeuvres* ed. K. Lettenhove (Brussels, 1866–1867)

Gesta Henrici Quinti eds F. Taylor and J. F. Roskell (Oxford, 1975)

Gesta Romanorum ed. C. Swan (London, [1824] 1964)

Gower, John, *The English Works of John Gower* ed. G. C. Macaulay, EETS e.s. 81, 82 (London, 1900–1901)

Les Grandes Chroniques de France ed. R. Delachenal (Paris, 1910–1920)

Handbook of British Chronology eds F. M. Powicke and E. B. Fryde (2nd edn, London, 1961)

Hayton, Prince, 'Flors Historiarum Terre Orientis' *Recueil de historiens des croisades: Historiens arméniens* (Paris, 1869–1906)

Higden, Ranulf, *Polychronicon* ed. J. R. Lumby, r.s. 41 (London, 1865–1886)

Historia Vitae et Regni Ricardi Secundi ed. G. B. Stow (Philadelphia, 1977)

Historical Letters and Papers from the Northern Registers ed. J. Paine, r.s. 61 (London, 1873)

HMC, *Calendar of MSS of the Dean and Chapter and Wells* (London, 1907–1914)

HMC, *Fifth Report* (London, 1887)

HMC, *Third Report* (London, 1872)

Hoccleve, Thomas, *Minor Poems* ed. F. J. Furnivall, rev. J. Mitchell and A. I. Doyle, EETS e.s. 61, 73 (London, 1970)

Horn, Andrew, *The Mirror of Justices* ed. W. J. Whittaker, Seldon Society 7 (London, 1895)

Indentures of Retinue with John of Gaunt, Duke of Lancaster ed. N. B. Lewis, Camden Miscellany 22 (London, fourth series 1964)

Ireland, Thomas of, *Manipulus Florum* (Venice, 1483)

Issues of the Exchequer ed. F. Devon (London, 1837)

Jean XXII, 1316–1334: Lettres communes ed. G. Mollat (Paris, 1904–1947)

John of Gaunt's Register, 1379–1383 eds E. C. Lodge and R. Somerville, Camden Society 56, 57 (London, 1911)

Joinville, John of, *Life of Louis* tr. M. R. B. Shaw *Chronicles of the Crusades* (Harmondsworth, 1963)

King of Tars ed. J. Perryman (Heidelberg, 1980)

Knighton, Henry, *Knighton's Chronicle, 1337–1396* ed. G. H. Martin (Oxford, 1995)

Letters of Margaret of Anjou ed. C. Munro, Camden Society 86 (London, first series 1863)

Lettres closes, patentes et curiales du pape Benoît XII se rapportant à la France ed. G. Daumet (Paris, 1899–1920)

Lettres closes, patentes et curiales du pape Clément VI intéressant les pays autres que la France eds E. Déprez et al. (Paris, 1960–1961)

Lettres closes, patentes et curiales du pape Clément VI se rapportant à la France eds E. Déprez et al. (Paris, 1901–1961)

Lettres closes, secrètes et curiales du pape Urbain V eds P. Lecacheux and G. Mollat (Paris, 1954–1955)

Lettres secrètes et curiales du pape Grégoire XI ... relatives à la France eds L. Mirot et al. (Paris, 1935–1957)

Lettres secrètes et curiales du pape Jean XXII relatives à la France eds A. Coulon et al. (Paris, 1906–)

Lettres d'Urbain V eds A. Fierens and C. Tihon (Rome, 1928–1932)

Liber ecclesiae Beati Terrenani de Arbuthnott. Missale secundum usum Ecclesiae Sancti Andreae in Scotia ed. A. P. Forbes (Burntisland, 1864)

Liber Pontificalis of Edmund Lacy, Bishop of Exeter ed. R. Barnes (Exeter, 1847)

List of Sheriffs for England and Wales, Public Record Office Lists and Indexes (London, 1898)

Livre de Seyntz Medicines ed. E. J. Arnould (Oxford, 1940)

Lull, Raymond, *The Book of the Ordre of Chyvalry* ed. A. T. P. Byles, EETS o.s. 168 (London, 1926)

Lüttich, Hugo von, *Peregrinarius* eds F. Unterkircher and P. G. Schmidt (Leiden, 1991)

Lydgate and Burgh's Secrees of Old Philisoffres ed. R. Steele, EETS e.s. 66 (London 1894)

Machaut, Guillaume de, *The Capture of Alexandria* tr. J. Shirley (Aldershot, 2001)

Mandements et actes divers de Charles V (1364–1380) ed. L. Delisle (Paris, 1874)

Manuale et Processionale ad usum insignis Ecclesiae Eborancensis ed. W. G. Henderson, Surtees Society (Durham, 1875)

Mézières, Phillipe de, *Le songe du vieil pèlerin* ed. G. W. Coopland (Cambridge, 1969)

——, *Letter to King Richard II* ed. G. W. Coopland (Liverpool, 1975)

——, *Life of St. Peter Thomas* ed. J. Smet (Rome, 1954)

Middle English Sermons ed. W. O. Ross, EETS o.s. 209 (London, 1940)

Mirk's Festial. A Collection of Homilies ed. T. Erbe, EETS e.s. 96 (London, 1905)

Missale ad usum Ecclesie Westmonasteriensis ed. J. W. Legg (London, 1891–1897)

Missale ad usum Insignis et Praeclarae Ecclesiae Sarum ed. F. H. Dickinson (Burntisland 1861–1883)

Missale ad usum Percelebris Ecclesiae Herfordensis ed. W. G. Henderson (Leeds, 1874)

Missale de Lesnes ed. P. Jebb (London, 1964)

Der mittelenglische Versroman über Richard Löwenherz ed. K. Brunner (Vienna and Leipzig, 1913)

Monumenta Germaniae Historica: Scriptores eds G. H. Pertz et al. (Hanover, 1826–1934)

Murimuth, Adam, *Continuatio Chronicarum* ed. E. M. Thompson, r.s. 93 (London, 1889)

Orationum ed. E. Moeller *Corpus Christianorum Series Latina* 160–1 (Turnhout, 1992–1999)

Orville, Cabaret d', *La Chronique du Bon Duc Loys de Bourbon* ed. A.-M. Chazaud (Paris, 1876)

Pageants of Richard Beauchamp, Earl of Warwick ed. W. P. Carysfoot, Roxburghe Club (Oxford, 1908)

Papsttum und untergang des Templeordens ed. H. Finke (Münster, 1907)

Paris, Matthew, *Chronicon Majora* ed. H. R. Luard, r.s. 57 (London, 1872–1883)

Petrarca, Francesco, *Prose* eds G. Martellotti et al. (Milan, 1955)

Pisan, Christine de, *The book of fayttes of armes and of chivalry* ed. A. T. P. Byles, EETS o.s. 189 (London, 1932)

Political Poems and Songs Relating to English History ed. T. Wright, r.s. 14 (London, 1859–1861)

Political Songs of England ed. T. Wright, Camden Society 6 (London, first series 1839)

Private Indentures for Life Service in Peace and War, 1278–1476 eds M. Jones and S. Walker, Camden Society 32 (London, fifth series 1994)

Proceedings of the Privy Council ed. N. H. Nicolas (London, 1834–1837)

Projets de Croisade (v. 1200–v. 1330) ed. J. Paviot (Paris, 2008)

Purvey, John, *Remonstrance against Romish Corruptions in the Church* ed. J. Forshall (London, 1851)

Raynaldi, O. *Annales Ecclesiastici* (Lucca, 1750)

Reading, John of, *Chronica Johannis de Reading et Anonymi Cantuarensis 1346–1367* ed. J. Tait (Manchester, 1914)

Recital concerning the Sweet Land of Cyprus entitled 'Chronicle' ed. R. W. Dawkins (Oxford, 1932)

Regestum Clementis Papae V ed. Ordinis St Benedicti (Rome, 1885–1892)

Register of Edward the Black Prince, 1346–1365 eds M. C. B. Dawes et al., HMSO (London, 1930–1933)

Register of Gilbert Welton, Bishop of Carlisle, 1353–1362 ed. R. L. Storey, Canterbury and York Society (Woodbridge, 1999)

Register of Henry Wakefield, Bishop of Worcester, 1375–1395 ed. W. P. Marett, Worcestershire Historical Society (Worcester, 1972)

Register of John de Droxford, Bishop of Bath and Wells, 1309–1329 ed. B. Hobhouse, Somerset Record Society (London, 1887)

Register of John de Halton, Bishop of Carlisle, 1292–1324 eds W. N. Thompson and T. F. Tout, Canterbury and York Society (London, 1913)

Register of John Kirkby, Bishop of Carlisle, 1332–1352 and the Register of John Ross, Bishop of Carlisle, 1325–1332 ed. R. L. Storey, Canterbury and York Society (Woodbridge, 1993–1995)

Register of John Trefnant, Bishop of Hereford, 1389–1404 ed. W. W. Capes, Cantilupe Society, and Canterbury and York Society (London, 1914–1916)

Register of Ralph of Shrewsbury, Bishop of Bath and Wells, 1329–1363 ed. T. S. Holmes (London, 1896)

Register of Simon de Montacute, Bishop of Worcester, 1334–1337 ed. R. M. Haines, Worcestershire Historical Society (Worcester, 1996)

Register of Thomas Langley, Bishop of Durham, 1406–1437 ed. R. L. Storey, Surtees Society (Durham, 1949–1962)

Register of the Trinity Guild, Coventry ed. M. Dormer-Harris, (London, 1935–1944)

Register of William Edington, Bishop of Winchester, 1346–1366 ed. S. F. Hockey (Winchester, 1986–1987)

Register of William Greenfield, Lord Archbishop of York, 1306–1315 eds W. Brown and A. H. Thompson, Surtees Society (Durham, 1931–1940)

Register of William Melton, Archbishop of York, 1317–1340 eds R. M. T. Hill et al. Canterbury and York Society (Woodbridge, 1977–)

Register of Wolstan de Bransford, Bishop of Worcester, 1339–1349 ed. R. M. Haines, Worcestershire Historical Society (London, 1966)

Registrum Hamonis Hethe, Diocesis Roffensis, 1319–1352 ed. C. Johnson, Canterbury and York Society (Oxford, 1948)

Registrum Henrici Woodlock, Diocesis Wintoniensis, 1305–1316 ed. A. W. Goodman, Canterbury and York Society (Oxford, 1940–1941)

Registrum Johannis Gilbert, Episcopi Herefordensis, 1375–1389 ed. J. H. Parry, Canterbury and York Society (London, 1915)

Registrum Johannis de Pontissara, Episcopi Wyntoniensis, 1282–1304 ed. C. Deedes, Canterbury and York Society (London, 1915–1924)

Registrum Palatinum Dunelmense ed. T. D. Hardy, r.s. 62 (London, 1873–1878)

Registrum Radulphi Baldock, Gilberti Segrave, Ricardi Newport et Stephani Gravesend ed. R. C. Fowler, Canterbury and York Society (London, 1911)

Registrum Roberti Winchelsey, Cantuariensis Archiepiscopi, 1294–1313 ed. R. Graham, Canterbury and York Society (Oxford, 1952–1956)

Registrum Simonis Gandavo, Diocesis Saresbiriensis, 1297–1315 eds C. T. Flower and M. C. B. Dawes, Canterbury and York Society (Oxford and London, 1914–1934)

Romance of Beves of Hamtoun ed. E. Kölbing, EETS e.s. 46, 48, 65 (London, 1885–1894)

Romance of Guy of Warwick ed. J. Zupitza, EETS e.s. 42, 49, 59 (London, 1883–1891)

Rotuli Parliamentum eds J. Strachey et al. ([London], 1783)

Rous, John, *Johanni Rossi antiquarii Warwicensis Historia regum* ... (Oxford, 1745)

Royal and Historical Letters of Henry IV eds F. C. Hingeston et al., r.s. 18 (London, 1860–1965)

Saint-Victor, John of, 'Memoriale' *Recueil des Historiens des Gaules et de la France* eds M. Bouquet et al. (Paris, 1737–1904) vol. XXI pp. 630–76

The Sarum Missal ed. J. W. Legg (Oxford, 1916)

Scriptores Rerum Prussicarum eds T. Hirsch et al. (Leipzig, 1861–)

Selections from English Wycliffite Writings ed. A. Hudson (Cambridge, 1978)

Servion, Jean, 'Chroniques de Savoy' *Monumenta Historiae Patriae* eds C. Albert et al. (Turin, 1836–1855) vol. III *Scriptores* 1

Sir Ferumbras ed. S. J. H. Herrtage, EETS e.s. 34 (London, 1966)

Six Middle English Romances ed. M. Mills (London, 1992)

Le Speculum laicorum: édition d'une collection d'exempla, composée en Angleterre à la fin du XIIIe siècle ed. J. Welter (Paris, 1914)

Testamenta Vetusta ed. N. H. Nicolas (London, 1826)

Torsello, Marino Sanudo, 'Liber secretorum fidelium crucis' *Gesta Dei per Francos* ... ed. J. Bongars (Hanover, 1611)

Travels of Sir John Mandeville ed. A. W. Pollard (London, 1915)

Trivet, Nicholas, *Annales* ed. T. Hog (London, 1845)

Urbain V: Lettres communes eds M.-H. Laurent et al. (Paris, 1954–1985)

Ursins, Juvenal des, *Histoire de Charles VI, roy de France* eds J. Michaud et al. (Paris, 1836)

Usk, Adam, *The Chronicle of Adam Usk* ed. C. Given-Wilson (Oxford, 1997)

Villani, Giovanni and Matteo, *Cronica* ed. F. Gheradi Dragomanni (Milan, 1846–1848)

De Visione Sancti Simonis Stock ed. B. M. Xiberta (Rome, 1950)

Vitae paparum Avenionensium ed. G. Mollat (Paris, 1914–1927)

Vitalis, Orderic, *Historia Ecclesiastica* ed. M. Chibnall (Oxford, 1969–1980)

Walsingham, Thomas, *Historia Anglicana* ed. H. T. Riley, r.s. 28 (London, 1863–1864)

——, *The* Chronica Maiora *of Thomas Walsingham, 1376–1422* tr. D. Preest with J. G. Clark (Woodbridge, 2005)

Westminster Chronicle, 1381–1394 eds L. C. Hector and B. F. Harvey (Oxford, 1982)

Wills of the Archdeaconry of Sudbury, 1439–1474, Wills from the Register 'Baldwyne' Part I (1439–1461) ed. P. Northeast (Woodbridge, 2001)

Wyclif, John, *Polemical Works in Latin* ed. R. Buddensieg (London, 1883)

Wykeham's Register ed. T. F. Kirby, Hampshire Record Society (London, 1896–1899)

Secondary Sources

The Age of Richard II ed. J. L. Gillespie (Stroud, 1997)

Ainsworth, P. F. *Jean Froissart and the Fabric of History* (Oxford, 1990)

Archer, R. E. 'The Mowbrays, Earls of Nottingham and Dukes of Norfolk to 1432' DPhil. thesis (Oxford, 1984)

Arms, Armies and Fortifications in the Hundred Years War eds A. Curry and M. Hughes (Woodbridge, 1994)

Aston, M. 'The Impeachment of Bishop Despenser' *BIHR* 38 (1965) pp. 127–48

Atiya, A. S. *The Crusade in the Later Middle Ages* (London, 1938)

Balard, M. *Les latins en Orient XIe–XVe siècle* (Paris, 2006)

Barber, M. 'The *Pastoureaux* of 1320' *Journal of Ecclesiastical History* 32 (1981) pp. 143–66

Barber, R. W. *Edward Prince of Wales and Aquitaine* (Woodbridge, 1996)

Barker, J. R. V. *The Tournament in England 1100–1400* (Woodbridge, 1986)

Barker, J. W. *Manuel II Palaeologus* (New Brunswick, 1969)

Barnie, J. *War in Medieval Society: Social Values and the Hundred Years War* (London, 1974)

Barron, W. R. J. *English Medieval Romance* (London, 1987)

Bartlett, R. *The Making of Europe* (London, 1993)

Bell, A. 'The English and the Crusade of Nicopolis' *Medieval Life* 4 pt. 2 (1996) pp. 18–22

——, *War and the Soldier in the Fourteenth Century* (Woodbridge, 2004)

Beltz, G. F. *Memorials of the Order of the Garter* (London, 1841)

Bengtson, J. 'St George and the Formation of English Nationalism' *Journal of Medieval and Early Modern Studies* 27 (1997) pp. 314–40

Bennett, M. J. 'Henry Bolingbroke and the Revolution of 1399' *Henry IV: The Establishment of a Regime* eds G. Dodd and D. Biggs (York, 2003) pp. 9–34

Biller, P. *The Measure of Multitude: Population in Medieval Thought* (Oxford, 2000)

Binkley, P. 'John Bromyard and the Hereford Dominicans' *Centres of Learning: Learning and Location in Pre-Modern Europe and the Near East* eds J. W. Drijvers and A. A. MacDonald (Leiden, 1995) pp. 255–64

Boase, T. S. R. *Boniface III* (London, 1933)

Boehlke, F. J. *Pierre de Thomas, Scholar, Diplomat and Crusader* (Philadelphia, 1966)

Boulton, D. J. D. *The Knights of the Crown* (2nd edn, Woodbridge, 2000)

Boyle, L. E. 'The Date of the *Summa Praedicantium* of John Bromyard' *Speculum* 48 (1978) pp. 533–7

Bridrey, E. *La Condition juridique des croisés et le privilège de croix* (Paris, 1900)

Brown, E. A. R. and N. F. Regalado, '*La grant feste*: Philip the Fair's Celebration of the Knighting of His Sons in Paris at Pentecost of 1313' *City and Spectacle in Medieval Europe* eds B. A. Hanawalt and K. L. Reyerson (Minneapolis, 1994) pp. 56–86

Brundage, J. A. 'Cruce Signari: The Rite for Taking the Cross in England' *Traditio* 22 (1966) pp. 289–310

——, 'The Crusader's Wife: A Canonistic Quandary' *Studia Gratiana* 12 (1967) pp. 425–42

——, *Medieval Canon Law and the Crusader* (Madison, 1969)

——, 'The Votive Obligations of Crusaders' *Traditio* 24 (1968) pp. 77–118

Bullough, D. A. 'Games People Played: Drama and Ritual as Propaganda in Medieval Europe' *TRHS* 24 (1974) pp. 97–119

Cardini, F. 'The Warrior and the Knight' *The Medieval World* ed. J. le Goff, tr. L. G. Cochrane (2nd edn, London, 1997) pp. 75–112

Catto, J. I. 'Religion and the English Nobility in the Later Fourteenth Century' *History and Imagination. Essays in Honour of H. R. Trevor-Roper* eds H. Lloyd-Jones et al. (London, 1981) pp. 43–55

Cavanaugh, S. *A Study of Books Privately Owned in England 1300–1450* (Ann Arbor, 1985)

Chaume, M. M. 'Une prophétie relative à Charles VI' *Revue du moyen âge latin* 3 (1947) pp. 27–42

Cherry, M. 'The Courtenay Earls of Devon: The Formation and Disintegration of a late Medieval Affinity' *Southern History* 1 (1979) pp. 71–91

Christiansen, E. *The Northern Crusades* (2nd edn, London, 1997)

Cipollone, G. *La liberazione dei 'captivi' tra Cristianità e Islam: Oltre la crociata e il Đihād: Toleranza e servizio umanitario* (Rome, 2000)

Clarke, M. V. *Fourteenth Century Studies* (Oxford, 1937)

Clifford, E. *A Knight of Great Renown* (Chicago, 1961)

Cole, P. J. *The Preaching of the Crusades* (Cambridge, Mass., 1991)

Collins, H. E. L. *The Order of the Garter, 1348–1461* (Oxford, 2000)

Constable, G. 'The Historiography of the Crusades' *The Crusades from the Perspective of Byzantium and the Muslim World* eds A. E. Laiou and R. P. Mottahedeh (Washington D. C., 2001) pp. 1–22

Coote, L. A. *Prophecy and Public Affairs in Later Medieval England* (York, 2000)

Coss, P. R. *The Knight in Medieval England, 1000–1400* (Stroud, 1993)

——, *The Origins of the English Gentry* (Cambridge, 2003)

Cottle, B. *The Triumph of English, 1350–1400* (London, 1969)

Cox, E. L. *The Green Count of Savoy* (Princeton, 1967)

Crusade and Conversion on the Baltic Frontier 1150–1500 ed. A. V. Murray (Aldershot, 2001)

Crusading in the Fifteenth Century: Message and Impact ed. N. Housley (Basingstoke and New York, 2004)

D'Avray, D. L. *Death and the Prince* (Oxford, 1994)

Delaville le Roulx, J. *La France en Orient au XIVe siècle* (Paris, 1885–1886)

Delogu, D. *Theorising the Ideal Sovereign: The Rise of the French Vernacular Royal Biography* (Toronto, 2008)

Déprez, E. *Les préliminaires de la guerre de cent ans. La papauté, la France et l'Angleterre, 1328–1342* (Paris, 1902)

DeVries, K. 'The Reasons for the Bishop of Norwich's attack on Flanders in 1383' *Fourteenth Century England III* ed. W. M. Ormrod (Woodbridge, 2004) pp. 155–65

Doyle, A. I. 'The Manuscripts' *Middle English Alliterative Poetry* ed. D. A. Lawton (Cambridge, 1982) pp. 88–100

Du Boulay, F. R. H. 'Henry of Derby's Expeditions to Prussia, 1390–1391 and 1392' *The Reign of Richard II* eds F. R. H. Du Boulay and C. M. Barron (London, 1971) pp. 153–72

Düll, S. et al. 'Faithful unto Death: The Tomb Slab of Sir William Neville and Sir John Clanvowe, Constantinople 1391' *Antiquities Journal* 71 (1991) pp. 174–90

Edbury, P. W. *The Kingdom of Cyprus and the Crusades 1191–1374* (Cambridge, 1991)

Ehlers, A. 'The Crusade against Lithuania Reconsidered' *Crusade and Conversion on the Baltic Frontier 1150–1500* ed. A. V. Murray (Aldershot, 2001) pp. 21–44

Ekdahl, S. 'Horses and Crossbows: Two Important Warfare Advantages of the Teutonic Order in Prussia' *Military Orders: II* ed. H. Nicholson (Aldershot, 1998) pp. 119–50

England and the Low Countries in the Late Middle Ages eds C. M. Barron and N. Saul (Stroud, 1995)

Evans, M. 'Crusades and Society in the English Midlands c.1150–1307' PhD thesis (Nottingham, 1997)

Ferguson, A. B. *The Indian Summer of English Chivalry* (Durham, N.C., 1960)

Fernandes, L. 'On Conducting the Affairs of the State: A Guideline of the Fourteenth Century' *Annales Islamologiques* 24 (1988) pp. 81–91

Finlayson, J. '*Richard, Coer de lyon*: Romance, History or Something in Between?' *Studies in Philology* 87 (1990) pp. 156–80

Fletcher, C. D. 'Manhood and Politics in the Reign of Richard II' *Past and Present* 189 (2005) pp. 3–39

——, *Richard II: Manhood, Youth and Politics, 1377–1399* (Oxford, 2008)

Fonnesburg-Schmidt, I. *The Popes and the Baltic Crusades, 1147–1254* (Leiden, 2007)

Forey, A. 'The Military Order of St. Thomas of Acre' *EHR* 92 (1977), pp. 481–503

Forrest, J. *The History of Morris Dancing, 1458–1750* (Cambridge, 1999)

Fowler, E. 'The Romance Hypothetical: Lordship and the Saracens in *Sir Isumbras*' *The Spirit of Medieval English Popular Romance* eds A. Rutter and J. Gilbert (Harlow, 2000) pp. 97–121

Fowler, K. A. 'Deux Entrepreneurs militaires au XIVe siècle: Bertrand du Guesclin et Sir Hugh Calveley' *Le Combattant au Moyen Age* (2nd edn, Paris, 1995) pp. 243–56

——, *The King's Lieutenant: Henry of Grosmont, First Duke of Lancaster* (London, 1969)

Fowler, R. C. 'Seals in the Public Record Office' *Archaeologia* 74 (1923–1924) pp. 103–16

France, J. *The Crusades and the Expansion of Catholic Christendom, 1000–1714* (London, 2005)

Fraser, C. M. *A History of Antony Bek, Bishop of Durham, 1283–1311* (Oxford, 1957)

Gennes, J.-P. *Les Chevaliers du Saint-Sépulcre de Jérusalem* (Herault, 1995)

Ghazarian, J. G. *The Armenian Kingdom in Cilicia during the Crusades* (Richmond, 2000)

Given-Wilson, C. *The Royal Household and the King's Affinity: Service, Politics and Finance in England, 1360–1413* (New Haven, 1986)

Glamorgan County History ed. T. B. Pugh (Cardiff, 1971)

Goodman, A. *John of Gaunt: The Exercise of Princely Power in Fourteenth-Century Europe* (Harlow, 1992)

——, *The Loyal Conspiracy: The Lords Appellant under Richard II* (London, 1971)

Gough, S. *Sepulchral Monuments in Great Britain* (London, 1796)

Gundy, A. 'The Rule of Thomas Beauchamp 1369–1398' PhD thesis (Cambridge, 2000)

Gutiérrez de Velasco, A. 'Los ingleses en España' *Estudios de Edad Media de la Corona de Aragon* vol. IV (Saragossa, 1951) pp. 213–319

Haines, R. M. *Archbishop Stratford: Political Revolutionary* (Toronto, 1986)

Halecki, O. *Un Empereur de Byzance à Rome, Vingt ans de travail pour l'Union des églises et pour la défence de l'empire d'orient, 1355–1373* (Warsaw, 1930)

Hamilton, B. 'Eleanor of Castile and the Crusading Movement' *Intercultural Contacts in the Medieval Mediterranean* ed. B. Arbel (London, 1996) pp. 92–103

Hamilton, J. S. 'Charter Witness Lists for the Reign of Edward II' *Fourteenth Century England* vol. I ed. N. Saul (Woodbridge, 2000) pp. 1–20

——, *Piers Gaveston: Earl of Cornwall, 1307–1312* (Detroit, 1988)

Harriss, G. L. *Shaping The Nation: England 1360–1461* (Oxford, 2005)

Harvey, L. P. *Islamic Spain, 1250–1500* (Chicago, 1990)

Hebgin-Barnes, P. 'A Triumphant Image: Henry Scrope's Window in Heydour Church' *Medieval Life* 4 (1996) pp. 26–8

Higounet, C. 'De la Rochelle à Torun: Aventure de barons en Prusse et relations économiques' *Le Moyen Age* 69 (1963) pp. 529–40

Hill, G. F. *A History of Cyprus* (Cambridge, 1940–1952)

Hillgarth, J. N. *The Spanish Kingdoms 1250–1516* (London, 1971)

Hirsch, T. *Danzigs Handels – und Gewerbs-geschichte* (Liepzig, 1858)

History of the Crusades ed. K. M. Setton (Madison, 1969–1989)

Hobhouse, E. 'The Register of Roger de Norbury' *Collections for a History of Staffordshire*, William Salt Society (Birmingham, 1880)

Hopkins, A. *The Sinful Knights: A Study of Middle English Penitential Romance* (Oxford, 1990)

Horner, P. J. 'A Sermon on the Anniversary of the Death of Thomas Beauchamp, Earl of Warwick' *Traditio* 34 (1978) pp. 381–401

Hornstein, L. H. 'The Historical Background of the *King of Tars*' *Speculum* 16 (1941) pp. 404–11

Housley, N. *The Avignon Papacy and the Crusades, 1305–1378* (Oxford, 1986)

——, *Contesting the Crusades* (Oxford, 2006)

——, 'The Crusading Movement, 1274–1700' *Oxford Illustrated History of the Crusades* ed. J. S. C. Riley-Smith (Oxford, 1995) pp. 260–95

——, *The Italian Crusades: The Papal-Angevin Alliance and the Crusades against Christian Lay Powers, 1254–1343* (Oxford, 1982)

——, *The Later Crusades, 1274–1580: From Lyons to Alcazar* (Oxford, 1992)

——, 'Mercenary Companies, the Papacy and the Crusades, 1356–1378' *Traditio* 38 (1982) pp. 253–80

——, 'Politics and Heretics in Italy: Anti-Heretical Crusades, Orders and Confraternities 1200–1500' *Journal of Ecclesiastical History* 33 (1982) pp. 193–208

——, 'Pope Clement and the Crusades of 1309–1310' *Journal of Medieval History* 8 (1982) pp. 29–43

——, *Religious Warfare in Europe 1400–1536* (Oxford, 2002)

Hudson, A. *Lollards and their Books* (London, 1985)

——, *The Premature Reformation: Wycliffite Texts and Lollard History* (Oxford, 1988)

Huizinga, J. H. *The Waning of the Middle Ages* tr. F. J. Hopman (London, 1938)

Ibn Jaldún: El Mediterráneo en el siglo XIV: La Peninsula Ibérica El entorno mediterráneo eds M. Viguera et al. (Seville, 2006)

Ibn Khaldun: The Mediterranean in the 14th Century: Rise and Fall of Empires eds M. Viguera et al. (Seville, 2006)

i-Lluch, R. S. 'Caballeros Cristianos en el Occidente europeo e islámico' *'Das kommt mir Spanisch vor': Eigenes und Fremdes in den deutsch-spanischen Beziehungen des späten mittelalters* eds N. Jaspert and K. Herbers (Münster, 2004) pp. 217–90

Imber, C. *The Ottoman Empire, 1300–1650* (2nd edn, Basingstoke, 2009)

Iorga, N. *Philippe de Mézières et la croisade au XIVe siècle* (Paris, 1896)

Jacob, E. F. *The Fifteenth Century, 1399–1485* (Oxford, 1961)

James, M. R. *The Ancient Libraries of Canterbury and Dover* (Cambridge, 1903)

Jensen, K. V. 'Robert Holkot's *Questio* on Killing Infidels' *Archivum Fratrum Praedicatorum* 63 (1993) pp. 207–28

Jones, M. K. 'The Fortunes of War: The Military Career of John, second Lord of Bourchier' *Transactions of the Essex Society for Archaeology and History* 26 (1995) pp. 145–61

Jones, T. *Chaucer's Knight* (London, 1980)

Jotischky, A. *Crusading and the Crusader States* (Harlow, 2004)

Kaeppeli, T. *Scriptores Ordinis Praedicatorum Medii Aevi* (Rome, 1970–1993)

Kafadar, C. *Between Two Worlds: The Construction of the Ottoman State* (Los Angeles and London, 1995)

Keen, M. H. 'Chaucer's Knight, the English Aristocracy and the Crusade' *English Court Culture in the Later Middle Ages* eds V. J. Scattergood and J. W. Sherborne (London, 1983) pp. 45–63

——, *Chivalry* (New Haven, 1984)

——, 'Chivalry and English Kingship in the Later Middle Ages' *War, Government and Aristocracy in the British Isles, c.1150–1500* eds C. Given-Wilson, A. Kettle and L. Scales (Woodbridge, 2008) pp. 250–66

——, *The Laws of War in the Late Middle Ages* (London, 1965)

——, *Nobles, Knights and Men-at-arms* (London, 1996)

——, *Origins of the English Gentleman: Heraldry, Chivalry and Gentility in Medieval England c.1300–1500* (Stroud, 2002)

Kipling, G. 'Richard II's "Sumptuous Pageants" and the Idea of Civic Triumph' *Pageantry in the Shakespearean Theater* ed. D. M. Bergeron (Athens, GA, 1985) pp. 83–103

Leopold, A. *How to Recover the Holy Land: The Crusade Proposals of the Late Thirteenth and Early Fourteenth Centuries* (Aldershot, 2000)

Lewis, N. B. 'Simon Burley and Baldwin of Raddington' *EHR* 52 (1937) pp. 662–9

Lewis, S. 'The Apocalypse of Isabella of France: Paris; Bibl. Nat. Ms. Fr. 13096' *Art Bulletin* 72 (1990) pp. 224–60

Lindenbaum, S. 'The Smithfield Tournament of 1390' *Journal of Medieval and Renaissance Studies* 20 (1990) pp. 1–20

Linder, A. *Raising Arms: Liturgy in the Struggle to Liberate Jerusalem in the Late Middle Ages* (Turnhout, 2003)

Linehan, P. *History and the Historians of Medieval Spain* (Oxford, 1993)

Lloyd, S. D. *English Society and the Crusade 1216–1307* (Oxford, 1988)

Lloyd, T. H. *England and the German Hanse, 1157–1611* (Cambridge, 1991)

Lock, P. *The Franks in the Aegean, 1204–1500* (London, 1995)

Lomax, D. W. *The Reconquest of Spain* (London, 1978)

Loomis, R. S. '*Richard Cœur de Lion* and the *Pas Saladin* in Medieval Art' *Publications of the Modern Language Association* 30 (1915) pp. 509–28

López de Coca, J. E. and B. Krauel, 'Cruzados escoceses en la frontera de Granada (1330)' *Anuario de Estudios Medievales* 18 (1988) pp. 245–61

Lunt, W. E. *Financial Relations of the Papacy with England* (Cambridge, Mass., 1939–1962)

——, *Papal Revenues in the Middle Ages* (New York, 1965)

Luttrell, A. 'Chaucer's Knight and the Mediterranean' *Library of Mediterranean History* 1 (1994) pp. 127–60

——, 'English Contributions to the Hospitaller Castle at Bodrum in Turkey: 1407–1437' *Military Orders: II* ed. H. Nicholson (Aldershot, 1998) pp. 163–72

——, 'English Levantine Crusaders, 1363–1367' *Renaissance Studies* 2 (1988) pp. 143–53

——, *The Hospitallers in Cyprus, Rhodes, Greece and the West, 1291–1440* (London, 1978)

——, 'Hospitallers in Rhodes, 1306–1421' *History of the Crusades* ed. K. M. Setton (Madison, 1969–1989) vol. III pp. 278–313

——, *Latin Greece, the Hospitallers and the Crusades, 1291–1440* (London, 1982)

Mackay, A. 'Religion, Culture and Ideology on the Late Medieval Castilian-Granadan Frontier' *Medieval Frontier Societies* eds R. Bartlett and A. Mackay (Oxford, 1989) pp. 228–43

Macquarrie, A. *Scotland and the Crusades: 1095–1560* (Edinburgh, 1985)

Maddicott, J. R. *Thomas of Lancaster, 1307–1322: A Study in the Reign of Edward II* (Oxford, 1970)

Magee, J. 'Politics, Society and the Crusade in England and France, 1378–1400' PhD thesis (Leicester, 1997)

Maier, C. T. *Crusade Propaganda and Ideology: Model Sermons for the Preaching of the Cross* (Cambridge, 2000)

——, *Preaching the Crusades* (Cambridge, 1994)

Manion, L. 'The Loss of the Holy Land and *Sir Isumbras*: Literary Contributions to Fourteenth-Century Crusade Discourse' *Speculum* 85 (2010) pp. 65–90

Manzano, M. *La intervención de los benimerines an la peninsula ibérica* (Madrid, 1992)

Mason, E. 'Legends of the Beauchamps' Ancestors: The Use of Baronial Propaganda in Medieval England' *Journal of Medieval History* 10 (1984) pp. 25–40

Matthews, D. *Writing to the King: Nation, Kingship and Literature in England, 1250–1350* (Cambridge, 2010)

McCarthy, J. *The Ottoman Turks* (London, 1997)

McFarlane, K. B. *Lancastrian Kings and Lollard Knights* (Oxford, 1972)

McHardy, A. K. 'Liturgy and Propaganda during the Hundred Years War' *Studies in Church History* 18 (Oxford, 1982) pp. 215–27

McKendrick, S. 'Tapestries from the Low Countries in England during the Fifteenth Century' *England and the Low Countries in the Late Middle Ages* eds C. M. Barron and N. Saul (Stroud, 1995) pp. 43–63

McKenna, J. W. 'How God Became an Englishman' *Tudor Rule and Revolution, Essays for G. R. Elton* eds D. J. Guth and J. W. McKenna (Cambridge, 1982) pp. 25–43

McNamee, C. *The Wars of the Bruces: Scotland, England and Ireland, 1306–1328* (East Linton, 1997)

Mehl, D. *The Middle English Romances of the Thirteenth and Fourteenth Centuries* (London, 1969)

Menache, S. *Clement V* (Cambridge, 1998)

Metin Kunt, I. 'The Rise of the Ottomans' *New Cambridge Medieval History* vol. VI ed. M. Jones (Cambridge, 2000) pp. 839–63

Michaud, J. *Histoire des croisades* (Paris, 1824–1829)

Mirot, M. L. *Le siège de Mahdia une expédition Française èn Tunisie au XIVe siècle* (Paris, 1932)

Molina, J. 'The Frontier of Granada' *Ibn Khaldun: The Mediterranean in the 14th Century: Rise and Fall of Empires* eds M. Viguera et al. (Seville, 2006) pp. 154–63

Molinier, A. 'Description de deux manuscrits contenant la règle de la "Militia Passionis Jhesu Christi"' *Archives de l'Orient Latin* 1 (1881) pp. 335–64

Moor, C. *Knights of Edward I*, Harleian Society (London, 1929–1932)

Morgan, N. 'The Signification of the Banner in the Wilton Diptych' *The Regal Image of Richard II* eds D. Gordon, C. Monnas and C. Elam (London, 1997) pp. 178–88

Nicholson, H. J. *Love, War and the Grail: Templars Hospitaller and Teutonic Knights* (Leiden, 2004)

Nicol, D. M. *The Last Centuries of Byzantium* (2nd edn, Cambridge, 1993)

Nolcken, C. von, 'Some Alphabetical Compendia and How Preachers Used them in Fourteenth-Century England' *Viator* 12 (1981) pp. 271–88

O'Callaghan, J. F. *Reconquest and Crusade in Medieval Spain* (Philadelphia, 2003)

Ordines Militares: Colloquia Torunensia Historica ed. Z. H. Nowark (Torún, 1981–)

Ormrod, W. M. *Edward III* (New Haven, 2011)

——, 'Finance and Trade under Richard II' *Richard II: The Art of Kingship* ed. A. Goodman and J. L. Gillespie (Oxford, 1999) pp. 155–86

Owst, G. R. *Literature and the Pulpit* (2nd edn, Oxford, 1961)

Oxford Dictionary of National Biography (Oxford, 2004–)

Paine, C. 'The Bishop of Norwich's Crusade: Its Origins and Participants' MLitt. thesis (Oxford, 1995)

Palmer, J. J. N. *England, France and Christendom 1377–1399* (London, 1972)

Pantin, W. A. 'The Letters of John Mason: Fourteenth-Century Formulary from St. Augustine's Canterbury' *Essays in Medieval History presented to B. Wilkinson* eds T. A. Sandquist and M. R. Powicke (Toronto, 1969) pp. 192–219

Paravicini, W. 'Die Preussenreisen des Europäischen Adels' *Historische Zeitschrift* 23 (1981) pp. 25–38

——, *Die Preussenreisen des Europäischen Adels* (Sigmaringen, 1989)

——, 'La Prusse et l'Europe occidentale: La participation de la noblesse d'Europe occidentale aux croisades de l'Order des Chevaliers Teutoniques contre la Lituanie' *Cahiers de Recherches Mèdievales (XIIIe-Xves.)* 1 (1996) pp. 177–91

Paviot, J. 'England and the Mongols (1260–1330)' *Journal of the Royal Asiatic Society* 3rd series 10 (2000) pp. 305–18

——, *Les Ducs de Bourgogne, la Croisade et l'Orient* (Paris, 2003)

Perroy, G. *L'Angleterre et la grand schisme d'Occident* (Paris, 1933)

Philippe de Mézières and His Age: Politics and Piety in the Fourteenth Century eds R. Blumenfeld-Kosinski and K. Petkov (Leiden, 2011)

Phillips, J. R. S. *Edward II* (New Haven, 2010)

——, 'Edward II and the Prophets' *England in the Fourteenth Century* ed. W. M. Ormrod (Woodbridge, 1986) pp. 189–201

Phillips, S. *The Prior of the Knights Hospitaller in Late Medieval England* (Woodbridge, 2009)

Postan, M. M. *Medieval Trade and Finance* (Cambridge, 1973)

Powicke, F. M. *The Medieval Books of Merton College* (Oxford, 1931)

——, *The Thirteenth Century, 1216–1307* (2nd edn, Oxford, 1962)

Pratt, J. H. *Chaucer and War* (Lanham, 2000)

Prawer, J. *World of the Crusaders* (London, 1972)

Pryor, J. H. *Geography, Technology and War: Studies in the Maritime History of the Mediterranean 649–1571* (Cambridge, 1988)

Purcell, M. *Papal Crusading Policy: The Chief Instruments of Papal Crusading Policy, 1244–1291* (Leiden, 1975)

Quellen und studien zur Geschichtes des Deutschen ordens eds U. Arnold et al. (Bonn, 1966–)

Regaldo, N. F. 'Kalila et Dimma, liber regius' *Satura: Studies in Medieval Literature* eds N. M. Reale and R. E. Sternglantz (Donington, 2001) pp. 103–23

Richard II: The Art of Kingship eds A. Goodman and J. L. Gillespie (Oxford, 1999)

Richard, J. *La Papauté et les Missions D'Orient au Moyen Âge* (2nd edn, Rome, 1998)

Richmond, V. B. *The Legend of Guy of Warwick* (New York, 1996)

Riquer, M. *Caballeros andantes españoles* (Madrid, 1967)

Romano, D. 'Un Inglés en la Guerra contro el Moro: 1324' *Al-Qantara* 2 (1981) pp. 457–9

Rouse, R. A. 'An Exemplary Life: Guy of Warwick as Medieval Culture Hero' *Guy of Warwick: Icon and Ancestor* eds A. Wiggins and R. Field (Cambridge, 2007) pp. 94–109

Rowell, S. C. 'Baltic Europe' *The New Cambridge Medieval History, 1300–1415* vol. VI ed. M. Jones (Cambridge, 2000) pp. 699–734

——, *Lithuania Ascending: A Pagan Empire within East-Central Europe, 1295–1345* (Cambridge, 1994)

——, 'Unexpected Contacts: Lithuanians at Western Courts, c.1316–c.1400' *EHR* III (1996) pp. 557–77

Ruiz, T. F. *Spain's Centuries of Crisis, 1300–1474* (Oxford, 2007)

Russell, P. E. *English Intervention in Spain during the Reigns of Edward III and Richard II* (Oxford, 1955)

——, *Henry the Navigator: A Life* (New Haven, 2000)

Rutland Magazine and County Historical Record ed. G. Phillips (Oakham, 1903–1912)

Sandquist, T. A. 'The Holy Oil of St Thomas of Canterbury' *Essays in Medieval History presented to B. Wilkinson* eds T. A. Sandquist and M. R. Powicke (Toronto, 1969) pp. 330–44

Saul, N. *For Honour and Fame: Chivalry in England 1066–1500* (London, 2011)

——, 'The Kingship of Richard II' *Richard II: The Art of Kingship* eds A. Goodman and J. L. Gillespie (Oxford, 1999) pp. 37–58

——, *Knights and Esquires: The Gloucestershire Gentry in the Fourteenth Century* (Oxford, 1981)

——, *Richard II* (New Haven, 1997)

——, *The Three Richards* (London, 2005)

Scattergood, V. J. 'Adam Davy's Dreams and Edward II' *Archiv für das Studium der Neuren Sprachen und Literaturen* 206 (1970) pp. 253–60

Scheifele, E. 'Richard II and the Visual Arts' *Richard II: The Art of Kingship* eds A. Goodman and J. L. Gillespie (Oxford, 1999) pp. 255–72

Schein, S. *Fideles Crucis: The Papacy, the West, and the Recovery of the Holy Land* (Oxford, 1991)

Setton, K. M. *Papacy and the Levant, 1204–1571* (Philadelphia, 1976–1984)

Sinclair, A. F. 'The Beauchamp Earls of the Middle Ages' PhD thesis (London, 1986)

Staley, L. 'Gower, Richard II, Henry of Derby, and the Business of Making Culture' *Speculum* 75 (2000) pp. 68–96

——, *Languages of Power in the Age of Richard II* (University Park, 2005)

Stapleton, T. 'A Brief Summary of the Wardrobe Accounts of the Tenth, Eleventh and Fourteenth Years of King Edward the Second' *Archaeologia* 26 (1836) pp. 318–44

Stretton, G. 'Some Aspects of Medieval Travel' *TRHS* 7 (1924) pp. 77–97

Strickland, M. 'Provoking or Avoiding Battle? Challenge, Duel and Single Combat in Warfare of the High Middle Ages' *Armies, Chivalry and Warfare in Medieval Britain and France* ed. M. Strickland (Stamford, 1998) pp. 317–43

Sumption, J. *The Hundred Years War* (London, 1990–2009)

Taymiyya, Ibn, *Lettre à un roi croisé (al-Risâlat al-Qubrusiyya)* ed. J. Michot (Louvain-la-Neuve and Lyon, 1995)

Their, L. *Kreuzzugsbemühungen unter Papst Clemens V, 1305–1314* (Düsseldorf, 1973).

Tipton, C. 'The English at Nicopolis' *Speculum* 37 (1962) pp. 528–40

Tout, T. F. *Chapters in Medieval Administrative History* (Manchester, 1920–1933)

Turville-Petre, T. 'Humphrey de Bohun and *William de Palerne*' *Neuphilologische Mitteilungen* 75 (1974) pp. 250–2

Tyerman, C. J. *The Debate on the Crusades* (Manchester, 2011)

——, *England and the Crusades 1095–1588* (Chicago, 1988)

——, 'The French and the Crusade 1313–1336' DPhil. thesis (Oxford, 1981)

——, *God's War: A New History of the Crusades* (London, 2006)

——, *The Invention of the Crusades* (Basingstoke, 1998)

——, 'Philip V of France, the Assemblies of 1319–1320 and the Crusade' *BIHR* 57 (1984) pp. 15–34

——, 'Philip VI and the Recovery of the Holy Land' *EHR* 100 (1985) pp. 25–52

Urban, W. L. *The Baltic Crusade* (2nd edn, Chicago, 1994)

——, *The Livonian Crusade* (2nd edn, Chicago, 2004)

——, *The Prussian Crusade* (Lanham, 1980)

——, *The Samogitian Crusade* (Chicago, 1989)

Vale, J. *Edward III and Chivalry: Chivalric Society and its Context 1270–1350* (Woodbridge, 1982)

——, 'Image and Identity in the Pre-History of the Order of the Garter', *St. George's Chapel Windsor in the Fourteenth Century* ed. N. Saul (Woodbridge, 2005) pp. 35–50

Vale, M. G. A. *War and Chivalry: Warfare and Aristocratic Culture in England, France, and Burgundy at the End of the Middle Ages* (London, 1981)

Victoria History of the County of Cambridge and the Isle of Ely eds A. F. Wareham, A. P. M. Wright et al. (London, 1978–)

Victoria History of the County of Rutland ed. W. Page (London, 1908–1936)

Victoria History of the County of Stafford eds M. W. Greenslade et al. (London, 1908–)

Valdeón, J. B. *Pedro I, el Cruel, y Enrique de Trastámara: la primera guerra civil española?* (Madrid, 2002)

Wagner, R. A. 'The Swan Badge and the Swan Knight' *Archaeologia* 97 (1959) pp. 127–38

Walker, S. *The Lancastrian Affinity, 1361–1399* (Oxford, 1990)

——, 'Richard's Views on Kingship' *Rulers and Ruled in Late Medieval England* eds R. Archer and S. Walker (London, 1995) pp. 49–63

Waller, J. G. 'The Lords of Cobham, their Monuments and the Church' *Archaeologia Cantiana* 11 (1877) pp. 49–112

War, Government and Aristocracy in the British Isles, c.1150–1500 eds C. Given-Wilson, A. Kettle and L. Scales (Woodbridge, 2008)

The Wars of Edward III: Sources and Interpretations ed. C. R. Rogers (Woodbridge, 1999)

Watt, J. L. *Henry VI* (Cambridge, 1996)

Whitwell, R. J. 'Italian Bankers and the English Crown' *TRHS* 17 (1903) pp. 175–233

Wright, J. R. *The Church and the English Crown, 1305–1334* (Toronto, 1980)

Wylie, J. H. *The History of England under Henry the Fourth* (London, 1884–1898)

Index

Warfare in History

The Battle of Yorktown, 1781: A Reassessment, *John D. Grainger*

Special Operations in the Age of Chivalry, 1100–1550, *Yuval Noah Harari*

Women, Crusading and the Holy Land in Historical Narrative, *Natasha R. Hodgson*

The English Aristocracy at War: From the Welsh Wars of Edward I to the Battle of Bannockburn, *David Simpkin*

The Calais Garrison: War and Military Service in England, 1436–1558, *David Grummitt*

Renaissance France at War: Armies, Culture and Society, c. 1480–1560, *David Potter*

Bloodied Banners: Martial Display on the Medieval Battlefield, *Robert W. Jones*

Alfred's Wars: Sources and Interpretations of Anglo-Saxon Warfare in the Viking Age, *Ryan Lavelle*

The Dutch Army and the Military Revolutions, 1588–1688, *Olaf van Nimwegen*

In the Steps of the Black Prince: The Road to Poitiers, 1355–1356, *Peter Hoskins*

Norman Naval Operations in the Mediterranean, *Charles D. Stanton*

Shipping the Medieval Military: English Maritime Logistics in the Fourteenth Century, *Craig L. Lambert*

Edward III and the War at Sea: The English Navy, 1327–1377, *Graham Cushway*

The Soldier Experience in the Fourteenth Century, *edited by Adrian R. Bell and Anne Curry*

Warfare in Tenth-Century Germany, *David S. Bachrach*

Chivalry, Kingship and Crusade: The English Experience in the Fourteenth Century, *Timothy Guard*

The Norman Campaigns in the Balkans, 1081–1108, *Georgios Theotokis*

Welsh Soldiers in the Later Middle Ages, 1282–1422, *Adam Chapman*

Merchant Crusaders in the Aegean, 1291–1352, *Mike Carr*

Printed and bound by CPI Group (UK) Ltd, Croydon, CR0 4YY

13/04/2025

14656522-0002